THE MACRO PLAYS

EARLY ENGLISH TEXT SOCIETY

No. 262

1969

PRICE 50s.

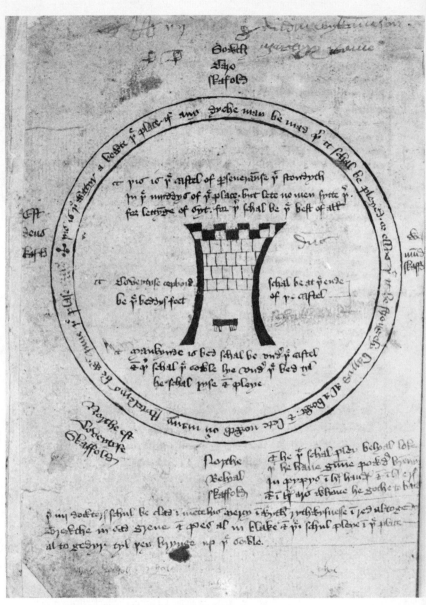

The plan of the theatre for *The Castle of Perseverance*:
Folger MS. V. a. 354, f. 191ᵛ

THE
MACRO PLAYS

THE CASTLE OF PERSEVERANCE

WISDOM · MANKIND

EDITED BY

MARK ECCLES

Published for

THE EARLY ENGLISH TEXT SOCIETY

by the

OXFORD UNIVERSITY PRESS

LONDON NEW YORK TORONTO

1969

PRINTED IN GREAT BRITAIN
AT THE UNIVERSITY PRESS, OXFORD
BY VIVIAN RIDLER
PRINTER TO THE UNIVERSITY

CONTENTS

ILLUSTRATIONS

The plan of the theatre for *The Castle of Perseverance*:
Folger MS. V.a. 354, f. 191ᵛ   *Frontispiece*

Folger MS. V.a. 354, f. 171ᵛ (*The Castle of Perseverance*) *facing p.* 58

Folger MS. V.a. 354, f. 121ʳ (*Wisdom*)   *facing p.* 151

Folger MS. V.a. 354, f. 124ʳ (*Mankind*)   *facing p.* 159

INTRODUCTION   vii

THE CASTLE OF PERSEVERANCE

Manuscript   viii
Date   x
Language   xi
Verse   xv
Sources and Analogues   xix
Staging   xxi
The Play   xxiv

WISDOM

Manuscripts   xxvii
Date   xxx
Language   xxx
Verse   xxxii
Sources   xxxiii
Staging   xxxiv
The Play   xxxv

MANKIND

Manuscript   xxxvii
Date   xxxviii
Language   xxxviii
Verse   xl
Sources and Analogues   xli
Staging   xlii
The Play   xliii

BIBLIOGRAPHY   xlvii

TABLE OF CORRESPONDING LINES   lii

CONTENTS

TEXTS

    THE CASTLE OF PERSEVERANCE   I

    WISDOM   113

    MANKIND   153

NOTES   185

    THE CASTLE OF PERSEVERANCE   185

    WISDOM   203

    MANKIND   216

ABBREVIATIONS IN THE NOTES   228

GLOSSARY   229

PROPER NAMES   279

INTRODUCTION

THE Macro plays are here re-edited from Folger MS. V. a. 354 (formerly MS. 5031) in the Folger Library, Washington, D.C. The manuscripts of *Wisdom* and *Mankind* once belonged to a monk named Hyngham and later to Robert Oliver. These manuscripts and that of *The Castle of Perseverance* were acquired by the Revd. Cox Macro (1683–1767, *D.N.B.*), a native of Bury St. Edmunds, who collected many manuscripts, some of which had belonged to Sir Henry Spelman. The three plays were bound in a volume with three other manuscripts when they were sold in 1819 by John Patteson, but Hudson Gurney, who bought them in 1820, had the plays bound in a separate volume. The Folger Library purchased this volume at the Gurney sale at Sotheby's, 30 March 1936, lot 170, for £440.[1]

The Castle of Perseverance was first published in full in *The Macro Plays* (EETS., Extra Series, xci, 1904), edited by F. J. Furnivall with an introduction by A. W. Pollard, who had included 408 lines in his *English Miracle Plays, Moralities and Interludes*, 1890. The Abbotsford Club in 1835 published *Wisdom*, lines 1–752, from the incomplete Bodleian Digby MS. 133, and in 1837 published the rest of the play from the Macro manuscript. Furnivall edited the Digby text in 1882 and the complete Macro text in 1904. The three Macro plays, then owned by J. H. Gurney of Keswick Hall near Norwich, had been transcribed before 1882 for Furnivall and the New Shakspere Society by Eleanor Marx, daughter of Karl Marx and a friend of Bernard Shaw. Furnivall generously allowed this transcript to be used for editions of *Mankind* by J. M. Manly in *Specimens of the Pre-Shaksperean Drama*, vol. i, 1897, and by Alois Brandl in *Quellen des weltlichen Dramas in England vor Shakespeare*, 1898. J. S. Farmer published reproductions of the Macro manuscripts in *The Tudor Facsimile Texts*, *Mankind* and *Wisdom* in 1907 and *The Castle of Perseverance* in 1908.

In the present edition the capitalization and punctuation are modern. Words are not divided as in the manuscripts, which have

---

[1] Seymour de Ricci, *Census of Medieval and Renaissance Manuscripts in the United States and Canada*, ii (New York, 1937), 2272.

such forms as *a geyn, an on, be hende, I now, I wys, so leyn*. The usual abbreviations are expanded without notice according to the scribes' spelling in full forms, and Roman numerals are replaced by the corresponding words. Initial *ff* is printed as *f* or *F*. The letter *i* is printed for the vowel and *j* for the consonant, but *u* and *v* are printed as written in the manuscripts. Latin words are printed as written except for obvious errors.

The line numbering of the present edition corrects that of the 1904 edition in *The Castle of Perseverance*, 362–3649, *Wisdom*, 510–1163, and *Mankind*, 125–914. The 1904 edition inconsistently counted as verse five of the many extra-metrical Latin quotations in *The Castle* (those here numbered 361*a*, 410*a*, 503*a*, 516*a*, 866*a*) and three of the missing lines in *Wisdom* (after 551, 579, 1136); made errors in dividing lines according to rhyme in *The Castle*, 785–8 and 1750–3, and *Wisdom*, 510–18; miscounted at *Wisdom*, 800; and omitted from the text seven lines added in the margin in *Mankind*, 125–8, 130, and 201–2. In the 1924 reprint the line numbers in *The Castle*, originally 2334–2739, were misprinted as 2434–2839. A table of corresponding lines is provided on p. lii.

For their help and counsel in preparing this edition I am especially grateful to Professor Norman Davis, Professor R. M. Wilson, Professor Angus McIntosh, N. R. Ker, and R. W. Burchfield. My friends at the Folger Library have given every assistance in my study of the manuscripts.

I. THE CASTLE OF PERSEVERANCE

1. *Manuscript*

The manuscript is written in a single hand, dated about 1440 by G. F. Warner and J. A. Herbert.[1] The thirty-eight leaves (ff. 154–91), measuring 210 by 143 mm. (trimmed to 140 mm. in the first gathering), consist of two gatherings of sixteen leaves each and six leaves of a third gathering. The scribe averaged 48 lines to a page. The paper shows two watermarks. That in the first and third gatherings Pollard describes as 'having four slightly concave sides, with a bend coming down from the left-hand top corner, and on the right-hand side a thumb-like projection'. The second

---

[1] *The Macro Plays*, ed. Furnivall and Pollard, pp. xxxi, xxxii; *The Castle of Perseverance*, ed. Farmer, p. v.

gathering has a mark of three mounds within a circle, somewhat resembling marks dated 1442 and 1451 in Briquet, *Les Filigranes*, nos. 11849 and 11850.

The text has two breaks in the sense, one after f. 170^v and one after f. 182^v. Each results from the loss of the contents of one leaf, between 90 and 100 lines, since the scribe averaged 48 lines to a page. Moreover, in the second quire the second and fourth sheets have changed places, and so have the seventh and eighth. The proper order of leaves is 170, 173, 172, 171, 174, 175, 177, 176, 179, 178, 180, 181, 184, 183, 182, 185. Pollard concluded that 'our present scribe simply copied an earlier manuscript, leaf by leaf, as he found it', because the second quire, where the missing leaves belong, has sixteen leaves like the first quire. N. R. Ker, however, believes it is more probable that the second quire originally had eighteen leaves. Since several speeches were now misassigned, speakers' names were added in different hands of the fifteenth and early sixteenth centuries: at the foot of f. 170^v 'malus angelus', crossed out and changed to 'Detraccio ad caro' to indicate the first speaker on f. 171; at the top of f. 177 'Ira'; and at the top of f. 178 'covetyse'. A stage direction was also added on f. 185, 'He aperith þe sowle', but the scribe probably wrote the directions for music on ff. 159, 160^v, and 161. Either the scribe or a reviser inserted words needed for the sense such as 'ladi' in line 124, 'be' (580), 'lyfe' (1172), 'in' (1314), 'grace' (1635), 'goode' (1844), 'not' (2562), all in lighter ink. The scribe used red ink on ff. 160^v and 161 for two stage directions and six names of speakers, and he touched the initials of the speakers' names with red on ff. 162^v, 163, 164, and 185. A later hand has written 'John Adams' on f. 158^v, and a few words have been scribbled at the foot of f. 155 and elsewhere.

The punctuation of the manuscript is light. A point separates clauses in the stage plan and names in the list of players, where .// is also used. // beneath the line marks an insertion, as in 80 and 378. Points under a letter are used to cancel it in 1921 and 3495. A *punctus elevatus* separates short verses written on one line, either two verses as in 785–6 or four verses as in 631–4. Everywhere else a horizontal line after each verse joins with a vertical line to indicate that two or three verses rhyme, as in 1:3, 2:4, 5:7, 6:8, 9:13, 10:11:12. A line across the page follows each speech, except in the banns. A paragraph mark resembling superior *a* appears in the margin before each stanza of the banns except the first and eighth, before line 148, before Latin quotations in 866*a*, 1644*a*, 2007*a*, 2599*a*, 2612*a*, 2638*a*, 2985*a*, and 3610*a*, and before three sentences in the stage plan; cf. *Ludus Coventriae*, EETS., E.S. cxx, p. 276. The sign ∴ is written in the margin before 1092, 1105, 1122, 1135, 1152, 1157, and many later lines, usually marking the fifth or tenth line of a stanza.

The scribe usually writes $þ^t$, $þ^u$, w^t, which are expanded in this edition to *þat*, *þou*, *wyth* (cf. *wyth* 558). He often writes a letter above the line when nothing is omitted, as in $boþ^e$, $þ^e$ def. art. and pron., $þ^ei$, $þ^i$, $þ^is$, w^as. He puts a vowel above the line when *r* is omitted, as in g^ace, p^ide, g^one, and *t* above the line for *th* or *yth*, as in $fyty^t$, $gader^t$. He uses the common signs for *and*, *con*, *per* or *par*, *pre*, *pro*, *-que*, *quod*, *re*, *-rum*, *-er* or *-yr*, *-or* or *-ur*, *-us*, and *-ys*. He indicates by a horizontal stroke the omission of *n* or *m*, the omission of *i* in *-cion*, and the contraction of Latin words. An occasional stroke through *h* and a flourish after *d* or *n* seem to have no significance.

2. Date

Pollard wrote: 'How early in the fifteenth century we may place the *Castle of Perseverance* is a question which must be decided by philologists, but on literary grounds I should like to place it as early as possible, not much later than 1425' (p. xxiv). Gayley suggested about 1400 or 1400–10, and Smart 'about the middle of the first decade of the fifteenth century, or in round numbers about 1405.'[1] Bennett concluded 'that the play was originally written some time before the turn of the century, perhaps in the latter half of the last decade of the fourteenth century', that the banns were added between 1398 and 1400, and that a revised ending (lines 3121–3649 as numbered in the present edition) was written between 1402 and 1405.[2] This theory of revision will be discussed in section 4 below.

[1] C. M. Gayley, *Plays of Our Forefathers*, 1907, pp. 281, 293; W. K. Smart, 'The *Castle of Perseverance*: Place, Date, and a Source', *Manly Anniversary Studies in Language and Literature*, 1923, pp. 42–53.

[2] Jacob Bennett, 'The "Castle of Perseverance": Redactions, Place, and Date', *Mediaeval Studies*, xxiv (1962), 141–52, and his unpublished thesis, 'A Linguistic Study of *The Castle of Perseverance*', Boston University, 1960.

The play can hardly be dated so precisely, but it may have been composed between 1400 and 1425. This is consistent with an allusion to *crakows*, pointed toes on shoes, which is discussed by Smart and in my note on line 1059. The known references to *crakows* as a current fashion were probably written between 1382 and 1425.

3. *Language*

The dialect of the extant version of *The Castle of Perseverance*, a variety of East Midland, suggested to Furnivall that the play was written in Norfolk. On the other hand, Smart, who observed that the gallows of Canwick (see the note on line 2421) stood just outside the city of Lincoln, argued that the play was written in or near Lincoln, and Bennett supported this view. The language, however, is quite different from that of any manuscript having known associations with that area. For example, the third person present singular verb ends in *-th*, *-t*, and only rarely in *-s*; 'shall' is written *schal*, not *sal*; and the object form of the third person plural pronoun is always *hem*, not *þam*, *þaim*, or *þem*, a usage totally alien to the city of Lincoln. The manuscript of *The Castle* could not have been written by a scribe from Lincolnshire, but it may very well have been written by a scribe from Norfolk.

The evidence from vocabulary, phonology, and accidence is consistent with such a provenance. The vocabulary of the play is East Midland with strong Northern influence. Smart claimed the following words as Northern: *bedene* 'immediately', *blodyr* 'blubber', *boun* 'ready', *brustun-gutte* 'burst-gut', *busk* 'hasten', *byggyng* 'dwelling', *gate* 'way', *kettys* 'carrions', *laykys* 'games', *lowe* 'flame', *mowle* 'earth', *prene* 'spike', *rakle* 'haste', *rappokys* 'wretches', *skowtys* 'trulls', *syke* 'stream', *tak* 'endurance', and *tyne* 'lose'. Nearly all these words, however, occur in East Midland as well as in Northern texts: *bedene* in Capgrave and *Palladius*, *blodyr* in Usk and *Beryn*, *boun* in Capgrave and *Beryn*, and so with the rest except that the noun *rakle* is found only here and *brustun-gutte* and *mowle* only here in Middle English. Other words are mainly Northern or North Midland, according to Rolf Kaiser:[1] *bolne* 'swell', *carpe* 'cry out', *drepe* 'strike', *fonde* 'fool', *fyle*

[1] *Zur Geographie des mittelenglischen Wortschatzes, Palaestra*, 205 (1937), pp. 178–278.

'wretch', *gere* 'equip', *grete* 'weep', *houte* 'shout', *irke* 'grow weary', *lende* 'remain', *mynne* 'lesser', *nerhand* 'almost', *ros* 'boasting', *schade* 'pour off', *solwyd* 'sullied', *tyl* 'to', *unquert* 'wicked', and *3one* 'that'. Probably also Northern are *crulle* 'crawl', *dagge* 'jog', *ded* 'death', *graythyd* 'dressed', *leykyn* 'play', and *pycke* 'pitch'.

The following are the principal points of interest in the treatment of sounds in spelling and rhymes:[1]

The reflex of OE. *a* before lengthening consonant groups is normally written *o*, as *bold* 416, *wombe* 3332, *hond* 4, *among* 436, *honge* 3066; but, except before *ld*, sometimes *a* as *hande* 2475, *land* 3605 (rhyming on *quenchand* pres. pt., but also on *honde*, *fonde*), and often *hange* 430, 2527, 2731.

The reflex of OE. *ā* is normally written *o*, sometimes *oo* as *doo* 188, *goo* 323; *more* 839 rhymes on *store*, *lore* 'lost'; *sore* 40 rhymes on *lore*, but *sare* 20 on *bare*, *3are*. It rhymes on the reflex of OE. *ō* in the series *also* 1119, *perto*, *do*, *go*, and *goo* 1832, *too* 'two', *doo*.

The reflex of OE. *æ* is normally written *a*, but *e* in *elmesdede* 2009, *ex* 2571, *gedelyng* 2980 beside *gad(e)lyng-* 463, 1769, *mes(se)* 1212, 2165.

The reflexes of OE. *ǣ¹/ē* and *ǣ²* rhyme together, and with the reflex of OE. *ē*, not only before dental consonants but before other consonants as well: *wede* 585, *fede*, *brede*, *strete*; *brede* 1174, *spede*, *lede*, *fede*; *wele* 661, *dele*, *mele*, *whele*; *fere* 997, *dere*, *here*, *lere*; *reche* 3022, *leche*, *teche*, *speche*. Cf. also *leve* (OE. *lēaf*) 3236 rhyming on *preve*, *leve* 'dear', *cheve*. When shortened these vowels are variously represented: *drede* pp. adj. 3025 (rhyming *red*, *ded*, *hed*), but *drad* 1051 (rhyming *glad*, etc.); *lefte* 2789 but *lafte* 1787 (rhyming *crafte*); *lent* 33 (rhyming *asent*, etc.) but *lante* 335 (rhyming *wante*). It is presumably on the model of *drede/drad*, and *lede/lad* (2584), that *fadde* was formed as an alternative past participle of *fede*, as 187 (rhyming *glad*, etc.), 1523 (rhyming *madde*, etc.) beside *fed(de)* 212, 1982.

The reflex of OE. *i* is normally written *i* or *y* but sometimes *e*: infin. *leue* 'live' 1081, *wetyn* 375; pp. *dreuyn* 1042, 2204 (rhyming *schreuyn* pp., *leuyn* infin.), *dreue* 1570 (rhyming *lyue* n., *schreue* pp.), *drewyn* 2824, *smete* 1846; adv. *sekyr* 1562, *hedyr* 2475, *þedyr* 135, 1561, *wedyr* 323, 1572; rel. pron. *weche* 1512. Here

---

[1] Professor Norman Davis has given valuable advice on the description of sounds and forms in each of the Macro plays.

belong also the probably ON. *mekyl* 76, 3614 and the OF. *preuy*, *-e* 691, 1365, *spetows* 2052. Some of these may represent the common lengthening in open syllables (cf. *ewyl* 312), but others, especially the group of adverbs and the French words, more probably reflect simple lowering of the short vowel.

The reflex of OE. *ȳ* is often written *i* or *y*, as *dyd* 2306, *knytte* 560, *synne* 196 (rhyming *chynne* but also *grenne*, *brenne*), *kyd* 2808 (rhyming *adred*, etc.), *kynde*, *mynde* 92, 94 (rhyming *behynde* but also *ende*; cf. the rhyme *fynde*:*ende*, etc. 15 ff.), *fyre* 1961 (rhyming *lere*), *pride*, *pryde* 159, 957, 1048 (rhyming *wyde*, etc., but also *brede*, *hed*, etc.). It is also written *e*, often in the same words, as *dedyst* 2944, *knet* 1239 (rhyming *beset*), *kende*, *mende* 786–7 (rhyming *wende*, etc.), *fer* 2289, *prede* 2079 (rhyming *rede*, etc.); similarly *bye* 852 but *bey* 3096, *drye* 528 but *dreye* 177—*drye* 2352 rhymes on *weye*, *teye*, *abeye*.

The reflex of OE. *ēg-* is written *y* in *dye* 1387 (rhyming *hye*, *eye*), *hy* 2034 (rhyming *by*), *yne* 1106 (rhyming *swyne*). It is written *ey* in *dey(e)* 556 (rhyming *trye*), 940 (rhyming *envye*), 2850 (rhyming *desteny*, etc.), 3164 (rhyming *mercye*), *eyn(e)* 1516, 2229, *eye* 1602 (rhyming *envye*, etc.). But *day* 638, *deye* 1758 rhyme on *say*, *sey*.

The reflex of OE. *-oht* is written *owt(h)* but sometimes rhymes on the reflex of *-aht*, though this is regularly written *awt(h)*. So *þowth* 713 rhymes *bowth*, *lawth*, *nowth*; *browth* 2274 rhymes *nowth*, *betawth*, *cawth*; *nowth* is normally so written, but rhymes on *-awt(h)* at 290, 362, 513 (*nout*), 2793.

In words containing earlier *-ht*, spellings such as *ght* or *ȝt* are never used: the fricative is often not shown in the spelling, as *fytyn* 70, *seuenenyt* 133, *syt* 1940, *whytt* 359 (rhyming *flyt*, *wryt*), *wytys* 157, *browt* 260, *dowtyr* 999, *tawt* 515. More commonly the spelling is *th*, as *bryth* 162, *knyth* 215, *myth* 1, *browth* 2267, *nowth* 2, *þowth* 292. This spelling is used only occasionally for *-t* in words which never contained the fricative, as *coueyth* 839, *knyth* 990 (rhyming *syth*, etc.), *dyspyth*, *delyth* 2310–11 (rhyming *dyth*). (The same spelling is simultaneously used for the dental fricative more commonly than *þ*, especially in the 3 sg. pres. indic. of verbs.)

The reflex of OE. *sc* initially is written *sch*, except in *sulde* 2480; but medially and finally sometimes *ch*, as *felechepys* 1304, *worchep* 1656.

The reflex of OE. *hw-* is usually written *wh*, but *w* in *wanne* 53, *weche* 1512, 1514 and *wyche* 383, *wedyr* 'whether' 281 and *weydyr* 3188, *wedyr* 'whither' 323, *were* 1125, *woso* 264, *wyth* 'white' in plan and 716.

The loss of certain consonants is occasionally shown in spelling: *l* before a consonant in *schat* 1572, *schudyst* 1591, *werd* 157, etc., *werdly* 180, *wytte* 1767; *r* before *s* in *mossel* 1171 (cf. rhymes like *fors* 1002 : *clos*, *wers* 3201 : *dystresse*); *w* in *syche* 480 beside *swyche* 1237, *to(o)* 'two' 18, etc.

The following are the most noteworthy points of accidence:[1]

Nouns. The genitive singular and the plural end mostly in *-ys*, but in some words, especially those ending in a vowel, in *-s*: gen. sg. *mannys* 655, but much oftener *mans* 23, 117, 257, 896, etc.; pl. *penys* 767, *pens* 798, *aungelys* 314, *aungels* 301, *ladys* 620, *vertus* 54, also *gounse* 2073, *ladyse* 2544, *vertuse* 2426, 2581. *Heuene, heueneryche, helle* before nouns are at this date combining forms rather than genitives. Exceptional plurals, other than the common mutated forms, are *breþeryn* 1019, 1037, *chyldyr* and *chyldryn* 956, 894, *eyn(e)* and *yne* 1516, 2229, 1106, *fon(e)* 1695, 3396.

Pronouns. Fem. sg. *sche, hyr, hyr(e)* or *here*; 2 pl. *ȝe, ȝour(e), ȝou*; 3 pl. *þei* or *þey, her(e), hem*.

Verbs. The ending *-(y)n* appears in the infinitive and present plural, and in the past participle of strong verbs. In both infinitive and present plural forms without *-n* are much commoner, but those with it form a substantial minority; e.g. infin. *faryn* 372, *fynden* 1237, *rewlyn* 311, *walkyn* 211, *wetyn* 375, *ben* 119, *gon* 435, *seyne* 256, *sen* 347; pl. *callyn* 47, *fytyn* 70, *gapyn* 200, *semyn* 799, *arn* 73, ben 309, *han* 216. In the strong past participle, on the other hand, forms with *-n* are rather more than half the total, e.g. *betyn* 588, *brokyn* 1481, *bowndyn* 3345, *castyn* 180, *dreuyn* 1042, *etyn* 1369, *gotyn* 2936, *ȝouyn* 2560, *holdyn* 194, *lorn* 2678, *wrokyn* 2135, *ben* 1521, *don* 538, *gon* 1756, *sen* 1516; of those without *-n* about a quarter are parts of verbs with a nasal at the end of the stem, as *bownde* 701, *com* 2934, *founde* 1255, *gunne* 1307, *wonne* 1717.

In the present indicative, the 2 sg. ends in *-(y)st* except for *woldys* 2321, *puttys* 3434; the 3 sg. ends mostly in *-(y)th*, occa-

---

[1] The vowel of unstressed inflexional syllables is usually written *y*, but *i* and *e* also occur. On final *e* see pp. xviii–xix.

sionally in -*yt/it* as *seruyt* 2614, *waxit* 418, and rarely in -(*y*)*s*: *dwellys* 3440, *dos* 1063, *seys* 3351; *knowe* 104, 105 is isolated. In the plural, in addition to the forms with and without -*n* mentioned above, there are occasional forms in -(*y*)*th*(*e*): *callyth* 52, *faryth* 2903, *mewythe* 3494, *hathe* 2293.

The imperative plural is usually without distinctive ending but sometimes has -(*y*)*th*: *syttyth* 163, 272, *leuyth*, *brewyth* 949–50, *cryeth* 2197, *seth* 273, *goth* 1002.

The present participle ends in -*yng*(*e*) except for *fyndende* 81, *takande* 144, *quenchand* 3603. The past participle of both weak and strong verbs sometimes has the prefix *i*-: *ilent* 238, *iment* 240, *ipyth* 209, *irent* 2026, *ispendyd* 1295; *ifounde* 1838, *iknowe* 222.

The glossary gives all forms of strong, preterite-present, and anomalous verbs.

Since *The Castle of Perseverance* was not printed until 1904, it contains several words not recorded in the *Oxford English Dictionary*: *begrete*, *dagge* v., *deseruiture*, *drulle*, *feterel*, *geyn-went*, *kewe*, *kynse*, *largyte*, *lathe*, *ouyrblyue*, *owle* v., *rakle* n., *rasche* n., *vnwolde*. For the following words *The Castle* provides an earlier example than any other cited in *OED.*, or in the parts of the *Middle English Dictionary* published by 1965, A to Hastie (parentheses give the date of the first other record): *cukke* (1440), *dapyrly* (1858), *devnesse* (1621), *dogge trot* (1664), *fesyl* (*c.* 1532), *flapyr* v. (1835), *fogge* v. (1588), *gogmagog* (*c.* 1580 as a common noun), *hory* (1530), *howtys* (1600), *kacke* (1436), *kyth* 'belly' (1540), *modyr* 'girl' (1440), *Penyman* (1610), *pytyr-patyr* (1561), *rouge* v. (1612), *ruble* v. (1637), *saggyd* (1440), *slugge* n. (*a.* 1500), *snowre* 'scowl' (*c.* 1440), *sompe* (1653), *sportaunce* (1584), *spud* (1440), *tak* 'spot' (1602).

4. Verse

Of the 318 complete stanzas, 235 contain thirteen lines, usually *ababababcdddc*, and 45 contain nine lines, usually *ababcdddc*. In the thirteen-line stanzas the rhymes of the first eight lines are *ababbcbc* in 2326 ff., *ababcbcb* in 1886 ff., 2261 ff., 3327 ff., and 3418 ff., and *ababcdcd* in 3164 ff., 3190 ff., and 3216 ff. Twelve of the nine-line stanzas use only three rhymes, *ababbcccb*. The nine-line stanzas have two parts, 1–5 and 6–9, each complete in sense and linked by the tail rhyme. The three parts of the thirteen-line stanzas are usually marked by completion of sentences in lines 4, 9, and 13. The sense runs on from line 4 only at 4, 121, 173, 1497, 1523, 2072, 2846, 3473, 3486, 3512, 3551, 3564, and 3614 and from line 9 only at 849, 1515, 2334, 3224, 3504, 3619, 3632, and possibly 2360.

One stanza (261–74 spoken by Flesh) has fourteen lines, beginning like a nine-line stanza and adding five lines, *efffe*. Four stanzas have eight lines, *aaabcccb*, with two stresses to a line in 623–46 (World, Pleasure, and Folly) and four and three stresses in 777–84 (Backbiter). Twenty-eight stanzas have four lines on one rhyme, with two or three stresses in the first and third lines and three or four stresses in the second and fourth lines, as in 1286–97, 3229–48. Though Pollard says that these quatrains are always divided between two speakers, this is true only of the first seven, which are divided between Mankind and World or a Deadly Sin. Two other four-line stanzas rhyme *abab* (1750–3, 2965–8). Three of the Deadly Sins make speeches of only two rhyming lines (1767–8, 1812–13, 1853–4).

The rhythms are strongly marked and vigorously varied. In the banns the lines have from two to six stresses, except that the ninth line of a stanza has either one or two. In the rest of the play most lines in the thirteen-line stanzas have four stresses, with three in the ninth and thirteenth lines of a stanza; but the four-stress lines are often varied with lines of three stresses (sometimes two or five, with six in 1970), and the ninth and thirteenth lines often have two stresses (sometimes four or five, with six in 3404), while the ninth line has only one stress in 464 ('Iwys'), 1946, 1977, 2308, and 3322. I cannot agree with Pollard that the thirteen-line stanzas are extremely uniform, or with Bennett, who believes that the original poet wrote only lines 157–3120, that 'the extreme metrical regularity of his lines creates considerable monotony', and that in 172 of his 188 thirteen-line stanzas, with four stresses to a line and three in lines 9 and 13, 'the number of accents in the lines is always rigidly adhered to'. I have not found a single stanza with this regular pattern of stresses in every line. As in all good drama, the rhythm is the rhythm of speech, not of the metronome.

The alliteration emphasizes the stressed words. In the thirteen-line stanzas of the banns eight lines on the average alliterate and three of the eight show triple or quadruple alliteration. The World,

Belial, Flesh, and the Seven Sins alliterate nearly all their lines; Mankind, feeble at first, soon learns the art from them (738 ff., 1238 ff.). Scenes of argument like the last two scenes show less alliteration, but it still occurs in every stanza of more than four lines. I do not find, as Bennett does, that the skill with which alliteration is used differs essentially in different parts of the play.

Bennett argues that different authors wrote these three parts: the original play, lines 157–3120 in this edition; the banns, 1–156; and a revised ending, 3121–3649. His seven criteria are stanza form, metre, alliterative technique, poetical style, grammar, syntax, and dramatic effectiveness. He observes that the thirteen-line stanzas of the original play are consistently divided into an exposition of nine lines and a conclusion of four lines: 'The continuity of thought is unbroken in the exposition, the pause is well defined, and the conclusion, though logically connected with the exposition, is a restatement or a new twist of thought, rather than a strict continuum.' In the banns, on the other hand, the continuity of sense is carried on through thirteen lines, and in the last two scenes almost half the stanzas do not separate the parts. He calls the original poet 'an extremely conscientious metrist' but finds the lines in the banns generally longer and in the ending sometimes longer and sometimes shorter. The alliteration in the original, he believes, has 'an ease and fluency which unquestionably set it apart from the alliteration of the redactions', though the reviser of the ending may have taken from the original some passages with frequent alliteration. The poetic style, Bennett thinks, is at its best in 2956–60. As for grammar and syntax, he says of the original writer that 'His sentences are all clear and concise, and errors of a grammatical nature are difficult to find, whereas most of the stanzas of both redactions are characterized by awkwardness of expression and grammatical confusion.' Finally, Bennett points out that the action moves in a series of effective scenes towards the climax and then, instead of ending with a climax, 'the play is extended in length by means of a dogmatic and actionless debate'. Since the banns do not mention the Four Daughters of God but hint that the Virgin Mary is to intercede, he suggests that 'the original ending consisted of a scene in which the Blessed Virgin Mary alone interceded for man before God'.

It seems to me quite likely that a second author wrote the banns.

The metre is rougher than in the rest of the play, and the long lines move less swiftly. The stanzas are linked by repeating one or more words from the last line of each in the first line of the following stanza, a device used only occasionally thereafter (as in 375, 504, 712, 1178). The syntax is awkward in line 4 (*he made*), in 80–83 (where the subject shifts from the Bad Angel to Covetousness), and in 84 (*þat if* for *If*). E. K. Chambers (see the note on 124) commented that 'The prologue does not quite square with the play itself and may be a later addition.'

On the other hand, one author could have written the rest of the play. Bennett finds the same dialect used throughout. Both the main part and the conclusion use the same stanza patterns of thirteen, nine, and four lines; and the thirteen-line stanzas of both, though Bennett thinks otherwise, show the same continuity for nine lines and then a well-defined pause, except for three or four stanzas in the main part and four in the conclusion. Both parts seem to me similar in metre, alliterative technique, and poetic style, and neither is always clear in syntax. As for dramatic effectiveness, the debate in heaven whether man should be saved or damned seemed dramatic to medieval writers, or they would not have imagined the scene so often (see note on 3129). The debate is not actionless, for the Four Daughters ascend to the throne of God, secure a decision, and act upon it when they rescue Mankind from the Bad Angel who is bearing him to hell. These two scenes, where opposing champions keep the fate of Mankind in suspense until near the end, are much more effective than the brief scene in *Ludus Coventriae*, no. xi, and more dramatic than a scene with a single intercessor would have been.

The techniques of rhyme, like the language and style, are consistent throughout the play. Each part, for instance, has rhymes on unstressed -*ynge* (41–7, 289–95, 1516–18, 3466–7, 3619) and on other unstressed syllables (54–56, 526–32, 888, 3414–16). The same word is used twice in one set of rhymes in the banns (once, in the first stanza), in the main part of the play (fifteen times), and in the last two scenes (five times). Most rhymes are masculine, but double rhymes are fairly common in each part (as in 10–12, 205–7, 3262–8).

Final unstressed *e* seems to be pronounced in one rhyme, *Rome*: *to me* 178–82, but forms with and without Early ME.

final *e* rhyme together, as in *schat* : *gate*, *hap* : *skape*. The author may have sounded this final *e* only occasionally, to provide a rhyme. The pronunciation of *r* was light enough to permit such rhymes as *synne* : *werne*, *fors* : *clos*, and so with *l* in *wylt* : *wryt*.

An unusual habit is the rhyming of a stressed syllable with another stressed syllable followed by an unstressed ending. Examples are *naylyd* 3556 : *avayle*, *takyth* 97 : *lake*, *wallys* 729 : *call*, *declaryt* 2103 : *fare*, *wrenchys* 2760 : *qwenche*, *atenyde* 2427 : *frende*, *sens* 799 : *commaundementys*, *hens* 1246 : *synnys*, *Trewpe* 3270 : *brewyth*, *Mankynd* 3558 : *pynyd*, and *bord* 3539 : *restoryd*. In the first five the rhyme is complete without the unstressed ending, while in the rest it is spread over two syllables which could be pronounced as one. These rhymes occur from the banns to the end of the play.

Rhyme-tags are common throughout: *as I gesse, as I trowe, as I þe say, as I wene, boþe in home and halle, day and nyth, fer and ner, for any þynge, forsoþe I sey, ful evyn, I fynde, I gesse, I lete, I say, I sey in my sawe, I trowe, I vndirstonde, in flode, in londe, in toure and toun, iwys* (ten times in rhyme), *more and lesse, nyth and day, on grounde, on hylle, on molde, saun dowte, sothe to sayn* (*sey*), *trewly I tell þe, trewly I trowe, trewly to tell, þe sothe for to seyne* (*sey*), *þe soþe may be sene, þe soþe to tell, vndyr gore, vndyr lende, vndyr lynde, vndyr schawe, vndyr sterre, vndyr sunne, upon grounde, wythout les*, and *wythoutyn dystaunce*. The author especially enjoys alliterative phrases with *be*: *be bankys bace, be bankys brede, be bankys ful bare, be bankys on brede, be buskys and bankys broun, be dale and be doun, be dale or downys drye, be dalys derne, be downe and dalys, be downe and dyche, be downe, dale, and dyche, be downe or be dale, be downys drye, be dykys and be denne, be feldys ferne, be fen and flode, be fen or flode, be flodys and be fenne, be greuys grene, be holtys and hethe, be holtys and hyll, be londe and lake, be londe ne lake, be se and sonde, be sompe and syke, be steppe and stalle, be strete and stalle, be strete and stronde, be strete and stye, be strete and style, be stye and strete, be stye nor strete*, and *be sty or be strete*.

5. *Sources and Analogues*

The Castle of Perseverance dramatizes themes which had been treated by many Christian writers. It is a divine comedy presenting a psychomachia, a conflict between good and evil forces for the soul of man. Mankind follows his bad angel to the world, the Devil, and the flesh; he repents with the help of confession and penitence; he perseveres in goodness while the virtues defend the castle against his enemies; he gives his heart to covetousness; he is overthrown by death; and the debate of the daughters of God ends with his salvation through God's mercy.

The author had probably read many treatises and heard many sermons on vices and virtues and on confession and penance. Though he made no specific borrowings, he may have known such widely read poems as the *Psychomachia* of Prudentius, where virtues overcome vices in a series of battles, and *Le Chasteau d'Amour* of Robert Grosseteste, Bishop of Lincoln (see note on line 52). He treated in his own way the familiar themes of man's temptation by the Devil, the world, the flesh, and the seven sins, their attack on a castle and defeat by seven virtues, death's sudden conquest, and the complaint of the soul to the body. His account of the daughters of God differs from the versions in Hugh of St. Victor, St. Bernard, *Le Chasteau d'Amour*, *Sawles Warde*, *Cursor Mundi*, and the *Meditationes Vitae Christi* attributed to Bonaventura (see note on line 3129). Sister Callista Reddoch in an unpublished thesis[1] finds parallel ideas in Gregory's *Moralia*, Bernard's *Sermones* and *Meditationes*, *De Pugna Spirituali contra Septem Vitia Capitalia* (*Opera S. Bonaventurae*, ed. 1864–71, xii, 158–64), *The Prick of Conscience*, and 'The Mirror of the Periods of Man's Life' (*Hymns to the Virgin and Christ*, ed. Furnivall, pp. 58–78). All these are analogues rather than sources.

The quotations are mainly from the Bible, though line 866 quotes a proverb of 'Caton, þe grete clerke', and line 2513 refers to 'þe bok of kendys', Alexander Nequam's *De Naturis Rerum*. Fourteen Latin texts come from the *Psalms*, nine from other books of the Old Testament, ten from the Gospels, and nine from other books of the New Testament. Half of these texts occur in the last two scenes, the debate in heaven.

The author drew on common speech for proverbial expressions, several of which have not been found elsewhere: 'We haue etyn garlek euerychone', 'Aforn mele men mete schul tyle', 'He helde

---

[1] 'Non-dramatic Sources and Analogues in a Typical English Morality, The Castell of Perseverance', Catholic University of America, 1944. See also E. N. S. Thompson, *The English Moral Plays*, 1910.

þe ex be þe helue'. He used an unusually large number of proverbial comparisons, like 'bold as a belle', 'wyth as swan', 'Werldys
wele is lyke a thre-fotyd stole', and 'bryther þanne blossum on
brere'.[1] His reliance on such comparisons and on rhyme-tags
suggests that he was familiar with secular verse in English as well
as with religious writings.

6. Staging

The stage plan for *The Castle of Perseverance* is of special interest
as the earliest known illustration in England to show how a play
was presented. The drawing pictures the castle and a bed under it
within a ring which represents 'the water about the place' or else
strong bars. The writing on the plan gives directions to the
players about the placing of five scaffolds and the cupboard of
Covetousness, the number of 'stytelerys' or marshals, the gunpowder to be used by Belial, and the mantles to be worn by the
Four Daughters of God. The frontispiece of this edition repro-
duces the plan by permission of the Folger Library.

Richard Southern in his valuable book *The Medieval Theatre in
the Round*, 1957, reconstructs the manner of performance from the
plan, the stage directions, and references in the play. Furnivall
supposed that 'The audience, if not let into the enclosure, must
have been a movable one, going from one scaffold to another as its
occupants spoke', but Southern makes it clear that the audience
stood or sat within 'the place', a theatrical term here meaning the
area within the circle. The purpose of the ring of water or bars was
probably to keep out spectators unless they paid to be admitted.
The scaffolds, though on the plan they appear to be outside the
ring, may have been inside it, since the actors move freely between
the scaffolds and 'the place' and they would need longer ramps if
they had to cross the ditch each time. Southern suggests that the
scaffolds were mounted by steps and that they may have been
enclosed with curtains, which opened to reveal first the World,
then the Devil, the Flesh, later Covetousness, and finally God. The
actors also played in 'the place' or 'green', since the Daughters of
God are to 'play in the place altogether till they bring up the Soul'.

It is clear from the banns that a travelling company acted the
play on tour, giving one performance in each village or town they

[1] B. J. Whiting, *Proverbs in the Earlier English Drama*, 1938.

visited. One week in advance, two men with banners and trumpets rode into town, gathered a crowd, and announced to 'the good commons of this town' that a play would be presented 'on the green in royal array'. The two banner-bearers told the story and urged all good neighbours to come early to the play. We may compare the banns for the Corpus Christi play called *Ludus Coventriae*, probably acted in Norfolk during the fifteenth century, which invite the people to see 'this game well played in good array' the next Sunday at six in the morning in 'N. town' (the name of the place to be inserted, as with the blanks in the *Castle* banns). *The Play of the Sacrament* also has two banner-bearers who announce that the play may be seen at Croxton on Monday.

How many players travelled with the company? The actors' list names thirty-three roles in addition to the two banner-bearers. Some doubling would be possible, but Bevington estimates that more than twenty-two players would be needed.[1] Twenty are on stage at the same time during the siege of the Castle (Mankind, two Angels, seven Virtues, three Enemies, and seven Sins), while the Soul is lying under the bed and God the Father may or may not be already on his scaffold. Bevington's suggestion that the roles 'may have been divided between professional strollers and an assortment of amateurs drafted from each locality' is not very likely, for only one character, Penance, speaks fewer than forty lines. The 'stytelerys', on the other hand, were probably local men chosen to control the crowd and to see that space was kept clear for the players.

The players probably brought with them their scaffolds and castle, costumes and banners, and trumpets and bagpipes. They either carried or borrowed a bed, cupboard, and benches for thrones, spears, bows, and a spade for Sloth. Other properties included a box for Backbiter, a faggot, coals, gunpowder, stones, roses for the Virtues, and coins for Covetousness. Kingly costumes were needed for God and for his three enemies, and wings for the angels and probably for the Virtues, since the Bad Angel compares them to geese and refers to their 'hakle' or feathers (2650). Lechery, the Virtues, and the Daughters of God were dressed as women but were no doubt played by men.

When the actors arrived at a village they would first find a place

---

[1] D. M. Bevington, *From Mankind to Marlowe*, 1962, pp. 49, 72.

to play in. The play refers to 'this proper plain place' (that is, this fine open space, 160), 'this green' (227, 1892, 2632), 'this croft' (1144, 2144), 'this ground' (2910), 'yon plain' (1764), 'yon field' (1914), and 'yon green grass' (1907). If the actors could find a meadow by a stream, the ditch would have to be dug only part of the way; or if necessary the place could be barred all around. Southern thinks that the ditch must have been ten feet wide and five feet deep and that the earth from the ditch formed a hill on which people could sit. I doubt that so large a ditch was needed and that loose earth would make very good seats. The phrase in 271–2, 'Therefore on hill Sit all still', may be only a rhyme-tag, and when there was no ditch there would be no hill. Southern's estimate that the circle was 110 feet across depends on his assumptions about a hill and on the diameter of the Cornish rounds, which ranged from 40 to 126 feet. There is not enough evidence to determine the size of this circle.

Within the circle most of the audience stood or sat on the grass, turning to follow the actors as they spoke from different scaffolds or from the ground or from the castle. They were not to sit in the middle of the place 'for letting of sight, for there shall be the best of all'. The World opens the play by telling 'worthy wights' and 'sirs seemly' to sit together 'on side' (156–63) and Pleasure says, 'Peace, people, of peace we you pray. Sit and see well to my saw' (491–2). The most worthy wights may have sat on stools or benches. A performance of the play would probably have lasted more than three hours and a half.

The stage directions are in Latin except for four in English: *pipe vp mu[syk]* after 455, *Trumpe vp* after 574, *trumpe vp* after 646, and a later addition, 'He aperith þe sowle', after 3059. The future tense is used in fourteen verbs, and perhaps it should have been written in *descendit* (490, 1446, 2556). Other verbs are abbreviated: *d'* and *dic'* (for *dicet*), *ascend'*, *descend'*. The following are probably errors: *vocauit* (1766), *verberauit* (1822 and 1863, for *verberabit* as in 1777), and *ascendet* and *dixit* (3228, for *ascendent* and *dicet*).[1]

The Castle of Perseverance has had several modern productions,

[1] James Willis, 'Stage Directions in "The Castell of Perseverance"', *Modern Language Review*, li (1956), 404–5; Southern, *The Medieval Theatre in the Round*, pp. 34–49; A. Henry, '"The Castle of Perseverance": The Stage Direction at Line 1767', *N. & Q.*, ccx (1965), 448.

including one at the Maddermarket Theatre in Norwich by Nugent
Monck and two at Oxford. C. R. B. Quentin produced it for the
Oxford University Experimental Theatre Club on 10–12 November
1938 at the Taylorian Institute, on 3–5 July 1939 in the quadrangle
of St. Edmund Hall, and on 7–8 July 1939 on the steps of St.
George's Chapel, Windsor. Nevill Coghill wrote in 1948 that this
production, 'modernized and produced entirely by undergraduates,
was one of the most memorable and striking I have ever seen.
Above all it revealed what an excellent and actable play it is,
full of character, variety, and excitement, and yet based in essential
Christian simplicities. That this was no fluke was proved by a
second production given in St. Mary's, Oxford, about three years
ago. Once again the thrill and majesty, and the comedy too, held
large audiences and gave scope to the imagination of actor and
producer alike.'[1]

7. The Play

The Castle of Perseverance is the earliest English moral play to
survive as a whole, since only the first half remains of *The Pride of
Life*, which may have been written about 1400. As drama it
surpasses the three other extant moral plays written in English
before 1500, *Wisdom*, *Mankind*, and *Nature*, as much as it is in
turn surpassed by *Everyman*, the sixteenth-century English
version of the Dutch *Elckerlijk*.[2] *The Castle of Perseverance*
dramatizes a single great theme, the battle between good and evil
powers for the soul of man. It ranges in mood from the mocking
laughter of Backbiter and the Bad Angel to the impressive solemnity
of Death and the majesty of God the Father. The author has at his
command a vigorous vocabulary, expressively varied rhythms, and
a power to create stage pictures which reinforce the appeal to the
ear by appeal to the eye.

The play opens with the World, the Devil, and the Flesh on
their thrones, the three kings who boast of their purpose to destroy
Mankind. He appears on the ground below as a new-born child,
naked and feeble, and is soon persuaded by his Bad Angel to go

---

[1] Preface to *The Castle of Perseverance*, adapted by Iwa Langentels, 1948;
Oxford Magazine, 17 Nov., 1938; letters from Nevill Coghill, Roy Porter,
J. W. Robinson, Richard Southern, and Gavin Townend.
[2] See the edition of *Everyman* by A. C. Cawley, Manchester, 1961.

to the World and become rich and lordlike. Clothed in fine array
by Pleasure and given gold and silver by Sir Covetousness, he hugs
all the sins to his bosom. When his Good Angel calls for help,
Penance pierces Mankind with a lance and Shrift gives him confession and absolution. The Virtues guard him in their castle
against the assaults of the Devil and the Flesh. Covetousness,
however, tempts Mankind in old age to forsake his hope of heaven
for gold. Death strikes him down and the World deceives him by
giving his treasure to a stranger, but he dies calling on God for
mercy. The Soul prays God to help as the Bad Angel carries him
to hell. Mercy and Peace plead for him in heaven against stern
Righteousness and Truth, till God the Father orders Mankind
saved from the fiend to sit at his right hand.

The main body of the play, lines 157–2777, dramatizes man's
life on earth as he wavers between good and evil, followed by a
second part on death and a third part on judgement. Ramsay in
his introduction to Skelton's *Magnyfycence*, p. clxv, calls these
three parts Conflict of the Vices and Virtues, The Coming of
Death, and The Debate of the Heavenly Graces, and divides the
first part into six sequences, Innocence, Temptation, Life-in-Sin,
Repentance, then again Temptation and Life-in-Sin. The banns
tell the story in nine stanzas, six on the life of man, two on his
death and call for mercy, and one on his salvation. They devote two
stanzas to the most dramatic action, the siege of the castle with the
combats between vices and virtues. On the other hand, they make
no mention of the declaration of war against man at the beginning
or of the debate of God's daughters at the end. The play begins by
showing the power of man's enemies, the World, the Devil, and
the Flesh; it ends by showing the greater power of God. But for
his mercy the drama would be a tragedy, the fall of man from
prosperity to death and damnation. The final scenes in heaven are
therefore essential to the Christian meaning of the play.

The unity of the play depends on Mankind, around whom the
action revolves until Death ends his earthly life and only the Soul
remains. The author carefully balances his thirty other characters,
fifteen bad against fifteen good. The Bad Angel from hell opposes
the Good Angel sent by Christ from heaven; the Seven Sins fight
in turn against the Seven Virtues; while the Devil, the Flesh and,
the World with four of his followers, Pleasure, Folly, Backbiter,

and Servant, make up another unholy alliance of seven who contrast with, though they do not confront, Shrift and Penance, the Four Daughters, and God the Father. Good and evil are more evenly matched than in Marlowe's *Faustus*, where the Good Angel and the Old Man are helpless against the Bad Angel, the Seven Sins, Mephistophilis, Lucifer, and Beelzebub. Mankind is in a like situation during the first third of *The Castle of Perseverance*, where the Good Angel stands alone against fourteen enemies, but the balance shifts while Mankind perseveres in goodness, and again when he faces damnation, till God at last swings the pendulum to the side of mercy.

The greater scope of the play and the long-windedness of its speeches keep *The Castle of Perseverance* from achieving the concentrated intensity of *Everyman*. The author dared beyond his strength in undertaking to present the whole life of man from birth to death and the judgement of the soul in heaven. He divided between two speakers only one long stanza and seven quatrains; otherwise every speech runs a full course of one to six stanzas, each usually thirteen or nine lines long. Fewer words would be more effective. Yet the author had a strong sense of pattern: the three kings begin with three stanzas apiece, the Good Angel speaks one stanza and the Bad Angel another, each Sin attacks a Virtue in a single stanza and each Virtue answers in two. When a speech is longer than three stanzas, it carries dramatic weight: the first speech of Mankind and of Backbiter, the single soliloquy of Death, the parting shot of the Bad Angel, the pleas of the Four Daughters, and the final speech of God.

The Castle of Perseverance rises at times to moving drama: Mankind saying in bewilderment, 'Whereto I was to þis werld browth/ I ne wot. . . . A, Lord Jhesu, wedyr may I goo?'; hoping that he may 'Make mery a ful great throwe./ I may leuyn many a day'; renouncing 'Sory synne, þou grysly gore'; saying of the Virtues, 'Here arn my best frendys', yet turning to Covetousness because 'Penyman is mekyl in mynde'; Death declaring, 'Ageyns me is no defens./ In þe grete pestelens/ þanne was I wel knowe'; Mankind begging desperately, 'World, World, haue me in mende!/ Good Syr Werld, helpe now Mankend!'; Mercy pleading that 'Mankynd is of oure kyn'; and God saying at the end, 'As a sparke of fyre in þe se/ My mercy is synne quenchand.' Backbiter and the Bad Angel are merry devils, and all man's enemies are both dangerous and absurd, for though man is no match for them, they are no match for God. The play is a mirror for every man to see himself:

> All men example hereat may take
> To mayntein þe goode and mendyn here mys.
> þus endyth oure gamys.

II. WISDOM

1. *Manuscripts*

The play has no title in the Macro manuscript or in the incomplete copy in Digby MS. 133 in the Bodleian. Thomas Sharp in 1835 gave it the title *Mind, Will, and Understanding*, and Furnivall in 1882 called it *A Morality of Wisdom, Who is Christ* and referred to it as *Wisdom*. Because of the two titles the play is listed as two different plays in C. J. Stratman's *Bibliography of Medieval Drama*.[1]

The Macro manuscript of *Wisdom* was copied in the late fifteenth century by the same scribe who copied the greater part of *Mankind* (ff. 122–32^r). This scribe wrote an average of 25 lines to a page in *Wisdom*. The twenty-four leaves (ff. 98–121), which measure 220 by 160 mm., are in two quires of twelve leaves each. The watermark on each quire is a pot with cover and handle, resembling Briquet's nos. 12476–80, used in France in 1471 and later. This watermark appears in a later form on two leaves which were added to the manuscript of *Ludus Coventriae*.[2]

A monk named Hyngham wrote these verses at the end of the Macro *Wisdom* and again at the end of *Mankind*:

> O liber si quis cui constas forte queretur
> Hynghamque monacho dices super omnia consto.

The abbreviation after Hyngham is expanded by Pollard to *que*, by Furnivall to *quem*, and by Manly to *quod*, but the sign stands for enclitic *-que*. The sense requires *queret* for *queretur*. The lines

---

[1] Nos. 2140–3, 2360–5; cf. nos. 36–38, 1384–6, 2080–2.
[2] *Ludus Coventriae*, ed. Block, p. xi. The Digby MS. of *Wisdom* is on paper marked with a gloved hand and star.

may be translated: 'O book, if anyone shall perhaps ask to whom you belong, you will say, "I belong above everything to Hyngham, a monk."' The hand is probably of the late fifteenth century. Thomas Hyngham, monk, wrote his name as owner ('constat') in a fifteenth-century manuscript of Boethius in English formerly at Bury St. Edmunds, and Thomas Hengham, monk of Norwich (? *fl.* 1447), owned two Latin manuscripts.[1] Richard Hengham or Hyngham, Doctor of Canon Law, was abbot of Bury from 1474 to 1479.[2]

In the first half of the sixteenth century various persons wrote in the margins or blank leaves of the Macro manuscript of *Wisdom*. Robert Oliver, who also owned *Mankind* (f. 134), used two ciphers in the manuscript of *Wisdom*. In one he represented a vowel by p with one to five cross-strokes for a, e, i, o, u; in the other he substituted for a vowel the next letter of the alphabet (b, f, k, p, or x). This second cipher is called 'grew' for 'Greek' in the first version and 'grw' in the second version of these rhymes on f. 121^v:

> B for a stondyng aye
> f for e in god fay
> k for j yt yss no nay
> p for o put therto
> and he y^t wyll wryght grw
> must put a x for a v.

In this second cipher Oliver wrote on f. 119^v: 'Iste liber pertinet ad me Robertum Oliuer' and another line now only partly legible. He began to write the same words on other leaves (ff. 99, 103–4, 117^v), and he wrote 'Robetum Oliuer' in his first cipher on f. 101. 'Rainold Wodles' is written in the same two ciphers and three others (ff. 99^v, 121^v) and 'gonolde' in the same two ciphers along with 'thomas gonnolld' written backwards (f. 108). Also written backwards are 'Thomas Wyllym book' (f. 115), 'Kis min arcs knave' (f. 114^v), and 'Thus me to cummande to wryght wyth my left hande' (f. 98^v, partly repeated on f. 114^v). 'Iohn Plandon' is

---

[1] N. R. Ker, *Medieval Libraries of Great Britain*, ed. 1964, pp. 234, 285. Cf. M. R. James, *Catalogue of MSS. in Corpus Christi College, Cambridge*, i. 506.

[2] W. K. Smart, *Some English and Latin Sources and Parallels for the Morality of Wisdom*, p. 86; A. B. Emden, *Biographical Register of the University of Cambridge to 1500* (1963).

written in Arabic numerals representing the twenty-four letters without *i* or *u* (f. 104). 'John' and 'Thomas' appear many times, once with 'Jamys' (f. 118ᵛ). The only mention of a place is in the opening lines of a will which began 'In the name of god amen I Rychard Cake of Bury senior . . .' (f. 105, partly repeated on f. 106).[1]

This ballad with a refrain is written on ff. 111ᵛ and 112:

ther wer iij lowely on pyllgrymag wolld goo a—
marya
the fyst was marymaudellen who*m* cryst forgaue her syn a—
marya
the secu*n*de was mary regypte[2] next of all hyr kyn a—
marya
yᵉ therde owʳ bllyssyde lady yᵉ flower of all wome*n* a—
marya.

The same hand writes onc line on f. 113: 'met & dry*n*ke thy had inowe but logynge' (written above cancelled 'clothyng'). Another hand writes on f. 117:

Wythe hufa
Wythe huffa wᵗ huffa wᵗ huffa onys agen
A gallant glorius.

A man surrounded by dragons is drawn on f. 98ᵛ and the head of a man on f. 121ᵛ.

Punctuation is rare, but a separating point is sometimes used for clarity, as in *all thre. on* (8), *sowll. of Gode* (143), *For. for loue* (268), *Jenet .N.* (834). A colon is written after *wythowt* in 325 s.d., and cancelling dots in 430, 483, and 1017. Lines sometimes join three consecutive rhymes, as in 325–411, and a line across the page follows every speech and stage direction.

The scribe uses the abbreviations *þᵗ*, *þᵘ*, *wᵗ* (written *wyth* in 863), and *i* above the line for *ri*, as in *tⁱnyte*. Letters may be written

[1] A Richard Cake (rector of Bradfield 1503–12?) was given Harley MS. 211 by Prior Waterpytte of Norwich Carmelite convent (Ker, *Medieval Libraries*, p. 286). A Thomas Gonnell of Croxton, Cambs., made a will proved in 1492 (British Record Soc. x. 242; cf. Thomas Gunnell in Emden and William Gonell in *D.N.B.*). A John Plandon was named in a Bury will of 1504 (Camden Soc. xlix. 98); a John Plandon wrote in 1530 about the lands of Wolsey's colleges at Oxford and Ipswich (*Letters and Papers, Henry VIII*, iv, pt. iii. 3018); and John Plandon of Eriswell, Suffolk, left a will proved in 1551 (British Record Soc. xi. 418; cf. xi. 585 for the will of William Wodles or Woodles of Ipswich).
[2] So written for 'mary of egypte'.

above the line even when nothing is omitted, as in $þ^{an}$, $þ^e$, $þ^{er}$, $þ^{es}$ $þ^{ey}$, $þ^i$, $þ^{is}$, y^e, 3^e. Besides using all the signs found in *The Castle of Perseverance*, the scribe also abbreviates *ser* and *sub*. He indicates a contraction or the omission of *n* or *m* or of *i* in -*cion* by a horizontal stroke, by a flourish, or by a flourish with a dot over the final letter. Often he ends a word with an ornamental flourish or adds a stroke over *ght* or *th*.

In Digby MS. 133 the first 752 lines of *Wisdom* and the stage direction following are written by one scribe on ff. 158–69, a gathering of twelve leaves. The play just before *Wisdom* is headed 'candelmes day & the kyllynge of the children of Israell. anno domini 1512', and *Wisdom* is in a hand of about that date.

The Digby MS., which contains four plays from the East Midlands and treatises on astronomy and astrology, was owned by Miles Blomefylde, a physician and alchemist born at Bury St. Edmunds in 1525. He signed his name at the head of *The Conversion of St. Paul* and his initials at the head of *Mary Magdalene* and of *Wisdom*. He also preserved the only known copy of *Fulgens and Lucres*, on which he wrote, 'I am Miles Blomefyldes booke.'[1]

The Digby text of *Wisdom* is independent of the Macro text, since it supplies five lines omitted from the earlier manuscript (66, 448, 496, 600, 720) and occasional words (as in 63, 176, 190). It gives one more stage direction, *Exient* in 518, and preserves words no longer present or legible in the Macro stage directions at 1, 16, 164, and 324. Both scribes make frequent errors, but the readings of the Digby manuscript must be taken into account.

2. *Date*

Pollard dated the composition of *Wisdom* somewhere about 1460 and Smart about 1460–3. We shall see that *Mankind* was probably written between 1465 and 1470, and the language of *Wisdom* seems to be of about the same period.

3. *Language*

The dialect of *Wisdom* is a variety of East Midland. The Macro scribe's most characteristic practices concern his representation of

[1] *D.N.B.*; Henry Medwall, *Fulgens and Lucres*, ed. F. S. Boas and A. W. Reed, 1926.

certain consonants, and show him to have been an East Anglian. In particular, the use of *x* for *sh-* in *xall* and *xulde* (e.g. 51, 340) is common in Norfolk and Suffolk.[1] The scribe often writes *w* instead of initial *wh* (*wyche* 5, *wyght* 'white' 16 s.d., *wat* 73)—but *h* in *how* 'who' 839—while on the other hand he has *wh* for *w* in *whoo* 'woe' 347 and for *h* in *whowe* 'how' 891. *W* is also common for consonantal *v*, as *wery* 15, *wertu* 378, *belowyde* 13. Earlier *-ht* is normally written *ght*, as *lyght* 22, *broughte* 23, but the *gh* is occasionally omitted, as in *sleyttys* 674, *sowte* 18 (rhyming *sowght* 21), *nowte* 950, *thowte* 955. The loss of the fricative thus indicated is confirmed by rhymes such as *sleyght*, *myght* 725–6 : *dyscheyit*, *qwytte* 849 : *fyght*, etc., and by numerous spellings with unhistorical *ght* such as *beyght* 'bait', *byght* 'bite', *endyght* 'indict', *lought* 'bow', *tyght* 'quickly', *wyght* 'white'.

The main points of interest in vowels are as follows:

The reflex of OE. *a* before lengthening groups is usually written *o*, as *olde* 956, *lombys* 490, *londe* 732, *longe* 242, but sometimes *a* as *stande*, *lande*, *hande* rhyming on *wynnande*, etc. 677–83, and *hangynge* 16 s.d.

The reflex of OE. *ā* is normally written *o*, as *go* 319, etc., *lore* 418 and *more* 1000 rhyming *before*, etc., *sorre* 331 rhyming *store*; but *a* also appears in *mare* 740, 814 rhyming *hare*, *bare*.

The reflex of OE. *ǣ²* rhymes with that of *ē* in *sprede* 453 : *hede*, etc.

The reflex of OE. *i*, normally *i* or *y*, is *e* in *Cresten* 177, *sekyr* 368, *hedyr*, *thedyr* 199 rhyming *togedyr* (but *hydyr*, *thedyr* rhyming *togydyr* 728–32). Cf. also *rebaldry* 749, *tenker* 752.

The reflex of OE. *y̆* is normally written *y*, as *synne* 158 rhyming *wythin*, *mynde* 42 rhyming *mankynde* but also *hende*, *ende*, and 189 rhyming *ende* (and similar rhymes at 294–9, 527–33); but *e(e)* in *knett* 196, 231 rhyming *dett*, *sett*, and *feer* 821 rhyming *yer*, etc. *Bye* 665 rhymes on *I*.

The reflex of OE. *ēg* is written *y* in *lye* 750 rhyming *by*, but *ey* 1086 rhyming *crye*, etc.

[1] For examples see S. B. Meech in *Speculum*, ix (1934), 73 and E. J. Dobson in *Medium Ævum*, ix (1940), 153. For this and other features of East Anglian English of the fifteenth century see N. Davis, *The Language of the Pastons* (Proceedings of the British Academy, xl, 1955), and references there.

The main points of interest in accidence are the following:

Nouns. The genitive singular ends in *-ys*, the plural in *-ys* (*-es*) or *-s*. Exceptional plurals are *bren* 'eyebrows' 196, *chylderne* 406.

Pronouns. Fem. sg. *sche, here, here*; 2 pl. *ye* (*ʒe*), *yowr, yow*; 3 pl. *they* (*þey*), *her(e), hem* (*them* 811).

Verbs. The infinitive with *n* occurs only in one rhyme (*sene* 59). In the present indicative, the 3 sg. ends in *-th, -t*, with *-s* only in rhyme (*tellys*, etc. 270–75, *conteynys* 1010, *has* 177, *hase, mase* 576–9). The present plural is usually without distinctive ending, but there are a few forms in *-n* (*bene* 56, *fallyn* 438, *endyn* 878), and in *-th(e)* (*bethe* 178, *doth* 1028, *hathe* 53), and *has* 1093 (rhyming *trespas*). About half the strong past participles end in *-n* (e.g. *foundon* 28, *yewyn* 576, *holdyn* 585, *ben* 109, *don* 915, *seen* 818); the prefix *i-* is not used. The present participle ends in *-ynge*, sometimes *-enge* as *knowenge* 155, *cryenge* 550 s.d., with *-ande* only in rhyme (677–83, 777–83).

The *Oxford English Dictionary* does not give *enbraces* 'briberies', *juge-partynge*, or *malewrye* and it cites only *Wisdom* for *grates* 'thanks', *informable*, and *tenderschyppe*. The following words have not been found earlier than *Wisdom* (parentheses give the date of the first other record in *OED*.): *affyable* 'affable' (1540), *per-ceyvable* (1567), *perverse* v. (1574), *recognycyon* (1473), *recordaunce* (1490), *recurable* (1608), *reporture* (c. 1485), *victoryall* (1501), *wy* interj. 'why' (1519), *wyppe* interj. 'whip' (1525), and *wyrry* n. 'worry' (1804).

4. *Verse*

All but ten of the 145 stanzas have eight lines: seventy-two stanzas rhyme *ababbcbc*, one *ababcbcb* (301–8), sixty *aaabaaab*, and two *aaabcccb*. A line is missing in three other stanzas, two with two rhymes (551–7, 574–80) and one with three rhymes (1133–9). Two stanzas have four lines rhyming *abab* (1053–6, 1081–4), three have ten lines rhyming *aaabaaabcc* (509–18, 725–34, 735–44), and two have twelve lines rhyming *ababbcbccdcd* (49–60, 881–92).

Wisdom and the Soul speak in dignified, regular rhythm, almost always with four stresses and rhyming *ababbcbc*. Lucifer prefers a tripping measure with two to five stresses and only two rhymes. Mind, Will, and Understanding begin and end by speaking as Wisdom does, but they speak in the rhythm and stanza form of

Lucifer when they talk with him or under his influence. Alliteration is not much used except in the scene of the devil's dance (685–776).

Pollard notes that 'The author has a very fair sense of rhythm and a good command of rimes.' About one line in four rhymes on a suffix: -*able* 28 times, -*all* 18, -*ance* or -*ence* 42, -*cion* 54, -*ent* 14, -*ly* 51, -*nes* 22, -*schyppe* 6, -*te* or -*ty* 24, -*ure* 10, -*ynge* 16, and participial -*ande* 9. Since most stanzas need either four or six words to rhyme together, the same word rhymes twice in thirteen stanzas. Rhymes like those found in *The Castle* occur in *wylde*: *exyled* and *mylde*: *reconsylyde* (616–20, 982–4).

5. Sources

Smart published a valuable study of the English and Latin sources for *Wisdom*.[1] He showed that the author based most of the first ninety lines on an English version of *Orologium Sapientiae* by the mystic Henry Suso, translated into English before 1411 by a Carthusian of Beauvale, Notts.[2] Walter Hilton's *Scale of Perfection*, written in English in Nottinghamshire before 1396, furnished many ideas and phrases for *Wisdom*, 103–70 and 1117–58, and Hilton's *Epistle on Mixed Life* was used in 401–29. Latin works drawn on in *Wisdom* include two treatises formerly attributed to St. Bernard, *Meditationes de Cognitione Humanae Conditionis* and *Tractatus de Interiori Domo*, St. Bonaventure's *Soliloquium*, and the anonymous *Novem Virtutes*. These religious writings are used mainly in the first and last scenes of the play. The author is more independent when he describes the temptation by Lucifer and especially when he satirizes the vices of his contemporaries.

The author quotes many Latin texts from the Vulgate, most often from *Sapientia* (*Wisdom of Solomon*) or *Cantica Canticorum Salamonis* (*Song of Solomon*) but also from *Psalms*, *Proverbs*, *Lamentations*, *Malachi*, *Ecclesiasticus*, *Matthew*, *Romans*, *Ephesians*, and *Colossians*. Eight of these texts are quoted in the *Scale of Perfection* and others are quoted in *Orologium Sapientiae* or the

[1] Walter K. Smart, *Some English and Latin Sources and Parallels for the Morality of Wisdom*, 1912.

[2] Karl Horstmann, 'Orologium Sapientiae or The Seven Poyntes of Trewe Wisdom', *Anglia*, x (1888), 123–89; G. Schleich ,'Auf den Spuren Susos in England', *Archiv*, clvi (1929), 184–94.

Meditationes. All but one occur in the first or fourth scene, while all but one of the proverbs or proverbial expressions occur in the second or third scene.

6. *Staging*

The stage directions in English for producing *Wisdom* are unusually full, unlike the brief notes in Latin (*Exient* in 518 and 776, *Et cantent* in 620, and *Hic recedunt demones* in 978). They describe the costumes of every character: Wisdom as a king in purple cloth of gold, Anima as a maid in white and black, the Five Wits and Three Mights all in white, Lucifer arrayed as a devil and then as a gallant, six retainers with red beards, six dressed as jurors, six as gallants or matrons, and small boys as devils. They tell what verses to sing during each procession, as the Five Wits enter after 164 and lead the going out after 324, and as the Soul sings sadly while she and her faculties go out after 996 and joyfully when they return to Wisdom after 1064. Most of the entrances and exits are marked, but no entrance is given for Mind, Will, and Understanding at 179, 381, or 551–66 or for Wisdom at 873.

Pollard counted thirty-eight players and supposed that twenty-four of these were on stage together during the dances. These numbers, however, include three minstrels. Bevington suggested that the play was 'intended for five to six speaking actors with six boy "mutes"', assuming that one player probably doubled as Wisdom and Lucifer and that the boys who played devils also played the Five Wits and all the dancers in turn. This would leave the player of Wisdom no time to change to the 'devil's array' of Lucifer. Boys might have played all the silent parts, and it seems likely that each set of dancers left the stage before the next entered, though there is only one *Exient* for them all (at 776). On the other hand, the direction after 752 begins, 'Here entreth vi women in sut, [iii] dysgysyde as galontys and iii as matrones', and it is not easy to see why three boys dressed as men should be called women. Probably these six dancers were women but all the dances might be omitted if necessary, as suggested by the marginal notes before 685 and 785 which together read 'vacat'.[1] A similar note after 164 suggests omission of the virgins who represented the Five Wits.

[1] In the Digby *Candlemas Day* (*Digby Plays*, pp. 2, 19–23) 'virgynes, as many as a man wyll', dance at the end of the play to 'shewe summe sport & plesure'.

The 'vi small boys' in the direction after 912 should probably read 'vii small boys', since they play the Seven Deadly Sins. The naughty boy carried off by Lucifer at 550 may have been taken from the audience. If this boy and the minstrels are omitted, the play would then have thirty-six roles, but without the dances it could have been acted by six men and seven boys.

There is no clear evidence that the play was acted before an audience of monks, as Smart supposed, or by schoolboys, as Chambers conjectured, or by students at an Inn of Court during Lent, as Molloy suggested. If it had been taken on tour, there would probably be either banns as in *The Castle* and *Ludus Coventriae*, or an appeal for money as in *Mankind*. *Wisdom* may have been presented by the men and women of a town or guild for a general audience.

7. *The Play*

Wisdom dramatizes the struggle between Christ and Lucifer to win man's soul. The play begins and ends as a sermon. Wisdom, richly dressed as Christ the King, speaks first to the audience and then to Anima, the Soul. The three powers of the Soul, Mind, Will, and Understanding, obey the command of Wisdom to declare their signification. Wisdom gives them good advice, but the fiend, Lucifer, gives the more friendly counsel. They make merry with song and dance, they boast of their wicked life, but in the end they listen to Wisdom and the Soul is saved. The war between Christ and Satan for the soul of man is a clear conflict between white and black.

After Wisdom opens the play by introducing himself as the Son of God, the maiden Anima kneels down to declare her love, and he assures her of God's love. Every soul here, he says, is like her, black through sin and white through the knowing of God. The Five Wits of the Soul enter as virgins, singing; then the Three Mights of the Soul, Mind, Will, and Understanding, tell how each is needed for knowing God. Wisdom warns them to beware of the World, the Flesh, and the Fiend, but no sooner is the stage clear than Lucifer reveals to the spectators how subtly he will tempt man. Disguised as a proud gallant, he soon persuades Mind to devote himself to pride, Understanding to covetousness, and Will to lechery. All agree that maintenance, perjury, and lust were never more flourishing in England. Each calls in six followers who dance. The Three Mights fall to fighting each other, but then resolve to be merry. Wisdom makes them repent by showing how they have disfigured Anima, who now looks 'fowlere þan a fende', but who drives out the devils of deadly sin by her contrition. After she has confessed her sins off stage, she returns with her Five Wits and Three Mights, all in white as at first but now wearing crowns as symbols of victory over sin. Anima rejoices that she has been cleansed from sin by the grace of the 'hye soueren Wysdam, my joy, Cristus'.

The play can be divided into four scenes, which picture in turn Innocence, Temptation, Sinful Life, and Repentance. Only six characters speak: Wisdom and Anima in the first and fourth scenes, Lucifer in the second, and Mind, Understanding, and Will in all four scenes. The play lacks the focus of a single character representing Mankind: Anima is a puppet who suffers rather than acts, the Five Wits do not even speak, while the choices between good and evil are made by Mind and accepted by Understanding and Will. This committee of three is all too unanimous, except when they come to blows in scene three; and it is hard to share the emotions of such abstract personifications. The use of monologue is overdone: Wisdom addresses the audience in 1–16 and in 997–1064, Lucifer in 325–80 and in 519–50. The dialogue is formal and didactic, except for the Devil's eloquence and the gay speeches of the third scene.

Wisdom is too intent on teaching moral virtue to have much concern with dramatic virtues. The author combines preaching with pageantry, offering the spectators a feast for the eye with cloth of gold and ermine, 'a rich imperial crown' and golden orb and sceptre. He brings in four processions with songs of joy or lamentation; Lucifer roaring, and later carrying off a naughty boy; a three-men's song by the Three Mights; and the wild dancing of six men with red beards, six jurors who wear two faces in a hood, and six women with wonderful visors. The play is a good show. Its main purpose is not political satire, as Ramsay supposed (introduction to *Magnyfycence*, p. lxxi), but exhortation to Christian living:

> Nowe ye mut euery soule renewe
> In grace, and vycys to eschew,
> Ande so to ende wyth perfeccyon.

III. MANKIND

1. *Manuscript*

One scribe wrote ff. 122–32ʳ and a second scribe wrote the last four pages, ff. 132ᵛ–4ʳ. Pollard thought that the same hand wrote the last four pages with a softer pen and different ink, but the letters are also formed differently, as may be seen in Farmer's facsimile. The first scribe crowded in an average of thirty-nine lines to a page, while the second scribe wrote only twenty-six or twenty-seven lines to a full page. The manuscript now contains thirteen leaves, which measure 220 by 160 mm. and consist of a single leaf (f. 122 in modern numbering) and a quire of twelve leaves. The original second leaf has been lost, since the surviving leaves are numbered i, iii, iv, v, vi, vii, viii, ix, x, with the last four leaves unnumbered. These numbers were written by the first scribe, for after writing *ix* he added three omitted lines above and below this number. The watermark is a hand and star, but it is not like any of the 988 forms of the hand shown in Briquet.

The monk Hyngham wrote the same inscription at the end of *Mankind* as at the end of *Wisdom*. Another writer wrote 'in the name of god amen' on f. 124 in the same hand which wrote in *Wisdom* 'In the name of god amen I Rychard Cake of Bury senior. . .'. An owner's inscription, later crossed out, appears on f. 134, 'Robertus olyuer est verus possessor hvius lybry', as well as 'Olyuer' and 'nouerint vniversi p', all in sixteenth-century writing. A 'John', who wrote his name many times (ff. 125–6, 134ᵛ), wrote this lament on f. 134ᵛ and then turned most of it into Latin[1]:

I trow I was cursyd in my motherys bely or ellys I was born a onhapy ower for I can neu*er* do thyng þat me*n* be plesid wythall now yff I do þe best I can oftetymys yt chancys onhapily I haue not knowne a felou so onhapi exsepte þe deuyll ware on hym for euyne now at þis tyme I am suer my master haue ii or iii greuys compleyntys on me at þis time yf yt be so my bottkes goo to wreke.

---

[1] Similar passages for boys to put into Latin are found in *A Fifteenth Century School Book*, ed. W. Nelson, 1956, nos. 172, 183, 222 ('I trowe I was borne in an unhappy season').

The first scribe often places a point within a line, with a bar in lines 5 and 6, and he adds cancelling dots in line 21. The second scribe, instead of a point, uses a bar in 819 and 838 and three bars before *amen* at the end, and he joins rhymes by lines in 823–34. Both scribes draw a line across the page to separate speeches.

The scribes abbreviate *þᵗ*, *þᵘ*, and *wᵗ*, employ the conventional signs for syllables, and write letters above the line without omission or to indicate omitted *r* or another letter (as in *nᶜlygence* 23 and *Wyllᵃm* 506). They mark a contraction or the omission of *n* or *m* either by a stroke or by a flourish, and they sometimes add a stroke through *h* or over *ght*. The first scribe, but not the second, often adds a dot to an ornamental flourish over final *n* or *m* (as in 3, 4, 5).

2. Date

Two passages have been used to date the composition of the play, 'Gyf ws rede reyallys' in 465 and 'Anno regni regitalis / Edwardi nullateni' in 689–90. Smart pointed out that royals were first coined in 1465 and Baker noted that the play mentions every English coin current during the reign of Edward IV except the angel, which appeared between 1468 and 1470, so that he would date *Mankind* within a year or two of 1466.[1] Smart dated the play in February 1471, during the time when Edward IV was not recognized as king. It could not, however, have been written at this time, since 'Master Alyngton of Botysam', mentioned in 514, was in exile with Edward from September 1470 to April 1471.[2] There is no proof that the play was revised. It may have been written between 1465 and 1470.

3. Language

Mankind is written in an East Midland dialect, with East Anglian *x* in *xall*, *xuld(e)* (the second scribe wrote both *xall* and *schall*). The place-names in 505–15 show that the play was acted in Cambridgeshire and Norfolk, and there is a reference in 274 to Bury in Suffolk.

[1] W. K. Smart, *Some English and Latin Sources and Parallels for the Morality of Wisdom*, p. 89 n., and 'Some Notes on *Mankind*', *Modern Philology*, xiv (1916), 45–58, 293–313; Donald C. Baker, 'The Date of *Mankind*', *Philological Quarterly*, xlii (1963), 90–91.
[2] J. C. Wedgwood, *History of Parliament*, i. 9.

Mankind differs from *Wisdom* in having *qw* for *wh* in *qwyll* 543, *qwyppe* 795, *qwyst* 557 beside *whyll* 414 and *wyll* 77, etc., *wher* 430 and *were* 502, with *who* for 'woe' 748. For *v*, both initial and medial, the first scribe wrote both *v* and *w*, as in *awyse, werse, rewelynge,* while the second preferred *w*, as in *wyle, weyn, wertu, welle,* and *wanite* (cf. *Wisdom, wertu, wery,* and *werely*). The first scribe wrote *moche* (*myche* 205) and *such,* while the second wrote *mech* 838, *-moche* 846, *sych* 831, and *swheche* 891. Earlier *-ht* is normally written *ght* by both scribes, but the first sometimes uses *ȝte* as *sowȝte* 493, *owȝte* 494, *nyȝte* 769, and both occasionally use *t(e)* only, as *bowte* 116, 255, *sowte* 296, *browt* 889. Reverse spellings are rare: *smyght* 442.

The reflex of OE. *a* before lengthening groups is usually written *o*, as *tolde* 671, *wombe* 36 rhyming *lambe, londe* 37, *long(e)* 262, 275, *honge* 791, but sometimes *a* as *hande* 684, *hange* 621, 655, etc.

The reflex of OE. *ā* is regularly written *o(o)* as *go* 469, *goo* 100, *more* 852 rhyming *before, sory* 200 rhyming *story.* It often rhymes on the reflex of OE. *ō,* as *both* 585: *soth, goo* 455: *onto, ston* 562: *don, anon* 575: *don, wott* 785: *fote.*

The reflex of OE. *ǣ²* rhymes on that of *ēo* in *clen* 340: *sen*; and the reflex of OE. *ēa* rhymes on those of *ǣ¹* and *ē* in *to-beton* 422: *wepyn* 'weapon' and *wepyn* 'weep'.

The reflex of OE. *i,* normally *i* or *y,* is *e* in *leuyng* 170, *sekyr* 660, *wretyn* 317, 335, *hedyr* 69 and *hethyr* 351, 519 rhyming *together.* Cf. also *pety* 364, 828, *reuer* 36.

The reflex of OE. *ȳ* is normally written *y,* as *-hyll* 204 rhyming *yll, hyryde* 54 rhyming *dysyryde*; but *e* in *besy* 565, *mankend* 823 (second scribe—the first writes *mankynde* 214, 448 rhyming *ende,* etc.), *ferys* 323 rhyming *frerys, feer* 287 rhyming *dysyer.*

The reflex of OE. *ēg* is written *ye* in *hye* 241 rhyming *dysobey, eyi* n *eyn* rhyming *reyn* 156, *eye* 876 (second scribe) rhyming *obey.*

Nouns. The genitive singular ends in *-ys* except for *faders* 728, *flyes* 790. The plural ends in *-ys* (*-es, -is*) or *-s* (*-se* in *felouse* 157, etc., *gallouse* 608). Exceptional plurals are *brothern* 29 and *brethern* 110 (rhyming *together*), *eyn* 156, *fon* 307, 407, 420.

Pronouns. Fem. sg. *sche, her(e), her(e)*; 2 pl. *ȝe* (*ye*), *yowr, yow* (*ye* 80); 3 pl. *þei* (*they*), *þer* (*there* 167, *her* 169), *þem* or *them* (*hem* 491, 883, 885). This preference for *þer* and *þem* distinguishes *Mankind* from *Wisdom,* which has only *her* and usually *hem.*

Verbs. The infinitive ends in -(*y*)*n* only in rhyme (*then* 304, *wepyn* 423, *gon* 708). In the present indicative, the 3 sg. ends in -*th* except for -*t* in *hat* 224, 500 and -*s* in *spekys* 253, *compellys* 560, *avows* 607, *weys* 699. *Hath* is plural in 176. The present plural ends in -*n* only twice (*arn* 706, *ben* 64), but slightly more than half the strong past participles have -*n* (e.g. *brokyn* 497, *etun* 131, *torn* 4, *ben* 640, *don* 389, *sen* 302, etc.); the prefix *i*- is not used. The present participle ends only in -*yng*(*e*).[1]

Since *Mankind* was not printed until 1897, it contains a number of words not in the *Oxford English Dictionary*: *allectuose, belymett, corn-threscher, dalyacyon, despectyble, dryff-draff, fote-mett, ho*(*y*)*lyke, interleccyon, ouerblysse, ouerdylew, ouerpysse*. Several words are cited in *OED.* only from *Mankind*: *peruersyose, pervercionatt, premyabyll, recreatory*. The following words have not been found earlier than *Mankind* (parentheses give the date of the first other record in *OED.*): *adjutory* (1612), *aprehensyble* (*a.* 1631), *bely-fyll* (1535), *bredynge* n. 'reproach' (1552), *calcacyon* (1656), *clerycall* (1592), *convicte* n. (1530), *curtly* (1654), *delusory* (1588), *demonycall* (1588), *dyspectuose* (1541), *expedycius* (1599), *inconsyderatt* (1549), *inexcusabyll* (1526), *monytorye* (1586), *myssemasche* (1585), *nekeverse* (1528), *obliuyows* (1535), *obsequyouse* (1530), *onredyly* (1599), *ouerface* (c. 1535), *partycypable* (1610), *partycypatt* (1567), *patrocynye* (1529), *predilecte* (1774), *propagacyon* (1526), *puerilite* (1512), *reducyble* (1529), *rune* n. 'run' (1581), *scottlynge* n. (1873), *smattrynge* a. (1526), *suavius* (1669), *superatt* (1515), *supplicatorie* (1550).

4. *Verse*

Ramsay observes that the dramatic use of contrasted metres found in *Wisdom* is further refined in *Mankind* with 'an increasing delicacy in fitting each scene with its appropriate metre'.[2] Mercy and Mankind speak sixty-four four-line stanzas rhyming *abab* and Mercy when alone speaks seven eight-line stanzas rhyming *ababbcbc*. Mischief and others use tail-rhyme stanzas of eight lines, fifty-five rhyming *aaabcccb* and two *aaabaaab*. Titivillus speaks two stanzas of twelve lines, two of three lines, and three

---

[1] Brandl describes the language in his edition, pp. xxii–xxiv.

[2] R. L. Ramsay, introduction to Skelton, *Magnyfycence*, EETS., pp. cxxxix–cxl.

couplets. A line is missing in 147–53, 202–4, 631–7, 687–93, and 772–8, and other irregular stanzas occur in 53–63, 122–30, 305–10, 331–43, 392–404, 445–50, 662–70, and 750–5. Mercy and Mankind often link their stanzas by rhyme, especially in soliloquy (1–44, 186–208, 734–59), and Mischief mockingly caps the rhyme at 45 and 772. While Mercy and Mankind speak in regular rhythm with four stresses, Mischief and his friends vary their rhythms with spirit and vigour.

Pollard criticizes the bad rhymes and assonances in *Mankind*, but they are not very different from those in *Wisdom*. Unstressed final syllables are rhymed, and the same word rhymes twice in fifteen stanzas.

5. *Sources and Analogues*

Brandl (p. xxx of his edition) saw parallels with *The Assembly of Gods* attributed to Lydgate (p. 31), where Sensuality sows a field with weeds, but this field is a battlefield. Mabel Keiller compared the ploughing of a half-acre and the beating of two mockers in *Piers Plowman*, B. vi, but the resemblances are slight.[1] Mackenzie found a closer parallel in 'Mercy Passith Riȝtwisnes' (*Hymns to the Virgin and Christ*, ed. Furnivall, pp. 95–100), a verse dialogue in which Mercy, a priest as in *Mankind*, saves a sinner from the Devil's temptation to despair and gives him hope of mercy through penance and repentance.[2] Sister Philippa suggested as an analogue a sermon in *Jacob's Well* (i. 256–8), but this is only another example of traditional teachings about mercy.[3] *Mankind* makes use of familiar doctrines rather than of any known source.

The author quotes sixteen texts from the Vulgate: five from *Psalms*, three from *Job*, and single texts from 1 *Samuel*, *Proverbs*, *Ecclesiastes*, *Ezekiel*, *Matthew*, *John*, 2 *Corinthians*, and *Revelation* or *Deuteronomy* (475). He also quotes Latin rhymes by an unidentified 'nobyll versyfyer' (753–5) and a Latin proverb (882). As

---

[1] 'The Influence of *Piers Plowman* on the Macro Play of *Mankind*', *PMLA*, xxvi (1911), 339–55.

[2] W. Roy Mackenzie, 'A New Source for *Mankind*', *PMLA*, xxvii (1912), 98–105.

[3] Sister M. P. Coogan, *An Interpretation of the Moral Play, Mankind*, 1947, pp. 38–45.

Whiting observes, New Guise 'uses two splendid Wellerisms' (325–6 and 618).[1]

6. Staging

Mankind, which was acted by travelling players, is the first English play to mention the gathering of money from the audience (457–70). The 'house' in which it was acted (209, 467) was evidently an inn, since New Guise calls for the hostler (732). Although Pollard thought it was played in the inn yard, it may have been played inside the inn, for Mankind says, 'I wyll into þi ʒerde, souerens' (561).[2] The audience is addressed as 'ʒe souerens þat sytt and ʒe brothern þat stonde ryght wppe' (29) and all the yeomanry are invited to join in singing (333). The play was acted at villages in Cambridgeshire and Norfolk, perhaps in February at Shrovetide.[3]

The seven parts could have been played by six men if, as Brandl suggested, one doubled as Mercy and Titivillus (not as Mischief and Titivillus, since they speak consecutively in 453–6). Men rather than boys played New Guise, Nowadays, and Nought, for though Mischief mocks them as 'fayer babys' (427) New Guise and Nowadays speak of their wives (135, 246, 381) and Nought haunts a tapster (274–6). Minstrels are called on to play dances (72). Mercy is dressed as a 'semely father' (209), probably as a priest; Mankind wears a long gown and later a short jacket; and Titivillus has a large head (461), probably a devil's mask. Pollard says that there is no mention of any properties beyond a net for Titivillus, but Mankind has a spade, seed grain, paper, and beads, Mercy a scourge, Titivillus a board and weeds, Mischief a weapon, fetters, dish and platter, rope, and a gallows, and the others have purses, a flute, a halter, church goods, and pen and paper. All these, however, could be easily carried or borrowed.

The only stage directions in English are 'Her þei daunce' (81) and 'Here Titivillus goth out wyth þe spade' (549). The directions in Latin include six exits but no entrances, 'Cantent' (161), 'Cantant omnes' (343), 'Clamant' (424), 'Loquitur ad New Gyse

---

[1] Proverbs in the Earlier English Drama, 1938, p. 73.

[2] Brandl, p. xxxii; T. W. Craik, The Tudor Interlude, p. 128.

[3] W. K. Smart, 'Some Notes on Mankind', Modern Philology, xiv (1916), 45–58; Sister M. P. Coogan, An Interpretation of the Moral Play, Mankind, 1947, pp. 1–56.

... Nowadays ... Nought' (478–86), 'Nought scribit' (672), and 'Dicant omnes' (725). Other actions can be inferred from the lines, such as Mankind kneeling and rising (209–18, 553–61, 650–61, 811–902), beating his enemies with the spade (380) and going to sleep and snoring (588–92).

7. The Play

Mankind has the most high-spirited fun of all the early moral plays. Five of the seven characters are comic villains, mockers of Mercy and tempters of Mankind. The merry devil Titivillus, who 'syngnyfyth the Fend of helle' (886), tricks Mankind into giving up labour and prayer, for 'Titivillus kan lerne yow many praty thynges' (572). The worldlings New Guise, Nowadays, and Nought are good for nothing, not even when they try to tempt, but although they are beaten they keep bobbing up again irrepressibly. Mischief ridicules Mercy and almost succeeds in getting Mankind to hang himself in despair. Although Mercy saves Mankind, 'the vices monopolize the theatrical life of the play—its diversified intrigue and its humor'.[1]

Mercy appears in an unusual guise, not as feminine, the daughter of God, but as masculine, the father confessor of Mankind. He tells the spectators at once the theme of the play: Repent your sins and God will show mercy. Mischief makes fun of Mercy and burlesques his preaching. After a gap in the manuscript, three rogues have come in because, they say, they heard Mercy call 'New Gyse, Nowadays, Nought', and these are their names. Dancing around Mercy they mock his language as 'full of Englysch Laten'. When they have gone, Mankind asks Mercy for 'gostly comforte' and is warned against the temptation of the flesh, of the world, and especially of Titivillus. He drives away the wicked worldlings with his spade and goes to fetch seed for sowing. Mischief advises the worldlings to call in Titivillus and to gather money from the spectators who wish to see 'hys abhomynabull presens'. After all have paid, Titivillus jests with the three rogues and sends them to steal horses and other booty in Cambridgeshire and west Norfolk. Invisible to Mankind, Titivillus hides a board under the ground to prevent digging, spoils

---

[1] Bernard Spivack, *Shakespeare and the Allegory of Evil*, 1958, p. 123.

the seed by mixing it with weeds, steals the spade, distracts Mankind from praying, and whispers that Mercy is a horse-thief and that Mankind should ask mercy of New Guise, Nowadays, and Nought. New Guise, who has just escaped hanging when the rope broke, dresses Mankind in the latest fashion, while Mischief, fresh from murder and manslaughter, summons him to a mock court at which Mankind swears to rob, steal, and kill. Despairing of mercy, Mankind is about to hang himself when Mercy rescues him and shows him the way to confession and forgiveness.

Although no divisions are marked in the manuscript, Furnivall divided the play into three scenes: the first dominated by Mercy (1–412), the second by Titivillus (413–733), and the third by Mercy once again (734–914). The stage is clear only once, after 412, but Mankind has a change of heart after 733. Ramsay suggested the same four parts as for *Wisdom*: Innocence (1–322), Temptation (323–606), Life-in-Sin (607–771), and Repentance (772–914). The comedy is much more exuberant in *Mankind* than in *Wisdom*; Mischief, the three rogues, and Titivillus are all boisterous and unrestrained. They are certainly not restrained in their speech, but though 'in language þei be large' (295) it should be remembered that the speakers represent the world and the Devil. The play may have been acted at Shrovetide, since it refers to winter and February (691), and Shrove Tuesday was a last fling before Lent, often celebrated with football (732) and with processions such as one in 1443 when the King of Christmas rode with Lent through Norwich.[1] The Lenten themes of the play have been well brought out by Sister Philippa, who believes that the author was a Dominican friar, whereas Smart suggests that he may have been a clergyman or lawyer living in or near Cambridge. There is nothing to support the conjecture by Adams that 'Possibly the author merely reworked an earlier and more serious morality, eliminating the moral element, and accentuating in his own way the comic features.'[2] As Sister Philippa observes (pp. 108–9):

The comic parts serve the serious parts by illustrating the allegory, and by underlining the moral teachings through parody and negative

[1] W. K. Smart, 'Some Notes on *Mankind*', *Modern Philology*, xiv (1916), 45–58; Sister M. P. Coogan, *An Interpretation of the Moral Play, Mankind*, pp. 7–21.
[2] J. Q. Adams, *Chief Pre-Shakespearean Dramas*, p. 304.

example. The vulgarities indulged in by the comic characters cannot be regarded as a sign that the moral aspects of the play are not to be taken seriously, even though Mercy is occasionally held up to ridicule in such passages. The certainty of the ultimate triumph of the Good prevented the medieval audience from being too much disturbed at its momentary discomfiture.

Mankind is a better play than critics until recently have recognized. The speeches of Mercy are tedious, but moralizing must be expected in a moral play. The author had a serious purpose, to warn men against the world and the Devil, but in achieving his purpose he made use of lively humour and of comic action. He could write with colloquial vigour and mocking irony. The play is amusing to read and would probably be even funnier when acted. Written for the common people, '*Mankind* is the most indisputably popular play of the fifteenth century'.[1]

[1] D. M. Bevington, *From Mankind to Marlowe*, p. 48.

BIBLIOGRAPHY

A. EDITIONS

1. The Castle of Perseverance

The Macro Plays, ed. F. J. Furnivall and Alfred W. Pollard, EETS., Extra Series, xci, London, 1904 (reprinted in 1924).

The Castle of Perseverance, ed. John S. Farmer, *The Tudor Facsimile Texts*, London and Edinburgh, 1908; Amersham, 1914.

2. Wisdom

Ancient Mysteries from the Digby Manuscripts, ed. Thomas Sharp, Abbotsford Club, Edinburgh, 1835.

Mind, Will, and Understanding: A Morality, ed. W. B. D. D. Turnbull, Abbotsford Club, Edinburgh, 1837.

The Digby Mysteries, ed. F. J. Furnivall, New Shakspere Society, London, 1882.

The Digby Plays, with an Incomplete 'Morality' of Wisdom, Who is Christ, ed. F. J. Furnivall, EETS., Extra Series, lxx, 1896 (reprinted in 1930).

The Macro Plays (see above).

Wisdom, ed. John S. Farmer, *The Tudor Facsimile Texts*, London and Edinburgh, 1907; Amersham, 1914.

3. Mankind

Specimens of the Pre-Shaksperean Drama, ed. John M. Manly, vol. i, Boston, 1897.

Quellen des weltlichen Dramas in England vor Shakespeare, ed. Alois Brandl, *Quellen und Forschungen*, lxxx, Strassburg, 1898.

The Macro Plays (see above).

Mankind, ed. John S. Farmer, *The Tudor Facsimile Texts*, London and Edinburgh 1907; Amersham, 1914.

Recently Recovered 'Lost' Tudor Plays, ed. John S. Farmer, London, 1907,

Chief Pre-Shakespearean Dramas, ed. Joseph Quincy Adams, Boston, 1924.

B. COMMENTARY

1. The Macro Plays

ADAMS, HENRY H., *English Domestic or Homiletic Tragedy, 1575–1642*. New York, 1943.

BEVINGTON, DAVID M., *From Mankind to Marlowe*, Cambridge, Mass., 1962.

BLOOMFIELD, MORTON W., *The Seven Deadly Sins*, East Lansing, Michigan, 1952.

BROOKE, C. F. TUCKER, *The Tudor Drama*, Boston, 1911.

CHAMBERS, E. K., *English Literature at the Close of the Middle Ages*, Oxford, 1945.

——*The Mediaeval Stage*, Oxford, 1903.

CHEW, S. C., *The Virtues Reconciled, An Iconographic Study*, Toronto, 1947.

Chief Pre-Shakespearean Dramas, ed. Joseph Quincy Adams, Boston, 1924.

COLE, DOUGLAS, *Suffering and Evil in the Plays of Christopher Marlowe*, Princeton, 1962.

COLLIER, J. P., *The History of English Dramatic Poetry*, ii, London, 1831; 1879.

COLLINS, SISTER MARY EMMANUEL, 'The Allegorical Motifs in the Early English Moral Plays', unpublished dissertation, Yale University, 1936.

CRAIG, HARDIN, *English Religious Drama of the Middle Ages*, Oxford, 1955.

CRAIK, T. W., *The Tudor Interlude: Stage, Costume, and Acting*, Leicester, 1958.

CUSHMAN, L. W., *The Devil and the Vice in the English Dramatic Literature before Shakespeare, Studien zur englischen Philologie*, vi, Halle, 1900.

ECKHARDT, EDUARD, *Die lustige Person im älteren englischen Drama, Palaestra*, xvii, Berlin, 1902.

——'Die metrische Unterscheidung von Ernst und Komik in den englischen Moralitäten', *Englische Studien*, lxii (1927), 152–69.

FARNHAM, WILLARD E., *The Medieval Heritage of Elizabethan Tragedy*, Berkeley, 1936.

GAYLEY, CHARLES M., *Plays of Our Forefathers*, New York, 1907.

LOMBARDO, AGOSTINO, *Il dramma pre-shakespeariano: studi sul teatro inglese dal Medioevo al Rinascimento*, Venice, 1957.

McCUTCHAN, J. WILSON, 'Personified Abstractions as Characters in Elizabethan Drama', unpublished dissertation, University of Virginia, 1949.

MACKENZIE, W. ROY, *The English Moralities from the Point of View of Allegory*, Boston, 1914.

The Macro Plays (see above, under Editions).

NICOLL, ALLARDYCE, *Masks, Mimes, and Miracles: Studies in the Popular Theatre*, London and New York, 1931.

OWST, G. R., *Literature and Pulpit in Medieval England*, Cambridge, 1933.

RAMSAY, ROBERT L., introduction to Skelton's *Magnyfycence*, EETS., 1906.

Representative English Comedies, ed. C. M. Gayley, vol. i, New York, 1903.

ROSSITER, A. P., *English Drama from Early Times to the Elizabethans*, London, 1950.

SHARP, THOMAS, *A Dissertation on the Pageants or Dramatic Mysteries Anciently Performed at Coventry*, Coventry, 1825.

SPIVACK, BERNARD, *Shakespeare and the Allegory of Evil*, New York, 1958.

STRATMAN, CARL J., *Bibliography of Medieval Drama*, Berkeley and Los Angeles, 1954.

THOMPSON, ELBERT N. S., 'The English Moral Plays', *Transactions of the Connecticut Academy of Arts and Sciences*, xvi (1910), 293–413.

WHITING, B. J., *Proverbs in the Earlier English Drama*, Cambridge, Mass., 1938.

WICKHAM, GLYNNE, *Early English Stages, 1300 to 1660*, i, London and New York, 1959.

WILLIAMS, ARNOLD, *The Drama of Medieval England*, East Lansing, Michigan, 1961.

——'The English Moral Play before 1500', *Annuale Medievale* (Duquesne University Press), iv (1963), 5–22.

2. *The Castle of Perseverance*

ALLISON, TEMPE E., 'On the Body and Soul Legend', *Modern Language Notes*, xlii (1927), 102–6.

ARNOTT, P. D., 'The Origins of Medieval Theatre in the Round', *Theatre Notebook*, xv (1961), 84–87.

BENNETT, JACOB, 'A Linguistic Study of *The Castle of Perseverance*', unpublished dissertation, Boston University, 1960.

——'The "Castle of Perseverance": Redactions, Place, and Date', *Mediaeval Studies*, xxiv (1962), 141–52.

The Castle of Perseverance, A Free Adaptation from the Macro Play, ed. Iwa Langentels, London, 1948.

The Castle of Perseverance, The Most Ancient Morality Extant, 1425 A.D., Translated, Adapted and Modified for Modern Church Use in Approximately the Original Manner, ed. Phillips E. Osgood, Boston, 1940.

1   BIBLIOGRAPHY

CORNELIUS, ROBERTA D., *The Figurative Castle*, Bryn Mawr, 1930.

English Miracle Plays, Moralities and Interludes, ed. Alfred W. Pollard, Oxford, 1890.

HAMMERLE, KARL, '*The Castle of Perseverance* und *Pearl*', *Anglia*, lx (1936), 401–2.

HENRY, AVRIL K., '"The Castle of Perseverance": the Stage Direction at line 1767', *Notes and Queries*, ccx (1965), 448.

McCUTCHAN, J. WILSON, 'Covetousness in "The Castle of Perseverance"', *Univ. of Virginia Studies*, iv (1951), 175–91.

——'Justice and Equity in the English Morality Play', *Journal of the History of Ideas*, xix (1958), 405–10.

MACKENZIE, W. ROY, 'The Origin of the English Morality', *Washington University Studies*, II, part ii. (1915), 141–64.

——'The Debate over the Soul in "The Pride of Life"', *Washington University Studies*, IX, part ii. (1922), 263–74.

Medieval Mystery Plays, Morality Plays, and Interludes, ed. Vincent F. Hopper and Gerald B. Lahey, Great Neck, New York, 1962.

NICOLL, ALLARDYCE, *The Development of the Theatre*, London and New York, 1927.

REDDOCH, SISTER M. CALLISTA, 'Non-dramatic Sources and Analogues in a Typical English Morality, *The Castell of Perseverance*', unpublished M.A. thesis, Catholic Univ. of America, 1944.

ROBINSON, J. W., 'Three Notes on Medieval Theatre', *Theatre Notebook*, xvi (1961), 60–62.

SMART, WALTER K., 'The "Castle of Perseverance": Place, Date, and a Source', in *The Manly Anniversary Studies in Language and Literature*, Chicago, 1923, pp. 42–53.

SOUTHERN, RICHARD, *The Medieval Theatre in the Round, A Study of the Staging of The Castle of Perseverance and Related Matters*, London, 1957.

STODDARD, HARRIET C., 'The Presentation of *The Castle of Perseverance*', unpublished M.A. thesis, Univ. of Chicago, 1929.

TRAVER, HOPE, *The Four Daughters of God*, Philadelphia, 1907.

WILLIS, JAMES, 'Stage Directions in "The Castell of Perseverance"', *Modern Language Review*, li (1956), 404–5.

WITHINGTON, ROBERT, '*The Castle of Perseverance*, line 695', *Philological Quarterly*, xiv (1935), 270.

3. *Wisdom*

BEVINGTON, DAVID M., 'Political Satire in the Morality *Wisdom Who is Christ'*, in *Renaissance Papers 1963*, Durham, North Carolina, 1964, pp. 41–51.

Earlier English Drama from Robin Hood to Everyman, edited and arranged for acting by F. J. Tickner, London and Edinburgh, 1926.

GREEN, JOSEPH C., *The Medieval Morality of Wisdom Who is Christ*, Nashville, Tennessee, 1938.

MOLLOY, JOHN J., *A Theological Interpretation of the Moral Play, Wisdom, Who is Christ*, Washington, 1952.

SCHMIDT, KARL, 'Die Digbyspiele', *Anglia*, viii (1885), 371–404.

SMART, WALTER K., *Some English and Latin Sources and Parallels for the Morality of Wisdom*, Menasha, Wisconsin, 1912.

SMITH, SISTER M. FRANCES, *Wisdom and Personification of Wisdom Occurring in Middle English Literature before 1500*, Washington, 1935.

4. *Mankind*

BAKER, DONALD C., 'The Date of *Mankind'*, *Philological Quarterly*, xlii (1963), 90–91.

BROWN, ARTHUR, 'Folklore Elements in the Medieval Drama', *Folk-Lore*, lxiii (1952), 65–78.

COOGAN, SISTER M. PHILIPPA, *An Interpretation of the Moral Play, Mankind*, Washington, 1947.

JONES, CLAUDE, 'Walsyngham Wystyll', *Journal of English and Germanic Philology*, xxxv (1936), 139.

KEILLER, MABEL M., 'The Influence of *Piers Plowman* on the Macro Play of *Mankind'*, *PMLA*, xxvi (1911), 339–55.

MACKENZIE, W. ROY, 'A New Source for *Mankind'*, *PMLA*, xxvii (1912), 98–105.

SMART, WALTER K., '*Mankind* and the Mumming Plays', *Modern Language Notes*, xxxii (1917), 21–25.

—— 'Some Notes on *Mankind'*, *Modern Philology*, xiv (1916), 45–58, 293–313.

TABLE OF CORRESPONDING LINES

As the line-numbers of the three plays in the 1904 edition and the present one differ in detail a table of corresponding lines is given below.

	ECCLES	FURNIVALL
C.	1–361	C. 1–361
	362–410	363–411
	411–503	413–505
	504–16	507–19
	517–784	521–788
	785–6	789
	787–8	790
	789–866	791–868
	867–1749	870–1752
	1750–1	1753
	1752–3	1754
	1754–3649	1755–3650[1]
W.	1–509	W. 1–509
	510	510–11
	511–16	512–17
	517–18	518
	519–51	520–52
	552–79	554–81
	580–799	583–802
	800–1136	804–1140
	1137–63	1142–68
M.	1–124	M. 1–124
	125–8	(in note)
	129	125
	130	(in note)
	131–200	126–95
	201–2	(in note)
	203–914	196–907

[1] The 1924 reprint misnumbers lines 2334–2739 as 2434–2839.

THE CASTLE OF PERSEVERANCE

Sowth
Caro
skafold

þis is þe watyr abowte þe place, if any dyche may be mad þer it schal
be pleyed, or ellys þat it be strongely barryd al abowt, and lete nowth
ouyrmany stytelerys be wythinne þe plase.

> þis is þe castel of perseueraunse þat stondyth
> In þe myddys of þe place, but lete no men sytte þer,
> for lettynge of syt, for þer schal be þe best of all.

Est	Coveytyse copbord be þe beddys feet	West
deus	schal be at þe ende of þe castel.	mundus
skafold		skaffold

> Mankyndeis bed schal be vndyr þe castel
> and þer schal þe sowlc lye vndyr þe bed tyl
> he schal ryse and pleye.

Northe est   Northe
Coveytyse   Belyal
skaffold   skaffold

and he þat schal pley belyal loke þat he haue gunnepowdyr brennynge
In pypys in hys handys and in hys erys and in hys ars whanne he gothe
to batayl.

þe iiij dowterys schul be clad in mentelys, Mercy in wyth, rythwysnesse in red altogedyr, Trewthe in sad grene, and Pes al in blake, and
þei schul pleye in þe place altogedyr tyl þey brynge up þc sowle.

Margins trimmed] Est deus ...kafold, Wes... mund... skaffo..., brennyn...,
batay...

Hec sunt nomina ludentium.   f. 191

In primis ij vexillatores.

Mundus et cum eo Voluptas, Stulticia, et Garcio.

Belyal et cum eo Superbia, Ira, et Invidia.

Caro et cum eo Gula, Luxuria, et Accidia.

Humanum Genus et cum eo Bonus Angelus et Malus Angelus.

Auaricia, Detraccio.

Confessio, Penitencia.

Humilitas, Paciencia, Caritas, Abstinencia, Castitas, Solicitudo, et Largitas.

Mors.

Anima.

Misericordia, Veritas, Justicia, et Pax.

Pater sedens in trono.

Summa xxxvj ludentium.

Margin trimmed] Accidi...

THE BANNS

PRIMUS VEXILLATOR. Glorious God, in all degres lord most of
    myth,
  þat heuene and erthe made of nowth, boþe se and lond,
þe aungelys in heuene hym to serue bryth
  And mankynde in mydylerd he made wyth hys hond,
And our lofly Lady, þat lanterne is of lyth,   5
  Save oure lege lord þe kynge, þe leder of þis londe,
And all þe ryall of þis revme and rede hem þe ryth,
  And all þe goode comowns of þis towne þat beforn us stonde
     In þis place.
     We mustyr ȝou wyth menschepe   10
     And freyne ȝou of frely frenchepe.
     Cryst safe ȝou all fro schenchepe
      þat knowyn wyl our case.

SECUNDUS VEXILLATOR. þe case of oure comynge ȝou to declare,
  Euery man in hymself forsothe he it may fynde: 15
Whou Mankynde into þis werld born is ful bare
  And bare schal beryed be at hys last ende.
God hym ȝeuyth to aungelys ful ȝep and ful ȝare,
  þe Goode Aungel and þe Badde to hym for to lende.
þe Goode techyth hym goodnesse, þe Badde synne and sare;   20
  Whanne þe ton hath þe victory, þe toþyr goth behende,
     Be skyll.
     þe Goode Aungel coueytyth euermore Mans saluacion
     And þe Badde bysytyth hym euere to hys dampnacion,
     And God hathe govyn Man fre arbritracion   25
      Wheþyr he wyl hymself saue or hys soule spyll.

PRIMUS VEXILLATOR. Spylt is Man spetously whanne he to
    synne asent.
  þe Bad Aungel þanne bryngyth hym thre enmys so stout:

The Banns] *not in MS.*   5 our lofly] ...fly *MS. faded*   7 ryall] *F* ryallis
16 Whou] *MS.* whou *or* whon *F* whon   17 last] ...ast *MS. faded*   18 God]
good *corrected in margin to* god   25 govyn] *MS.* govym   26 hymself]
hym se... *MS. trimmed*   spyll] sp... ll *MS. faded F* peryll   28 thre]
MS. iij *Roman numerals throughout are changed to words*

þe Werlde, þe Fende, þe foul Flesche so joly and jent.
  þei ledyn hym ful lustyly wyth synnys al abowt.   30
Pyth wyth Pride and Coueytyse, to þe Werld is he went,
  To meynten hys manhod all men to hym lout.
Aftyr Ire and Envye þe Fend hath to hym lent,
  Bakbytynge and endytynge wyth all men for to route,
    Ful evyn.   35
      But þe fowle Flesch, homlyest of all,
      Slawth, Lust and Leccherye gun to hym call,
      Glotony and oþyr synnys boþe grete and small.
        þus Mans soule is soylyd wyth synnys moo þanne seuyn.

SECUNDUS VEXILLATOR. Whanne Mans sowle is soylyd wyth
    synne and wyth sore,   40
  þanne þe Goode Aungyl makyth mykyl mornynge
þat þe lofly lyknesse of God schulde be lore
  þorwe þe Badde Aungellys fals entysynge.
He sendyth to hym Concyens, pryckyd ful pore,   f. 154ᵛ
  And clere Confescyon wyth Penauns-doynge.   45
þei mevyn Man to mendement þat he mysdyd before.
  þus þei callyn hym to clennesse and to good levynge,
    Wythoutyn dystaunce.
      Mekenesse, Pacyense, and Charyte,
      Sobyrnesse, Besynesse, and Chastyte,   50
      And Largyte, uertuys of good degre,
        Man callyth to þe Castel of Good Perseueraunce.

PRIMUS VEXILLATOR. þe Castel of Perseuerauns wanne Man-
    kynde hath tan,
  Wel armyd wyth vertus and ouyrcome all vycys,
þere þe Good Aungyl makyth ful mery þanne   55
  þat Mankynde hath ouyrcome hys gostly enmiis.
þe Badde Aungyl mornyþ þat he hath myssyd Man.
  He callyth þe Werld, þe Fende, and þe foule Flesch iwys
And all þe seuene synnys to do þat þey canne
  To brynge Mankynd ageyn to bale out of blys,   60

32 meynten] *MS.* meyten   ˙39 þus] *F* þis   43 Aungellys] *MS.* aungell
53 PRIMUS] secundus *erased and corrected to* Primus   56 enmiis] *MS.* emijs
58 iwys] þan *corrected to* I wys

Wyth wronge.
Pride asaylyth Meknesse wyth all hys myth,
Ire ageyns Paciensse ful fast ganne he fyth,
Envye ageyn Charyte strywyth ful ryth,
But Coveytyse ageyns Largyte fytyth ouyrlonge.   65

SECUNDUS VEXILLATOR. Coveytyse Mankynd euere coueytyth
    for to qwell.
He gaderyth to hym Glotony aȝeyns Sobyrnesse,
Leccherye wyth Chastyte fytyth ful fell
And Slawthe in Goddys seruyse ageyns Besynesse.
þus vycys ageyns vertues fytyn ful snelle.   70
Euery buskyth to brynge Man to dystresse.
But Penaunce and Confescion wyth Mankynd wyl melle,
    þe vycys arn ful lyckely þe vertues to opresse,
        Saun dowte.
        þus in þe Castel of Good Perseuerance   75
    Mankynd is maskeryd wyth mekyl varyaunce.
    þe Goode Aungyl and þe Badde be euere at dystaunce;
        þe Goode holdyth hym inne, þe Badde wold brynge hym
        owte.

PRIMUS VEXILLATOR. Owt of Good Perseueraunce whanne
    Mankynde wyl not come,
ȝyt þe Badde Aungyl wyth Coveytyse hym gan asayle,   80
Fyndende hym in pouerte and penaunce so benome,
    And bryngyth hym in beleue in defaute for to fayle.
þanne he profyrth hym good and gold so gret a sowme,
    þat if he wyl com ageyn and wyth þe Werld dayle,
þe Badde Aungyl to þe Werld tollyth hym downe   85
    þe Castel of Perseueraunce to fle fro þe vayle
        And blysse.
        þanne þe Werld begynnyth hym to restore.
    Haue he neuere so mykyl, ȝyt he wold haue more;
    þus þe Badde Aungyl leryth hym hys lore.   90
        þe more a man agyth, þe harder he is.

---

66 SECUNDUS] primus *erased and corrected to* ijᵘˢ   79 PRIMUS] secundus
erased and corrected to jᵘˢ   80 gan *added above the line*   86 vayle] *F*
dayle

SECUNDUS VEXILLATOR. Hard a man is in age and   f. 155
    covetouse be kynde.
  Whanne all oþyr synnys Man hath forsake,
Euere þe more þat he hath þe more is in hys mynde
    To gadyr and to gete good wyth woo and wyth wrake.   95
þus þe Goode Aungyl caste is behynde
  And þe Badde Aungyl Man to hym takyth,
þat wryngyth hym wrenchys to hys last ende
    Tyl Deth comyth foul dolfully and loggyth hym in a lake
      Ful lowe.   100
    þanne is Man on molde maskeryd in mynde.
    He sendyth afftyr hys sekkatours, ful fekyl to fynde,
    And hys eyr aftyrward comyth euere behynde,
      I Wot Not Who is hys name, for he hym nowt knowe.

PRIMUS VEXILLATOR. Man knowe not who schal be hys eyr and
    gouerne hys good.   105
  He caryth more for hys catel þanne for hys cursyd synne.
To putte hys good in gouernaunce he mengyth hys mod,
  He wolde þat it were scyfftyd amongys hys ny kynne.
But þer schal com a lythyr ladde wyth a torne hod,
    I Wot Neuere Who schal be hys name, hys cloþis be ful
      þynne,   110
Schal eryth þe erytage þat neuere was of hys blod,
  Whanne al hys lyfe is lytyd upon a lytyl pynne
      At þe laste.
    On lyue whanne he may no lenger lende,
    Mercy he callyth at hys laste ende: 115
    'Mercy, God! be now myn frende!'
      Wyth þat Mans spyryt is paste.

SECUNDUS VEXILLATOR. Whanne Manys spyryt is past, þe
    Badde Aungyl ful fell
Cleymyth þat for couetyse Mans sowle schuld ben hys
And for to bere it ful boystowsly wyth hym into hell.   120
  þe Good Aungyl seyth nay, þe spyryt schal to blys
For at hys laste ende of mercy he gan spell
  And þerfore of mercy schal he nowth mysse,

    92 SECUNDUS VEXILLATOR] MS. Primus vexillator The next four stanzas are
also misassigned   114 he may] MS. may F he may

And oure lofly Ladi if sche wyl for hym mell,
 Be mercy and be menys in purgatory he is,   125
  In ful byttyr place.
 þus mowthys confession
 And hys hertys contricion
 Schal saue Man fro dampnacion
  Be Goddys mercy and grace.   130

PRIMUS VEXILLATOR. Grace if God wyl graunte us of hys
 mykyl myth,
 þese parcellys in propyrtes we purpose us to playe
þis day seuenenyt before ʒou in syth
 At . . . on þe grene in ryal aray.
ʒe haste ʒou þanne þedyrward, syrys, hendly in hyth,   f. 155ᵛ
 All goode neyborys ful specyaly we ʒou pray,   136
And loke þat ʒe be þere betyme, luffely and lyth,
 For we schul be onward be vnderne of þe day,
  Dere frendys.
 We thanke ʒou of all good dalyaunce   140
 And of all ʒoure specyal sportaunce
 And preye ʒou of good contynuaunce
  To oure lyuys endys.

SECUNDUS VEXILLATOR. Os oure lyuys we loue ʒou, þus
 takande oure leue.
ʒe manly men of . . ., þer Crist saue ʒou all!   145
He maynten ʒoure myrthys and kepe ʒou fro greve
 þat born was of Mary myld in an ox stall.
Now mery be all . . . and wel mote ʒe cheve,
 All oure feythful frendys, þer fayre mote ʒe fall!
ʒa, and welcum be ʒe whanne ʒe com prys for to preve   150
 And worþi to be worchepyd in boure and in hall
  And in euery place.
 Farewel, fayre frendys,
 þat lofly wyl lystyn and lende.
 Cryste kepe ʒou fro fendys!   155
  Trumpe up and lete vs pace.

124 Ladi *added above the line in different ink*   132 parcellys] *MS.* parcell
134 *Any place-name could be inserted here, and in 145 and 148*   142 contynu-
aunce] *F* contynnaunce   144 Os] *F* Deus   145, 149 þer] *F* þus   148 mery]
F mercy   154 lende] *MS.* lendys   156 *The rest of f. 155ᵛ is blank*

SCENE I

MUNDUS. Worthy wytys in al þis werd wyde,
  Be wylde wode wonys and euery weye-went,
Precyous prinse, prekyd in pride,
  þorwe þis propyr pleyn place in pes be ʒe bent!   160
Buske ʒou, bolde bachelerys, vndyr my baner to abyde
  Where bryth basnetys be bateryd and backys ar schent.
ʒe, syrys semly, all same syttyth on syde,
  For bothe be see and be londe my sondys I haue sent,
     Al þe world myn name is ment.   165
     Al abowtyn my bane is blowe,
     In euery cost I am knowe,
     I do men rawyn on ryche rowe
      Tyl þei be dyth to dethys dent.

Assarye, Acaye, and Almayne,   170
  Cauadoyse, Capadoyse, and Cananee,
Babyloyne, Brabon, Burgoyne, and Bretayne,
  Grece, Galys, and to þe Gryckysch See,
I meue also Masadoyne in my mykyl mayne,
  Frauns, Flaundrys, and Freslonde, and also Normande,   175
Pyncecras, Parys, and longe Pygmayne,
     And euery toun in Trage, euyn to þe Dreye Tre,
     Rodys and ryche Rome.
     All þese londys at myn avyse
     Arn castyn to my werdly wyse.   180
     My tresorer, Syr Coueytyse,
      Hath sesyd hem holy to me.

þerfor my game and my gle growe ful glad.
  þer is no wythe in þis werld þat my wytte wyl me warne.
Euery ryche rengne rapyth hym ful rad   185
  In lustys and in lykyngys my lawys to lerne.
Wyth fayre folke in þe felde freschly I am fadde.
  I dawnse doun as a doo be dalys ful derne.

---

157 *Scene-divisions are not in the MS.*   159 prinse *above the line over* pride *canc. F* in prise   171 Cauadoyse] *MS.* Cauadoyse *or* Canadoyse *F* Canadoyse   184 is no] *MS. F* is

What boy bedyth batayl or debatyth wyth blad
  Hym were betyr to ben hangyn hye in hell herne   190
    Or brent on lyth leuene.
    Whoso spekyth aȝeyn þe Werd
    In a presun he schal be sperd.
    Myn hest is holdyn and herd
      Into hyȝe heuene.   195

SCENE II

BELYAL. Now I sytte, Satanas, in my sad synne,
  As deuyl dowty, in draf as a drake.
I champe and I chafe, I chocke on my chynne,
  I am boystows and bold, as Belyal þe blake.
What folk þat I grope þei gapyn and grenne,   f. 156ᵛ
  Iwys fro Carlylle into Kent my carpynge þei take,   201
Bothe þe bak and þe buttoke brestyth al on brenne,
  Wyth werkys of wreche I werke hem mykyl wrake.
    In woo is al my wenne.
    In care I am cloyed   205
    And fowle I am anoyed
    But Mankynde be stroyed
      Be dykys and be denne.

Pryde is my prince in perlys ipyth;
  Wretthe, þis wrecche, wyth me schal wawe;   210
Enuye into werre wyth me schal walkyn wyth;
  Wyth þese faytourys I am fedde, in feyth I am fawe.
As a dyngne deuyl in my dene I am dyth.
  Pryde, Wretthe, and Enuye, I scy in my sawe,
Kyngys, kayserys, and kempys and many a kene knyth,   215
  þese louely lordys han lernyd hem my lawe.
    To my dene þei wyl drawe.
    Alholy Mankynne
    To helle but I wynne,
    In bale is my bynne   220
      And schent vndyr schawe.

198 chafe] MS. F chase   215 knyth] kyth *changed to* knyth

On Mankynde is my trost, in contre iknowe,
 Wyth my tyre and wyth my tayl tytly to tene.
þorwe Flaundris and Freslonde faste I gan flowe,
 Fele folke on a flokke to flappyn and to flene. 225
Where I graspe on þe grounde, grym þer schal growe.
 Gadyr ȝou togedyr, ȝe boyis, on þis grene!
In þis brode bugyl a blast wanne I blowe,
 Al þis werld schal be wood iwys as I wene
  And to my byddynge bende. 230
  Wythly on syde
  On benche wyl I byde
  To tene, þis tyde,
   Alholy Mankende.

SCENE III

CARO. I byde as a brod brustun-gutte abouyn on þese tourys. 235
 Euerybody is þe betyr þat to myn byddynge is bent.
I am Mankyndys fayre Flesch, florchyd in flowrys.
 My lyfe is wyth lustys and lykynge ilent.
Wyth tapytys of tafata I tymbyr my towrys.
 In myrthe and in melodye my mende is iment. 240
þou I be clay and clad, clappyd vndir clowrys,
 ȝyt wolde I þat my wyll in þe werld went,
  Ful trew I ȝou behyth.
  I loue wel myn ese,
  In lustys me to plese; 245
  þou synne my sowle sese
   I ȝeue not a myth.

In Glotony gracyous now am I growe; f. 157
 þerfore he syttyth semly here be my syde.
In Lechery and Lykynge lent am I lowe, 250
 And Slawth, my swete sone, is bent to abyde.
þese thre are nobyl, trewly I trowe,
 Mankynde to tenyn and trecchyn a tyde.
Wyth many berdys in bowre my blastys are blowe,
 Be weys and be wodys, þorwe þis werld wyde, 255

þe sothe for to seyne.
But if mans Flesch fare wel
Bothe at mete and at mel,
Dyth I am in gret del
    And browt into peyne. 260

And aftyr good fare in feyth þou I fell,
  þou I drywe to dust, in drosse for to drepe,
þow my sely sowle were haryed to hell,
    Woso wyl do þese werkys iwys he schal wepe
      Euyr wythowtyn ende. 265
    Behold þe Werld, þe Deuyl, and me!
    Wyth all oure mythis we kyngys thre
    Nyth and day besy we be
      For to distroy Mankende
        If þat we may. 270
    þerfor on hylle
    Syttyth all stylle
    And seth wyth good wylle
      Oure ryche aray.

SCENE IV

HUMANUM GENUS. Aftyr oure forme-faderys kende 275
  þis nyth I was of my modyr born.
Fro my modyr I walke, I wende,
  Ful feynt and febyl I fare ʒou beforn.
I am nakyd of lym and lende
  As Mankynde is schapyn and schorn. 280
I not wedyr to gon ne to lende
  To helpe myself mydday nyn morn.
    For schame I stonde and schende.
  I was born þis nyth in blody ble
  And nakyd I am, as ʒe may se. 285
  A, Lord God in trinite,
    Whow Mankende is vnthende!

Whereto I was to þis werld browth
  I ne wot, but to woo and wepynge

    258 Bothe] *MS.* bote   270 we may] *MS.* w...

I am born and haue ryth nowth   290
    To helpe myself in no doynge.
I stonde and stodye al ful of þowth.   f. 157ᵛ
    Bare and pore is my clothynge.
A sely crysme myn hed hath cawth
    þat I tok at myn crystenynge.   295
       Certys I haue no more.
      Of erthe I cam, I wot ryth wele,
      And as erthe I stande þis sele.
      Of Mankende it is gret dele.
       Lord God, I crye þyne ore!   300

To aungels bene asynyd to me:
    þe ton techyth me to goode;
On my ryth syde ȝe may hym se;
    He cam fro Criste þat deyed on rode.
Anoþyr is ordeynyd her to be   305
    þat is my foo, be fen and flode;
He is about in euery degre
    To drawe me to þo dewylys wode
       þat in helle ben thycke.
      Swyche to hath euery man on lyue
      To rewlyn hym and hys wyttys fyue.   310
      Whanne man doth ewyl, þe ton wolde schryue,
       þe tothyr drawyth to wycke.

But syn þese aungelys be to me falle,
    Lord Jhesu, to ȝou I bydde a bone   315
þat I may folwe, be strete and stalle,
    þe aungyl þat cam fro heuene trone.
Now, Lord Jesu in heuene halle,
    Here whane I make my mone.
Coryows Criste, to ȝou I calle.   320
      As a grysly gost I grucche and grone,
       I wene, ryth ful of thowth.
      A, Lord Jhesu, wedyr may I goo?
      A crysyme I haue and no moo.
      Alas, men may be wondyr woo   325
       Whanne þei be fyrst forth browth.

       308 To drawe] *MS.* do drawe *F* to drawe

BONUS ANGELUS. 3a forsothe, and þat is wel sene.
Of woful wo man may synge,
For iche creature helpyth hymself bedene
Saue only man at hys comynge. 330
Neuyrþelesse turne þe fro tene
And serue Jhesu, heuene kynge,
And þou schalt, be greuys grene,
Fare wel in all thynge.
þat Lord þi lyfe hath lante. 335
Haue hym alwey in þi mynde f. 158
þat deyed on rode for Mankynde
And serue hym to þi lyfes ende
And sertys þou schalt not wante.

MALUS ANGELUS. Pes, aungel, þi wordys are not wyse. 340
þou counselyst hym not aryth.
He schal hym drawyn to þe Werdys seruyse
To dwelle wyth caysere, kynge, and knyth,
þat in londe be hym non lyche.
Cum on wyth me, stylle as ston. 345
þou and I to þe Werd schul goon
And þanne þou schalt sen anon
Whow sone þou schalt be ryche.

BONUS ANGELUS. A, pes, aungel, þou spekyst folye.
Why schuld he coueyt werldys goode, 350
Syn Criste in erthe and hys meynye
All in pouert here þei stode?
Werldys wele, be strete and stye,
Faylyth and fadyth as fysch in flode,
But heuerychc is good and trye, 355
þer Criste syttyth bryth as blode,
Wythoutyn any dystresse.
To þe World wolde he not flyt
But forsok it euery whytt.
Example I fynde in holy wryt, 360
He wyl bere me wytnesse.
Diuicias et paupertates ne dederis michi, Domine.

340 MALUS] MS. Maluus   356 syttyth] MS. syttyht   361a Latin texts
added to a stanza are not counted in numbering the lines

MALUS ANGELUS. 3a, 3a, man, leue hym nowth,
  But cum wyth me, be stye and strete.
Haue þou a gobet of þe werld cawth,
  þou schalt fynde it good and swete.   365
A fayre lady þe schal be tawth
  þat in bowrc þi bale schal bete.
Wyth ryche rentys þou schalt be frawth,
  Wyth sylke sendel to syttyn in sete.
      I rede, late bedys be.   370
    If þou wylt haue wel þyn hele
    And faryn wel at mete and mele,
    Wyth Goddys seruyse may þou not dele
      But cum and folwe me.

HUMANUM GENUS. Whom to folwe wetyn I ne may.   375
  I stonde and stodye and gynne to raue.
I wolde be ryche in gret aray
  And fayn I wolde my sowle saue.
      As wynde in watyr I wave.
    þou woldyst to þe Werld I me toke,   f. 158ᵛ
    And he wolde þat I it forsoke.   381
    Now so God me helpe and þe holy boke,
      I not wyche I may haue.

MALUS ANGELUS. Cum on, man, whereof hast þou care?
  Go we to þe Werld, I rede þe, blyue,   385
For þer þou schalt mow ryth wel fare,
  In case if þou þynke for to thryue,
      No lord schal be þe lyche.
    Take þe Werld to þine entent
    And late þi loue be þeron lent.   390
    Wyth gold and syluyr and ryche rent
      Anone þou schalt be ryche.

HUMANUM GENUS. Now syn þou hast behetyn me so,
  I wyl go wyth þe and asay.
I ne lette, for frende ner fo,   395
  But wyth þe Werld I wyl go play,

367 bale] schal *canc. before* bale   376 and stodye] *F* in stodye   378 fayn
added in margin   379 *The scribe wrote and then cancelled* þou woldyst to þe
werld þat I me toke

Certys a lytyl þrowe.
In þis World is al my trust
To lyuyn in lykyng and in lust.
Haue he and I onys cust,   400
We schal not part, I trowe.

BONUS ANGELUS. A, nay, man, for Cristys blod,
Cum agayn, be strete and style.
þe Werld is wyckyd and ful wod
And þou schalt leuyn but a whyle.   405
What coueytyst þou to wynne?
Man, þynke on þyn endynge day
Whanne þou schalt be closyd vndyr clay,
And if þou thenke of þat aray,
Certys þou schalt not synne.   410
Homo, memento finis et in eternum non peccabis.

MALUS ANGELUS. 3a, on þi sowle þou schalt þynke al betyme.
Cum forth, man, and take non hede.
Cum on, and þou schalt holdyn hym inne.
þi flesch þou schalt foster and fede
Wyth lofly lyuys fode.   415
Wyth þe Werld þou mayst be bold
Tyl þou be sexty wyntyr hold.
Wanne þi nose waxit cold,
þanne mayst þou drawe to goode.

HUMANUM GENUS. I vow to God, and so I may   420
Make mery a ful gret throwe.
I may leuyn many a day;
I am but 3onge, as I trowe,
For to do þat I schulde.
Myth I ryde be sompe and syke   425
And be ryche and lordlyke,
Certys þanne schulde I be fryke
And a mery man on molde.

MALUS ANGELUS. 3ys, be my feyth, þou schalt be a lord, f. 159
And ellys hange me be þe hals!   430

426 lordlyke] F lord [i-]lyke

But þou muste be at myn acord.
  Oþyrwhyle þou muste be fals
    Amonge kythe and kynne.
  Now go we forth swythe anon,
  To þe Werld us must gon,   435
  And berc þe manly euere among
    Whanne þou comyst out or inne.

HUMANUM GENUS. 3ys, and ellys haue þou my necke,
  But I be manly be downe and dyche;
And þou I be fals, I ne recke,   440
  Wyth so þat I be lordlyche.
    I folwe þe as I can.
  þou schalt be my bote of bale,
  For were I ryche of holt and hale
  þanne wolde I 3eue neuere tale   445
    Of God ne of good man.

BONUS ANGELUS. I weyle and wrynge and make mone.
  þis man wyth woo schal be pylt.
I sye sore and grysly grone
  For hys folye schal make hym spylt.   450
    I not wedyr to gone.
  Mankynde hath forsakyn me.
  Alas, man, for loue of the!
  3a, for þis gamyn and þis gle
    þou schalt grocchyn and grone.   455

                         Pipe vp musyk

SCENE V

MUNDUS. Now I sytte in my semly sale;
  I trotte and tremle in my trew trone;
As a hawke I hoppe in my hende hale;
  Kyng, knyth, and kayser to me makyn mone.
Of God ne of good man 3yf I neuere tale.   460
  As a lykynge lord I leyke here alone.
Woso brawle any boste, be downe or be dale,
  þo gadlyngys schal be gastyd and gryslych grone

441 lordlyche] *F* lord [i-]lyche   455 s.d. Pipe vp musyk] *MS* pipe vp mu...

Iwys.
Lust, Foly, and Veynglory,   465
All þese arn in myn memory.
þus begynnyth þe nobyl story
    Of þis werldys blys.

Lust, Lykyng, and Foly,
    Comly knytys of renoun,   470
Belyue þorwe þis londe do crye
    Al abowtyn in toure and toun.
If any man be fer or nye
    þat to my seruyse wyl buske hym boun,
If he wyl be trost and trye   475
    He schal be kyng and were þe croun
        Wyth rycchest robys in res.
        Woso to þe Werld wyl drawe   f. 159ᵛ
        Of God ne of good man ȝeuyt he not a hawe,
        Syche a man, be londys lawe,   480
            Schal syttyn on my dees.

VOLUPTAS. Lo, me here redy, lord, to faryn and to fle,
    To sekyn þe a seruaunt dynge and dere.
Whoso wyl wyth foly rewlyd be
    He is worthy to be a seruaunt here   485
        þat drawyth to synnys seuene.
    Whoso wyl be fals and covetouse
    Wyth þis werld he schal haue lond and house.
    þis werldys wysdom ȝeuyth not a louse
        Of God nyn of hye heuene.   490
                    Tunc descendit in placeam pariter

Pes, pepyl, of pes we ȝou pray.
    Syth and sethe wel to my sawe.
Whoso wyl be ryche and in gret aray
    Toward þe Werld he schal drawe.
Whoso wyl be fals al þat he may,   495
    Of God hymself he hath non awe,

---

467 þus] *F* þer   477 rycchest] *MS.* rycches *F* rycchest   488 haue
added above the line   489 wysdom] *MS.* wydom   not] *MS.* no

And lyuyn in lustys nyth and day
　þe Werld of hym wyl be ryth fawe,
　　Do dwelle in his howse.
　Whoso wyl wyth þe Werld haue hys dwellynge　　　500
　And ben a lord of hys clothynge
　He muote nedys, ouyr al þynge,
　　Eueremore be couetowse.
Non est in mundo diues qui dicit 'habundo'.

STULTICIA. 3a, couetouse he muste be
　And me, Foly, muste haue in mende,　　　505
For whoso wyl alwey foly fle
　In þis werld schal ben vnthende.
þorwe werldys wysdom of gret degre
　Schal neuere man in werld moun wende
But he haue help of me　　　510
　þat am Foly fer and hende.
　　He muste hangyn on my hoke.
　Werldly wyt was neuere nout
　But wyth foly it were frawt.
　þus þe wysman hath tawt　　　515
　　Abotyn in his boke.
Sapiencia penes Domini.

VOLUPTAS. Now all þe men þat in þis werld wold thryue,
　For to rydyn on hors ful hye,
Cum speke wyth Lust and Lykynge belyue
　And hys felaw, 3onge Foly.　　　520
　　Late se whoso wyl vs knowe.
　Whoso wyl drawe to Lykynge and Luste
　And as a fole in Foly ruste,
　On vs to he may truste
　　And leuyn louely, I trowe.　　　525

MALUS ANGELUS. How, Lust, Lykyng, and Folye,　　　f. 160
　Take to me good entent!
I haue browth, be downys drye,
　To þe Werld a gret present.

I haue gylyd hym ful qweyntly, 530
 For syn he was born I haue hym blent.
He schal be serwaunt good and try,
 Amonge ӡou his wyl is lent,
  To þe Werld he wyl hym take.
  For syn he cowde wyt, I vndirstonde, 535
  I haue hym tysyd in euery londe.
  Hys Goode Aungel, be strete and stronde,
   I haue don hym forsake.

þerfor, Lust, my trewe fere,
 þou art redy alwey iwys 540
Of worldly lawys þou hym lere
 þat he were browth in werldly blys.
  Loke he be ryche, þe soþe to tell.
  Help hym, fast he gunne to thrywe,
  And whanne he wenyth best to lywe 545
  þanne schal he deye and not be schrywe
   And goo wyth vs to hell.

VOLUPTAS. Be Satan, þou art a nobyl knawe
 To techyn men fyrst fro goode.
Lust and Lykynge he schal haue, 550
 Lechery schal ben hys fode,
  Metys and drynkys he schal haue trye.
  Wyth a lykynge lady of lofte
  He schal syttyn in sendel softe
  To cachen hym to helle crofte 555
   þat day þat he schal deye.

STULTICIA. Wyth ryche rentys I schal hym blynde
 Wyth þe Werld tyl he be pytte,
And þanne schal I, longe or hys ende,
 Make þat caytyfe to be knytte 560
  On þe Werld whanne he is set sore.
  Cum on, man, þou schalt not rewe
  For þou wylt be to vs trewe.
  þou schalt be clad in clothys newe
   And be ryche eueremore. 565

553 lofte] last *canc. before* lofte 561 set sore] *MS.* set s... *F* set sore

HUMANUM GENUS. Mary, felaw, gramercy!
  I wolde be ryche and of gret renoun.
I ʒeue no tale trewly
  So þat I be lord of toure and toun,
    Be buskys and bankys broun.   570
    Syn þat þou wylt make me   f. 160ᵛ
    Boþe ryche of gold and fee,
    Goo forthe, for I wyl folow þe
      Be dale and euery towne.

               Trumpe vp. Tunc ibunt VOLUPTAS
               et STULTICIA, MALUS ANGELUS et
               HUMANUM GENUS ad MUNDUM, et
               dicet

VOLUPTAS. How, lord, loke owt! for we haue browth   575
  A serwant of nobyl fame.
Of worldly good is al hys þouth,
  Of lust and folye he hath no schame.
    He wolde be gret of name.
    He wolde be at gret honour   580
    For to rewle town and toure.
    He wolde haue to hys paramoure
      Sum louely dynge dame.

MUNDUS. Welcum, syr, semly in syth!
  þou art welcum to worthy wede.   585
For þou wylt be my serwaunt day and nyth,
  Wyth my seruyse I schal þe foster and fede.
þi bak schal be betyn wyth besawntys bryth,
  þou schalt haue byggyngys be bankys brede,
To þi cors schal knele kayser and knyth   590
  Where þat þou walke, be sty or be strete,
    And ladys louely on lere.
    But Goddys seruyse þou must forsake
    And holy to þe Werld þe take
    And þanne a man I schal þe make   595
      þat non schal be þi pere.

    567 and *added above the line*   568 I ʒeue] *F* [Of God] I ʒeue   574 s.d.
written in red, angelus ad *changed to* angelus et   580 be *added above the line*
in another hand   584 MUNDUS *in red, as are the next five speech-headings*
585 welcum] *MS.* welcun   591–2 *F prints these two lines in reverse order*

HUMANUM GENUS. ȝys, Werld, and þerto here myn honde
　To forsake God and hys seruyse.
To medys þou ȝeue me howse and londe
　þat I regne rychely at myn enprise.   600
So þat I fare wel be strete and stronde
　Whyl I dwelle here in werldly wyse,
I recke neuere of heuene wonde
　Nor of Jhesu, þat jentyl justyse.
　　　Of my sowle I haue non rewthe.   605
　　What schulde I recknen of domysday
　　So þat I be ryche and of gret aray?
　　I schal make mery whyl I may,
　　　And þerto here my trewthe.

MUNDUS. Now sertys, syr, þou seyst wel.   610
　I holde þe trewe fro top to þe too.
But þou were ryche it were gret del
　And all men þat wyl fare soo.
Cum up, my serwaunt trew as stel.
　　　Tunc ascendet HUMANUM GENUS ad MUNDUM
þou schalt be ryche, whereso þou goo.   615
Men schul seruyn þe at mel
　Wyth mynstralsye and bemys blo,
　　Wyth metys and drynkys trye.
　　Lust and Lykynge schal be þin ese.
　　Louely ladys þe schal plese.   620
　　Whoso do þe any disesse
　　　He schal ben hangyn hye.

Lykynge, beluye   f. 161
Late clothe hym swythe
In robys ryve   625
　Wyth ryche aray.
Folye, þou fonde,
Be strete and stronde,
Serue hym at honde
　Bothe nyth and day.   630

597 GENUS] MS. geus   603 recke] F reeke   614 s.d. GENUS] MS. geus
625 wyth rych at end of line, canc.

VOLUPTAS. Trostyly,
Lord, redy,
Je vous pry,
  Syr, I say.
In lyckynge and lust   635
He schal rust
Tyl dethys dust
  Do hym to day.

STULTICIA. And I, Folye,
Schal hyen hym hye   640
Tyl sum enmye
  Hym ouyrgoo.
In worldys wyt
þat in Foly syt
I þynke ʒyt   645
  Hys sowle to sloo.

                                            Trumpe vp

SCENE VI

DETRACCIO. All þyngys I crye agayn þe pes
  To knyt and knaue, þis is my kende.
ʒa, dyngne dukys on her des
  In byttyr balys I hem bynde.   650
Cryinge and care, chydynge and ches
  And sad sorwe to hem I sende,
ʒa, lowde lesyngys lacchyd in les,
  Of talys vntrewe is al my mende.
        Mannys bane abowtyn I bere.   655
    I wyl þat ʒe wetyn, all þo þat ben here,
    For I am knowyn fer and nere,
    I am þe Werldys messengere,
        My name is Bacbytere.

Wyth euery wyth I walke and wende   660
  And euery man now louyth me wele.
Wyth lowde lesyngys vndyr lende
  To dethys dynt I dresse and dele.

---

*631–46 written as four lines with dividing marks after the first three rhyme-
words in each line*   639 STULTICIA] *MS.* Stultic...   646 *s.d. in red*

To speke fayre beforn and fowle behynde
  Amongys men at mete and mele   665
Trewly, lordys, þis is my kynde.
    þus I renne upon a whele,
      I am feller þanne a fox.
      Fleterynge and flaterynge is my lessun,
      Wyth lesyngys I tene boþe tour and town,   670
      Wyth letterys of defamacyoun
        I bere here in my box.

I am lyth of lopys þorwe euery londe,
  Myn holy happys may not ben hyd.
To may not togedyr stonde   675
  But I, Bakbyter, be þe thyrde.
I schape ȝone boyis to schame and schonde,
  All þat wyl bowyn whanne I hem bydde.
To lawe of londe in feyth I fonde.
    Whanne talys vntrewe arn betydde   680
      Bakbytere is wyde spronge.
    þorwe þe werld, be downe and dalys,
    All abowtyn I brewe balys.
    Euery man tellyth talys
      Aftyr my fals tunge.   685

þerfore I am mad massenger   f. 161ᵛ
  To lepyn ouyr londys leye
þorwe all þe world, fer and ner,
  Vnsayd sawys for to seye.
In þis holte I hunte here   690
  For to spye a preuy pley,
For whanne Mankynde is cloþyd clere,
  þanne schal I techyn hym þe wey
    To þe dedly synnys seuene.
    Here I schal abydyn wyth my pese   695
    þe wronge to do hym for to chese,
    For I þynke þat he schal lese
      þe lyth of hey heuene.

667 þus] *F* þer   668 a *added above the line*

SCENE VII

VOLUPTAS. Worthy World, in welthys wonde,
   Here is Mankynde ful fayr in folde.   700
In bryth besauntys he is bownde
And hon to bowe to ȝou so bolde.
He leuyth in lustys euery stounde;
   Holy to ȝou he hathe hym ȝolde.
For to makyn hym gay on grounde,   705
   Worthy World, þou art beholde.
      þis werld is wel at ese.
     For to God I make avow
     Mankynde had leuer now
     Greue God wyth synys row   710
      þanne þe World to dysplese.

STULTICIA. Dysplese þe he wyl for no man.
   On me, Foly, is al hys þowth.
Trewly Mankynde nowth nen can
   þynke on God þat hathe hym bowth.   715
Worthy World, wyth as swan,
   In þi loue lely is he lawth.
Sythyn he cowde and fyrste began
   þe forsakyn wolde he nowth,
      But ȝeue hym to Folye.   720
     And syþyn he hathe to þe be trewe,
     I rede þe forsakyn hym for no newe.
     Lete us plesyn hym tyl þat he rewe
      In hell to hangyn hye.

MUNDUS. Now, Foly, fayre þe befall,   725
   And Luste, blyssyd be þou ay!
ȝe han browth Mankynde to myn hall
   Sertys in a nobyl aray.
Wyth werldys welthys wythinne þese wallys
   I schal hym feffe if þat I may.   730
Welcum, Mankynde! to þe I call,
   Clenner cloþyd þanne any clay,

713 al hys] *MS.* al hys al hys   729 wallys] *MS. F* wall   730 if] *F* of

Be downe, dale, and dyche.
Mankynde, I rede þat þou reste   f. 162
Wyth me, þe Werld, as it is beste.   735
Loke þou holde myn hende heste
And euere þou schalt be ryche.

HUMANUM GENUS. Whou schuld I but I þi hestys helde?
  þou werkyst wyth me holy my wyll.
þou feffyst me wyth fen and felde   740
  And hye hall, be holtys and hyll.
In werldly wele my wytte I welde,
  In joye I jette wyth juelys jentyll,
On blysful banke my boure is bylde,
  In veynglorye I stonde styll.   745
      I am kene as a knyt.
      Whoso ageyn þe Werld wyl speke
      Mankynde schal on hym be wreke,
      In stronge presun I schal hym steke,
      Be it wronge or ryth.   750

MUNDUS. A, Mankynde, wel þe betyde
  þat þi loue on me is sette!
In my bowrys þou schalt abyde
  And ȝyt fare mekyl þe bette.
I feffe þe in all my wonys wyde   755
  In dale of dros tyl þou be deth.
I make þe lord of mekyl pryde,
  Syr, at þyn owyn mowthis mette.
      I fynde in þe no tresun.
      In all þis worlde, be se and sonde,   760
      Parkys, placys, lawnde and londe,
      Here I ȝyfe þe wyth myn honde,
      Syr, an opyn sesun.

Go to my tresorer, Syr Couetouse.
  Loke þou tell hym as I seye.   765
Bydde hym make þe maystyr in hys house
  Wyth penys and powndys for to pleye.

Loke þou ȝeue not a lous
    Of þe day þat þou schalt deye.
Messenger, do now þyne vse;   770
    Bakbytere, teche hym þe weye.
        þou art swetter þanne mede.
    Mankynde, take wyth þe Bakbytynge.
    Lefe hym for no maner thynge.
    Flepergebet wyth hys flaterynge   775
        Standyth Mankynde in stede.

DETRACCIO. Bakbytynge and Detracion
Schal goo wyth þe fro toun to toun.
Haue don, Mankynde, and cum doun.
        I am þyne owyn page.   780
I schal bere þe wyttnesse wyth my myth
Whanne my lord þe Werlde it behyth.
Lo, where Syr Coueytyse sytt
        And bydith us in his stage.

HUMANUM GENUS. Syr Worlde, I wende,   f. 162ᵛ
In Coueytyse to chasyn my kende.   786

MUNDUS. Haue hym in mende,
And iwys þanne schalt þou be ryth þende.

BONUS ANGELUS. Alas, Jhesu, jentyl justyce,
    Whedyr may mans Good Aungyl wende?   790
Now schal careful Coueytyse
    Mankende trewly al schende.
Hys sely goste may sore agryse;
    Bakbytynge bryngyth hym in byttyr bonde.
Worldly wyttys, ȝe are not wyse,   795
    Ȝour louely lyfe amys ȝe spende
        And þat schal ȝe sore smert.
    Parkys, ponndys, and many pens
    þei semyn to ȝou swetter þanne sens,
        But Goddys seruyse nyn hys commaundementys   800
        Stondyth ȝou not at hert.

785–8 *written as two lines with dividing marks after* wende *and* mende   *The
initial of each speech-heading on f. 162ᵛ is touched with red*   792 schende]
F [to-]schende   798 ponndys] F poundys

MALUS ANGELUS. 3a, whanne þe fox prechyth, kepe wel 3ore
 gees!
He spekyth as it were a holy pope.
Goo, felaw, and pyke of þo lys
 þat crepe þer upon þi cope!   805
þi part is pleyed al at þe dys
 þat þou schalt haue here, as I hope.
Tyl Mankynde fallyth to podys prys,
 Coueytyse schal hym grype and grope
  ' Tyl sum schame hym schende.   810
  Tyl man be dyth in dethys dow
  He seyth neuere he hath inow.
  þerfore, goode boy, cum blow
   At my neþer ende!

SCENE VIII

DETRACCIO. Syr Coueytyse, God þe saue,   815
 þi pens and þi poundys all!
I, Bakbyter, þyn owyn knaue,
 Haue browt Mankynde vnto þine hall.
þe Werlde bad þou schuldyst hym haue
 And feffyn hym, whatso befall.   820
In grene gres tyl he be graue
 Putte hym in þi precyous pall,
  Coueytyse, it were ell rewthe.
  Whyl he walkyth in worldly wolde
  I, Bakbyter, am wyth hym holde.   825
  Lust and Folye, þo barouns bolde,
   To hem he hath plyth hys trewthe.

AUARICIA. Ow, Mankynde, blyssyd mote þou be!
 I haue louyd þe derworthly many a day,
And so I wot wel þat þou dost me.   830
 Cum up and se my ryche aray.
It were a gret poynte of pyte   f. 163
 But Coueytyse were to þi pay.
Sit up ryth here in þis se.
 I schal þe lere of werldlys lay   835

804 þo] F þe   823 ell] F all   834 here] hele *changed to* here

þat fadyth as a flode.
Wyth good inow I schal þe store,
And ʒyt oure game is but lore
But þou coueyth mekyl more
    þanne euere schal do þe goode.   840

þou muste ʒyfe þe to symonye,
    Extorsion, and false asyse.
Helpe no man but þou haue why.
    Pay not þi serwauntys here serwyse.
þi neyborys loke þou dystroye.   845
    Tythe not on non wyse.
Here no begger þou he crye;
    And þanne schalt þou ful sone ryse.
        And whanne þou vsyste marchaundyse
        Loke þat þou be sotel of sleytys,   850
        And also swere al be deseytys,
        Bye and sell be fals weytys,
            For þat is kynde coueytyse.

Be not agaste of þe grete curse.
    þis lofly lyfe may longe leste.   855
Be þe peny in þi purs,
    Lete hem cursyn and don here beste.
What deuyl of hell art þou þe wers
    þow þou brekyste Goddys heste?
Do aftyr me, I am þi nors.   860
    Alwey gadyr and haue non reste.
        In wynnynge be al þi werke.
        To pore men take none entent,
        For þat þou haste longe tyme hent
        In lytyl tyme it may be spent;   865
            þus seyth Caton, þe grete clerke.

Labitur exiguo quod partum tempore longo.

HUMANUM GENUS. A, Auaryce, wel þou spede!
    Of werldly wytte þou canst iwys.
þou woldyst not I hadde nede
    And schuldyst be wrothe if I ferd amys.   870

I schal neuere begger bede
  Mete nyn drynke, be heuene blys;
Rather or I schulde hym cloþe or fede
  He schulde sterue and stynke iwys.
      Coueytyse, as þou wylt I wyl do.   875
      Whereso þat I fare, be fenne or flod,
      I make avow be Goddys blod
      Of Mankynde getyth no man no good
        But if he synge si dedero.

AUARICIA. Mankynd, þat was wel songe.   f. 163ᵛ
  Sertys now þou canst sum skyll.   881
Blyssyd be þi trewe tonge!
  In þis bowre þou schalt byde and byll.
Moo synnys I wolde þou vndyrfonge:
  Wyth coveytyse þe feffe I wyll;   885
And þanne sum pryde I wolde spronge,
  Hyȝe in þi hert to holdyn and hyll
    And abydyn in þi body.
    Here I feffe þe in myn heuene
    Wyth gold and syluyr lyth as leuene.   890
    þe dedly synnys, all seuene,
      I schal do comyn in hy.

Pryde, Wrathe, and Envye,
  Com forthe, þe Deuelys chyldryn þre!
Lecchery, Slawth, and Glotonye,   895
  To mans flesch ȝe are fendys fre.
Dryuyth downne ouyr dalys drye,
  Beth now blyþe as any be,
Ouyr hyll and holtys ȝe ȝou hyȝe
  To com to Mankynde and to me   900
    Fro ȝoure dowty dennys.
    As dukys dowty ȝe ȝou dresse.
    Whanne ȝe sex be comne, I gesse,
    þanne be we seuene and no lesse
      Of þe dedly synnys.   905

SCENE IX

SUPERBIA. Wondyr hyȝe howtys on hyll herd I houte;
  Koueytyse kryeth, hys karpynge I kenne.
Summe lord or summe lordeyn lely schal loute
  To be pyth wyth perlys of my proude penne.
Bon I am to braggyn and buskyn abowt,   910
  Rapely and redyly on rowte for to renne.
Be doun, dalys, nor dennys no duke I dowt,
  Also fast for to fogge, be flodys and be fenne.
      I rore whanne I ryse.
    Syr Belyal, bryth of ble,   915
    To ȝou I recomaunde me.
    Haue good day, my fadyr fre,
      For I goo to Coveytyse.

IRA. Whanne Coveytyse cried and carpyd of care,
  þanne must I, wod wreche, walkyn and wend   920
Hyȝe ouyr holtys, as hound aftyr hare.
  If I lette and were þe last, he schuld me sore schend.
I buske my bold baston, be bankys ful bare.
  Sum boy schal be betyn and browth vndyr bonde.
Wrath schal hym wrekyn and weyin hys ware.   925
  Forlorn schal al be for lusti laykys in londe,
      As a lythyr page.
    Syr Belyal, blak and blo,   f. 164
    Haue good day, now I goo
    For to fell þi foo   930
      Wyth wyckyd wage.

INVIDIA. Whanne Wrath gynnyth walke in ony wyde wonys,
  Envye flet as a fox and folwyth on faste.
Whanne þou steryste or staryste or stumble upon stonys,
  I lepe as a lyon; me is loth to be þe laste.   935
Ȝa, I breyde byttyr balys in body and in bonys,
  I frete myn herte and in kare I me kast.
Goo we to Coveytyse, all þre at onys,
  Wyth oure grysly gere a grome for to gast.

911 rapely] F raþely   912 duke] F dukis   926 in] F &   934 steryste
or staryste] MS. F sterystis or starystis

þis day schal he deye. 940
Belsabubbe, now haue good day,
For we wyl wendyn in good aray,
Al þre in fere, as I þe say,
Pride, Wrath, and Envye.

BELIAL. Farewel now, chyldryn fayre to fynde! 945
Do now wel ȝoure olde owse.
Whanne ȝe com to Mankynde
Make hym wroth and envyous.
Leuyth not lytly vndyr lynde;
To his sowle brewyth a byttyr jous. 950
Whanne he is ded I schal hym bynde
In hell, as catte dothe þe mows.
Now buske ȝou forþe on brede.
I may be blythe as any be,
For Mankynde in euery cuntre 955
Is rewlyd be my chyldyr þre,
Envye, Wrathe, and Pryde.

SCENE X

GULA. A grom gan gredyn gayly on grounde.
Of me, gay Glotoun, gan al hys gale.
I stampe and I styrte and stynt upon stounde, 960
To a staunche deth I stakyr and stale.
What boyes wyth here belys in my bondys ben bownd,
Boþe here bak and here blod I brewe al to bale.
I fese folke to fyth tyl here flesch fond.
Whanne summe han dronkyn a drawth þei drepyn in a dale; 965
In me is here mynde.
Mans florchynge flesch,
Fayre, frele, and fresch,
I rape to rewle in a rese
To kloye in my kynde. 970

LUXURIA. In mans kyth I cast me a castel to kepe. f. 164ᵛ
I, Lechery, wyth lykynge, am lovyd in iche a lond.
Wyth my sokelys of swettnesse I sytte and I slepe.
Many berdys I brynge to my byttyr bonde.

945 chyldryn] *MS.* chyrdryn   970 kloye] *MS.* kloyet

In wo and in wrake wyckyd wytys schal wepe   975
þat in my wonys wylde wyl not out wende.
Whanne Mankynde is castyn undyr clourys to crepe,
þanne þo ledrouns for here lykynge I schal al to-schende,
Trewly to tell.
Syr Flesch, now I wende,   980
Wyth lust in my lende,
To cachyn Mankynde
To þe Devyl of hell.

ACCIDIA. 3a, what seyst þou of Syr Slawth, wyth my soure syth?
Mankynde louyth me wel, wys as I wene.   985
Men of relygyon I rewle in my ryth;
I lette Goddys seruyse, þe soþe may be sene.
In bedde I brede brothel wyth my berdys bryth;
Lordys, ladys, and lederounnys to my lore leene.
Mekyl of mankynd in my clokys schal be knyth   990
Tyl deth dryuyth hem down in dalys bedene.
We may non lenger abyde.
Syr Flesch, comly kynge,
In þe is al oure bredynge.
3eue us now þi blyssynge,   995
For Coveytyse hath cryde.

CARO. Glotony and Slawth, farewel in fere,
Louely in londe is now 3our lesse;
And Lecherye, my dowtyr so dere,
Dapyrly 3e dresse 3ou so dyngne on desse.   1000
All þre my blyssynge 3e schal haue here.
Goth now forth and gyue 3e no fors.
It is no nede 3ou for to lere
To cachyn Mankynd to a careful clos
Fro þe bryth blysse off heuene.   1005
þe Werld, þe Flesch, and þe Devyl are knowe
Grete lordys, as we wel owe,
And þorwe Mankynd we settyn and sowe
þe dedly synnys seuene.

978 þo] F þe   984 what] MS. F waht   syth] snowt canc. before syth

SCENE XI

Tunc ibunt SUPERBIA, IRA, INVIDIA, GULA, LUXURIA, et
ACCIDIA ad AUARICIAM et dicet SUPERBIA:

SUPERBIA. What is þi wyll, Syr Coveytyse?   1010
   Why hast þou afftyr vs sent?
Whanne þou creydyst we ganne agryse
   And come to þe now par asent.
      Oure loue is on þe lent.
     I, Pryde, Wrath, and Envye,   1015
     Gloton, Slawth, and Lecherye,
     We arn cum all sex for þi crye
      To be at þi commaundement.

AUARICIA. Welcum be ȝe, breþeryn all,   f. 165
   And my systyr, swete Lecherye!   1020
Wytte ȝe why I gan to call?
   For ȝe must me helpe and þat in hy.
Mankynde is now com to myn hall
   Wyth me to dwell, be downys dry.
þerfore ȝe must, whatso befall,   1025
   Feffyn hym wyth ȝoure foly,
     And ell ȝe don hym wronge.
     For whanne Mankynd is kendly koueytous
     He is provd, wrathful, and envyous;
     Glotons, slaw, and lecherous   1030
      þei arn oþyrwhyle amonge.

þus euery synne tyllyth in oþyr
   And makyth Mankynde to ben a foole.
We seuene fallyn on a fodyr
   Mankynd to chase to pynyngys stole.   1035
þerfore, Pryde, good broþyr,
   And breþyryn all, take ȝe ȝour tol.
Late iche of vs take at othyr
   And set Mankynd on a stomlynge stol

1020 systyr] *MS.* sytyr   1035 pynyngys] *MS.* pynygys
C 4343   D

Whyl he is here on lyve.   1040
Lete vs lullyn hym in oure lust
Tyl he be dreuyn to dampnynge dust.
Colde care schal ben hys crust
To deth whanne he schal dryve.

SUPERBIA. In gle and game I growe glad.   1045
  Mankynd, take good hed
And do as Coveytyse þe bad,
  Take me in þyn hert, precyous Pride.
Loke þou be not ouyrlad,
  Late no bacheler þe mysbede,   1050
Do þe to be dowtyd and drad,
  Bete boyes tyl þey blede,
    Kast hem in careful kettys.
    Frende, fadyr and modyr dere,
    Bowe hem not in non manere,   1055
    And hold no maner man þi pere,
    And vse þese new jettys.

Loke þou blowe mekyl bost
  Wyth longe crakows on þi schos.
Jagge þi clothis in euery cost,   1060
  And ell men schul lete þe but a goos.
It is þus, man, wel þou wost,
  þerfore do as no man dos
And euery man sette at a thost
  And of þiself make gret ros.   1065
    Now se þiself on euery syde.
    Euery man þou schalt schende and schelfe   f. 165ᵛ
    And holde no man betyr þanne þiselfe.
    Tyl dethys dynt þi body delfe
    Put holy þyn hert in Pride.   1070

HUMANUM GENUS. Pryde, be Jhesu, þou seyst wel.
  Whoso suffyr is ouyrled al day.
Whyl I reste on my rennynge whel
  I schal not suffre, if þat I may.

1043 crust] *MS.* curst   1068 man] ma *canc. before* man

Myche myrthe at mete and mel   1075
  I loue ryth wel, and ryche aray.
Trewly I þynke, in euery sel,
  On grounde to be graythyd gay
    And of myselfe to take good gard.
  Mykyl myrthe þou wylt me make,   1080
  Lordlyche to leue, be londe and lake.
  Myn hert holy to þe I take
    Into þyne owyn award.

SUPERBIA. I þi bowre to abyde
I com to dwelle be þi syde.   1085

HUMANUM GENUS. Mankynde and Pride
Schal dwell togedyr euery tyde.

IRA. Be also wroth as þou were wode.
  Make þe be dred, be dalys derne.
Whoso þe wrethe, be fen or flode,   1090
  Loke þou be avengyd ȝerne.
Be redy to spylle mans blod.
  Loke þou hem fere, be feldys ferne.
Alway, man, be ful of mod.
  My lothly lawys loke þou lerne,   1095
    I rede, for any þynge.
  Anon take venjaunce, man, I rede,
  And þanne schal no man þe ouyrlede,
  But of þe þey schul haue drede
    And bowe to þi byddynge.   1100

HUMANUM GENUS. Wrethe, for þi councel hende,
  Haue þou Goddys blyssynge and myn.
What caytyf of al my kende
  Wyl not bowe, he schal abyn.
Wyth myn venjaunce I schal hym schende   1105
  And wrekyn me, be Goddys yne.
Raþyr or I schulde bowe or bende
  I schuld be stekyd as a swyne

1084–7 *written as two lines with dividing marks*   1086 GENUS] *MS.* geus
1092 spylle] *MS.* spydle *with* d *blotted out*   1094 ful of mod] feld & flod
canc. before ful of mod

Wyth a lothly launce.
Be it erly or late,   1110
Whoso make wyth me debate
I schal hym hyttyn on þe pate
And takyn anon venjaunce.

IRA. Wyth my rewly rothyr   f. 166
I com to þe, Mankynde, my broþyr.   1115

HUMANUM GENUS. Wrethe, þi fayr foþyr
Makyth iche man to be vengyd on oþyr.

INVIDIA. Envye wyth Wrathe muste dryve
To haunte Mankynde also.
Whanne any of þy neyborys wyl þryve   1120
Loke þou haue Envye þerto.
On þe hey name I charge þe belyue
Bakbyte hym, whowso þou do.
Kyll hym anon wythowtyn knyve
And speke hym sum schame were þou go,   1125
Be dale or downys drye.
Speke þi neybour mekyl schame,
Pot on hem sum fals fame,
Loke þou vndo hys nobyl name
Wyth me, þat am Envye.   1130

HUMANUM GENUS. Envye, þou art boþe good and hende
And schalt be of my counsel chefe.
þi counsel is knowyn þorwe mankynde,
For ilke man callyth oþyr hore and thefe.
Envye, þou arte rote and rynde,   1135
þorwe þis werld, of mykyl myschefe.
In byttyr balys I schal hem bynde
þat to þe puttyth any reprefe.
Cum vp to me above.
For more envye þanne is now reynynge   1140
Was neuere syth Cryst was kynge.
Cum vp, Envye, my dere derlynge.
þou hast Mankyndys love.

1109 *The scribe wrote and then cancelled the next line*   1114–17 *written as two*
lines with dividing marks   1116 GENUS] *MS.*g ...   Wrethe] w *blotted. F* and
Wrethe

INVIDIA. I clymbe fro þis crofte
Wyth Mankynde to syttyn on lofte.   1145

HUMANUM GENUS. Cum, syt here softe,
For in abbeys þou dwellyst ful ofte.

GULA. In gay Glotony a game þou begynne,
Ordeyn þe mete and drynkys goode.
Loke þat no tresour þou part atwynne   1150
But þe feffe and fede wyth al kynnys fode.
Wyth fastynge schal man neuere heuene wynne,
þese grete fasterys I holde hem wode.
þou þou ete and drynke, it is no synne.
Fast no day, I rede, be þe rode,   1155
þou chyde þese fastyng cherlys.
Loke þou haue spycys of goode odoure
To feffe and fede þy fleschly floure
And þanne mayst þou bultyn in þi boure
And serdyn gay gerlys.   1160

HUMANUM GENUS. A, Glotony, wel I þe grete!   f. 166ᵛ
Soth and sad it is, þy sawe.
I am no day wel, be sty nor strete,
Tyl I haue wel fyllyd my mawe.
Fastynge is fellyd vndyr fete,   1165
þou I neuere faste, I ne rekke an hawe,
He seruyth of nowth, be þe rode, I lete,
But to do a mans guttys to gnawe.
To faste I wyl not fonde.
I schal not spare, so haue I reste,   1170
To haue a mossel of þe beste.
þe lenger schal my lyfe mow leste
Wyth gret lykynge in londe.

GULA. Be bankys on brede,
Oþyrwhyle to spew þe spede!   1175

1144–7 written as two lines with dividing marks   1145 Mankynde followed
in MS. by a diamond-shaped mark (probably not o)   1146 HUMANUM
GENUS] MS. Humanum . . .   1150 þou] MS. F þe   1166 ne rekke]
MS. rekke F rekke [not]   1168 guttys] F gieays   1172l yfe added
above the line   1174–7 written as two lines with dividing marks

HUMANUM GENUS. Whyl I lyf lede
Wyth fayre fode my flesche schal I fede.

LUXURIA. 3a, whanne þi flesche is fayre fed,
   þanne schal I, louely Lecherye,
Be bobbyd wyth þe in hed;   1180
   Hereof serue mete and drynkys trye.
In loue þi lyf schal be led;
   Be a lechour tyl þou dye.
þi nedys schal be þe better sped
   If þou 3yf þe to fleschly folye   1185
      Tyl deth þe down drepe.
     Lechery syn þe werld began
     Hath avauncyd many a man.
   þerfore, Mankynd, my leue lemman,
     I my cunte þou schalt crepe.   1190

HUMANUM GENUS. A, Lechery, wel þe be.
   Mans sed in þe is sowe.
Fewe men wyl forsake þe
   In any cuntre þat I knowe.
Spousebreche is a frend ryth fre,   1195
   Men vse þat mo þanne inowe.
Lechery, cum syt be me.
   þi banys be ful wyd iknowe,
     Lykynge is in þi lende.
     On nor oþyr, I se no wythte   1200
    þat wyl forsake þe day ner nyth.
    þerfore cum vp, my berd bryth,
     And reste þe wyth Mankynde.

LUXURIA. I may soth synge
'Mankynde is kawt in my slynge'.   1205

HUMANUM GENUS. For ony erthyly þynge,
To bedde þou muste me brynge.

ACCIDIA. 3a, whanne 3e be in bedde boþe,   f. 167
   Wappyd wel in worthy wede,

1180 in] *F* in [þi]   1183 þou] *MS.* þu   1185 If þou] *MS.* If
1201 forsake þe] *MS.* forsake   1204–7 *written as two lines*   1206 GENUS]
MS. g...   1208 boþe] browth *canc. before* boþe

þanne I, Slawthe, wyl be wrothe   1210
  But to brothelys I may brede.
Whanne þe messe-belle goth
  Lye stylle, man, and take non hede.
Lappe þyne hed þanne in a cloth
  And take a swet, I þe rede,   1215
     Chyrche-goynge þou forsake.
    Losengerys in londe I lyfte
    And dyth men to mekyl vnthryfte.
    Penaunce enjoynyd men in schryfte
     Is vndone, and þat I make.   1220

HUMANUM GENUS. Owe, Slawthe, þou seyst me skylle.
  Men vse þe mekyl, God it wot.
Men lofe wel now to lye stylle
  In bedde to take a morowe swot.
To chyrcheward is not here wylle;   1225
  Here beddys þei þynkyn goode and hot.
Herry, Jofferey, Jone, and Gylle
  Arn leyd and logyd in a lot
    Wyth þyne vnþende charmys.
    Al mankynde, be þe holy rode,   1230
    Are now slawe in werkys goode.
    Com nere þerfore, myn fayre foode,
     And lulle me in þyne armys.

ACCIDIA. I make men, I trowe,
In Goddys seruyse to be ryth slowe.   1235

HUMANUM GENUS. Com up þis þrowe.
Swyche men þou schalt fynden inowe.

HUMANUM GENUS. Mankynde I am callyd be kynde,
  Wyth curssydnesse in costys knet.
In sowre swettenesse my syth I sende,   1240
  Wyth seuene synnys sadde beset.
Mekyl myrþe I moue in mynde,
  Wyth melody at my mowþis met.
My prowd pouer schal I not pende
  Tyl I be putte in peynys pyt,   1245

1224 morowe] F þorowe   1234-7 *written as two lines*   1236 Com] *MS.* con

To helle hent fro hens.
In dale of dole tyl we are downe
We schul be clad in a gay gowne.
I se no man but þey vse somme
    Of þese seuene dedly synnys.   1250

For comounly it is seldom seyne,
    Whoso now be lecherows
But of oþyr men he schal haue dysdeyne
    And ben prowde or covetous.
        In synne iche man is founde.   1255
    þer is pore nor ryche, be londe ne lake,   f. 167ᵛ
    þat alle þese seuene wyl forsake,
      But wyth on or oþyr he schal be take
      And in here byttyr bondys bownde.

BONUS ANGELUS. So mekyl þe werse, weleawoo,   1260
    þat euere good aungyl was ordeynyd þe.
þou art rewlyd aftyr þe fende þat is þi foo
    And noþynge certys aftyr me.
Weleaway, wedyr may I goo?
    Man doth me bleykyn blody ble.   1265
Hys swete sowle he wyl now slo.
    He schal wepe al hys game and gle
        At on dayes tyme.
      ʒe se wel all sothly in syth
      I am abowte boþe day and nyth   1270
    To brynge hys sowle into blis bryth,
      And hymself wyl it brynge to pyne.

MALUS ANGELUS. No, Good Aungyl, þou art not in sesun,
    Fewe men in þe feyth þey fynde.
For þou hast schewyd a ballyd resun,   1275
    Goode syre, cum blowe myn hol behynde.
Trewly man hathe non chesun
    On þi God to grede and grynde,
For þat schuld cunne Cristis lessoun
    In penaunce hys body he muste bynde   1280

1253 But of] MS. F of   1266 slo] F sle

And forsake þe worldys mende.
Men arn loth on þe to crye
Or don penaunce for here folye.
þerfore haue I now maystrye
    Welny ouyr al mankynde.   1285

BONUS ANGELUS. Alas, Mankynde
Is bobbyd and blent as þe blynde.
In feyth, I fynde,
To Crist he can nowt be kynde.

Alas, Mankynne   1290
Is soylyd and saggyd in synne.
He wyl not blynne
Tyl body and sowle parte atwynne.

Alas, he is blendyd,
Amys mans lyf is ispendyd,   1295
Wyth fendys fendyd.
Mercy, God, þat man were amendyd!

CONFESSIO. What, mans Aungel, good and trewe,
    Why syest þou and sobbyst sore?
Sertys sore it schal me rewe   1300
    If I se þe make mornynge more.
May any bote þi bale brewe
    Or any þynge þi stat astore?
For all felechepys olde and newe
    Why makyst þou grochynge vndyr gore   1305
        Wyth pynynge poyntys pale?
    Why was al þis gretynge gunne
    Wyth sore syinge vndyr sunne?
    Tell me and I schal, if I cunne,
        Brewe þe bote of bale.   1310

BONUS ANGELUS. Of byttyr balys þou mayste me bete,   f. 168
    Swete Schryfte, if þat þou wylt.
For Mankynde it is þat I grete;
    He is in poynt to be spylt.

1286–97 *written as six lines*   1304 all] olde *crossed out and* all *written*
in margin   1314 in *added above the line*

He is set in seuene synnys sete   1315
  And wyl certys tyl he be kylt.
Wyth me he þynkyth neueremore to mete,
  He hath me forsake, and I haue no gylt.
    No man wyl hym amende.
    þerfore, Schryfte, so God me spede,   1320
    But if þou helpe at þis nede
    Mankynde getyth neuere oþyr mede
    But peyne wythowtyn ende.

CONFESCIO. What, Aungel, be of counfort stronge,
  For þi lordys loue þat deyed on tre.   1325
On me, Schryfte, it schal not be longe
  And þat þou schalt þe sothe se.
If he wyl be aknowe hys wronge
  And noþynge hele, but telle it me,
And don penaunce sone amonge,   1330
  I schal hym stere to gamyn and gle
    In joye þat euere schal last.
    Whoso schryue hym of hys synnys alle
    I behete hym heuene halle.
    þerfor go we hens, whatso befalle,   1335
    To Mankynde fast.

          Tunc ibunt ad HUMANUM GENUS et dicet

CONFESSIO. What, Mankynde, whou goth þis?
  What dost þou wyth þese deuelys seuene?
Alas, alas, man, al amys!
  Blysse in þe name of God in heuene,   1340
    I rede, so haue I rest.
    þese lotly lordeynys awey þou lyfte
    And cum doun and speke wyth Schryfte
    And drawe þe ȝerne to sum thryfte.
    Trewly it is þe best.   1345

HUMANUM GENUS. A, Schryfte, þou art wel be note
  Here to Slawthe þat syttyth here-inne.
He seyth þou mytyst a com to mannys cote
  On Palme Sunday al betyme.

  1322 getyth] *MS.* getyh   1324 stronge] good *canc. before* stronge
  1333 schryue] *MS.* schyue   1340 name] *MS.* F mane

þou art com al to sone.   1350
þerfore, Schryfte, be þi fay,
Goo forthe tyl on Good Fryday.
Tente to þe þanne wel I may;
    I haue now ellys to done.

CONFESCIO. Ow, þat harlot is now bold!   1355
    In bale he byndyth Mankynd belyue.
Sey Slawthe I preyd hym þat he wold
    Fynd a charter of þi lyue.
Man, þou mayst ben vndyr mold
Longe or þat tyme, kyllyd wyth a knyue,   1360
Wyth podys and froskys manyfold.
    þerfore schape þe now to schryue
        If þou wylt com to blys.
    þou synnyste, or sorwe þe ensense.   f. 168ᵛ
    Behold þynne hert, þi preue spense,   1365
    And þynne owyn consyense,
        Or sertys þou dost amys.

HUMANUM GENUS. 3a, Petyr, so do mo!
    We haue etyn garlek euerychone.
þou I schulde to helle go,   1370
    I wot wel I schal not gon alone,
        Trewly I tell þe.
    I dyd neuere so ewyl trewly
    But oþyr han don as ewyl as I.
    þerfore, syre, lete be þy cry   1375
        And go hens fro me.

PENITENCIA. Wyth poynt of penaunce I schal hym prene
    Mans pride for to felle.
Wyth þis launce I schal hym lene
    Iwys a drope of mercy welle.   1380
Sorwe of hert is þat I mene;
    Trewly þer may no tunge telle
What waschyth sowlys more clene
    Fro þe foul fend of helle

1374 But] MS. F þat   1377 prene] preve *canc. before* prene

þanne swete sorwe of hert.   1385
God, þat syttyth in heuene on hye,
Askyth no more or þat þou dye
But sorwe of hert wyth wepynge eye
For all þi synnys smert.

þei þat syh in synnynge,   1390
In sadde sorwe for here synne,
Whanne þei schal make here endynge,
Al here joye is to begynne.
þanne medelyth no mornynge
But joye is joynyd wyth jentyl gynne.   1395
þerfore, Mankynde, in þis tokenynge,
Wyth spete of spere to þe I spynne,
Goddys lawys to þe I lerne.
Wyth my spud of sorwe swote
I reche to þyne hert rote.   1400
Al þi bale schal torne þe to bote.
Mankynde, go schryue þe ȝerne.

HUMANUM GENUS. A sete of sorwe in me is set;
Sertys for synne I syhe sore.
Mone of mercy in me is met;   1405
For werldys myrþe I morne more.
In wepynge wo my wele is wet.
Mercy, þou muste myn stat astore.
Fro oure lordys lyth þou hast me let,
Sory synne, þou grysly gore,   1410
Owte on þe, dedly synne!
Synne, þou haste Mankynde schent.
In dedly synne my lyfe is spent.
Mercy, God omnipotent!
In ȝoure grace I begynne.   1415

For þou Mankynde haue don amys,   f. 169
And he wyl falle in repentaunce,
Crist schal hym bryngyn to bowre of blys
If sorwe of hert lache hym wyth launce.

1386 syttyth] *MS*. syttyh   1404 syhe] *MS*. F shye   1408 stat] F fatt

Lordyngys, ȝe se wel alle þys, 1420
  Mankynde hathe ben in gret bobaunce.
I now forsake my synne iwys
  And take me holy to Penaunce.
      On Crist I crye and calle.
    A, mercy, Schryfte! I wyl no more. 1425
    For dedly synne myn herte is sore.
    Stuffe Mankynde wyth þyne store
      And haue hym to þyne halle.

CONFESCIO. Schryffte may no man forsake.
  Whanne Mankynde cryeth I am redy. 1430
Whanne sorwe of hert þe hathe take
  Schryfte profytyth veryly.
Whoso for synne wyl sorwe make
  Crist hym heryth whanne he wyl criye.
Now, man, lete sorwe þyn synne slake 1435
  And torne not ageyn to þi folye,
      For þat makyth dystaunce.
    And if it happe þe turne ageyn to synne,
    For Goddys loue lye not longe þerinne.
    He þat dothe alwey ewyl and wyl not blynne, 1440
      þat askyth gret venjaunce.

HUMANUM GENUS. Nay sertys þat schal I not do,
  Schryfte, þou schalte þe sothe se;
For þow Mankynde be wonte þerto
  I wyl now al amende me. 1445
        Tunc descendit ad CONFESSIONEM
I com to þe, Schryfte, alholy, lo!
  I forsake ȝou, synnys, and fro ȝou fle.
ȝe schapyn to man a sory scho;
  Whanne he is begylyd in þis degre
      ȝe bleykyn al hys ble. 1450
    Synne, þou art a sory store.
    þou makyst Mankynd to synke sore.
    þerfore of ȝou wyl I no more.
    I aske schryfte for charyte.

1422 my] *MS.* I *F* my   1423 Penaunce] *MS.* penaune

CONFESCIO. If þou wylt be aknowe here   1455
    Only al þi trespas,
I schal þe schelde fro helle fere
    And putte þe fro peyne vnto precyouse place.
If þou wylt not make þynne sowle clere
    But kepe hem in þyne hert cas,   1460
Anoþyr day þey schul be rawe and rere
    And synke þi sowle to Satanas
       In gastful glowynge glede.
      þerfore, man, in mody monys,   f. 169ᵛ
      If þou wylt wende to worþi wonys,   1465
      Schryue þe now, al at onys,
       Holy of þi mysdede.

HUMANUM GENUS. A, ȝys, Schryfte, trewly I trowe,
    I schal not spare, for odde nor even,
þat I schal rekne al on a rowe   1470
    To lache me up to lyuys leuene.
To my Lord God I am aknowe
    þat syttyth abouen in hey heuene
þat I haue synnyd many a þrowe
    In þe dedly synnys seuene,   1475
       Boþe in home and halle.
      Pride, Wrathe, and Envye,
      Coueytyse and Lecherye,
      Slawth and also Glotonye,
       I haue hem vsyd alle.   1480

þe ten comaundementys brokyn I haue
    And my fyue wyttys spent hem amys.
I was þanne wood and gan to raue.
    Mercy, God, forgeue me þys!
Whanne any pore man gan to me craue   1485
    I gafe hym nowt, and þat forþynkyth me iwys.
Now, Seynt Saueour, ȝe me saue
    And brynge me to ȝour boure of blys!
      I can not alle sav.
      But to þe erthe I knele adown,   1490

Boþe wyth bede and orisoun,
And aske myn absolucioun,
Syr Schryfte, I ȝou pray.

CONFESCIO. Now Jhesu Cryste, God holy,
And all þe seyntys of heuene hende,   1495
Petyr and Powle, apostoly,
To whom God ȝafe powere to lese and bynde,
He forȝeue þe þi foly
þat þou hast synnyd wyth hert and mynde.
And I up my powere þe asoly   1500
þat þou hast ben to God vnkynde,
Quantum peccasti.
In Pride, Ire, and Envye,
Slawthe, Glotony, and Lecherye,
And Coveytyse continuandelye   1505
Vitam male continuasti.

I þe asoyle wyth goode entent
Of alle þe synnys þat þou hast wrowth
In brekynge of Goddys commaundement
In worde, werke, wyl, and þowth.   1510
I restore to þe sacrament   f. 170
Of penauns weche þou neuere rowt;
þi fyue wyttys mysdyspent
In synne þe weche þou schuldyst nowt,
Quicquid gesisti,   1515
Wyth eyne sen, herys herynge,
Nose smellyd, mowthe spekynge,
And al þi bodys bad werkynge,
Vicium quodcumque fecisti.

I þe asoyle wyth mylde mod   1520
Of al þat þou hast ben ful madde
In forsakynge of þyn aungyl good,
And þi fowle Flesche þat þou hast fadde,
þe Werld, þe Deuyl þat is so woode,
And folwyd þyne aungyl þat is so badde.   1525

1511 þee] *F* þee [þe]

To Jhesu Crist þat deyed on rode
I restore þe ageyn ful sadde.
　　Noli peccare.
And all þe goode dedys þat þou haste don
And all þi tribulacyon　　　　　　　　　　　　　　　1530
Stonde þe in remyssion.
　　Posius noli viciare.

HUMANUM GENUS. Now, Syr Schryfte, where may I dwelle
To kepe me fro synne and woo?
A comly counseyl ȝe me spelle　　　　　　　　　　　　1535
To fende me now fro my foo.
If þese seuene synnys here telle
þat I am þus fro hem goo,
þe Werld, þe Flesche, and þe Deuyl of hell
Schul sekyn my soule for to sloo　　　　　　　　　　1540
　　Into balys bowre.
　　þerfore I pray ȝou putte me
　　Into sum place of surete
　　þat þei may not harmyn me
　　Wyth no synnys sowre.　　　　　　　　　　　　1545

CONFESCIO. To swyche a place I schal þe kenne
þer þou mayst dwelle wythoutyn dystaunsce
And alwey kepe þe fro synne,
　　Into þe Castel of Perseueraunce.
If þou wylt to heuene wynne　　　　　　　　　　　　1550
　　And kepe þe fro werldyly dystaunce,
Goo to ȝone castel and kepe þe þerinne,
　　For it is strenger þanne any in Fraunce.
　　　　To ȝone castel I þe seende.
　　þat castel is a precyous place,　　　　　　　　　1555
　　Ful of vertu and of grace;
　　Whoso leuyth þere hys lyuys space
　　　　No synne schal hym schende.

HUMANUM GENUS. A, Schryfte, blessyd mote þou be!　f. 170ᵛ
þis castel is here but at honde.　　　　　　　　　　1560
þedyr rapely wyl I tee,
　　Sekyr ouyr þis sad sonde.

1552 Goo to] MS. F goo　　1553 it is] MS. is F it is　　1561 rapely] F raþely

Good perseueraunce God sende me
  Whyle I leue here in þis londe.
Fro fowle fylthe now I fle,   1565
  Forthe to faryn now I fonde
    To ȝone precyous port.
  Lord, what man is in mery lyue
  Whanne he is of hys synnys schreue!
  Al my dol adoun is dreue.   1570
    Criste is myn counfort.

MALUS ANGELUS. Ey, what deuyl, man, wedyr schat?
  Woldyst drawe now to holynesse?
Goo, felaw, þi goode gate,
  þou art forty wyntyr olde, as I gesse.   1575
Goo ageyn, þe deuelys mat,
  And pleye þe a whyle wyth Sare and Sysse.
Sche wolde not ellys, ȝone olde trat,
  But putte þe to penaunce and to stresse,
    ȝone foule feterel fyle.   1580
    Late men þat arn on þe pyttys brynke
    Forberyn boþe mete and drynke
    And do penaunce as hem good þynke,
      And cum and pley þe a whyle.

BONUS ANGELUS. ȝa, Mankynde, wende forthe þi way   1585
  And do noþynge aftyr hys red.
He wolde þe lede ouyr londys lay
  In dale of dros tyl þou were ded.
Of cursydnesse he kepyth þe key
  To bakyn þe a byttyr bred.   1590
In dale of dol tyl þou schudyst dey
  He wolde drawe þe to cursydhed,
    In synne to haue myschaunce.
    þerfor spede now þy pace
    Pertly to ȝone precyouse place   1595
    þat is al growyn ful of grace,
      þe Castel of Perseueraunce.

1581 þe *added above the line*
Perseueraunce   1597 Perseueraunce] *MS.* perseraunce *F*

C 4343   E

HUMANUM GENUS. Goode Aungyl, I wyl do as þou wylt,
  In londe whyl my lyfe may leste,
For I fynde wel in holy wryt   1600
  þou counseylyste euere for þe beste.

*   *   *   *   *

SCENE XII

CARITAS. To Charyte, man, haue an eye   f. 173
  In al þynge, man, I rede.
Al þi doynge as dros is drye
  But in Charyte þou dyth þi dede.   1605
I dystroye alwey Envye;
  So dyd þi God whanne he gan blede;
For synne he was hangyn hye
  And ȝyt synnyd he neuere in dede,
      þat mylde mercy welle.   1610
    Poulc in hys pystyl puttyth þe prefe,
    'But charyte be wyth þe chefe'.
  þerfore, Mankynde, be now lefe
    In Charyte for to dwelle.

ABSTINENCIA. In Abstinens lede þi lyf,   1615
  Take but skylful refeccyon;
For Gloton kyllyth wythoutyn knyf
  And dystroyeth þi complexion.
Whoso ete or drynke ouyrblyue
  It gaderyth to corrupcion.   1620
þis synne browt us alle in stryue
  Whanne Adam fel in synne down
      Fro precyous paradys.
    Mankynd, lere now of oure lore.
    Whoso ete or drynke more   1625
  þanne skylfully hys state astore,
    I holde hym noþynge wys.

1601 *A leaf is missing from the MS. Two later hands add a speech-heading
for the misplaced f. 171 which follows,* malus angelus *canc. above* Detraccio ad
caro   1606 Envye] eny *canc. before* envye   1621 stryue] *MS. F* strye

CASTITAS. Mankynd, take kepe of Chastyte
And moue þe to maydyn Marye.
Fleschly foly loke þou fle,   1630
  At þe reuerense of Oure Ladye.
Quia qui in carne viuunt Domino placere non possunt.
þat curteys qwene, what dyd sche?
  Kepte hyre clene and stedfastly,
And in here was trussyd þe Trinite;
  þorwe gostly grace sche was worthy,   1635
    And al for sche was chaste.
    Whoso kepyt hym chast and wyl not synne,
    Whanne he is beryed in bankys brymmne
    Al hys joye is to begynne.
      þerfore to me take taste.   1640

SOLICITUDO. In Besynesse, man, loke þou be,
  Wyth worþi werkys goode and þykke.
To Slawthe if þou cast þe
  It schal þe drawe to þowtys wyckke.
Osiositas parit omne malum.
It puttyth a man to pouerte   f. 173ᵛ
  And pullyth hym to peynys prycke.   1646
Do sumwhat alwey for loue of me,
  þou þou schuldyst but thwyte a stycke.
    Wyth bedys sumtyme þe blys.
    Sumtyme rede and sumtyme wryte   1650
    And sumtyme pleye at þi delyte.
    þe Deuyl þe waytyth wyth dyspyte
      Whanne þou art in idylnesse.

LARGITAS. In Largyte, man, ley þi loue.
  Spende þi good, as God it sent.   1655
In worchep of hym þat syt above
  Loke þi goodys be dyspent.
In dale of dros whanne þou schalt droue
  Lytyl loue is on þe lent;

1629 Marye] to *canc. before* marye   1634 Trinite] *MS.* trinte   1635 grace
added in margin   1638 brymmne] F brynnne   1644 wyckke] þy *canc.*
before wyckke   1648 thwyte] tw *canc. before* thwyte

þe sekatourys schul seyn it is here behoue   1660
 To make us mery, for he is went
  þat al þis good gan owle.
  Ley þi tresour and þy trust
  In place where no ruggynge rust
  May it dystroy to dros ne dust   1665
  But al to helpe of sowle.

HUMANUM GENUS. Ladys in londe, louely and lyt,
 Lykynge lelys, 3e be my leche.
I wyl bowe to 3our byddynge bryth;
 Trewe tokenynge 3e me teche.   1670
Dame Meknes, in 3our myth
 I wyl me wryen fro wyckyd wreche.
Al my purpos I haue pyt,
 Paciens, to don as 3e me preche;
  Fro Wrathe 3e schal me kepe.   1675
  Charyte, 3e wyl to me entende.
  Fro fowle Envye 3e me defende.
  Manns mende 3e may amende,
  Whethyr he wake or slepe.

Abstynens, to 3ou I tryst;   1680
 Fro Glotony 3e schal me drawe.
In Chastyte to leuyn me lyst,
 þat is Oure Ladys lawe.
Besynes, we schul be cyste;
 Slawthe, I forsake þi sleper sawe.   1685
Largyte, to 3ou I tryst,
 Coveytyse to don of dawe.
  þis is a curteys cumpany.
  What schuld I more monys make?
  þe seuene synnys I forsake   1690
  And to þese seuene vertuis I me take.
  Maydyn Meknes, now mercy!

HUMILITAS. Mercy may mende al þi mone.
 Cum in here at þynne owyn wylle.

   1669 3our] my *canc. below* 3our

We schul þe fende fro þi fon 1695
  If þou kepe þe in þis castel stylle.

Cum sancto sanctus eris, et cetera.   Tunc intrabit

Stonde hereinne as stylle as ston;   f. 172
  þanne schal no dedly synne þe spylle.
Wheþyr þat synnys cumme or gon,
  þou schalt wyth us þi bourys bylle,   1700
    Wyth vertuse we schul þe vaunce.
    þis castel is of so qweynt a gynne
    þat whoso euere holde hym þerinne
    He schal neuere fallyn in dedly synne;
      It is þe Castel of Perseueranse.   1705

Qui perseuerauerit usque in finem, hic saluus erit.
      Tunc cantabunt 'Eterne rex altissime', et dicet

HUMILITAS. Now blyssyd be Oure Lady, of heuene Emperes!
  Now is Mankynde fro foly falle
And is in þe Castel of Goodnesse.
  He hauntyth now heuene halle
    þat schal bryngyn hym to heuene.   1710
    Crist þat dyed wyth dyen dos
    Kepe Mankynd in þis castel clos
    And put alwey in hys purpos
      To fle þe synnys seuene!

MALUS ANGELUS. Nay, be Belyals bryth bonys,   1715
  þer schal he no whyle dwelle.
He schal be wonne fro þese wonys
  Wyth þe Werld, þe Flesch, and þe Deuyl of hell.
    þei schul my wyl awreke.
    þe synnys seuene, þo kyngys thre,   1720
    To Mankynd haue enmyte.
    Scharpely þei schul helpyn me
      þis castel for to breke.

Howe, Flypyrgebet, Bakbytere!
  3erne oure message loke þou make.   1725

1696 s.d. Tunc intrabit] F tunc mutabit *misplaced after 1908*   1699 cumme]
MS. cunne   1705 s.d. et dicet] *MS.* et . . . F &[c]   1707 HUMILITAS]
MS. Humilita...   1708 foly] h *canc. before* foly   1720 þo] F þe

Blythe about loke þou bere.
  Sey Mankynde hys synnys hath forsake.
Wyth ȝene wenchys he wyl hym were,
  Al to holynesse he hath hym take.
In myn hert it doth me dere,   1730
    þe host þat þo moderys crake;
      My galle gynnyth to grynde.
    Flepyrgebet, ronne upon a rasche.
    Byd þe Werld, þe Fend, and þe Flesche
    þat þey com to fytyn fresche   1735
      To wynne aȝeyn Mankynde.

DETRACCIO. I go, I go, on grounde glad,
  Swyftyr þanne schyp wyth rodyr.
I make men masyd and mad
  And euery man to kyllyn odyr   1740
    Wyth a sory chere.
    I am glad, be Seynt Jamys of Galys,
    Of schrewdnes to tellyn talys
    Boþyn in Ingelond and in Walys,
      And feyth I haue many a fere.   1745
              Tunc ibit ad BELIAL

SCENE XIII

Heyl, set in þyn selle!
Heyl, dynge Deuyl in þi delle!
Heyl, lowe in helle!
I cum to þe talys to telle.

BELYAL. Bakbyter, boy,   f. 172ᵛ
  Alwey be holtys and hothe,   1751
Sey now, I sey,
  What tydyngys? Telle me þe sothe.

DETRACCIO. Teneful talys I may þe sey,
  To þe no good, as I gesse: 1755
Mankynd is gon now awey
  Into þe Castel of Goodnesse.

1745 s.d. ibit] F ibu[nt]   1746–53 *written as four lines with dividing marks*
after selle, helle, boy, sey   1751 hothe] F hethe

þer he wyl boþe lyuyn and deye
  In dale of dros tyl deth hym dresse;
Hathe þe forsakyn, forsoþe I sey,   1760
  And all þi werkys more and lesse;
    To ӡone castel he gan to crepe.
  Ӡone modyr Meknes, sothe to sayn,
  And all ӡene maydnys on ӡone playn
For to fytyn þei be ful fayn   1765
    Mankynd for to kepe.
          Tunc vocabit SUPERBIAM, INUIDIAM, et IRAM

SUPERBIA. Syr kynge, what wytte?
We be redy þrotys to kytte.

BELYAL. Sey, gadelyngys—haue ӡe harde grace
  And euyl deth mote ӡe deye!—   1770
Why lete ӡe Mankynd fro ӡou pase
  Into ӡene castel fro us aweye?
    Wyth tene I schal ӡou tey.
  Harlotys, at onys
  Fro þis wonys!   1775
  Be Belyals bonys,
    Ӡe schul abeye.
          Et verberabit eos super terram

DETRACCIO. Ӡa, for God, þis was wel goo,
  þus to werke wyth bakbytynge.
I werke boþe wrake and woo   1780
  And make iche man oþyr to dynge.
I schal goo abowte and makyn moo
  Rappys for to route and rynge.
Ӡe bakbyterys, loke þat ӡe do so.
  Make debate abowtyn to sprynge   1785
    Betwene systyr and broþyr.
  If any bakbyter here be lafte,
  He may lere of me hys crafte.
  Of Goddys grace he schal be rafte
    And euery man to kyllyn oþyr.   1790

1766 s.d. vocabit SUPERBIAM, INUIDIAM, et IRAM] *MS.* vocauit sperbia
inuida et Ira *F* vertunt Superbia, Inuidia, & Ira   1767–8 *written as one line*

SCENE XIV

Ad CARNEM:

Heyl, kynge, I calle!
Heyl, prinse, proude prekyd in palle!
Heyl, hende in halle!
Heyl, syr kynge, fayre þe befalle!

CARO. Boy Bakbytynge,   1795
Ful redy in robys to rynge,
Ful glad tydynge,
Be Belyalys bonys, I trow þow brynge.

DETRACCIO. ȝa, for God, owt I crye
    On þi too sonys and þi dowtyr ȝynge: 1800
Glotoun, Slawthe, and Lechery
    Hath put me in gret mornynge.
þey let Mankynd gon up hye   f. 171
    Into ȝene castel at hys lykynge,
þerin for to leue and dye,   1805
    Wyth þo ladys to make endynge,
        þo flourys fayre and fresche.
    He is in þe Castel of Perseuerauns
    And put hys body to penauns.
    Of hard happe is now þi chauns,   1810
        Syre kynge, Mankyndys Flesche.

Tunc CARO clamabit ad GULAM, ACCIDIAM, et LUXURIAM

LUXURIA. Sey now þi wylle.
Syr Flesch, why cryest þou so schylle?

CARO. A, Lechery, þou skallyd mare!
    And þou Gloton, God ȝeue þe wo!   1815
And vyle Slawth, euyl mote þou fare!
    Why lete ȝe Mankynd fro ȝou go
        In ȝone castel so hye?
    Euele grace com on þi snowte!

1791–8 written as four lines   1795 Boy] F Roy   1807 þo] F þe
1812–13 written as one line

Now I am dressyd in gret dowte. 1820
Why ne had ȝe lokyd betyr abowte?
Be Belyalys bonys, ȝe schul abye.

              Tunc uerberabit eos in placeam

DETRACCIO. Now, be God, þis is good game!
  I, Bakbyter, now bere me wel.
If I had lost my name, 1825
  I vow to God it were gret del.
I schape þese schrewys to mekyl schame;
  Iche rappyth on oþyr wyth rowtynge rele.
I, Bakbyter, wyth fals fame
  Do brekyn and brestyn hodys of stele. 1830
      þorwe þis cuntre I am knowe.
  Now wyl I gynne forth to goo
  And make Coueytyse haue a knoke or too,
  And þanne iwys I haue doo
      My deuer, as I trowe. 1835

SCENE XV

               Ad MUNDUM:

Heyl, styf in stounde!
Heyl, gayly gyrt upon grounde!
Heyl, fayre flowr ifounde!
Heyl, Syr Werld, worþi in wedys wonde!

MUNDUS. Bakbyter in rowte, 1840
þou tellyst talys of dowte,
So styf and so stowte.
What tydyngys bryngyst þou abowte?

DETRACCIO. Noþynge goode, þat schalt þou wete.
  Mankynd, Syr Werld, hath þe forsake. 1845
Wyth Schryfte and Penauns he is smete
  And to ȝene castel he hath hym take

1821 ne had] *MS.* had *F* nad   1822 s.d. uerberabit] *MS.* uerberauit *F*
uerberant   1836–43 *written as four lines*   1839 wedys] *F* wodis
1844 goode *added above the line*

Amonge ȝene ladys whyt as lake.
Lo, Syr Werld, ȝe moun agryse
þat ȝe be seruyd on þis wyse.   1850
Go pley ȝou wyth Syr Coyeytyse
Tyl hys crowne crake.

            Tunc buccinabit cornu ad AUARICIAM

AUARICIA. Syr bolnynge bowde,
Tell me why blowe ȝe so lowde!

MUNDUS. Lewde losel, þe Deuel þe brenne!   1855
I prey God ȝeue þe a fowl hap!
Sey, why letyst þou Mankynd
Into ȝene castel for to skape?
    I trowe þou gynnyst to raue.
    Now, for Mankynd is went,   f. 171ᵛ
    Al oure game is schent.   1861
    þerfore a sore dryuynge dent,
    Harlot, þou schalt haue.

                                    Tunc verberabit eum

AUARICIA. Mercy, mercy! I wyl no more.
þou hast me rappyd wyth rewly rowtys.   1865
I snowre, I sobbe, I sye sore.
    Myn hed is clateryd al to clowtys.
In al ȝoure state I schal ȝou store
If ȝe abate ȝoure dyntys dowtys.
Mankynd, þat ȝe haue forlore,   1870
    I schal do com owt fro ȝone skowtys
        To ȝoure hende hall.
    If ȝe wyl no more betyn me,
    I schal do Mankynd com out fre.
    He schal forsake, as þou schalt se,   1875
        þe fayre vertus all.

MUNDUS. Haue do þanne, þe Deuyl þe tere!
þou schalt ben hangyn in hell herne.
Bylyue my baner up þou bere
And besege we þe castel ȝerne   1880

1848 lake] MS. la...   1852 s.d. buccinabit cornu] F buccinabunt cornuo
1853-4 written as one line   1855 Lewde] MS. F lowde   1862 a]
þou canc. before a   1863 s.d. verberabit] MS. verberauit F verberant

note for mankynd is went
al oure game is schent
þyng þ a sory spynynge dent

harlot þou schalt haue tue ...

Anapora

weyr woy I kyll no more
þu haff me rappys þe rightly porht
I snorh I sobbe I crye sore
my hed is clatteryd al to clottys
in al zoure stutte I schal zon store
if ze akette zoure spyrit do ...
mankynd þ ze haue for loye

to zoure hende halt

I schal do com owt fro zone scottys
if ze kyl no more beþy me
I schal do mankynd com owt fre
he schal for sake as þu schalt ...

þ sayd ... all

Amen

haue do rune þ deuyl þ tere
þu schalt ben hangyn I hett here
by lyue my bau up þu bere
þ he sege the þ castel zeue
I haue mankynd yrobryth good
of þ world am kyng & lord
þ brothyr schul bless in her blood
zeue lete flewyr up my fame
I schape the schaune I schome
I schal brynge þ me þ brothyr haue
þ schal no vertu stelly in my londe
sche schal dey up on þis ...
wekenes is þ modyr þ I mene
to bryng a heele a bytt bonde
sche schal dey up on þis grene
if þ sche com al in my honde
I am þ kyng it is my crist
þ castel of vertu for to spryll
hastyth lyue up on zone hyst

mankynd for to stele

þ flawyr felle & fele

zeue pupos þ her uppo

ze harreth in zour guppys

the mund capisvac & stabac the is castellio & veyulo & þ demon

Belyal

I here guppys hebelen al of tene
þ kest world halbrch to heyye
for to clymy zou castel dene
þ maydnys medyry for to meye
fyede my penow up on a prene
& pyke the forthe nok awam heyye
schapyth nok zoury schelbyr schene
zeue skallyd skowt for to skeyye

up on zone grene grese

Mankynd for to stele.
Whanne Mankynd growyth good,
I, þe Werld, am wyld and wod.
þo bycchys schul bleryn in here blood
    Wyth flappys felle and fele. 1885

3erne lete flapyr up my fane
And schape we schame and schonde.
I schal brynge wyth me þo bycchys bane;
þer schal no vertus dwellyn in my londe.
Mekenes is þat modyr þat I mene, 1890
    To hyre I brewe a byttyr bonde.
Sche schal dey upon þis grene
    If þat sche com al in myn honde,
        3ene rappokys wyth here rumpys.
    I am þe Werld. It is my wyll 1895
    þe Castel of Vertu for to spyll.
    Howtyth hye upon 3ene hyll,
        3e traytours, in 3oure trumpys.

SCENE XVI

Tunc MUNDUS, CUPIDITAS, et STULTICIA ibunt ad castellum cum vexillo et dicet DEMON:

BELYAL. I here trumpys trebelen al of tene.
    þe worþi Werld walkyth to werre 1900
For to clyuyn 3one castel clene,
    þo maydnys meyndys for to merre.
Sprede my penon upon a prene
    And stryke we forthe now vndyr sterre.
Schapyth now 3oure scheldys schene 1905
    3ene skallyd skoutys for to skerre
        Upon 3one grene grese.
    Buske 3ou now, boyes, belyue. f. 174

1887 schame] F schance   1890 The scribe wrote and then crossed out line
1892   1894 3ene] F 3eue   1898 s.d. dicet] MS. d' F domino
1902 þo] F þe

For euere I stonde in mekyl stryue;
Whyl Mankynd is in clene lyue   1910
    I am neuere wel at ese.

Make ȝou redy, all þre,
    Bolde batayl for to bede.
To ȝone feld lete us fle
    And bere my baner forthe on brede.   1915
To ȝone castel wyl I te;
    þo mamerynge modrys schul haue here mede.
But þei ȝeld up to me,
    Wyth byttyr balys þei schul blede,
        Of here reste I schal hem reue.   1920
    In woful watyrs I schal hem wasche.
    Haue don, felaus, and take ȝoure trasche
    And wende we þedyr on a rasche
        þat castel for to cleue.

SUPERBIA. Now, now, now, go now!   1925
    On hyc hyllys lete us howte;
For in pride is al my prow
    þi bolde baner to bere abowte.
To Golyas I make avow
    For to schetyn ȝone iche skowte.   1930
On hyr ars, raggyd and row,
    I schal boþe clatyr and clowte
        And ȝeue Meknesse myschanse.
    Belyal bryth, it is þyn hest
    þat I, Pride, goo þe nest   1935
    And bere þi baner beforn my brest
        Wyth a comly contenaunce.

SCENE XVII

CARO. I here an hydowse whwtynge on hyt.
    Belyue byd my baner forth for to blase.
Whanne I syt in my sadyl it is a selkowth syt;   1940
    I gape as a gogmagog whanne I gynne to gase.

1921 woful] *written* wowful, *second* w *subpuncted*   1940 Whanne] *MS. F*
wahanne

þis worthy wylde werld I wagge wyth a wyt;
  ӡone rappokys I ruble and al to-rase;
Boþe wyth schot and wyth slynge I caste wyth a sleyt
    Wyth care to ӡone castel to crachen and to crase   1945
        In flode.
    I am mans Flesch; where I go
    I am mans most fo;
    Iwys I am euere wo
        Whane he drawyth to goode.   1950

þerfor, ӡe bolde boyes, buske ӡou abowte.
  Scharply on scheldys ӡour schaftys ӡe scheuere.
And Lechery ledron, schete þou a skoute.
  Help we Mankynd fro ӡone castel to keuere.
      Helpe we moun hym wynne.   1955
    Schete we all at a schote
    Wyth gere þat we cunne best note
    To chache Mankynd fro ӡene cote
      Into dedly synne.

GULA. Lo, Syr Flesch, whov I fare to þe felde,   f. 174ᵛ
  Wyth a faget on myn hond for to settyn on a fyre.   1961
Wyth a wrethe of þe wode wel I can me welde;
  Wyth a longe launce þo loselys I schal lere.
    Go we wyth oure gere.
    þo bycchys schul blcykyn and blodyr;   1965
    I schal makyn swyche a powdyr,
    Boþe wyth smoke and wyth smodyr,
      þei schul schytyn for fere.
               Tunc descendent in placeam

SCENE XVIII

MALUS ANGELUS dicet ad BELYAL:

As armys! as an herawd, hey now I howte.
  Deuyl, dyth þe as a duke to do þo damyselys dote.   1970
Belyal, as a bolde boy þi brodde I bere abowte;
  Helpe to cache Mankynd fro caytyfys cote.

1963, 1965, 1970 þo] F þe   1967 smodyr] F somodyr   1969 herawd]
MS. F heyward   1970 damyselys] MS. damysely F damyselys

Pryd, put out þi penon of raggys and of rowte.
Do þis modyr Mekenes meltyn to mote.
Wrethe, prefe Paciens, þe skallyd skowte.   1975
 Envye, to Charyte schape þou a schote
  Ful ȝare.
 Wyth Pryde, Wrethe, and Envye,
 þese deuelys, be downys drye,
 As comly kyngys I dyscrye   1980
  Mankynd to kachyn to care.

Ad CARNEM:

Flesch, frele and fresche, frely fed,
 Wyth Gloton, Slawthe, and Lechery mans sowle þou slo.
As a duke dowty do þe to be dred.
 Gere þe wyth gerys fro toppe to þe too.   1985
Kyth þis day þou art a kynge frely fedde.
 Gloton, sle þou Abstynensce wyth wyckyd woo.
Wyth Chastyte, þou Lechour, be not ouyrledde.
 Slawthe, bete þou Besynes on buttokys bloo.
  Do now þi crafte, in coste to be knowe.   1990

Ad MUNDUM:

 Worthy, wytty, and wys, wondyn in wede,
 Lete Coueytyse karpyn, cryen, and grede.
 Here ben bolde bacheleris batyl to bede,
  Mankynd to tene, as I trowe.

HUMANUM GENUS. þat dynge Duke þat deyed on rode   1995
 þis day my sowle kepe and safe!
Whanne Mankynd drawyth to goode
 Beholde what enmys he schal haue!
þe Werld, þe Deuyl, þe Flesche arn wode;
 To men þei casten a careful kaue;   2000
Byttyr balys þei brewyn on brode
 Mankynd in wo to weltyr and waue,
  Lordyngys, sothe to sey.
  þerfore iche man be war of þis,
  For whyl Mankynd clene is   2005
  Hys enmys schul temptyn hym to don amys
   If þei mown be any wey.

1980 kyngys] *MS. F* kynge   1987 Abstynensce] *MS.* abstynesce
2000 þei] *MS. F* ben 2001 brewyn] *F* brekyn

Omne gaudium existimate cum variis temptacionibus insideritis.

þerfore, lordys, beth now glad
  Wyth elmesdede and orysoun
For to don as Oure Lord bad,   2010
  Styfly wythstonde ȝoure temptacyoun.
Wyth þis foul fende I am ner mad.   f. 175
  To batayle þei buskyn hem bown.
Certys I schuld ben ouyrlad,
  But þat I am in þis castel town,   2015
    Wyth synnys sore and smerte.
    Whoso wyl leuyn oute of dystresse
    And ledyn hys lyf in clennesse
    In þis Castel of Vertu and of Goodnesse
      Hym muste haue hole hys hert.   2020
Delectare in Domino et dabit tibi peticiones cordis tui.

BONUS ANGELUS. A, Mekenesse, Charyte, and Pacyens,
  Prymrose pleyeth parlasent.
Chastyte, Besynes, and Abstynens,
  Myn hope, ladys, in ȝou is lent.
Socoure, paramourys, swetter þanne sens,   2025
  Rode as rose on rys irent.
þis day ȝe dyth a good defens.
  Whyl Mankynd is in good entent
    His þoutys arn vnhende.
    Mankynd is browt into þis walle   2030
    In freelte to fadyn and falle.
    þerfore, ladys, I pray ȝou alle,
      Helpe þis day Mankynde.

HUMILITAS. God, þat syttyth in heuene on hy,
  Saue al Mankynd be se and sonde!   2035
Lete hym dwellyn here and ben vs by
  And we schul puttyn to hym helpynge honde.
Ȝyt forsoþe neuere I sy
  þat any fawte in vs he fonde
But þat we sauyd hym fro synne sly   2040
  If he wolde be us styfly stonde

2025 Socoure] F so come

In þis castel of ston.
þerfor drede þe not, mans aungel dere.
If he wyl dwellyn wyth vs here
Fro seuene synnys we schul hym were   2045
And his enmys ichon.

Now, my seuene systerys swete,
þis day fallyth on us þe lot
Mankynd for to schylde and schete
Fro dedly synne and schamely schot.   2050
Hys enmys strayen in þe strete
To spylle man wyth spetows spot.
þerfor oure flourys lete now flete
And kepe we hym, as we haue het,
Among vs in þis halle.   2055
þerfor, seuene systerys swote,
Lete oure vertus reyne on rote.
þis day we wyl be mans bote
Ageyns þese deuelys alle.

BELYAL. þis day þe vaward wyl I holde.   2060
Avaunt my baner, precyous Pride,
Mankynd to cache to karys colde.
Bold batayl now wyl I byde.
Buske ʒou, boyes, on brede.
Alle men þat be wyth me wytholde,   f. 175ᵛ
Boþe þe ʒonge and þe olde,   2066
Envye, Wrathe, ʒe boyes bolde,
To rounde rappys ʒe rape, I rede.

SUPERBIA. As armys, Mekenes! I brynge þi bane,
Al wyth pride peyntyd and pyth.   2070
What seyst þou, faytour? be myn fayr fane,
Wyth robys rounde rayed ful ryth,
Grete gounse, I schal þe gane.
To marre þe, Mekenes, wyth my myth,
No werldly wyttys here ar wane.   2075
Lo, þi castel is al beset!
Moderys, whov schul ʒe do?
Mekenes, ʒeld þe to me, I rede.

Myn name in londe is precyous Prede.
Myn bolde baner to þe I bede.   2080
   Modyr, what seyste þerto?

HUMILITAS. Ageyns þi baner of pride and bost
   A baner of meknes and mercy
I putte ageyns pride, wel þou wost,
   þat schal schende þi careful cry.   2085
þis meke kynge is knowyn in euery cost
   þat was croysyd on Caluary.
Whanne he cam doun fro heuene ost
   And lytyd wyth mekenes in Mary,
     þis lord þus lytyd lowe.   2090
    Whanne he cam fro þe Trynyte
    Into a maydyn lytyd he,
    And al was for to dystroye þe,
     Pride, þis schalt þou knowe.
Deposuit potentes de sede et cetera.

For whanne Lucyfer to helle fyl,   2095
   Pride, þerof þou were chesun,
And þou, deuyl, wyth wyckyd wyl
   In paradys trappyd us wyth tresun.
So þou us bond in balys ille,
   þis may I preue be ryth resun,   2100
Tyl þis duke þat dyed on hylle
   In heuene man myth neuere han sesun;
     þe gospel þus declaryt.
    For whoso lowe hym schal ben hy,
    þerfore þou schalt not comen us ny,   2105
    And þou þou be neuere so sly,
     I schal felle al þi fare.
Qui se exaltat humiliabitur et cetera.

IRA. Dame Pacyens, what seyst þou to Wrathe and Ire?
   Putte Mankynd fro þi castel clere,
Or I schal tappyn at þi tyre   2110
   Wyth styffe stonys þat I haue here.

2109 fro þi] MS. fro þi fro þi

I schal slynge at þe many a vyre   f. 177
  And ben avengyd hastely here.
þus Belsabub, oure gret syre,
  Bad me brenne þe wyth wyld fere,   2115
    þou bycche blak as kole.
    þerfor fast, fowlc skowle,
    Putte Mankynd to us owte,
    Or of me þou schalt haue dowte,
      þou modyr, þou motyhole!   2120

PACIENCIA. Fro þi dowte Crist me schelde
  þis iche day, and al mankynde!
þou wrecchyd Wrethe, wood and wylde,
  Pacyens schal þe schende.

Quia ira viri justiciam Dei non operatur.

For Marys sone, meke and mylde,   2125
  Rent þe up, rote and rynde,
Whanne he stod meker þanne a chylde
  And lete boyes hym betyn and byndc,
    þerfor, wrecche, be stylle.
    For þo pelourys þat gan hym pose,   2130
    He myth a dreuyn hem to dros,
    And ȝyt, to casten hym on þe cros,
      He sufferyd al here wylle.

þowsentys of aungellys he myth han had
  To a wrokyn hym þer ful ȝerne,   2135
And ȝyt to deyen he was glad
  Us pacyens to techyn and lerne.
þerfor, boy, wyth þi boystous blad,
  Fare awey be feldys ferne.
For I wyl do as Jhesu bad,   2140
  Wrecchys fro my wonys werne
    Wyth a dyngne defens.
    If þou fonde to comyn alofte
    I schal þe cacche fro þis crofte
    Wyth þese rosys swete and softe,   2145
      Peyntyd wyth pacyens.

2112 Ira *is added in another contemporary hand at the top of f. 177, the leaf which
should have followed f. 175*   2123 Wrethe] *F* wreche   2134 aungellys]
MS. aungell   2145 rosys] *F* rolys

INUIDIA. Out, myn herte gynnyth to breke,
  For Charyte þat stondyth so stowte.
Alas, myn herte gynnyth to wreke.
  ʒelde up þis castel, þou hore clowte.   2150
It is myn offyce fowle to speke,
  Fals sklaundrys to bere abowte.
Charyte, þe Deuyl mote þe cheke
  But I þe rappe wyth rewly rowte,
    þi targe for to tere.   2155
    Let Mankynde cum to us doun
    Or I schal schetyn to þis castel town
    A ful fowle defamacyoun.
      þerfore þis bowe I bere.

CARITAS. þou þou speke wycke and fals fame,   2160
  þe wers schal I neuere do my dede.
Whoso peyryth falsly anoþyr mans name,
  Cristys curs he schal haue to mede.
Ve homini illi per quem scandalum venit.
Whoso wyl not hys tunge tame,   f. 177ᵛ
  Take it sothe as mes-crede,   2165
Wo, wo to hym and mekyl schame!
  In holy wrytte þis I rede.
    For euere þou art a schrewe.
    þou þou speke euyl, I ne ʒeue a gres;
    I schal do neuere þe wers.   2170
    At þe last þe sothe vers
      Certys hymself schal schewe.

Oure louely Lord wythowtyn lak
  ʒaf example to charyte,
Whanne he was betyn blo and blak   2175
  For trespas þat neuere dyd he.
In sory synne had he no tak
  And ʒyt for synne he bled blody ble.
He toke hys cros upon hys bak,
  Synful man, and al for þe.   2180

2149 wreke] breke *canc.*, wreke *written in margin*   2163a venit] *MS.*
ven...   2164 not *followed by* tame *canc.*   2177 had he] *MS. (blot)*
he (?) had he *F* had he

þus he mad defens.
Envye, wyth þi slaundrys þycke,
I am putte at my Lordys prycke;
I wyl do good aȝeyns þe wycke
    And kepe in sylens.   2185

BELYAL. What, for Belyalys bonys,
    Whereabowtyn chyde ȝe?
Haue don, ȝe boyes, al at onys.
    Lasche don þese moderys, all þre.
Werke wrake to þis wonys.   2190
    þe vaunward is grauntyd me.
Do þese moderys to makyn monys.
    Ȝoure dowty dedys now lete se.
        Dasche hem al to daggys.
        Haue do, boyes blo and blake.   2195
        Wirke þese wenchys wo and wrake.
        Claryouns, cryeth up at a krake,
        And blowe ȝour brode baggys!

                              Tunc pugnabunt diu

SUPERBIA. Out, my proude bak is bent!
    Mekenes hath me al forbete.   2200
Pride wyth Mekenes is forschent.
    I weyle and wepe wyth wondys wete;
        I am betyn in þe hed.
    My prowde pride adoun is dreuyn;
    So scharpely Mekenes hath me schreuyn   2205
        þat I may no lengyr leuyn,
        My lyf is me bereuyd.

INVIDIA. Al myn enmyte is not worth a fart;
    I schyte and schake al in my schete.
Charyte, þat sowre swart,   2210
    Wyth fayre rosys myn hed gan breke.
        I brede þe malaundyr.
    Wyth worthi wordys and flourys swete

2189 all þre] at onys *canc. before* þre
vannward   2198 s.d. diu] *F* domini
cancelled line 2221
2191 vaunward] *MS.* vaunward *or*
2203 *The scribe wrote and then*

Charyte makyth me so meke
I dare neyþyr crye nore crepe,   2215
  Not a schote of sklaundyr.

IRA. I, Wrethe, may syngyn weleawo.   f. 176
  Pacyens me ȝaf a sory dynt.
I am al betyn blak and blo
Wyth a rose þat on rode was rent.   2220
    My speche is almost spent.
    Hyr rosys fel on me so scharpe
    þat myn hed hangyth as an harpe.
    I dar neyþyr crye nor carpe,
      Sche is so pacyent.   2225

MALUS ANGELUS. Go hens, ȝe do not worthe a tord.
  Foule falle ȝou, alle foure!
ȝerne, ȝerne, let fall on bord,
  Syr Flesch, wyth þyn eyn soure.
    For care I cukke and koure.   2230
    Syr Flesch, wyth þyn company,
    ȝerne, ȝerne, make a cry.
    Helpe we haue no velony
      þat þis day may be oure.

CARO. War, war, late mans Flesche go to!   2235
  I com wyth a company.
Haue do, my chyldryn, now haue do,
  Glotoun, Slawth, and Lechery.
Iche of ȝou wynnyth a scho.
  Lete not Mankynde wynne maystry.   2240
Lete slynge hem in a fowl slo
  And fonde to feffe hym wyth foly.
    Dothe now wel ȝoure dede.
    ȝerne lete se whov ȝe schul gynne
    Mankynde to temptyn to dedly synne.   2245
    If ȝe muste þis castelle wynne
      Hell schal be ȝour mede.

GULA. War, Syr Gloton schal makyn a smeke
  Aȝeyns þis castel, I vowe.

2228 ȝerne] be *canc. before* ȝerne   2240 wynne] *MS.* wᵗ *F* with

Abstynens, þou þou bleyke,   2250
  I loke on þe wyth byttyr browe.
I haue a faget in myn necke
  To settyn Mankynd on a lowe.
My foul leye schalt þou not let,
  I wou to God, as I trowe.   2255
      þerfor putte hym out here.
    In meselynge glotonye,
    Wyth goode metys and drynkys trye,
    I norche my systyr Lecherye
      Tyl man rennyth on fere.   2260

ABSTINENCIA. þi metys and drynkys arn vnthende
  Whanne þei are out of mesure take.
þei makyn men mad and out of mende
  And werkyn hem bothe wo and wrake.
þat for þi fere þou þou here kyndyl,   2265
  Certys I schal þi wele aslake
Wyth bred þat browth us out of hell
  And on þe croys sufferyd wrake: ·
      I mene þe sacrament.
    þat iche blysful bred   f. 176ᵛ
    þat hounge on hyl tyl he was ded   2271
    Schal tempere so myn maydynhed
      þat þi purpos schal be spent.

In abstynens þis bred was browth,
  Certys, Mankynde, and al for þe.   2275
Of fourty dayes ete he nowth
  And þanne was naylyd to a tre.
Cum jejunasset quadraginta diebus et cetera.
Example us was betawth,
  In sobyrnesse he bad us be.
þerfor Mankynd schal not be cawth,   2280
  Glotony, wyth þy degre.
      þe sothe þou schalt se.
    To norysch fayre þou þou be fawe,
    Abstynens it schal wythdrawe
    Tyl þou be schet vndyr schawe   2285
      And fayn for to fle.

LUXURIA. Lo, Chastyte, þou fowle skowte!
 þis ilke day here þou schalt deye.
I make a fer in mans towte
 þat launcyth up as any leye.   2290
þese cursyd colys I bere abowte
 Mankynde in tene for to teye.
Men and wommen hathe no dowte
 Wyth pyssynge pokys for to pleye.
   I bynde hem in my bondys.   2295
  I haue no reste, so I rowe,
  Wyth men and wommen, as I trowe,
  Tyl I, Lechery, be set on a lowe
   In al Mankyndys londys.

CASTITAS. I, Chastyte, haue power in þis place 2300
 þe, Lechery, to bynd and bete.
Maydyn Marye, well of grace,
 Schal qwenche þat fowle hete.
Mater et Virgo, extingue carnales concupiscentias!
Oure Lord God mad þe no space
 Whanne his blod strayed in þe strete.   2305
Fro þis castel he dyd þe chase
 Whanne he was crounyd wyth þornys grete
   And grene.
  To drery deth whanne he was dyth
  And boyes dyd hym gret dyspyth,   2310
  In lechery had he no delyth,
   And þat was ryth wel sene.

At Oure Lady I lere my lessun
 To haue chaste lyf tyl I be ded.
Sche is qwene and beryth þe croun,   2315
 And al was for hyr maydynhed.
þerfor go fro þis castel toun,
 Lechery, now I þe rede,
For Mankynd getyst þou nowth doun

 2291 *The scribe wrote this line opposite 2289, then cancelled it and wrote it in
its right place* 2303 concupiscentias] *MS.* concupisce . . .

To soloyen hym wyth synful sede.   2320
  In care þou woldys hym cast.
And if þou com up to me,   f. 179
Trewly þou schalt betyn be
Wyth þe ȝerde of Chastyte
  Whyl my lyf may last.   2325

ACCIDIA. Ware, war, I delue wyth a spade.
  Men calle me þe lord Syr Slowe.
Gostly grace I spylle and schade;
  Fro þe watyr of grace þis dyche I fowe.
Ȝe schulyn com ryth inowe   2330
  Be þis dyche drye, be bankys brede.
Thyrti thousende þat I wel knowe
  In my lyf louely I lede
    þat had leuere syttyn at þe ale
    Thre mens songys to syngyn lowde   2335
    þanne toward þe chyrche for to crowde.
    þou Besynesse, þou bolnyd bowde,
      I brewe to þe þyne bale.

SOLICITUDO. A, good men, be war now all
  Of Slugge and Slawthe, þis fowl þefe!   2340
To þe sowle he is byttyrer þanne gall;
  Rote he is of mekyl myschefe.
Goddys seruyse, þat ledyth us to heuene hall,
  þis lordeyn for to lettyn us is lefe.
Whoso wyl schryuyn hym of hys synnys all,   2345
  He puttyth þis brethel to mykyl myschefe,
    Mankynde he þat myskaryed.
    Men moun don no penauns for hym þis,
    Nere schryue hem whanne þey don amys,
    But euyr he wold in synne iwys   2350
      þat Mankynd were taryed.

þerfor he makyth þis dyke drye
  To puttyn Mankynde to dystresse.
He makyth dedly synne a redy weye
  Into þe Castel of Goodnesse.   2355

    2320 soloyen] *F* sowen   hym wyth] *MS. F* hym   2329, 2340 þis] *F* þe
2336 for] *MS.* fror

But wyth tene I schal hym teye,
  þorwe þe helpe of heuene emperesse.
Wyth my bedys he schal abeye,
  And oþyr ocupacyons more and lesse
    I schal schape hym to schonde,   2360
    For whoso wyle Slawth putte doun
    Wyth bedys and wyth orysoun
    Or sum oneste ocupacyoun,
      As boke to haue in honde.
Nunc lege nunc ora nunc disce nuncque labora.

CARO. Ey, for Belyalys bonys, þe kynge,   2365
  Whereabowte stonde ȝe al-day?
Caytyuys, lete be ȝour kakelynge
  And rappe at rowtys of aray.
Glotony, þou fowle gadlynge,
  Sle Abstynens, if þou may.   2370
Lechery, wyth þi werkynge,
  To Chastyte make a wyckyd aray
    A lytyl þrowe.
    And whyl we fyth   f. 179^v
    For owre ryth,   2375
    In bemys bryth
      Late blastys blowe.
                        Tunc pugnabunt diu
GULA. Out, Glotoun, adown I dryue.
  Abstynens hathe lost my myrth.
Syr Flesch, I schal neuere thryue;   2380
  I do not worthe þe deuelys dyrt;
    I may not leuyn longe.
    I am al betyn, toppe and tayl;
    Wyth Abstynens wyl I no more dayl;
    I wyl gon cowche qwayl   2385
      At hom in ȝour gonge.

LUXURIA. Out on Chastyte, be þe rode!
  Sche hathe mc dayschyd and so drenchyd.

2364a Nunc ... nuncque] F nec ... neque ora] MS. hora   2365 Bel-
yalys] MS. Blyalys   2377 s.d. diu] F domini   2379 Abstynens] MS.
abstynes   myrth] MS. F myth   2385 qwayl] F [&] qwayl   2388
hathe me] MS. F hathe

3yt haue sche þe curs of God
   For al my fere þe qwene hath qwenchyd.   2390
      For ferd I fall and feynt.
    In harde ropys mote sche ryde!
    Here dare I not longe abyde.
    Sumwhere myn hed I wolde hyde
      As an irchoun þat were schent.   2395

ACCIDIA. Out, I deye! ley on watyr!
   I swone, I swete, I feynt, I drulle!
3ene qwene wyth hyr pytyr-patyr
   Hath al to-dayschyd my skallyd skulle.
      It is as softe as wulle.   2400
    Or I haue here more skathe,
    I schal lepe awey, be lurkynge lathe,
    þere I may my ballokys bathe
      And leykyn at þe fulle.

MALUS ANGELUS. 3a, þe Deuyl spede 3ou, al þe packe!   2405
   For sorwe I morne on þe mowle,
I carpe, I crye, I coure, I kacke,
   I frete, I fart, I fesyl fowle.
      I loke lyke an howle.

                           Ad MUNDUM:

   Now, Syr World, whatso it cost,   2410
   Helpe now, or þis we haue lost;
   Al oure fare is not worth a thost;
      þat makyth me to mowle.

MUNDUS. How, Coveytyse, banyour avaunt!
   Here comyth a batayl nobyl and newe;   2415
For syth þou were a lytyl faunt,
   Coveytyse, þou hast ben trewe.
Haue do þat damysel, do hyr dawnt.
   Byttyr balys þou hyr brewe.
þe medys, boy, I þe graunt,   2420
   þe galows of Canwyke to hangyn on newe,
      þat wolde þe wel befalle.
    Haue don, Syr Coueytyse.

    2400 as wulle] *MS.* a wulle   2420 medys] md *canc. before* medys

Wyrke on þe best wyse.
Do Mankynde com and aryse   2425
   Fro ӡone vertuse all.

AUARICIA. How, Mankynde! I am atenyde
  For þou art þere so in þat holde.
Cum and speke wyth þi best frende,
  Syr Coueytyse, þou knowyst me of olde.   2430
What deuyl schalt þou þer lenger lende   f. 178
  Wyth grete penaunce in þat castel colde?
Into þe werld if þou wylt wende,
  Amonge men to bere þe bolde,
    I rede, be Seynt Gyle.   2435
    How, Mankynde! I þe sey,
    Com to Coueytyse, I þe prey.
    We to schul togedyr pley,
      If þou wylt, a whyle.

LARGITAS. A, God helpe! I am dysmayed,   2440
  I curse þe, Coveytyse, as I can;
For certys, treytour, þou hast betrayed
  Nerhand now iche erthely man.
So myche were men neuere afrayed
  Wyth Coueytyse, syn þe werld began.   2445
God almythy is not payed.
  Syn þou, fende, bare þe Werldys bane,
    Ful wyde þou gynnyst wende.
    Now arn men waxyn ner woode;
    þey wolde gon to helle for werldys goode.   2450
    þat Lord þat restyd on þe rode
      Is maker of an ende.
Maledicti sunt auariciosi hujus temporis.

þer is no dysese nor debate
  þorwe þis wyde werld so rounde,
Tyde nor tyme, erly nor late,   2455
  But þat Coveytyse is þe grounde.

2431 *A later hand adds the speech-heading* covetyse   2448 wende] g *canc.*
before wende   2452 an ende] *MS.* an h ende   2456 Coveytyse] *MS.*
Coveyse

þou norchyst pride, envye, and hate,
    þou Coueytyse, þou cursyd hounde.
Criste þe schelde fro oure gate
    And kepe us fro þe saf and sounde   2460
        þat þou no good here wynne!
    Swete Jhesu, jentyl justyce,
    Kepe Mankynde fro Coueytyse,
    For iwys he is, in al wyse,
        Rote of sorwe and synne.   2465

AUARICIA. What eylyth þe, Lady Largyte,
    Damysel dyngne upon þi des?
And I spak ryth not to þe,
    þerfore I prey þe holde þi pes.
How, Mankynde! cum speke wyth me,   2470
    Cum ley þi loue here in my les.
Coueytyse is a frend ryth fre,
    þi sorwe, man, to slake and ses.
        Coueytyse hathe many a ȝyfte.
    Mankynd, þyne hande hedyr þou reche.   2475
    Coueytyse schal be þi leche.
    þe ryth wey I schal þe teche
        To thedom and to þryfte.

HUMANUM GENUS. Coueytyse, whedyr schuld I wende?
    What wey woldyst þat I sulde holde?   2480
To what place woldyst þou me sende?
    I gynne to waxyn hory and olde.
My bake gynnyth to bowe and bende,   f. 178ᵛ
    I crulle and crepe and wax al colde.
Age makyth man ful vnthende,   2485
    Body and bonys and al vnwolde;
        My bonys are febyl and sore.
    I am arayed in a sloppe,
    As a ȝonge man I may not hoppe,
    My nose is colde and gynnyth to droppe,   2490
        Myn her waxit al hore.

2481 luxurya *added in a later hand, then crossed out*   2482 olde] *MS. F*
colde

AUARICIA. Petyr! þou hast þe more nede
  To haue sum good in þyn age:
Markys, poundys, londys and lede,
  Howsys and homys, castell and cage.   2495
þerfor do as I þe rede;
  To Coueytyse cast þi parage.
Cum, and I schal þyne erdyn bede;
  þe worthi Werld schal ȝeue þe wage,
    Certys not a lyth.   2500
    Com on, olde man, it is no reprefe
    þat Coueytyse be þe lefe.
    If þou deye at any myschefe
      It is þiselfe to wyth.

HUMANUM GENUS. Nay, nay, þese ladys of goodnesse   2505
  Wyl not lete me fare amys,
And þou I be a whyle in dystresse,
  Whanne I deye I schal to blysse.
It is but foly, as I gesse,
  Al þis werldys wele iwys.   2510
þese louely ladys, more and lesse,
  In wyse wordys þei telle me þys.
    þus seyth þe bok of kendys.
    I wyl not do þese ladys dyspyt
    To forsakyn hem for so lyt.   2515
    To dwellyn here is my delyt;
      Here arn my best frendys.

AUARICIA. ȝa, up and don þou take þe wey
  þorwe þis werld to walkyn and wende
And þou schalt fynde, soth to sey,   2520
  þi purs schal be þi best frende.
þou þou syt al-day and prey,
  No man schal com to þe nor sende,
But if þou haue a peny to pey,
  Men schul to þe þanne lystyn and lende   2525
    And kelyn al þi care.
    þerfore to me þou hange and helde

2521 frende] *MS.* fremde

And be coueytous whylys þou may þe welde.
If þou be pore and nedy in elde
    þou schalt oftyn euyl fare.   2530

HUMANUM GENUS. Coueytyse, þou seyst a good skyl.
    So grete God me avaunce,
Al þi byddynge don I wyl.
I forsake þe Castel of Perseueraunce.
In Coueytyse I wyl me hyle   f. 180
    For to gete sum sustynaunce.   2536
Aforn mele men mete schul tyle;
    It is good for al chaunce
        Sum good owhere to hyde.
        Certys þis 3e wel knowe,   2540
        It is good, whouso þe wynde blowe,
        A man to haue sumwhat of hys owe,
            What happe so-euere betyde.

BONUS ANGELUS. A, ladyse, I prey 3ou of grace,
    Helpyth to kepe here Mankynne.   2545
He wyl forsake þis precyous place
    And drawe a3eyn to dedly synne.
Helpe, ladys, louely in lace.
    He goth fro þis worthi wonnynge.
Coueytyse awey 3e chace   2550
    And schyttyth Mankynd sumwhere here-inne,
        In 3oure worþi wyse.
        Ow, wrechyd man, þou schalt be wroth,
        þat synne schal be þe ful loth.
        A, swete ladys, helpe, he goth   2555
            Awey wyth Coueytyse.

                        Tunc descendit ad AUARICIAM

HUMILITAS. Good Aungyl, what may I do þerto?
    Hymselfe may hys sowle spylle.
Mankynd to don what he wyl do,
    God hath 3ouyn hym a fre wylle.   2560

2529 be pore] po r *canc. before* be pore   in] *F* &   2532 me] *F* me [wyl]
2541 whouso] *F* whon-so   2550 chace] chach *with final* h *erased*

þou he drenche and hys sowle slo,
Certys we may not do þeretylle.
Syn he cam þis castel to,
We dyd to hym þat vs befelle
And now he hath us refusyd. 2565
As longe as he was wythinne þis castel walle,
We kepte hym fro synne, ȝe sawe wel alle;
And now he wyl aȝeyn to synne falle,
I preye ȝou holde us excusyd.

PACIENCIA. Resun wyl excusyn us alle. 2570
He helde þe ex be þe helue.
þou he wyl to foly falle,
It is to wytyn but hymselue.
Whyl he held hym in þis halle,
Fro dedly synne we dyd hym schelue. 2575
He brewyth hymselfe a byttyr galle;
In dethys dynt whanne he schal delue
þis game he schal begrete.
He is endewyd wyth wyttys fyue
For to rewlyn hym in hys lyue. 2580
We vertuse wyl not wyth hym stryue,
Avyse hym and hys dede.

CARITAS. Of hys dede haue we nowt to done;
He wyl no lenger wyth us be lad.
Whanne he askyd out, we herd hys bone, 2585
And of hys presens we were ryth glad.
But, as þou seste, he hath forsakyn us sone; f. 180ᵛ
He wyl not don as Crist hym bad.
Mary, þi Sone abouyn þe mone
As make Mankynd trewe and sad, 2590
In grace for to gon.
For if he wyl to foly flyt,
We may hym not wythsyt.
He is of age and can hys wyt,
ȝe knowe wel euerychon. 2595

ABSTINENCIA. Ichon ȝe knowyn he is a fole,
In Coueytyse to dyth hys dede.

2562 not *added above the line*   2593 may] *F* [ne] may

Werldys wele is lyke a thre-fotyd stole,
  It faylyt a man at hys most nede.
Mundus transit et concupiscencia ejus.
Whanne he is dyth in dedys dole,   2600
  þe ryth regystre I schal hym rede;
He schal be tore wyth teneful tole;
  Whanne he schal brenne on glemys glede
    He schal lere a new lawe.
      Be he neuere so ryche of werldys wone,   2605
      Hys seketouris schul makyn here mone:
      'Make us mery and lete hym gone!
      He was a good felawe.'

CASTITAS. Whanne he is ded here sorwe is lest.
  þe ton sekatour seyth to þe tothyr: 2610
'Make we mery and a ryche fest
  And lete hym lyn in dedys fodyr.'
Et sic relinquent alienis diuicias suas.
So hys part schal be þe lest;
  þe systyr seruyt þus þe brothyr.
I lete a man no betyr þanne a best,   2615
  For no man can be war be oþyr
    Tyl he hathe al ful spunne.
    þou schalt se þat day, man, þat a bede
    Schal stonde þe more in stede
    þanne al þe good þat þou mytyst gete,   2620
    Certys vndyr sunne.

SOLICITUDO. Mankynde, of on þynge haue I wondyr:
  þat þou takyst not into þyn mende,
Whanne body and sowle schul partyn on sundyr
  No werldys good schal wyth þe wende.   2625
Non descendet cum illo gloria ejus.
Whanne þou art ded and in þe erthe leyd vndyr
  Mysgotyn good þe schal schende;
It schal þe weyen as peys in pundyr
  þi sely sowle to bryngyn in bende

2598 lyke] MS. kyke   2612a relinquent] MS. relinquam F relinquat
2614 seruyt] F semyt   2619 stonde þe] F þee stonde

And make it ful vnþende. 2630
And ȝyt Mankynd, as it is sene,
Wyth Coueytyse goth on þis grene.
þe treytor doth us al þis tene
Aftyr hys lyuys ende.

LARGITAS. Out, I crye, and noþynge lowe, 2635
On Coueytyse, as I wel may.
Mankynd seyth he hath neuere inowe
Tyl hys mowthe be ful of clay.
Auarus numquam replebitur pecunia.
Whane he is closyd in dethis dow f. 181
What helpyt ryches or gret aray? 2640
It flyet awey as any snow
Anon aftyr þye endynge day,
To wylde werldys wyse.
Now, good men alle þat here be,
Haue my systerys excusyd and me, 2645
þou Mankynde fro þis castel fle.
Wyte it Coueytyse.

MALUS ANGELUS. Ȝa, go forthe and lete þe qwenys cakle!
þer wymmen arn are many wordys.
Lete hem gon hoppyn wyth here hakle! 2650
þer ges syttyn are many tordys.
Wyth Coueytyse þou renne on rakle
And hange þyne hert upon hys hordys.
þou schalt be schakyn in myn schakle;
Vnbynde þi baggys on hys bordys, 2655
On hys benchys aboue.
Parde, þou gost owt of Mankynde
But Coueytyse be in þi mende.
If euere þou þynke to be thende,
On hym þou ley þi loue. 2660

HUMANUM GENUS. Nedys my loue muste on hym lende,
Wyth Coueytyse to waltyr and wave.
I knowe non of al my kynde
þat he ne coueytyth for to haue.

Penyman is mekyl in mynde;   2665
  My loue in hym I leye and laue.
Where þat euere I walke or wende
  In wele and woo he wyl me haue;
      He is gret of grace.
        Whereso I walke in londe or lede   2670
        Penyman best may spede;
        He is a duke to don a dede
            Now in euery place.

BONUS ANGELUS. Alas, þat euere Mankynde was born!
  On Coueytyse is al hys lust.   2675
Nyth and day, mydnyth and morn,
  In Penyman is al hys trust.
Coueytyse schal makyn hym lorn
  Whanne he is doluen al to dust;
To mekyl schame he schal be schorn,   2680
  Wyth foule fendys to roten and rust.
        Alas, what schal I do?
        Alas, alas, so may I say.
        Man goth wyth Coueytyse away.
        Haue me excusyd, for I ne may   2685
            Trewly not do þerto.

MUNDUS. A, a, þis game goth as I wolde.
  Mankynde wyl neuere þe Werld forsake.
Tyl he be ded and vndyr molde
  Holy to me he wyl hym take.   2690
To Coueytyse he hath hym ȝolde;   f. 181ᵛ
  Wyth my wele he wyl awake;
For a thousende pounde I nolde
  But Coveytyse were Mans make,
        Certys on euery wyse.   2695
        All þese gamys he schal bewayle,
        For I, þe Werld, am of þis entayle,
        In hys moste nede I schal hym fayle,
            And al for Coveytyse.

        2693 I nolde] of golde *canc. before* I nolde

SCENE XIX

AUARICIA. Now, Mankynd, be war of þis: 2700
  þou art a-party wele in age.
I wolde not þou ferdyst amys;
  Go we now knowe my castel cage.
In þis bowre I schal þe blys;
  Worldly wele schal be þi wage;   2705
More mucke þanne is þyne iwys
  Take þou in þis trost terage
    And loke þat þou do wronge.
   Coveytyse, it is no sore,
   He wyl þe feffen ful of store,   2710
   And alwey, alwey sey 'more and more',
    And þat schal be þi songe.

HUMANUM GENUS. A, Coveytyse, haue þou good grace!
  Certys þou beryst a trewe tonge.
'More and more', in many a place,   2715
  Certys þat songe is oftyn songe.
I wyste neuere man, be bankys bace,
  So seyn in cley tyl he were clonge:
'Inow, inow' hadde neuere space,
  þat ful songe was neuere songe,   2720
    Nor I wyl not begynne.
   Goode Coveytyse, I þe prey
   þat I myth wyth þe pley.
   Ʒeue me good inow, or þat I dey,
    To wonne in werldys wynne.   2725

AUARICIA. Haue here, Mankynd, a thousend marke.
  I, Coveytyse, haue þe þis gote.
þou mayst purchase þerwyth bothe ponde and parke
  And do þerwyth mekyl note.
Lene no man hereof, for no karke,   2730
  þou he schulde hange be þe þrote,
Monke nor frere, prest nor clerke,
  Ne helpe þerwyth chyrche nor cote,
    Tyl deth þi body delue.
   þou he schuld sterue in a caue,   2735

Lete no pore man þerof haue.
In grene gres tyl þou be graue
Kepe sumwhat fore þiselue.

HUMANUM GENUS. I vow to God, it is gret husbondry.   f. 184
Of þe I take þese noblys rownde.   2740
I schal me rapyn, and þat in hye,
To hyde þis gold vndyr þe grownde.
þer schal it ly tyl þat I dye,
It may be kepte þer saue and sownde.
þou my neygbore schuld be hangyn hye,   2745
þerof getyth he neythyr peny nor pownde.
      3yt am I not wel at ese.
Now wolde I haue castel wallys,
, Stronge stedys and styf in stallys.
Wyth hey holtys and hey hallys,   2750
Coveytyse, þou muste me sese.

AUARICIA. Al schalt þou haue al redy, lo,
At þyn owyn dysposycyoun.
Al þis good take þe to,
Clyffe and cost, toure and toun.   2755
þus hast þou gotyn in synful slo
Of þyne neygborys be extorcyoun.
'More and more' sey 3yt, haue do,
Tyl þou be ded and drepyn dounn;
      Werke on wyth werldys wrenchys.   2760
'More and more' sey 3yt, I rede,
To more þanne inow þou hast nede.
Al þis werld, bothe lenthe and brede,
      þi coveytyse may not qwenche.

HUMANUM GENUS. Qwenche neuere no man may;   2765
Me þynkyth neuere I haue inow.
þer ne is werldys wele, nyth nor day,
But þat me thynkyth it is to slow.
'More and more' 3it I say
And schal euere whyl I may blow;   2770
On Coveytyse is al my lay
And schal tyl deth me ouyrthrow.

2757 be *added above the line*

'More and more', þis is my steuene.
If I myth alwey dwellyn in prosperyte,
Lord God, þane wel were me.   2775
I wolde, þe medys, forsake þe
  And neuere to comyn in heuene.

SCENE XX

MORS. Ow, now it is tyme hye
  To castyn Mankynd to Dethys dynt.
In all hys werkys he is vnslye;   2780
  Mekyl of hys lyf he hath myspent.
To Mankynd I ney ny,
  Wyth rewly rappys he schal be rent.
Whanne I com iche man drede forþi,
  But ȝyt is þer no geyn-went,   2785
    Hey hyl, holte, nyn hethe.
  ȝe schul me drede euerychone;   f. 184ᵛ
  Whanne I come ȝe schul grone;
  My name in londe is lefte alone:
    I hatte drery Dethe.   2790

Drery is my deth-drawth;
  Ageyns me may no man stonde.
I durke and downbrynge to nowth
  Lordys and ladys in euery londe.
Whomso I haue a lessun tawth,   2795
  Onethys sythen schal he mowe stonde;
In my carful clothys he schal be cawth,
  Ryche, pore, fre and bonde;
    Whanne I come þei goo no more.
  Whereso I wende in any lede,   2800
  Euery man of me hat drede.
  Lette I wyl for no mede
    To smyte sadde and sore.

Dyngne dukys arn adred
  Whanne my blastys arn on hem blowe.   2805

2785 geyn-went] F geyn [i-]went   2793 downbrynge] MS. down brynge
F down [I] brynge   2805 blastys] MS. bastys

Lordys in londe arn ouyrled;
  Wyth þis launce I leye hem lowe.
Kyngys kene and knytys kyd,
  I do hem deluyn in a throwe,
In banke I buske hem abed,   2810
  Sad sorwe to hem I sowe,
    I tene hem, as I trowe.
    As kene koltys þow þey kynse,
    Ageyns me is no defens.
    In þe grete pestelens   2815
      þanne was I wel knowe.

But now almost I am forȝete;
  Men of Deth holde no tale.
In coveytyse here good þey gete;
  þe grete fyschys ete þe smale.   2820
But whane I dele my derne dette
  þo prowde men I schal avale.
Hem schal helpyn noþyr mel nor mete
  Tyl þey be drewyn to dethys dale;
    My lawe þei schul lerne.   2825
    þer ne is peny nor pownde
    þat any of ȝou schal saue sownde.
    Tyl ȝe be grauyn vndyr grownde
      þer may no man me werne.

To Mankynde now wyl I reche;   2830
  He hathe hole hys hert on Coveytyse.
A newe lessun I wyl hym teche
  þat he schal bothe grwcchyn and gryse.
No lyf in londe schal ben hys leche;   f. 183
  I schal hym proue of myn empryse;   2835
Wyth þis poynt I schal hym broche
  And wappyn hym in a woful wyse.
    Nobody schal ben hys bote.
    I schal þe schapyn a schenful schappe.
    Now I kylle þe wyth myn knappe!   2840
    I reche to þe, Mankynd, a rappe
      To þyne herte rote.

HUMANUM GENUS. A, Deth, Deth! drye is þi dryfte.
  Ded is my desteny.
Myn hed is cleuyn al in a clyfte;   2845
  For clappe of care now I crye;
Myn eyeledys may I not lyfte;
  Myn braynys waxyn al emptye;
I may not onys myn hod up schyfte;
    Wyth Dethys dynt now I dey!   2850
      Syr Werld, I am hent.
    Werld, Werld, haue me in mende!
    Goode Syr Werld, helpe now Mankend!
    But þou me helpe, Deth schal me schende.
      He hat dyth to me a dynt.   2855

Werld, my wyt waxyt wronge;
  I chaunge boþe hyde and hewe;
Myn eyeledys waxyn al outewronge;
  But þou me helpe, sore it schal me rewe.
Now holde þat þou haste behete me longe,   2860
  For all felechepys olde and newe,
Lesse me of my peynys stronge.
  Sum bote of bale þou me brewe
      þat I may of þe ȝelpe.
    Werld, for olde aqweyntawns,   2865
    Helpe me fro þis sory chawns.
    Deth hathe lacchyd me wyth hys launce.
      I deye but þou me helpe.

MUNDUS. Owe, Mankynd, hathe Dethe wyth þe spoke?
  Ageyns hym helpyth no wage.   2870
I wolde þou were in þe erthe beloke
  And anoþyr hadde þyne erytage.
Oure bonde of loue schal sone be broke;
  In colde clay schal be þy cage;
Now schal þe Werld on þe be wroke   2875
  For þou hast don so gret outrage.
      þi good þou schalt forgoo.
    Werldlys good þou hast forgon
    And wyth tottys þou schalt be torn.

þus haue I seruyd here-beforn   2880
   A hundryd thousand moo.

HUMANUM GENUS. Ow, Werld, Werld, euere worthe wo!   f. 183ᵛ
   And þou, synful Coveytyse!
Whanne þat a man schal fro ȝou go
   Ȝe werke wyth hym on a wondyr wyse.   2885
þe wytte of þis werld is sorwe and wo.
   Be ware, good men, of þis gyse!
þus hathe he seruyd many on mo.
   In sorwe slakyth al hys asyse;
      He beryth a tenynge tungge.   2890
      Whyl I leyd wyth hym my lott
      Ȝe seyn whou fayre he me behott;
      And now he wolde I were a clott
      In colde cley for to clynge.

MUNDUS. How, boy, aryse! now þou muste wende   2895
   On myn erdyn, be steppe and stalle.
Go brewe Mankynd a byttyr bende
   And putte hym oute of hys halle.
Lete hym þerinne no lenger lende.
   Forbrostyn, I trowe, be hys galle   2900
For þou art not of hys kende.
   All hys erytage wyl þe wele befalle.
      þus faryth myn fayre feres.
      Oftyn tyme I haue ȝou told,
      þo men þat ȝe arn to lest behold   2905
      Comynly schal ȝoure wonnynge wold
      And ben ȝoure next eyrys.

GARCIO. Werld worthy, in wedys wounde,
   I þanke þe for þi grete ȝyfte.
I go glad upon þis grounde   2910
   To putte Mankynde out of hys þryfte.
I trowe he stynkyth þis ilke stounde.
   Into a lake I schal hym lyfte.
Hys parkys, placys, and penys rounde,
   Wyth me schul dryuen in þis dryfte   2915

2892 behott] MS. F be hett

In baggys as þei ben bownde.
For I þynke for to dele,
I vow to God, neythyr corn nore mele.
If he haue a schete he beryth hym wele
   Whereinne he may be wounde.   2920

Tunc iet ad HUMANUM GENUS

Whou faryst, Mankynde? art þou ded?
  Be Goddys body, so I wene.
He is heuyer þanne any led.
  I wold he were grauyn vndyr grene.

HUMANUM GENUS. Abyde, I breyd uppe wyth myn hed.   2925
  What art þou? what woldyst þou mene?
Wheydyr comyst þou for good or qwed?
  Wyth peynys prycke þou doste me tene,
    þe sothe for to sey.
    Telle me now, so God þe saue,   f. 182
    Fro whom comyst þou, good knaue?   2931
      What dost þou here? what woldyst þou hauc?
      Telle me or I deye.

GARCIO. I am com to haue al þat þou hast,
  Ponndys, parkys, and euery place.   2935
Al þat þou hast gotyn fyrst and last,
  þe Werld hathe grauntyd it me of hys grace
    For I haue ben hys page.
    He wot wel þou schalt be ded,
    Neueremore to ete bred;   2940
    þerfore he hath for þe red
      Who schal haue þyne erytage.

HUMANUM GENUS. What deuyl! þou art not of my kyn.
  þou dedyst me neuere no maner good.
I hadde leuer sum nyfte or sum cosyn   2945
  Or sum man hadde it of my blod.
    In sum stede I wold it stod.

2920 wounde] *MS.* wou...   2932 what woldyst] *MS.* wha woldyst
2935 Ponndys] *F* poundys

Now schal I in a dale be delue
And haue no good þerof myselue.
Be God and be hys apostelys twelue,   2950
    I trowe þe Werld be wod.

GARCIO. 3a, 3a, þi parte schal be þe lcste.
Deye on, for I am maystyr here.
I schal þe makyn a nobyl feste
And þanne haue I do myn deuere.   2955
þe Werld bad me þis gold areste,
    Holt and hallys and castell clere.
þe Werldys joye and hys jentyl jeste
    Is now þyne, now myn, boþe fere and nere.
        Go hens, for þis is myne.   2960
        Syn þou art ded and browth of dawe,
        Of þi deth, syr, I am ryth fawe.
        þou þou knowe not þe Werldys lawe,
        He hath 3oue me al þat was þyne.

HUMANUM GENUS. I preye þe now, syn þou þis good
    schalt gete,   2965
    Telle þi name or þat I goo.

GARCIO. Loke þat þou it not for3ete:
    My name is I Wot Neuere Whoo.

HUMANUM GENUS. I Wot Neuere Who! so welaway!
Now am I sory of my lyf.   2970
I haue purchasyd many a day
    Londys and rentys wyth mekyl stryf.
I haue purchasyd holt and hay,
    Parkys and ponndys and bourys blyfe,
Goode gardeynys wyth gryffys gay,   2975
    To myne chyldyr and to myn wyfe
        In dethe whanne I were dyth.
        Of my purchas I may be wo,   f. 182ᵛ
        For, as þout, it is not so,
        But a gedelynge I Wot Neuere Who   2980
        Hath al þat þe Werld me behyth.

2965 þe *added above the line*   2969 welaway] *MS.* welesay *F* wele say
2974 ponndys] *F* poundys

Now, alas, my lyf is lak.
 Bittyr balys I gynne to brewe.
Certis a vers þat Dauid spak
 I þe sawter I fynde it trewe: 2985
Tesauriȝat et ignorat cui congregabit ea.
Tresor, tresor, it hathe no tak;
 It is oþyr mens, olde and newe.
Ow, ow, my good gothe al to wrak!
 Sore may Mankynd rewe.
  God kepe me fro dyspayr!   2990
  Al my good, wythout fayle,
  I haue gadryd wyth gret trauayle,
  þe Werld hathe ordeynyd of hys entayle
  I Wot Neuere Who to be myn eyr.

Now, good men, takythe example at me. 2995
 Do for ȝoureself whyl ȝe han spase.
For many men þus seruyd be
 þorwe þe werld in dyuerse place.
I bolne and bleyke in blody ble
 And as a flour fadyth my face.   3000
To helle I schal bothe fare and fle
 But God me graunte of hys grace.
  I deye certeynly.
  Now my lyfe I haue lore.
  Myn hert brekyth, I syhe sore.   3005
  A word may I speke no more.
  I putte me in Goddys mercy.

SCENE XXI

ANIMA. 'Mercy', þis was my last tale
 þat euere my body was abowth.
But Mercy helpe me in þis vale,   3010
 Of dampnynge drynke sore I me doute.
Body, þou dedyst brew a byttyr bale
 To þi lustys whanne gannyst loute.
þi sely sowle schal ben akale;
 I beye þi dedys wyth rewly rowte,   3015

And al it is for gyle.
Euere þou hast be coueytows
Falsly to getyn londe and hows.
To me þou hast browyn a byttyr jows.
    So welaway þe whyle!   3020

Now, swet Aungel, what is þi red?
þe ryth red þou me reche.
Now my body is dressyd to ded
    Helpe now me and be my leche.
Dyth þou me fro deuelys drede.   3025
    þy worthy weye þou me teche.
I hope þat God wyl helpyn and be myn hed
    For 'mercy' was my laste speche;
        þus made my body hys ende.

*   *   *   *   *   *   *

MALUS ANGELUS. Wyttnesse of all þat ben abowte,   f. 185
    Syr Coueytyse he had hym owte.   3031
    þerfor he schal, wythoutyn dowte,
        Wyth me to helle pytt.

BONUS ANGELUS. 3e, alas, and welawo!
    A3eyns Coueytyse can I not telle.   3035
Resun wyl I fro þe goo,
    For, wrechyd sowle, þou muste to helle.
Coueytyse, he was þi fo;
    He hathe þe schapyn a schameful schelle;
þus hathe seruyd many on mo   3040
    Tyl þei be dyth to dethys delle,
        To byttyr balys bowre.
    þou muste to peyne, be ryth resun,
    Wyth Coveytyse, for he is chesun.
    þou art trappyd ful of tresun   3045
        But Mercy be þi socowre.

For ryth wel þis founde I haue
    A3eyns Rythwysnesse may I not holde.
þou muste wyth hym to careful caue
    For grete skyllys þat he hathe tolde.   3050

3019 browyn] F brokyn   3029 A leaf is missing from the MS.
3030 MALUS ANGELUS not in MS.   3047 I] MS. F he

Fro þe awey I wandyr and waue;
 For þe I clynge in carys colde.
Alone now I þe laue
 Whylyst þou fallyst in fendys folde,
  In helle to hyde and hylle.   3055
  Rytwysnesse wyl þat þou wende
  Forthe awey wyth þe fende.
  But Mercy wyl to þe sende,
   Of þe can I no skylle.

ANIMA. Alas, Mercy, þou art to longe!   3060
 Of sadde sorwe now may I synge.
Holy wryt it is ful wronge
 But Mercy pase alle þynge.
I am ordeynyd to peynys stronge,
 In wo is dressyd myn wonnynge,   3065
In helle on hokys I schal honge,
 But mercy fro a welle sprynge.
  þis deuyl wyl hauc me away.
  Weleaway! I was ful wod
  þat I forsoke myn Aungyl Good   3070
  And wyth Coueytyse stod
   Tyl þat day þat I schuld dey.

MALUS ANGELUS. 3a, why woldyst þou be coueytous
 And drawe þe agayn to synne?
I schal þe brewe a byttyr jous;   3075
 In bolnynnge bondys þou schalt brenne.
In hye helle schal be þyne hous,   f. 185ᵛ
 In pycke and ter to grone and grenne;
þou schalt lye drenkelyd as a movs;
 þer may no man þerfro þe werne   3080
  For þat ilke wyll.
  þat day þe ladys þou forsoke
  And to my counsel þou þe toke,
  þou were betyr anhangyn on hoke
   Upon a jebet hyll.   3085

3053 I] *F* I [must] 3059 He aperith þᵉ sowle *added in later hand*
3084 were] be *canc. before* were

Farter fowle, þou schalt be frayed
  Tyl þou be frettyd and al forbled.
Foule mote þou be dysmayed
  þat þou schalt þus ben ouyrled.
For Coueytyse þou hast asayed   3090
  In byttyr balys þou schalt be bred.
Al mankynd may be wel payed
  Whou Coueytyse makyth þe adred.
      Wyth rappys I þe rynge.
    We schul to hell, bothe to,   3095
    And bey in inferno.
    Nulla est redempcio
      For no kynnys þynge.

Now dagge we hens a dogge trot.
  In my dongion I schal þe dere.   3100
On þe is many a synful spot;
  þerfore þis schame I schal þe schere
    Whanne þou comyst to my neste.
    Why woldyst þou, schrewe schalt neuere þe,
    But in þi lyue don aftyr me?   3105
    And þi Good Aungyl tawth þe
      Alwey to þe beste.

3a, but þou woldyst hym not leue;
  To Coueytyse alwey þou drow.
þerfore schalt þou euyl preue;   3110
  þat foul synne þi soule slow.
I schal fonde þe to greue
  And putte þe in peynnys plow.
Haue þis, and euyl mote þou scheue,
  For þou seydyst neuere 'inow, inow'   3115
    þus lacche I þe þus lowe.
    þow þou kewe as a kat,
    For þi coueytyse haue þou þat!
    I schal þe bunche wyth my bat
      And rouge þe on a rowe.   3120

3093 Whou] *MS*. whou *or* whon *F* whon   3096 bey] *F* bey [for euer]
3106 tawth] *F* [he] tawth   3113 peynnys] *MS*. peymys   3120 rouge]
MS. rouge *or* ronge *F* ronge

Lo, synful tydynge,
Boy, on þi bak I brynge.
Spedely þou sprynge.
þi placebo I schal synge.

To deuelys delle   3125
I schal þe bere to helle.
I wyl not dwelle.
Haue good day! I goo to helle.

SCENE XXII

MISERICORDIA. A mone I herd of mercy meve   f. 186
    And to me, Mercy, gan crye and call;   3130
But if it haue mercy, sore it schal me greve,
    For ell it schal to hell fall.
Rythwysnes, my systyr cheve,
    þys ʒe herde; so dyde we all.
For we were mad frendys leve   3135
    Whanne þe Jevys proferyd Criste eysyl and gall
        On þe Good Fryday.
        God grauntyd þat remission,
        Mercy, and absolicion,
        þorwe vertu of hys passion,   3140
            To no man schuld be seyd nay.

þerfore, my systyr Rytwysnes,
    Pes, and Trewthe, to ʒou I tell,
Whanne man crieth mercy, and wyl not ses,
    Mercy schal be hys waschynge-well: 3145
        Wytnesse of Holy Kyrke.
        For þe leste drope of blode
        þat God bledde on þe rode
        It hadde ben satysfaccion goode
            For al Mankyndys werke.   3150

JUSTICIA. Systyr, ʒe sey me a good skyl,
    þat mercy pasyt mannys mysdede.

3127-8 *written as one line*   3134 we] ʒe *changed to* we   3149 goode]
gode *changed to* goode   3152 mysdede] *MS.* mysdode

But take mercy whoso wyl
　He muste it aske wyth love and drede;
And eueryman þat wyl fulfyll   3155
　þe dedly synnys and folw mysdede,
To graunte hem mercy me þynkyth it no skyl;
　And þerfore, systyr, þou I rede
　　Lete hym abye hys mysdede.
　　For þou he lye in hell and stynke,   3160
　　It schal me neuere ouyrþynke.
　　As he hath browyn, lete hym drynke;
　　　þe Devyl schal qwyte hym hys mede.
Vnusquisque suum honus portabit.

Trowe ȝe þat whanne a man schal deye,
　þanne þow þat he mercy craue,   3165
þat anon he schal haue mercye?
　Nay, nay, so Crist me saue!
Non omne qui dicit 'Domine, Domine' intrabit regnum celorum.
For schuld no man do no good
　All þe dayes of hys lyve
But hope of mercy be þe rode   3170
　Schulde make boþe werre and stryve
　　And torne to gret grewaunse.
　　Whoso in hope dothe any dedly synne   f. 186ᵛ
　　To hys lyvys ende, and wyl not blynne,
　　Rytfully þanne schal he wynne   3175
　　　Crystis gret vengaunse.

VERITAS. Rytwysnes, my systyr fre,
　ȝour jugement is good and trewe.
In good feyth so þynkyth me;
　Late hym hys owyn dedys rewe.   3180
I am Veritas and trew wyl be
　In word and werke to olde and newe.
Was neuere man in fawte of me
　Dampnyd nor savyd, but it were dew.

I am euere at mans ende.   3185
Whanne body and sowle partyn atwynne,
þanne wey I hys goode dedys and hys synne,
And weydyr of hem be more or mynne
    He schal it ryth sone fynde.

For I am Trewþe and trewþe wyl bere,   3190
    As grete God hymself vs byd.
þer schal noþynge þe sowle dere
    But synne þat þe body dyd.
Syth þat he deyed in þat coveytous synne,
    I, Trewþe, wyl þat he goo to pyne.   3195
Of þat synne cowde he not blynne;
    þerfore he schal hys sowle tyne
        To þe pytte of hell.
    Ellys schuld we, boþe Trewþe and Rytwysnes,
    Be put to ouyrmekyl dystresse   3200
    And euery man schuld be þe wers
        þat þerof myth here tell.

PAX. Pes, my systyr Verite!
    I preye ȝou, Rytwysnes, be stylle!
Lete no man be ȝou dampnyd be   3205
    Nor deme ȝe no man to helle.
He is on kyn tyl vs thre,
    þow he haue now not al hys wylle.
For hys loue þat deyed on tre,
    Late saue Mankynd fro al peryle   3210
        And schelde hym fro myschaunsse.
    If ȝe tweyne putte hym to dystresse
    It schuld make gret hevynesse
    Betwene vs tweyne, Mercy and Pes,
        And þat were gret grevaunce.   3215

Rytwysnes and Trewthe, do be my red,   f. 187
    And Mercy, go we to ȝone hey place.
We schal enforme þe hey Godhed
    And pray hym to deme þis case.

3187 goode] *MS.* goodys   3200 put] *MS. F* pud

3e schal tell hym 3oure entent   3220
  Of Trewthe and of Rytwysnesse,
And we schal pray þat hys jugement
  May pase be vs, Mercy and Pes.
    All foure, now go we hens
    Wytly to þe Trinite   3225
    And þer schal we sone se
    What þat hys jugement schal be,
      Wythovtyn any deffens.

        Tunc ascendent ad PATREM omnes pariter
        et dicet VERITAS:

SCENE XXIII

VERITAS. Heyl, God almyth!
We cum, þi dowterys in syth,   3230
Trewth, Mercy, and Ryth,
And Pes, pesyble in fyth.

MISERICORDIA. We cum to preve
If Man, þat was þe ful leve,
If he schal cheve   3235
To hell or heuene, be þi leve.

JUSTICIA. I, Rytwysnes,
þi dowtyr as I ges,
Late me, neuereþelesse,
At þi dom putte me in pres.   3240

PAX. Pesyble kynge,
I, Pes, þi dowtyr 3ynge,
Here my preyinge
Whanne I pray þe, Lord, of a thynge.

DEUS. Welcum in fere,   3245
Bryther þanne blossum on brere!
My dowterys dere,
Cum forth and stand 3e me nere.

3228 s.d. ascendent] *MS.* ascendet *F* ascendent   dicet VERITAS] *MS.*
dixit verita. . .   3229–48 *written as ten lines*

VERITAS. Lord, as þou art Kyng of kyngys, crownyd wyth
   crowne,
  As þou lovyste me, Trewthe, þi dowtyr dere,   3250
Lete neuere me, Trewþe, to fall adowne,
  My feythful Fadyr, saunz pere!
Quoniam veritatem dilexisti.
For in all trewthe standyth þi renowne,
  þi feyth, þi hope, and þi powere,
Lete it be sene, Lord, now at þi dome,   3255
  þat I may haue my trewe prayere
     To do trewþe to Mankynd.
    For if Mankynd be dempte be ryth
    And not be mercy, most of myth,
    Here my trewthe, Lord, I þe plyth,   3260
     In presun man schal be pynyd.

Lord, whov schuld Mankynd be savyd,
  Syn he dyed in dedly synne
And all þi comaundementys he depravyd
  And of fals covetyse he wolde neuere blynne?   3265
Aurum sitisti, aurum bibisti.
þe more he hadde, þe more he cravyd,   f. 187ᵛ
  Whyl þe lyf lefte hym wythinne.
But he be dampnyd I am abavyd
  þat Trewthe schuld com of rytwys kynne,
     And I am þi dowtyr Trewþe.   3270
    þou he cried mercy, moriendo,
    Nimis tarde penitendo,
    Talem mortem reprehendo.
     Lete hym drynke as he brewyth!

Late repentaunce if man saue scholde,   3275
  Wheyþyr he wrouth wel or wyckydnesse,
þanne euery man wold be bolde
  To trespas in trost of forȝevenesse.
For synne in hope is dampnyd, I holde;
  Forgevyn is neuere hys trespase.   3280

3252 feythful] *MS.* feyᵗfful   3252a Quoniam] *MS.* Qm̄ *F* Quia
3253 standyth] *MS.* standᵗ   3260 trewthe] *MS.* threwthe

He synnyth in þe Holy Gost manyfolde.
  þat synne, Lord, þou wylt not reles
    In þis werld nor in þe toþyr.
  Quia veritas manet in eternum,
    Tendit homo ad infernum,   3285
    Nunquam venit ad supernum,
    þou he were my broþyr.

For man on molde halt welthe and wele,
  Lust and lykynge in al hys lyfe,
Techynge, prechynge, in euery sele,   3290
  But he forgetyth þe Lord belyve.
Hye of hert, happe and hele,
  Gold and syluyr, chyld and wyf,
Denteth drynke at mete and mele,
  Vnnethe þe to þanke he can not kyth   3295
    In any maner thynge.
    Whanne mans welþe gynnyth awake
    Ful sone, Lord, þou art forsake.
    As he hathe browne and bake,
      Trewthe wyl þat he drynke.   3300

For if Man haue mercy and grace
  þanne I, þi dowtyr Sothfastnesse,
At þi dom schal haue no place
  But be putte abak be wronge dures.
Lord, lete me neuere fle þi fayr face   3305
  To make my power any lesse!
I pray þe, Lord, as I haue space,
  Late Mankynd haue dew dystresse
    In helle fere to be brent.
    In peyne loke he be stylle,   3310
    Lord, if it be þi wylle,
    Or ell I haue no skylle
      Be þi trew jugement.
                        f. 188

MISERICORDIA. O Pater misericordiarum et Deus tocius con-
solacionis, qui consolatur nos in omni tribulacione nostra!

3285 infernum] supernum *canc. before* infernum   3313a misericordia-
rum] *F* maxime

O þou Fadyr, of mytys moste,
 Mercyful God in Trinite!   3315
I am þi dowtyr, wel þou woste,
 And mercy fro heuene þou browtyst fre.
Schew me þi grace in euery coste!
 In þis cas my counforte be!
Lete me, Lord, neuere be loste   3320
 At þi jugement, whovso it be,
  Of Mankynd.
  Ne had mans synne neuere cum in cas
  I, Mercy, schuld neuere in erthe had plas.
  þerfore graunte me, Lord, þi grace,   3325
   þat Mankynd may me fynd.

And mercy, Lord, haue on þis man
 Aftyr þi mercy, þat mekyl is,
Vnto þi grace þat he be tan,
 Of þi mercy þat he not mys!   3330
As þou descendyst fro þi trone
 And lyth in a maydyns wombe iwys,
Incarnat was in blod and bone,
 Lat Mankynd cum to þi blys,
  As þou art Kynge of heuene!   3335
  For werldly veynglory
  He hathe ben ful sory,
  Punchyd in purgatory
   For all þe synnys seuene.

Si pro peccato vetus Adam non cecidisset,
Mater pro nato numquam grauidata fuisset.
Ne had Adam synnyd here-before   3340
 And þi hestys in paradys had offent,
Neuere of þi modyr þou schuldyst a be bore,
 Fro heuene to erthe to haue be sent.
But thyrti wyntyr here and more,
 Bowndyn and betyn and al to-schent,   3345
Scornyd and scovrgyd sadde and sore,
 And on þe rode rewly rent,

3339a peccato] *MS.* ppeccato grauidata] *MS.* grauidada 3345 to-
schent] schent *written above* rent *canc.*

Passus sub Pilato Poncio.
As þou henge on þe croys
On hye þou madyste a voys,   3350
Mans helthe, þe gospel seys,
    Whanne þou seydyst 'Scitio'.

                                            scilicet, salutem animarum.

þane þe Jeves þat were vnquert
    Dressyd þe drynke, eysyl and galle.
It to taste þou myth nowth styrt   3355
    But seyd 'Consummatum est' was alle.
A knyt wyth a spere so smert,
    Whanne þou forgafe þi fomen þrall,
He stonge þe, Lord, vnto þe hert.
    þanne watyr and blod gan ovte wall,   3360
        Aqua baptismatis et sanguis redempcionis.
        þe watyr of baptomm,   f. 188ᵛ
        þe blod of redempcioun
        þat fro þin herte ran doun
            Est causa saluacionis.   3365

Lord, þou þat man hathe don more mysse þanne good,
    If he dey in very contricioun,
Lord, þe lest drope of þi blod
    For hys synne makyth satysfaccioun.
As þou deydyst, Lord, on þe rode,   3370
    Graunt me my peticioun!
Lete me, Mercy, be hys fode,
    And graunte hym þi saluacion,
        Quia dixisti 'Misericordiam seruabo'.
        'Mercy' schal I synge and say   3375
        And 'miserere' schal I pray
        For Mankynd euere and ay.
            Misericordias Domini in eternum cantabo.

JUSTICIA. Rythwys Kynge, Lord God almyth,
    I am þi dowtyr Rythwysnesse.   3380
þou hast louyd me euere, day and nyth,
    As wel as oþyr, as I gesse.

<hr>

3373 saluacion] *MS.* salucion   3374 seruabo] *F* amabo

Justicias Dominus justicia dilexit.

If þou mans kynde fro peyne aquite,
  þou dost ageyns þyne owyn processe.
Lete hym in preson to be pyth   3385
  For hys synne and wyckydnesse,
    Of a bone I þe pray.
    Ful oftyn he hathe þe, Lord, forsake
    And to þe Devyl he hathe hym take.
    Lete hym lyn in hell lake,   3390
      Dampnyd for euere and ay.
Quia Deum, qui se genuit, dereliquit.

For whanne Man to þe werld was bornn
  He was browth to Holy Kyrke,
Feythly followd in þe funte-ston
  And wesch fro orygynal synne so dyrke.   3395
Satanas he forsok as hys fone,
  All hys pompe and al hys werke,
And hyth to serue þe alone;
  To kepe þi commandementys he schuld not irke,
    Sicut justi tui.   3400
    But whanne he was com to mans astate
    All hys behestys he þanne forgate.
    He is worþi be dampnyd for þat,
      Quia oblitus est Domini creatoris sui.

For he hathe forgetyn þe þat hym wrout   3405
  And formydiste hym lyke þyne owyn face
And wyth þi precyous blod hym bowth
  And in þis world þou ȝeue hym space.
All þi benefetys he set at nowth
  But toke hym to þe Deuelys trase,   3410
þe Flesch, þe World, was most in his þowth
  And purpose to plese hem in euery plase,
    So grymly on grounde.

3382a Justicias] quia *partly erased before* Justicias   3383 fro] *MS.* fre
3385 be] þe *canc. before* be   3389 to] do *canc. before* to   3397 pompe]
MS. ponpe   3404 Domini] *MS. F* deum   3408 space] *written above*
grace *canc.*   3411 Flesch] *MS.* flsch   his] *MS.* Is

I pray þe, Lord lovely,   f. 189
Of man haue no mercy,   3415
But, dere Lord, lete hym ly,
   In hell lete hym be bounde!

Man hathe forsake þe Kynge of heuene
And hys Good Aungels gouernaunce
And solwyd hys sovle wyth synnys seuene   3420
   Be hys Badde Aungels comberaunce.
Vertuis he putte ful evyn away
   Whanne Coveytyse gan hym avaunce.
He wende þat he schulde a levyd ay,
   Tyl Deth trypte hym on hys daunce,   3425
      He loste hys wyttys fyve.
      Ouyrlate he callyd Confescion;
      Ouyrlyt was hys contricioun;
      He made neuere satisfaccioun.
        Dampne hym to helle belyve!   3430

For if þou take Mans sowle to þe
   Ageyns þi Rythwysnesse,
þou dost wronge, Lorde, to Trewth and me
   And puttys us fro oure devnesse.
Lord, lete vs neuere fro þe fle,   3435
   Ner streyne vs neuere in stresse,
But late þi dom be by vs thre
   Mankynde in hell to presse,
      Lord, I þe beseche!
      For Rytwysnes dwellys euere sure   3440
      To deme Man aftyr hys deseruiture,
      For to be dampnyd it is hys vre,
        On Man I crie wreche.

Letabitur justus cum viderit vindictam.

MISERICORDIA. Mercy, my systyr Rythwysnes!
   þou schape Mankynde no schonde.   3445
Leve systyr, lete be þi dresse.
   To saue Man lete vs fonde.

3421 comberaunce] governaunce *canc. and* comberaunce *written in margin*
3422 ful evyn away] a wey *canc. before* ful evyn   3440 dwellys] *MS.* dwell
F dwellis

For if Man be dampnyd to hell dyrknes,
  þanne myth I wryngyn myn honde
þat euere my state schulde be les,   3450
  My fredam to make bonde.
      Mankynd is of oure kyn.
    For I, Mercy, pase al thynge
    þat God made at þe begynnynge
    And I am hys dowtyr ȝynge,   3455
      Dere systyr, lete be þi dyn!
Et misericordia ejus super omnia opera ejus.

Of Mankynde aske þou neuere wreche
  Be day ner be nyth,
For God hymself hath ben hys leche,
  Of hys mercyful myth.   3460
To me he gan hym beteche,
  Besyde al hys ryth.
For hym wyl I prey and preche
  To gete hym fre respyth,
      And my systyr Pese.   3465
    For hys mercy is wythout begynnynge
    And schal be wythoutyn endynge,
    As Dauid seyth, þat worthy kynge;
      In scriptur is no les.
Et misericordia ejus a progenie in progenies et cetera.

VERITAS. Mercy is Mankynde non worthy,   f. 189ᵛ
  Dauid þou þou recorde and rede,   3471
For he wolde neuere þe hungry
  Neyþyr clothe nor fede,
Ner drynke gyf to þe þrysty,
  Nyn pore men helpe at nede.   3475
For if he dyd non of þese, forþy
  In heuene he getyth no mede.
      So seyth þe gospel.
    For he hathe ben vnkynde
    To lame and to blynde   3480
    In helle he schal be pynde.
      So is resun and skyl.
     3467 endynge] *MS.* begynnynge *F* endynge

PAX. Pesible Kyng in majeste,
  I, Pes þi dowtyr, aske þe a bonn
Of Man, whouso it be.   3485
  Lord, graunte me myn askynge sonn,
þat I may euermore dwelle wyth þe
  As I haue euerc ȝyt donn,
And lat me neuere fro þe fle,
  Specialy at þi dome   3490
    Of Man, þi creature.
    þou my systyr Ryth and Trewthe
    Of Mankynd haue non rewthe,
    Mercy and I ful sore vs mewythe
      To cacche hym to our cure.   3495

For whanne þou madyst erthe and hevyn,
  Ten orderys of aungelys to ben in blys,
Lucyfer, lyter þanne þe leuyn
  Tyl whanne he synnyd, he fel iwys.
To restore þat place ful evyn   3500
  þou madyst Mankynd wyth þys
To fylle þat place þat I dyd nevene.
  If þy wyl be resun it is,
    In pes and rest,
    Amonge þyne aungels bryth   3505
    To worchep þe in syth,
    Graunt, Lord God almyth!
    And so I holde it best.

For þou Truthe, þat is my systyr dere,
  Arguyth þat Man schuld dwell in wo   3510
And Rytwysnes wyth hyr powere
  Wolde fayn and fast þat it were so,
But Mercy and I, Pes, bothe in fere,
  Schal neuere in feyth acorde þerto,
þanne schuld we euere dyscorde here   3515
  And stande at bate for frend or foo
    And euere at dystaunce.
    þerfore my counseyl is

3490 Specialy] *MS.* spcialy   3495 cacche] chacche *corrected to* cacche

Lete vs foure systerys kys
And restore Man to blys,   3520
    As was Godys ordenaunce.

Misericordia et Veritas obuiauerunt sibi, Justicia et Pax osculate
    sunt.

For if 3e, Ryth and Truthe, schuld haue 3our wylle,   f. 190
    I, Pes, and Mercy schuld euere haue trauest.
þanne vs betwene had bene a gret perylle
    þat oure joyes in heuene schuld a ben lest.   3525
þerfore, gentyl systerys, consentyth me tyll,
    Ellys betwene oureself schuld neuere be rest.
Where schuld be luf and charite, late þer cum non ille.
    Loke oure joyes be perfyth, and þat I holde þe best,
        In heueneryche blys.   3530
        For þer is pes wythowtyn were,
        þere is rest wythowtyn fere,
        þer is charite wythowtyn dere.
        Our Fadyris wyll so is.

Hic pax, hic bonitas, hic laus, hic semper honestas.

þerfore, jentyl systerys, at on word,   3535
    Truth, Ryth, and Mercy hende,
Lete us stonde at on acord,
    At pes wythowtyn ende.
Late loue and charyte be at oure bord,
    Alle venjauns awey wende,   3540
To heuene þat Man may be restoryd,
    Lete us be all hys frende
        Before oure Fadyrs face.
        We schal deuoutly pray
        At dredful domysday   3545
        And I schal for vs say
        þat Mankynd schal haue grace.

Et tuam, Deus, deposcimus pietatem ut ei tribuere digneris
    lucidas et quietas mansiones.

Lord, for þi pyte and þat pes
    þou sufferyst in þi pascioun,

3541 *The scribe repeated line 3537 and then cancelled it*   3547 quietas]
MS. quie...

Boundyn and betyn, wythout les,   3550
  Fro þe fote to þe croun,
Tanquam ouis ductus es
  Whanne gutte sanguis ran adoun,
3yt þe Jves wolde not ses
  But on þyn hed þei þryst a croun   3555
    And on þe cros þe naylyd.
    As petously as þou were pynyd,
    Haue mercy of Mankynd,
    So þat he may fynde
      Oure preyer may hym avayle.   3560

PATER sedens in trono.
Ego cogito cogitaciones pacis, non affliccionis.

Fayre falle þe, Pes, my dowtyr dere!
  On þe I þynke and on Mercy.
Syn 3e acordyd beth all in fere,
  My jugement I wyl 3eue 3ou by
Not aftyr deseruynge to do reddere,   3565
  To dampne Mankynde to turmentry,
But brynge hym to my blysse ful clere
  In heuene to dwelle endelesly,
    At 3our prayere forþi.
    To make my blysse perfyth   3570
    I menge wyth my most myth
    Alle pes, sum treuthe, and sum ryth,
      And most of my mercy.

Misericordia Domini plena est terra. Amen!   f. 190ᵛ
                  Dicet filiabus:

My dowters hende,
Lufly and lusti to lende,   3575
Goo to 3one fende
And fro hym take Mankynd.

Brynge hym to me
And set hym here be my kne,
In heuene to be,   3580
In blysse wyth gamyn and gle.

   3553 sanguis] F sangu[in]is   3574–97 *written as twelve lines*

VERITAS. We schal fulfylle
þin hestys, as resun and skylle,
Fro 30ne gost grylle
Mankynde to brynge þe tylle.   3585

       Tunc ascendent ad MALUM ANGELUM
       omnes pariter et dicet

PAX. A, þou foule wyth,
Lete go þat soule so tyth!
In heuene lyth
Mankynde sone schal be pyth.

JUSTICIA. Go þou to helle,   3590
þou devyl bold as a belle,
þerin to dwelle,
In bras and brimston to welle!

              Tunc ascendent ad tronum

MISERICORDIA. Lo here Mankynd,
Lyter þanne lef is on lynde,   3595
þat hath ben pynyd.
þi mercy, Lord, lete hym fynde!

PATER sedens in judicio.
Sicut sintilla in medio maris.

My mercy, Mankynd, 3eue I þe.
  Cum syt at my ryth honde.
Ful wel haue I louyd þe,   3600
  Vnkynd þow I þe fonde.
As a sparke of fyre in þe se
  My mercy is synne-quenchand.
þou hast cause to love me
  Abovyn al thynge in land,   3605
    And kepe my comaundement.
    If þou me loue and drede
    Heuene schal be þi mede;
    My face þe schal fede:
      þis is myn jugement.   3610
Ego occidam et viuificabo, percuciam et sanabo, et ncmo est qui
  de manu mea possit eruere.

3588 heuene] MS. hene   3591 þou] MS. þu   3597a judicio] MS.
Judi...   sintilla] MS. sintill

Kyng, kayser, knyt, and kampyoun,
  Pope, patriark, prest, and prelat in pes,
Duke dowtyest in dede, be dale and be doun,
  Lytyl and mekyl, þe more and þe les,
All þe statys of þe werld is at myn renoun;   3615
  To me schal þei ȝeue acompt at my dygne des.
Whanne Myhel hys horn blowyth at my dred dom
  þe count of here conscience schal putten hem in pres
      And ȝeld a reknynge
    Of here space whou þey han spent,   3620
    And of here trew talent,
    At my gret jugement
      An answere schal me brynge.

Ecce, requiram gregem meum de manu pastoris.   f. 191

And I schal inquire of my flok and of here pasture
  Whou þey haue leuyd and led here peple sojet.   3625
þe goode on þe ryth syd schul stond ful sure;
  þe badde on þe lyfte syd þer schal I set.
þe seuene dedys of mercy whoso hadde vre
  To fylle, þe hungry for to geue mete,
Or drynke to þrysty, þe nakyd, vesture,   3630
  þe pore or þe pylgrym hom for to fette,
    þi neybour þat hath nede;
    Whoso doth mercy to hys myth
    To þe seke, or in presun pyth,
      He doth to me; I schal hym qvyth;   3635
      Heuene blys schal be hys mede.

Et qui bona egerunt ibunt in vitam eternam; qui vero mala, in
  ignem eternum.

And þei þat wel do in þis werld, here welthe schal awake;
  In heuene þei schal be heynyd in bounte and blys;
And þei þat evyl do, þei schul to helle lake
  In byttyr balys to be brent: my jugement it is.   3640
My vertus in heuene þanne schal þei qwake.
  þer is no wyth in þis werld þat may skape þis.
All men example here-at may take
  To mayntein þe goode and mendyn here mys.

3626 ryth] MS. F ryde   3638 be heynyd] MS. heynyd F heynyd [be]

þus endyth oure gamys.   3645
To saue ȝou fro synnynge
Evyr at þe begynnynge
Thynke on ȝoure last endynge!
   Te Deum laudamus!

WISDOM

THE NAMES OF THE PLAYERS

Persons who speak:

WISDOM

ANIMA

MIND, WILL, UNDERSTANDING

LUCIFER

Persons who do not speak:

The Five Wits, as virgins

A shrewd boy

Six men dancers with MIND,

six men dancers with UNDERSTANDING,

and six women dancers with WILL

Minstrels: trumpeters, a bagpiper, and a hornpiper

Seven small boys, as devils

The title and the full list of persons are not in the MSS., but the Macro MS. lists
ten persons at the end of the play (p. 152).

SCENE I

Fyrst enteryde WYSDOME in a ryche purpull clothe of golde
wyth a mantyll of the same ermynnyde wythin, hawynge abowt hys
neke a ryall hood furrcd wyth ermyn, wpon hys hede a cheweler
wyth browys, a berde of golde of sypres curlyed, a ryche imperyall
crown þerwpon sett wyth precyus stonys and perlys, in hys leyfte
honde a balle of golde wyth a cros þerwppon and in hys ryght
honde a regall schepter, thus seyenge:

WYSDOM. Yff ȝe wyll wet þe propyrte
    Ande þe resun of my nayme imperyall,
I am clepyde of hem þat in erthe be
    Euerlastynge Wysdom, to my nobley egalle;
    Wyche name acordyt best in especyall   5
        And most to me ys convenyent,
    Allthow eche persone of þe Trinyte be wysdom eternall
        And all thre on euerlastynge wysdome togedyr present.

Neuerþeles, forasmoche as wysdom ys propyrly
    Applyede to þe Sune by resune,   10
And also yt fallyt to hym specyally
    Bycause of hys hye generacyon,
    Therfor þe belowyde Sone hathe þis sygnyficacyon
        Custummaly Wysdom, now Gode, now man,
    Spows of þe chyrche and wery patrone,   15
        Wyffe of eche chose sowle. Thus Wysdom begane.

Here entrethe ANIMA as a mayde, in a wyght clothe of golde
gysely purfyled wyth menyver, a mantyll of blake þerwppeon, a
cheueler lyke to WYSDOM, wyth a ryche chappelet lasyde behynde

The scene-divisions are not in the MSS.
  S.d. *These words and letters, faded or cut off in the Macro MS. (MS.), are
supplied from the Digby MS. (D):* wyth a mantyll of the ... ryall hood furred ... of
sypres . . per . . . *and the last* hys   enteryde] *D* entreth   precyus]
D precious riche (riche *added above the line*)   3 of hem] in erthe *canc. before*
of hem   4 nobley] *MS.* noble. *F* noblé. *D* nobley   11 yt fallyt]
yt fallyt yt fa *changed to* yt fallyt   12 hye] *D* highest   15 wery] *D*
verray   16 s.d. *These words and letters are supplied from D:* r *in* cheueler,
wn *in* hangynge down, eyng *in* seyng   gysely] *MS.* gyedly. *D* gytely. *F* gyntely
menyver] menver *canc. before* menyver chappelet] *MS.* chappetelot. *D.* chapetelet

hangynge down wyth to knottys of golde and syde tasselys,
knelynge down to WYSDOM, thus seyng:

ANIMA. Hanc amaui et exquisiui: f. 99
    Fro my yougthe thys haue I sowte
To haue to my spowse most specyally,
    For a louer of yowr schappe am I wrowte.   20
    Aboue all hele and bewty þat euer was sowght
        I haue louyde Wysdom as for my lyght,
    For all goodnes wyth hym ys broughte.
        In wysdom I was made all bewty bryghte.

Off yowr name þe hye felycyte   25
    No creature knowyt full exposycyon.
WYSDAM. Sapiencia specialior est sole.
    I am foundon lyghte wythowt comparyson,
    Off sterrys aboue all þe dysposicyon,
        Forsothe of lyght þe very bryghtnes,   30
    Merowre of þe dyvyne domynacyon,
        And þe image of hys goodnes.

Wysdom ys better þan all worldly precyosnes,
    And all þat may dysyryde be
Ys not in comparyschon to my lyknes.   35
    The lengthe of þe yerys in my ryght syde be
    Ande in my lefte syde ryches, joy, and prosperyte.
        Lo, þis ys þe worthynes of my name.
ANIMA. A, soueren Wysdom, yff yowur benygnyte
        Wolde speke of loue, þat wer a game.   40

WYSDOM. Off my loue to speke, yt ys myrable.   f. 99ᵛ
    Beholde now, Sowll, wyth joyfull mynde,
How louely I am, how amyable,
    To be halsyde and kyssyde of mankynde.
    To all clene sowlys I am full hende   45
        And euer present wer þat þey be;
    I loue my lovers wythowtyn ende
        That þer loue haue stedfast in me.

s.d. (*cont.*) knelynge] ke *canc. before* knelynge   17 ANIMA *not in MSS.*
18 yougthe] *MS.* thowte. *D* yougthe   23 ys] *MS.* ys (n *canc.*). *D* he
24 In] *MS.* I. *D* In   33 worldly] *MS.* worldy *canc. before* worldly. *D* wordly
36 lengthe] lenthe *changed to* lengthe   ryght] ryth *canc. before* ryght
41 yt] *D* it. *F* þat   47 my] *D* the

The prerogatyff of my loue ys so grett
  þat wo tastyt þerof þe lest droppe sure   50
All lustys and lykyngys worldly xall lett;
  They xall seme to hym fylthe and ordure.
They þat of þe hewy burthen of synne hathe cure
  My loue dyschargethe and puryfycthe clene,
It strengtheth þe mynde, þe sowll makyt pure,   55
  And yewyt wysdom to hem þat perfyghte bene.
Wo takyt me to spowse may veryly wene,
  Yff aboue all thynge 3e loue me specyall,
That rest and tranqwyllyte he xall sene
  And dey in sekyrnes of joy perpetuall.   60

The hye worthynes of my loue
  Angell nor man can tell playnly.
Yt may be felt in experyens from aboue
  But not spoke ne tolde as yt ys veryly.
The godly loue no creature can specyfye.   65
  What wrech is that louyth not this love
þat louyt hys louers euer so tendyrly   f. 100
  That hys syght from them neuer can remowe ?

ANIMA. O worthy spowse and soueren fayer,
  O swet amyke, owr joy, owr blys!   70
To yowr loue wo dothe repeyer,
  All felycyte yn þat creature ys.
Wat may I yeue yow ageyn for þis,
  O Creator, louer of yowr creature?
Though be owr freelte we do amys,   75
  Yowr grett mercy euer sparyth reddure.

A, soueren Wysdom, sanctus sanctorum,
  Wat may I yeue to yowr most plesaunce?
WYSDOM. Fili, prebe michi cor tuum.
  I aske not ellys of all þi substance.   80

50 wo tastyt] *D* who tast   51 xall] *D* shall (*so throughout*)   52 to]
D tyll   55 strengtheth] strenthe *changed to* strength *and canc. before*
strengtheth   58 3e] *D* ye. *F* he   specyall] *MS. F* specyally. *D* specially
61 hye] *D* hey loue of my   63 in experyens from aboue] *MS. F.* from
experyens aboue. *D* in experience from above   66 *line supplied from D,*
reading wrech *for* wreth   69 fayer] *MS.* faye *canc. before* father. *D* fayre

Thy clene hert, þi meke obeysance,
  Yeue me þat and I am contente.
ANIMA. A, soueren joy, my hertys affyance,
  The fervowre of my loue to yow I present.

That mekyt my herte, yowr loue so ferwent.   85
  Teche me þe scolys of yowr dyvynyte.
WYSDOM. Dysyer not to sauour in cunnynge to excellent
  But drede and conforme yowr wyll to me.
  For yt ys þe heelfull dyscyplyne þat in Wysdam may be,
    The drede of God, þat ys begynnynge.   90
  The wedys of synne yt makyt to flee,
    And swete wertuus herbys in þe sowll sprynge.

ANIMA. O endles Wysdom, how may I haue knowynge   f. 100ᵛ
  Off þi Godhede incomprehensyble?
WYSDOM. By knowynge of yowrsylff ȝe may haue felynge 95
  Wat Gode ys in yowr sowle sensyble.
  The more knowynge of yowr selff passyble,
    þe more veryly ȝe xall God knowe.
  ANIMA. O soueren Auctoure most credyble,
    Yowr lessun I attende, as I owe,   100

I þat represent here þe sowll of man.
  Wat ys a sowll, wyll ȝe declare?
WYSDOM. Yt ys þe ymage of Gode þat all began;
  And not only ymage, but hys lyknes ȝe are.
  Off all creaturys þe fayrest ȝe ware   105
    Into þe tyme of Adamys offence.
  ANIMA. Lorde, sythe we thy sowlys yet nowt wer þer,
    Wy of þe fyrst man bye we þe vyolence?

WYSDOM. For euery creature þat hath ben or xall
  Was in natur of þe fyrst man, Adame,   110
Off hym takynge þe fylthe of synne orygynall,
  For of hym all creaturys cam.
  Than by hym of reson ȝe haue blame
    And be made þe brondys of helle.

83 my] *D* myn   84 present] *D* represente   87 cunnynge] *D* cunnynges
91 yt] *D* it. *F* þat   107 yet] *MS.* yᵗ. *D* that. *F* þat

Wen ȝe be bore fyrst of yowr dame,   115
  ȝe may in no wyse in hewyn dwell,

For ȝe be dysvyguryde be hys synne,   f. 101
  Ande dammyde to derknes from Godys syghte.
ANIMA. How dothe grace þan ageyn begynne?
  Wat reformythe þe sowll to hys fyrste lyght?   120
WYSDOM. Wysdam, þat was Gode and man ryght,
  Made a full sethe to þe Fadyr of hewyn
By þe dredfull dethe to hym was dyght,
  Off wyche dethe spronge þe sacramentys sevyn,

Wyche sacramentys all synne wasche awey: 125
  Fyrst, baptem clensythe synne orygynall
And reformyt þe sowll in feythe verray
  To þe gloryus lyknes of Gode eternall
Ande makyt yt as fayer and as celestyall
  As yt neuer dyffowlyde had be,   130
Ande ys Crystys own specyall,
  Hys restynge place, hys plesant see.

ANIMA. In a sowle watt thyngys be
  By wyche he hathe hys very knowynge?
WYSDOM. Tweyn partyes: þe on, sensualyte,   135
  Wyche ys clepyde þe flechly felynge.
The fyve owtewarde wyttys to hym be serwynge.
  Wan þey be not rewlyde ordynatly
The sensualyte þan, wythowte lesynge,
  Ys made þe ymage of synne then of hys foly.   140

The other parte, þat ys clepyde resone,   f. 101ᵛ
  Ande þat ys þe ymage of Gode propyrly,
For by þat þe sowll of Gode hathe cognycyon
  And be þat hym serwyt and louevyt duly.
Be þe neyther parte of reson he knowyt dyscretly   145
  All erthely thyngys how þey xall be vsyde,
Wat suffysyth to hys myghtys bodely,
  Ande wat nedyt not to be refusyde.

---

126 baptem] *MS.* bapten. *D* baptem   133 In] *MS.* I. *D* In   135 þe
on] *D* the on is the   141 The] *D* That   143 cognycyon] g *added above*
the line

Thes tweyn do sygnyfye
  Yowr dysgysynge and yowr aray,   150
Blake and wyght, fowll and fayer vereyly,
  Euery sowll here, þis ys no nay,
Blake by sterynge of synne þat cummyth all-day,
  Wyche felynge cummythe of sensualyte,
Ande wyght by knowenge of reson veray   155
  Off þe blyssyde infenyt Deyte.

Thus a sowle ys bothe fowlle and fayer:
  Fowll as a best be felynge of synne,
Fayer as a angell, of hewyn þe ayer,
  By knowynge of Gode by hys reson wythin.   160
  ANIMA. Than may I sey thus and begynne
    Wyth fyve prudent vyrgyns of my reme—
  Thow be þe fyve wyttys of my sowll wythinne—:
    'Nigra sum sed formosa, filia Jerusalem.'

f. 102

Her enteryd fyve vyrgynes in white kertyllys and mantelys,
wyth cheuelers and chappelettys, and synge 'Nigra sum sed for-
mosa, filia Jerusalem, sicut tabernacula cedar et sicut pelles Salamonis'.

ANIMA. The doughters of Jerusalem me not lake   165
  For þis dyrke schadow I bere of humanyte,
That as þe tabernacull of cedar wythowt yt ys blake
  Ande wythine as þe skyn of Salamone full of bewty.
  'Quod fusca sum, nolite considerare me,
    Quia decolorauit me sol Jouis.'   170
  WYSDOM. Thus all þe sowlys þat in þis lyff be
    Stondynge in grace be lyke to thys.

A, quinque prudentes, yowr wyttys fyve
  Kepe yow clene and ȝe xall neuer deface,
Ye Godys ymage neuer xall ryve,   175
  For þe clene sowll ys Godys restynge place.

---

159 as a] *D* as   ayer] *D* hayr   164 sed] *D* et   164 s.d. *These
letters are supplied from D*: elers *in* cheuelers, cut *in* sicut   enteryd] *D* entreth
in white] *MS.* w^t. *D* in white   *After the s.d. another hand in M writes* va va va
(*vacat*, 'it is void'); see note at 685 s.d.   172 be] *MS.* by. *D* be   175 neuer]
MS. D euer. *F* neuer   176 sowll ys] *MS.* sowll. *D* soule is

Thre myghtys euery Cresten sowll has,
　　Wyche bethe applyede to þe Trinyte.
MYNDE. All thre here, lo, byfor yowr face!
　　Mynde.
　　　　WYLL. Wyll.
　　　　　　WNDYRSTONDYNGE. Ande Vndyrstondynge, we
　　　　　　thre.　　　　　　　　　　　　　　　　　　180

WYSDAM. 3e thre, declare þan thys,
　　Yowr syngnyfycacyon and yowr propyrte.
MENDE. I am Mynde, þat in þe sowle ys　　　　　f. 102ᵛ
　　The veray fygure of þe Deyte.
Wen in myselff I haue mynde and se　　　　　　185
　　The benefyttys of Gode and hys worthynes,
How holl I was mayde, how fayere, how fre,
　　How gloryus, how jentyll to hys lyknes,

Thys insyght bryngyt to my mynde
　　Wat grates I ough to God ageyn　　　　　　　190
þat thus hathe ordenyde wythowt ende
　　Me in hys blys euer for to regne.
Than myn insuffycyens ys to me peyn
　　That I haue not werof to yelde my dett,
Thynkynge myselff creature most veyn;　　　　195
　　Than for sorow my bren I knett.

Wen in my mynde I brynge togedyr
　　þe yerys and dayes of my synfullnes,
The vnstabullnes of my mynde hedyr and thedyr,
　　My oreble fallynge and freellnes,　　　　　200
Myselff ryght nought than I confes,
　　For by myselff I may not ryse
Wythowt specyall grace of Godys goodnes.
　　Thus mynde makyt me myselff to dyspyse.

---

180 Vndyrstondynge] wns *canc. before* vndyrstondynge　　　　188 how jentyll]
D and how gentyll　　　　190 ough to God] *MS.* ought. *D* ough to God. *F* ought
to God　　　　191 wythowt] *D* wythouten　　　　199 vnstabullnes] *MS. F*
sustabullnes. *D* sustabylnesse　　　　200 My oreble fallynge] *D* Myn horrible
fallynges　　　　204 myselff] *MS.* me selff. *D* my self

I seke and fynde nowere comforte   205
  But only in Gode, my Creator.
Than onto hym I do resorte
  Ande say, 'Haue mynde of me, my Sauowr!'
  Thus mynde to mynde bryngyth þat fawowre;   f. 103
    Thus, by mynde of me, Gode I kan know.   210
  Goode mynde of Gode yt ys þe fygure;
    Ande thys mynde to haue all Crysten ow.

WYLL. And I of þe soull am þe Wyll,
  Off þe Godhede lyknes and fygure.
Wyth goode wyll no man may spyll   215
  Nor wythowt goode wyll of blys be sure.
  Wat soule wyll gret mede recure,
    He must grett wyll haue, in thought or dede,
  Wertuusly sett wyth consyens pure,
    For in wyll stondyt only mannys dede.   220

Wyll for dede oft ys take;
  Therfor þe wyll must weell be dysposyde.
Than þer begynnyt all grace to wake,
  Yff wyth synne yt be not anosyde.
  Therfor þe wyll must be wele apposyde   225
    Or þat yt to þe mevynge yewe consent:
  The lybrary of reson must be wnclosyde
    Ande aftyr hys domys to take entent.

Owr wyll in Gode must be only sett
  And for Gode to do wylfully.   230
Wan gode wyll resythe, Gode ys in ws knett,
  Ande he performyt þe dede veryly.
  Off hym cummyth all wyll sett perfyghtly,
    For of owrselff we haue ryght nought   f. 103ᵛ
  But syne, wrechydnes, and foly.   235
    He ys begynner and gronde of wyll and thought.

---

206 Creator] *MS. D* creature   214 fygure] *D* a fygure   215 Wyth]
MS. Wyt. *D* wyth   216 wythowt] *D* wythouten   218 in thought or
dede] in dede and in thought *changed to* in thought or dede   220 stondyt
only] *D* onely standyth   224 wyth synne yt] *D* it wyth synne   225 wele]
MS. wyll. *D* wele   226 mevynge yewe consent] *MS.* mevynge yewe cosent.
D mevynges yeve consent   230 wylfully] *MS. F* wysly. *D* wylfully

Than þis goode wyll seyde before
Ys behoueable to yche creature
Iff he cast hym to restore
    The soule þat he hath take of cure,   240
    Wyche of God ys þe fygure,
      As longe as þe fygure ys kept faycr,
    Ande ordenyde euer for to endure
      In blys, of wyche ys he þe veray hayer.

WNDYRSTONDYNGE. The thyrde parte of þe soule ys Wndyr-
    stondynge,   245
    For by wndyrstondyng I beholde wat Gode ys,
In hymselff begynnyng wythowt begynnynge
Ande ende wythowt ende þat xall neuer mys.
Incomprehensyble in hymselff he ys;
    Hys werkys in me I kan not comprehende.   250
How xulde I holly hym þan þat wrought all þis?
    Thus by knowynge of me to knowynge of Gode I assende.

I know in angelys he ys desyderable,
    For hym to beholde þei dysyer souerenly;
In hys seyntys most dylectable,   255
    For in hymm þei joy assyduly;
    In creaturys hys werkys ben most wondyrly,
      For all ys made by hys myght,
    By hys wysdom gouernyde most souerenly,   f. 104
      And hys benygnyte inspyryt all soullys wyth lyght.   260

Off all creaturys he ys lowyde souereyn,
    For he ys Gode of yche creature,
And þey be his peple þat euer xall reynge,
    In wom he dwellyt as hys tempull sure.
Wan I of thys knowynge make reporture   265
    Ande se þe loue he hathe for me wrought,
Yt bryngyt me to loue þat Prynce most pure,
    For, for loue, þat Lorde made a man of nought.

238 behoueable] *D* behouefull   240 he hath] *D* hath   243 for to] *D* to
244 ys he] *D* is   247 begynnynge] *MS.* begynnyge   248 wythowt] *D*
wythouten   254 þei] *MS.* þe. *D* thei   256 þei] *MS.* þer. *D* thei
257 wondyrly] *D* wonderfully   258 all] *D* all this   259 By hys] *MS.* By. *D*
bi his   260 hys benygnyte inspyryt] *D* be his benygnyte inspired   264 as]
D as in   265 of thys] *MS.* thys. *D* of this   268 a man] *D* man

Thys ys þat loue wyche ys clepyde charyte,
   For Gode ys charyte, as awtors tellys,   270
Ande woo ys in charyte, in Gode dwellyt he,
   Ande Gode, þat ys charyte, in hym dwellys.
   Thus wndyrstondynge of Gode compellys
      To cum to charyte; than haue hys lyknes, lo!
   Blyssyde ys þat sowll þat þis speche spellys: 275
      'Et qui creauit me requieuit in tabernaculo meo.'

WYSDOM. Lo, thes thre myghtys in on Soule be:
Mynde, Wyll, and Wndyrstondynge.
By Mynde of Gode þe Fadyr knowyng haue ye;
   By Wndyrstondynge of Gode þe Sone ye haue knowynge; 280
By Wyll, wyche turnyt into loue brennynge,
   Gode þe Holy Gost, þat clepyde ys lowe:
Not thre Godys but on Gode in beynge.
   Thus eche clene soule ys symylytude of Gode abowe. f. 104ᵛ

By Mynde feythe in þe Father haue we,   285
   Hoppe in owr Lorde Jhesu by Wndyrstondynge,
Ande be Wyll in þe Holy Gost charyte:
   Lo, thes thre pryncypall wertus of yow thre sprynge.
Thys þe clene soule stondyth as a kynge;
   Ande abowe all þis ȝe haue free wyll;   290
Off þat be ware befor all thynge,
   For yff þat perverte, all þis dothe spyll.

Ye haue thre enmyes; of hem be ware:
   The Worlde, þe Flesche, and þe Fende.
Yowr fywe wyttys from hem ȝe spare,   295
   That þe sensualyte þey brynge not yow byhynde.
Nothynge xulde offende Gode in no kynde;
   Ande yff þer do, se þat þe nether parte of resone
In no wys þerto lende;
   Than þe ouer parte xall haue fre domynacyon.   300

Wan suggestyon to þe Mynde doth apere,
   Wndyrstondynge, delyght not ȝe þerin;

---

270 tellys] *MS.* tell. *D* telles   277 WYSDOM] *MS.* Wydom. *D* Wysdam
on] *D* o   281 into] *MS.* in. *D* into   289 Thys] *D* thus   296 yow
byhynde] *D* to mynde   298 do, se] *F* dose   302 ȝe] *D* the

Consent not, Wyll, yll lessons to lere,
  Ande than suche steryngys be no syn.
    Thei do but purge þe soule wer ys suche contrauersye.   305
    Thus in me, Wysdom, yowr werkys begynne.
Fyght and ȝe xall haue þe crown of glory,
  That ys euerlastynge joy, to be parteners þerinne.

ANIMA. Soueren Lorde, I am bownde to the!   f. 105
  Wan I was nought þou made me thus gloryus;   310
Wan I perysschede thorow synne þou sauyde me;
  Wen I was in grett perell þou kept me, Cristus;
  Wen I erryde þou reducyde me, Jhesus;
    Wen I was ignorant þou tawt me truthe;
  Wen I synnyde þou corecte me thus;   315
    Wen I was hewy þou comfortede me by ruthe;

Wan I stonde in grace þou holdyste me þat tyde;
  Wen I fall þou reysyst me myghtyly;
Wen I go wyll þou art my gyde;
  Wen I cum þou reseywyste me most louynly.   320
  Thou hast anoyntyde me with þe oyll of mercy;
    Thy benefyttys, Lorde, be innumerable;
  Werfor lawde endeles to þe I crye,
    Recomendynge me to þin endles powre durable.

Here in þe goynge owt þe FYVE WYTTYS synge 'Tota pulcra es'
et cetera, they goyng befor, ANIMA next, and her folowynge
WYSDOM, and aftyr hym MYNDE, WYLL, and WNDYRSTON-
DYNGE, all thre in wyght cloth of golde, cheveleryde and crestyde
in sute.

   304 be] *MS.* by. *D* be   305 Thei] *MS.* The. *D* thei   308 ys
euerlastynge] *MS.* euer ys lastynge. *D* is euerlastyng   311 sauyde me]
MS. sauyde. *D* sauyd me   316 comfortede me] *MS.* comfortede. *D*
conforted me. *MS. adds* este *in margin*   319 wyll] *D* wele   321 anoyntyde me] *MS.* anoyntyde. *D* anoynted me   324 þin] *D* thi   324 s.d.
These letters are supplied from D: oyng *in* goyng, YLL *in* WYLL, es *in* crestyde
cheveleryde] *MS.* theveleryde. *D* chevelered   in sute] *F* in on sute

SCENE II

And aftyr þe songe entreth LUCYFER in a dewyllys aray wythowt
and wythin as a prowde galonte, seynge thus on thys wyse:

LUCYFER. Owt harow I rore, 325
For envy I lore.
My place to restore
    God hath mad a man.
All cum þey not thore, f. 105ᵛ
Woode and þey wore, 330
I xall tempte hem so sorre,
    For I am he þat syn begane.

I was a angell of lyghte;
Lucyfeer I hyght,
Presumynge in Godys syght, 335
    Werfor I am lowest in hell.
In reformynge of my place ys dyght
Man, whom I haue in most dyspyght,
Euer castynge me wyth hem to fyght
    In þat hewynly place he xulde not dwell. 340

I am as wyly now as than;
þe knowynge þat I hade, yet I can;
I know all compleccyons of a man
    Werto he ys most dysposyde;
Ande þerin I tempte ay-whan; 345
I marre hys myndys to þer wan,
That whoo ys hym þat God hym began;
    Many a holy man wyth me ys mosyde.

Of Gode man ys þe fygure,
Hys symylytude, hys pyctowre, 350
Gloryosest of ony creature
    þat euer was wrought;

s.d. (cont.) *These letters are supplied from D:* a *in* aray, se *in* wyse   dewyllys]
D deuely   328 a man] D man   333 a angell] D aungell   338 whom
I haue in] MS. whan I haue. DF whan I haue in   339 to] D for to
340 he] D that he   343 a man] D man   345 tempte] D tempte hym
346 þer] D thei   347 whoo ys hym þat] D wo is hym (that *crossed out*)

Wyche I wyll dysvygure
Be my fals conjecture;
Yff he tende my reporture   355
    I xall brynge hym to nought.

In þe soule ben thre partyes iwys:
Myndc, Wyll, Wndyrstondynge of blys,
Fygure of þe Godhede, I know well thys;
    And þe flesche of man þat ys so changeable   360
That wyll I tempte, as I gees;
Thow þat I perwert, synne non ys
But yff þe Soule consent to mys,
    For in þe Wyll of þe Soule the dedys ben damnable.

To þe Mynde of þe Soule I xall mak suggestyun,   f. 106
Ande brynge hys Wndyrstondynge to dylectacyon,   366
So þat hys Wyll make confyrmacyon;
    Than am I sekyr inowe
That dethe xall sew of damnacyon;
Than of þe Sowll þe Dewll hath dominacyon.   370
I wyll go make hys examynacyon,
    To all þe dewllys of helle I make awow.

For, for to tempte man in my lyknes,
Yt wolde brynge hym to grett feerfullnes,
I wyll change me into bryghtnes,   375
    And so hym to-begyle,
Sen I xall schew hym perfyghtnes,
And wertu prove yt wykkydnes;
Thus wndyr colors all thynge perverse;
    I xall neuer rest tyll þe Soule I defyle.   380

    Her LUCYFER dewoydyth and cummyth in ageyn as a goodly
galont.

MYNDE. My mynde ys euer on Jhesu
That enduyde ws wyth wertu.
Hys doctrine to sue

    363 to mys] *MS. F* to þis. *D* vnto mys   364 the dedys ben] *D* ben the
dedys   369 dethe] *D* dede   371 hys] *D* this   372 helle] *MS.* he...
D helle   373 For] *D* But   375 bryghtnes] *MS.* bryghtne. *D* brightnesse
376 begyle] *MS.* begyl... *D* begyle   378 prove yt] *MS.* provyt yt. *D* prove
it   380 þe] *MS.* þ... *D* the

Euer I purpos.

WNDYRSTONDYNGE. My wndyrstondynge ys in trew   385
That wyth feyth ws dyd renew.
Hys laws to pursew
    Ys swetter to me þan sawowre of þe rose.

WYLL. And my wyll ys hys wyll veraly
That made ws hys creaturys so specyally,   390
Yeldynge onto hym laude and glory
    For hys goodnes.
LUCYFER. Ye fonnyde fathers, founders of foly,
Vt quid hic statis tota die ociosi?
ȝe wyll perysche or ȝe yt aspye.   395
    The Dewyll hath acumberyde yow expres.

Mynde, Mynde, ser, haue in mynde thys!   f. 106ᵛ
MYNDE. He ys not ydyll þat wyth Gode ys.
LUCYFER. No, ser! I prowe well yis.
    Thys ys my suggestyun.   400
All thynge hat dew tymes
Prayer, fastynge, labour, all thes.
Wan tyme ys not kept, þat dede ys amys,
    þe more pleynerly to yowr informacyon.

Here ys a man þat lywyt wordly,   405
Hathe wyffe, chylderne, and serwantys besy,
And other chargys þat I not specyfye.
    Ys yt leeffull to þis man
To lewe hys labour wsyde truly,
Hys chargys perysche þat Gode gaff duly,   410
Ande yewe hym to preyer and es of body?
    Woso do thus wyth God ys not than.

Mertha plesyde Gode grettly thore.
MYNDE. Ye, but Maria plesyde hymm moche more.

385 My] D Myn   388 þan] D than the   389 ys] hys *changed to* ys
391 onto] MS. on. D vnto   395 perysche] MS. pyse. D pisshe. F peryse
397 MS. *repeats the heading* lucyfer   in mynde] D mynde of   399 yis] MS.
F thys. D yis   400 Thys] D lo this   401 thynge hat] MS. thnge hat. D thynge
hath   403 amys] D mys   404 þe more pleynerly] MS. F be more pleynerly.
D be more plenerly   408 Ys yt] MS. yt ys. D Is it   414 Maria] MS. Mara.
D Maria

LUCYFER. Yet þe lest hade blys for euermore.   415
    Ys not þis anow?
MYNDE. Contemplatyff lyff ys sett befor.
LUCYFER. I may not belewe þat in my lore,
For God hymselff, wan he was man borre,
    Wat lyff lede he? answer þou now.   420

Was he euer in contemplacyon?
MYNDE. I suppos not, by my relacyon.
LUCYFER. And all hys lyff was informacyon   f. 107
    Ande example to man.
Sumtyme wyth synners he had conversacyon;   425
Sumtyme wyth holy also comunycacyon;
Sumtyme he laboryde, preyde; sumtyme tribulacyon;
    Thys was vita mixta þat Gode here began;

Ande þat lyff xulde ye here sewe.
MYNDE. I kan not belewe thys ys trew.   430
LUCYFER. Contemplatyff lyff for to sewe
    Yt ys grett drede, and se cause why:
They must fast, wake, and prey, euer new,
Wse harde lywynge and goynge wyth dyscyplyne dew,
Kepe sylence, wepe, and surphettys eschewe,   435
    Ande yff þey fayll of thys þey offende Gode hyghly.

Wan þey haue wastyde by feyntnes,
Than febyll þer wyttys and fallyn to fondnes,
Sum into dyspeyer and sum into madnes.
    Wet yt well, God ys not plesyde wyth thys.   440
Lewe, lewe, suche syngler besynes.
Be in þe worlde, vse thyngys nesesse.
The comyn ys best expres.
    Who clymyt hye, hys fall gret ys.

MYNDE. Truly, me seme ȝe haue reson.   445
LUCYFER. Aplye yow then to þis conclusyun.
MYNDE. I kan make no replicacyon.   f. 107ᵛ
    Your resons be grete.

416 þis] D that   430 Contemp subpuncted before I kan not belewe thys].
D I can beleve that ye say   534 lywynge] D levynges   442 vse] wse
canc. before vse   448 line supplied from D

I kan not forgett þis informacyon.
LUCYFER. Thynke þerwppon, yt ys yowr saluacyon.   450
Now and Wndyrstondynge wolde haue delectacyon,
    All syngler deuocyons he wolde lett.

Yowr fyve wyttys abrode lett sprede.
Se how comly to man ys precyus wede;
Wat worschype yt ys to be manfull in dede;   455
    þat bryngyt in dominacyon.
Off þe symple what profyght yt to tak hede?
Beholde how ryches dystroyt nede;
It makyt man fayer, hym wele for to fede;
    And of lust and lykynge commyth generacyon.   460

Wndyrstondynge, tender ye þis informacyon.
WNDYRSTONDYNGE. In thys I fele in manere of dylectacyon.
LUCYFER. A, ha, ser, then þer make a pawsacyon.
    Se and beholde þe worlde abowte.
Lytyll thynge suffysyt to saluacyon;   465
All maner synnys dystroyt contryscyon;
They þat dyspeyer mercy haue grett compunccyon;
    Gode plesyde best wyth goode wyll, no dowte.

Therfor, Wyll, I rede yow inclyne;
Lewe yowr stodyes, þow ben dywyn;   470
Yowr prayers, yowr penance, of ipocryttys þe syne,
    Ande lede a comun lyff.
What synne ys in met, in ale, in wyn?
Wat synne ys in ryches, in clothynge fyne?
All thynge Gode ordenyde to man to inclyne.   f. 108
    Lewe yowr nyse chastyte and take a wyff.   476

Better ys fayer frut þan fowll pollucyon.
What seyth sensualite to þis conclusyon?
WYLL. As þe fyue wyttys gyff informacyon,
    Yt semyth yowr resons be goode.   480

454 comly] MS. comunly. D comly   455 yt ys] D it   456 bryngyt]
MS. brygyt. D bryngeth   459 wele] MS. werkys. D wele   462 in manere]
D a manere   469 Wyll] well canc., wyll above line   470 þow] D tho.
F þow [þey]   473 ys in met, in ale] MS. in met in hale. D is in mete in
ale   479 As] MS. At. D As

LUCYFERE. The Wyll of þe Soule hathe fre dominacyon;
Dyspute not to moche in þis wyth reson;
Yet þe nethyr parte to þis taketh sum instruccyon,
   And so xulde þe ouer parte but he were woode.

WYLL. Me seme, as ȝe sey, in body and soule,   485
   Man may be in þe worlde and be ryght goode.
LUCYFER. Ya, ser, by Sent Powle!
   But trust not þes prechors, for þey be not goode,
   For þey flatter and lye as þey wore woode;
      Ther ys a wolffe in a lombys skyn.   490
   WYLL. Ya, I woll no more row ageyn þe floode.
   I woll sett my soule on a mery pynne.

LUCYFER. Be my trowthe, than do ye wyslye.
Gode lowyt a clene sowll and a mery.
Acorde yow thre togedyr by   495
   And ye may not mysfare.
MYNDE. To þis suggestyon agre we.
WNDYRSTONDYNGE. Delyght þerin I haue truly.   f. 108ᵛ
WYLL. And I consent þerto frelye.
   LUCYFER. A, ser, all mery þan! awey care!   500

Go in þe worlde, se þat abowte;
Geet goode frely, cast no dowte;
To þe ryche ye se men lowly lought.
   Yeue to yowr body þat ys nede,
Ande euer be mery; let reuell rowte!   505
MYNDE. Ya, ellys I beschrew my snowte!
WNDYRSTONDYNGE. And yff I care, cache I þe gowte!
   WYLL. And yff I spare, þe Dewyll me spede!

LUCYFER. Go yowr wey than and do wysly.
Change þat syde aray.
       MYNDE. I yt dyfye.   510
WNDYRSTONDYNGE. We woll be fresche, hanip la plu joly!
   Farwell penance!

487 Ya, ser] MS. Ser. D ya ser. F Ser, [ȝis,]   490 lombys] bo canc.
before lombys. D lombe   492 on a] MS. a. D on a   493 than] D that
496 line supplied from D   497 we] D me   500 A] D A ha   awey] D
and awey   507 I] D me   511 hanip] D and it hap. F hamp

MYNDE. To worschyppys I wyll my mynde aplye.
WNDYRSTONDYNGE. My wndyrstondynge in worschyppys and
    glory.
WYLL. And I in lustys of lechery,   515
    As was sumtyme gyse of Frawnce.
        Wyth wy wyppe,
        Farwell, quod I, þe Dewyll ys wppe!   Exient

LUCYFER. Off my dysyere now haue I summe   f. 109
Wer onys brought into custume,   520
Then farwell consyens, he wer clumme,
    I xulde haue all my wyll.
Resone I haue made both deff and dumme;
Grace ys owt and put arome;
Wethyr I wyll haue, he xall cum.   525
    So at þe last I xall hym spyll.

I xall now stere hys mynde
To þat syne made me a fende,
Pryde, wyche ys ageyn kynde
    And of synnys hede.   530
So to couetyse he xall wende,
For þat enduryth to þe last ende,
And onto lechery, and I may hymm rende,
    Than am I seker þe Soule ys dede.

That Soule Gode made incomparable,   535
To hys lyknes most amyable,
I xall make yt most reprouable,
    Ewyn lyke to a fende of hell.
At hys deth I xall apere informable,
Schewynge hym all hys synnys abhomynable,   540
Prewynge hys Soule damnable,
    So wyth dyspeyer I xall hym qwell.

Wyll clennes ys mankyn,
Verely, þe soule God ys wythin;
Ande wen yt ys in dedly synne,   545
    Yt ys werely þe Deuelys place.   f. 109ᵛ

514 My] D Myn   517–18 one line] D two lines   518 s.d. only in D
523 deff] MS. dethe. D deff   530 of] D of all   543 Wyll] D Whgll
546 Yt ys] MS. Yt. D It is

Thus by colours and false gynne
Many a soule to hell I wyn.
Wyde to go I may not blyne
    Wyth þis fals boy, God gyff hym euell grace!   550

    Her he takyt a schrewde boy wyth hym and goth hys wey
cryenge.

SCENE III

MYNDE. Lo, me here in a new aray!
Wyppe, wyrre, care awey!
    Farwell perfeccyon!
Me semyt myselff most lyghly ay.
It ys but honest, no pryde, no nay.   555
I wyll be freshest, by my fay,
    For þat acordyt wyth my complexccyon.

WNDYRSTONDYNGE. Ande haue here one as fresche as yow!
All mery, mery, and glade now.
I haue get goode, Gode wott how.   560
    For joy I sprynge, I sckyppe.
Goode makyt on mery, to Gode avowe.
Farewell consyens, I know not yow!
I am at eas, hade I inow.
    Truthe on syde I lett hym slyppe.   565

WYLL. Lo, here on as jolye as ȝe!
I am so lykynge, me seme I fle.
I haue atastyde lust: farwell chastyte!
    My hert ys euermore lyght.
I am full of felycyte.   570
My delyght ys all in bewte.
þer ys no joy but þat in me.
    A woman me semyth a hewynly syght.

---

547 and false gynne] *MS*. gyane. *D* and false gynne   548 to hell] *D* to
hevyn   550 euell] *D* ille   550 s.d. schrewde boy] *MS*. boy *canc. before*
screwde boy. *D* shrewed boy   551 a new] *D* newe   554 lyghly] *MS*.
lyghtly. *D* lykly   558 one] *MS*. me. *D* one   559 mery, mery] mery
and mery *changed to* mery mery   564 at eas, hade I inow] *MS*. a eas hade I
now. *D* at ease had I Inowe   569 My] *D* Myn   570 full of] *MS*. full of
full of. *D* full of

MYNDE. Ande thes ben my syngler solace:
Kynde, fortune, and grace.   575
Kynde nobley of kynrede me yewyn hase,
    Ande þat makyt me soleyn.
Fortune in worldys worschyppe me doth lace.
Grace yewyt curryus eloquens, and þat mase
    That all oncunnynge I dysdeyn.   580

WNDYRSTONDYNGE. And my joy ys especyall
To hurde wppe ryches, for fer to fall,
To se yt, to handyll yt, to tell yt all,
    And streight to spare.
To be holde ryche and reyall   585
I bost, I avawnt wer I xall.
Ryches makyt a man equall
    To hem sumtyme hys souereyngys wer.

WYLL. To me ys joy most laudable
Fresche dysgysynge to seme amyable,   590
Spekynge wordys delectable
    Perteynynge onto loue.
It ys joy of joys inestymable
To halse, to kys þe affyable.
A louer ys son perceyvable   595
    Be þe smylynge on me, wan yt doth remove.

MYNDE. To avaunte thus me semyth no schame,
For galontys now be in most fame.
Curtely personys men hem proclame.
    Moche we be sett bye.   600
WNDYRSTONDYNGE. The ryche covetouse wo dare blame, f. 110ᵛ
Off govell and symony thow he bere þe name?
To be fals, men report yt game;
    Yt ys clepyde wysdom, 'Ware þat!' quod Ser Wyly.

576 nobley] *MS. F* nobyll. *D* nobley   yewyn] *D* yovyn. *F* ioy yovyn
582 for] *F* fro   584 streight] *MS.* strenght. *D* streightly   588 hys] *MS.*
to *changed to* hys   589 laudable] *MS.* delectable. *D* laudable   597 avaunte]
MS. avaynte. *D* avaunte   600 *line supplied from D*   601 covetouse]
MS. couetyse. *D* covetouse   603 report] *D* reportith   604 Ser Wyly]
D F Wyly

WYLL. Ande of lechory to make avawnte 605
Men fors yt no more þan drynke atawnt.
Thes thyngys be now so conversant,
    We seme yt no schame.
MYNDE. Curyous aray I wyll euer hante.
WNDYRSTONDYNGE. Ande I falsnes, to be passante. 610
WYLL. Ande I in lust my flesche to daunte.
    No man dyspyes thes; þey be but game.

MYNDE. I rejoys of thes; now let ws synge!
WNDYRSTONDYNGE. Ande yff I spar, ewell joy me wrynge!
WYLL. Haue at, quod I, lo, howe I sprynge! 615
    Lust makyth me wondyr wylde.
MYNDE. A tenowr to yow bothe I brynge.
WNDYRSTONDYNGE. And I a mene for ony kynge.
WYLL. And but a trebull I owtwrynge,
    The Deuell hym spede þat myrthe exyled! 620

                        Et cantent

MYNDE. How be þis trow ye nowe?
WNDYRSTONDYNGE. At þe best, to God avowe.
WYLL. As mery as þe byrde on bow,
    I take no thought. 624
MYNDE. The welfare of þis worlde ys in ws, I ma vowe. f. 111
WNDYRSTONDYNGE. Lett eche man tell hys condycyons howe.
WYLL. Begynne ye, ande haue at yow,
    For I am aschamyde of ryght nought.

MYNDE. Thys ys a cause of my worschyppe:
I serue myghty lordeschyppe 630
Ande am in grett tenderschyppe;
    Therfor moche folke me dredys.
Men sew to my frendeschyppe
For meyntnance of her schendeschyppe.
I support hem by lordeschyppe. 635
    For to get goode þis a grett spede ys.

WNDYRSTONDYNGE. And I vse jorowry,
Enbrace questys of perjury,
Choppe and chonge wyth symonye,
 And take large yeftys. 640
Be þe cause neuer so try,
I preue yt fals, I swere, I lye,
Wyth a quest of myn affye.
 The redy wey þis now to thryfte ys.

WYLL. And wat trow 3e be me? 645
More þan I take spende I threys thre.
Sumtyme I yeff, sumtyme þey me,
 Ande am euer fresche and gay.
Few placys now þer be
But onclennes we xall þer see; 650
It ys holde but a nysyte.
 Lust ys now comun as þe way.

MYNDE. Law procedyth not for meyntnance. f. 111ᵛ
WNDYRSTONDYNGE. Trowthe recurythe not for habundance.
WYLL. And lust ys in so grett vsance, 655
 We fors yt nought.
MYNDE. In vs þe worlde hathe most affyance.
WNDYRSTONDYNGE. Non thre be in so grett aqweynttance.
WYLL. Few þer be outhe of owr allyance.
 Wyll þe worlde ys thus, take we no thought! 660

MYNDE. Thought! nay, þerageyn stryve I.
WNDYRSTONDYNGE. We haue þat nedyt vs, so thryve I.
WYLL. And yff þat I care, neuer wyve I.
 Let them care þat hathe for to sewe!
MYNDE. Wo lordschyppe xall sew must yt bye. 665
WNDYRSTONDYNGE. Wo wyll haue law must haue monye.
WYLL. Ther pouert ys þe malewrye,
 Thow ryght be, he xall neuer renewe.

637–52 *In MS. Will speaks next, in D Understanding, but MS. corrects the error by marking the speech of Understanding A and the speech of Will B* 637 jorowry] *MS.* jerowry. *D* jorourry 641 Be þe cause] *MS.* By þe cause. *D* be the case 645 and] *MS.* A. *D* and 650 we] *D* ye *added above the line* 652 þe] *D* thei 663 yff] *D* gyve 664 them] *D* hem

MYNDE. Wronge ys born wpe boldly,
Thow all þe worlde know yt opynly,   670
Mayntnance ys now so myghty,
    Ande all for mede.
WNDYRSTONDYNGE. The law ys so coloryde falsly
By sleyttys and by perjury,
Brybys be so gredy,   675
    þat to þe pore trowth ys take ryght nought a hede.

WYLL. Wo gett or loose, ye be ay wynnande.   f. 112
Mayntnance and perjury now stande.
Thei wer neuer so moche reynande
    Seth Gode was bore.   680
MYNDE. Ande lechery was neuer more vsande
Off lernyde and lewyde in þis lande.
WNDYRSTONDYNGE. So we thre be now in hande.
    WYLL. Ya, and most vsyde eauerywere.

MYNDE. Now wyll we thre do make a dance   685
Off thow þat longe to owr retenance,
Cummynge in by contenance.
    þis were a dysporte.
WNDYRSTONDYNGE. Therto I geve acordance
Off thow þat ben of myn affyance.   690
WYLL. Let se bytyme þe meyntnance.
    Clepe in fyrst yowr resorte.

    Here entur six dysgysyde in þe sute of MYNDE, wyth rede
berdys, and lyouns rampaunt on here crestys, and yche a warder
in hys honde; her mynstrallys, trumpes. Eche answere for hys
name.

MYNDE. Let se cum in Indignacyon and Sturdynes,
Males also and Hastynes,

672 all] *D* all Is   676 to þe] *MS.* þe. *D* to the   nought a] *D* non
679 Thei] *MS. D* ther   685 *A contemporary hand in MS. wrote* va. *in the
margin here and* cat *before* 785, vacat *indicating that the speeches and dances
between these lines were to be omitted*   691 þe] *MS. D* þe *or* ye   692 s.d.
lyouns] *MS.* lyoun... *D* lyons   mynstrallys] *MS.* mynstrall. *D* menstrall

Wreche and Dyscorde expres,   695
    And þe sevente am I, Mayntennance.
Seven ys a numbyr of dyscorde and inperfyghtnes.
Lo, here ys a yomandrye wyth loweday to dres!
Ande þe Deule hade swore yt, þey wolde ber wp falsnes   f. 112ᵛ
    Ande maynten yt at þe best. þis ys þe Deullys dance.   700

Ande here menstrellys be convenyent,
For trumpys xulde blow to þe jugemente;
Off batell also yt ys on instrumente,
    Yevynge comfort to fyght.
Therfor þey be expedyente   705
To þes meny of meyntement.
Blow! lett see Madam Regent,
    Ande daunce, ye laddys! yowr hertys be lyght.

Lo, þat other spare, thes meny wyll spende.
WNDYRSTONDYNGE. Ya, wo ys hym xall hem offende!   710
WYLL. Wo wyll not to hem condescende,
    He xall haue threttys.
MYNDE. They spyll þat law wolde amende.
WNDYRSTONDYNGE. Yit mayntnance no man dare reprehende.
WYLL. Thes meny thre synnys comprehende: 715
    Pryde, Invy, and Wrathe in hys hettys.

WNDYRSTONDYNGE. Now wyll I than begyn my traces.
Jorowrs in on hoode beer to facys.
Fayer speche and falsehede in on space ys.
    Is it not ruthe?   720
The quest of Holborn cum into þis placys.
Ageyn þe ryght euer þey rechases.
Off wom þey holde not, harde hys grace ys.
    Many a tyme haue dammyde truthe.

---

697 dyscorde] *MS.* dycorde. *D* discorde   703 ys *added above the line*
706 þes] *D* these   mcyntement] *MS.* meyntnance. *D* mayntement. *F* meyntement   709 thes] *D* this   715 Thes] *D* these   716 hettys] *MS. D*
hestys   718 Jorowrs ... beer] *MS.* Jorowr ... beer. *D* Jorour ... berith
720 *line supplied from D*   722 rechases] *MS.* rechase. *D* rechases

f. 113

Here entrethe six jorours in a sute, gownyde, wyth hodys abowt
her nekys, hattys of meyntenance þervpon, vyseryde dyuersly;
here mynstrell, a bagpype.

WNDYRSTONDYNGE. Let se fyrst Wronge and Sleyght;   725
Dobullnes and Falsnes, schew yowr myght;
Now Raveyn and Dyscheyit;
      Now holde yow here togydyr.
Thys menys consyens ys so streytt
That þey report as mede yewyt beyght.   730
Here ys þe quest of Holborn, an euyll entyrecte.
      They daunce all þe londe hydyr and thedyr,
           And I, Perjury, yowr fownder.
      Now dance on, ws all! The worlde doth on ws wondyr.

Lo, here ys a menye loue wellfare.   735
MYNDE. Ye, þey spende þat tru men spare.
WYLL. Haue þey a brybe, haue þey no care
      Wo hath wronge or ryght.
MYNDE. They fors not to swere and starre.
WYLL. Though all be false, les and mare.   740
WNDYRSTONDYNGE. Wyche wey to þe woode wyll þe hare
      They knewe, and þey at rest sett als tyghte.
           Some seme hem wyse
           For þe fadyr of vs, Covetyse.

WYLL. Now Meyntnance and Perjury   745
Hathe schewyde þe trace of þer cumpeny,
Ye xall se a sprynge of Lechery,
      þat to me attende.
Here forme ys of þe stewys clene rebaldry.   f. 113ᵛ
They wene sey sothe wen þat þey lye.   750
Off þe comyn þey synge eche wyke by and by.
      They may sey wyth tenker, I trow, 'Lat amende.'

---

724 s.d. bagpype] *MS.* ba...pyp....*D* bagpy...   725 WNDYRSTON-
DYNGE.] Mynde *changed to* Wndyr. *D* Mynde   726 Falsnes] *D* falsehed
730 That þey] *D* that   731 entyrecte] *D F* endyrecte   732 þe] *D* this
733 And] *MS.* A. *D* and   737 haue þey no care] *D* thei haue no
care   740 Though] *MS.* Thouht. *D* though   746 þer] *D* her
750 wene] *MS.* veyn. *D* wene   752 tenker] *D* tynker

Here entreth six women in sut, thre dysgysyde as galontys and
thre as matrones, wyth wondyrfull vysurs congruent; here mynstrell, a hornepype.

WYLL. Cum slepers, Rekleshede and Idyllnes,
All in all, Surfet and Gredynes,
For þe flesche, Spousebreche and Mastres,   755
      Wyth jentyll Fornycacyon.
Yowr mynstrell a hornepype mete
þat fowll ys in hymselff but to þe erys swete.
Thre fortherers of loue; 'Hem schrew I!' quod Bete.
      Thys dance of þis damesellys ys thorow þis regyn.   760

MYNDE. Ye may not endure wythowt my meyntenance.
WNDYRSTONDYNGE. That ys bought wyth a brybe of owr
      substance.
WYLL. Whow, breydest þou vs of þin aqueyntance?
      I sett þe at nought!
MYNDE. On þat worde I woll tak vengeaunce.   765
Wer vycys be gederyde, euer ys sum myschance.
Hurle hens thes harlottys! Here gyse ys of France.
      þey xall abey bytterly, by hym þat all wrought!

WNDYRSTONDYNGE. Ill spede þe ande þou spare!
þi longe body bare   770
To bett I not spare.
      Haue the ageyn!
WYLL. Holde me not! let me go! ware!   f. 114
I dynge, I dasche! þer, go ther!
Dompe deuys, can ye not dare?   775
      I tell yow, outwarde, on and tweyn!   Exient

MYNDE. Now I schrew yow thus dansaunde!
WNDYRSTONDYNGE. Ye, and ewyll be þou thryvande!
WYLL. No more let vs be stryvande.
      Nowe all at on!   780

752 s.d. entreth] D entre   thre dysgysyde] MS. D dysgysyde. F [thre]
dysgysyde   congruent] MS. D F conregent   mynstrell] D mynstrallys
D ends after this s.d.   755 Spousebreche] and mast canc. before breche
759 schrew] scre canc. before schrew   762 substance] F festance
763 Whow] MS. F Whom   766 gederyde] gat canc. before gederyde
775 deuys] F Denys

MYNDE. Here was a meny onthryvande.
WNDYRSTONDYNGE. To þe Deull be þey drywande.
WYLL. He þat ys yll wywande,
    Wo hys hym, by þe bon!

MYNDE. Leue then þis dalyance   783
Ande set we a ordenance
Off better chevesaunce
    How we may thryve.
WNDYRSTONDYNGE. At Westmyster, wythowt varyance,
þe nex terme xall me sore avawnce,   790
For retornys, for enbraces, for recordaunce.
    Lyghtlyer to get goode kan no man on lyue.

MYNDE. Ande at þe parvyse I wyll be
A Powlys betwyn to ande thre,
Wyth a menye folowynge me,   795
    Entret, juge-partynge, and to-supporte.
WYLL. Ande euer þe latter, þe leuer me.
Wen I com lat to þe cyte
I walke all lanys and weys to myn affynyte;
    And I spede not þer, to þe stews I resort.   800

MYNDE. Ther gettys þou nouhte, but spendys.   f. 114ᵛ
WYLL. Yis, sumtyme I take amendys
Off hem þat nought offendys,
    I engrose vpe here purs.
MYNDE. And I arest þer no drede ys,   805
Preve forfett þer no mede ys,
Ande take to me þat nede ys;
    I reke not thow þey curs.

WNDYRSTONDYNGE. Thow þey curs, never þe wers I fare.
Thys day I endyght them I herde of neuer are;   810
To-morow I wyll aqwyt them, yff nede were.
    Thys lede I my lyff.

785 cat *in margin. See note on 685*   790 me sore avawnce] my sowraunce
canc. before sore avawnce, me *above line*   797 *The scribe of MS. wrote and
then cancelled line 802*   802 amendys] *MS.* amende *but* amendys *when first
written and cancelled*   804 engrose] *MS.* engose   808 curs] cr *canc.
before* curs   809 never] *MS.* nther *or* uther. *F* uther

WYLL. Ye, but of vs thre I haue lest care.
Met and drynke and ease, I aske no mare,
Ande a praty wenche, to se here bare;   815
    I reke but lytyll be sche mayde or wyffe.

MYNDE. Thys on a soper
I wyll be seen rycher,
Set a noble wyth goode chere
    Redyly to spende.   820
WNDYRSTONDYNGE. And I tweyn, be þis feer,
To moque at a goode dyner.
I hoope of a goode yer,
    For euer I trost Gode wyll send.

WYLL. And best we haue wyne,   825
Ande a cosyn of myn
Wyth ws for to dyne.
    Thre nobles wyll I spende frely.
MYNDE. We xall acorde well and fyne.   f. 115
WNDYRSTONDYNGE. Nay, I wyll not passe schylyngys nyne. 830
WYLL. No, þou was neuer but a swyn.
    I woll be holdyn jentyll, by Sent Audre of Ely.

Ande now in my mynde I haue
My cosyn Jenet N., so Gode me save;
Sche mornyth wyth a chorle, a very knaue,   835
    And neuer kan be mery.
I pley me þer wen I lyst rawe;
Than þe chorle wyll here dysprawe.
Who myght make hym thys to lawe,
    I wolde onys haue hym in þe wyrry.   840

MYNDE. For thys I kan a remedye:
I xall rebuk hym thus so dyspytuusly
þat of hys lyff he xall wery
    And qwak for very fcre.

821 And] A changed to And   825 And] MS. A. F And   828 spende]
F spede   830 nyne] MS. nyne ix   839 Who] MS. How   840 hym]
MS. hy...   843 wery] MS. very. F wery

Ande yff he wyll not leve þerby,   845
On hys bodye he xall abye
Tyll he leue þat jelousy.
    Nay, suche chorlys I kan lere.

WNDYRSTONDYNG. Nay, I kan better hym qwyttc:
Arest hym fyrst to pes for fyght,   850
Than in another schere hym endyght,
    He ne xall wete by wom ne howe.
Haue hym in þe Marschalsi seyn aryght,
Than to þe Amralte, for þey wyll byght,
A preuenire facias than haue as tyght,   855
    Ande þou xalt hurle hym so þat he xall haue inow.

WYLL. Wat and þes wrongys be espyede?
WNDYRSTONDYNGE. Wyth þe crose and þe pyll I xall   f. 115ᵛ
    wrye yt
That þer xall neuer man dyscrey yt
    þat may me appeyere.   860
MYNDE. Ther ys no craft but wc may trye yt.
WNDYRSTONDYNGE. Mede stoppyt, be yt neuer so allyede.
WYLL. Wyth yow tweyn wo ys replyede,
    He may sey he hathe a schrewde seyer.

MYNDE. Thow woldyst haue wondyr of sleyghtys þat be.   865
WNDYRSTONDYNGE. Thys make sume ryche and summe
    neuer the.
WYLL. þey must nedys grett goodys gett þe.
    Now go we to þe wyne!
MYNDE. In trewþe I grante; haue at wyth þe!
WNDYRSTONDYNGE. Ande for a peny or to, I wyll not fle.   870
WYLL. Mery, mery, all mery þan be we!
    Who þat ws tarythe, curs haue he and myn!

SCENE IV

WYSDOM. O thou Mynde, remembyr the!
    Turne þi weys, þou gost amyse.
Se what þi ende ys, þou myght not fle: 875
    Dethe to euery creature certen ys.

They þat lyue well, þey xall haue blys;
   Thay þat endyn yll, þey goo to hell.
I am Wysdom, sent to tell yow thys:
   Se in what stat þou doyst indwell.   880

MYNDE. To my mynde yt cummyth from farre
   That dowtles man xall dey.
Ande thes weys we go, we erre.   f. 116
   Wndyrstondynge, wat do ye sey?
   WNDYRSTONDYNGE. I sey, man, holde forthe þi wey!   885
      The lyff we lede ys sekyr ynowe.
I wyll no wndyrstondynge xall lett my pley.
      Wyll, frende, how seyst thowe?
      WYLL. I wyll not thynke þeron, to Gode avowe!
         We be yit but tender of age.   890
      Schulde we leve þis lyue? Ya, whowe?
      We may amende wen we be sage.

WYSDOM. Thus many on vnabylythe hym to grace.
   They wyll not loke, but slumber and wynke.
þey take not drede before þer face,   895
   Howe horryble þer synnys stynke.
Wen they be on þe pyttys brynke,
   Than xall þey trymbull and qwake for drede.
Yit Mynde, I sey, yow bethynke
   In what perell ye be now! Take hede!   900

Se howe ye haue dysvyguryde yowr soule!
   Beholde yowrselff; loke veryly in mynde!
Here ANIMA apperythe in þe most horrybull wyse, fowlere þan
a fende.
MYNDE. Out! I tremble for drede, by Sent Powle!
   Thys ys fowler þan ony fende.
WYSDOM. Wy art þou creature so onkynde,   905
      Thus to defoule Godys own place,
þat was made so gloryus wythowt ende?
      Thou hast made þe Deullys rechace.

879 am] an *canc. before* am   899 yow] *F* [to] yow   901 dysvyguryde]
MS. dyvyguryde

As many dedly synnys as ye haue vsyde,　　　　　　　f. 116ᵛ
　　So many deullys in yowr soule be.　　　　　　　　910
Beholde wat ys þerin reclusyde!
　　Alas, man, of þi Soule haue pyte!

Here rennyt owt from wndyr þe horrybyll mantyll of þe SOULI.
seven small boys in þe lyknes of dewyllys and so retorne ageyn.

　WYSDAM. What haue I do? why lowyste þou not me?
　　Why cherysyste þi enmye? why hatyst þou þi frende?
　Myght I haue don ony more for þe?　　　　　　　　915
　　But loue may brynge drede to mynde.

þou hast made the a bronde of hell
　Whom I made þe ymage of lyght.
Yff þe Deull myght, he wolde þe qwell,
　But þat mercy expellyt hys myght.　　　　　　　　920
　Wy doyst þou, Soule, me all dyspyght?
　　Why yewyst þou myn enmy þat I haue wrought?
　Why werkyst þou hys consell? by myn settys lyght?
　　Why hatyst þou vertu? why louyst þat ys nought?

MYNDE. A, lorde! now I brynge to mynde　　　　　925
　My horryble synnys and myn offens,
I se how I haue defowlyde þe noble kynde
　þat was lyke to þe by intellygens.
　Wndyrstondynge, I schew to your presens
　　Owr lyff wyche þat ys most synfull.　　　　　　930
　Sek yow remedye, do yowr dylygens
　　To clense þe Soull wyche ys þis fowll.

WNDYRSTONDYNGE. Be yow, Mynde, I haue very　　f. 117
　　knowenge
　That grettly Gode we haue offendyde,
Endles peyn worthyi be owr dysyrvynge,　　　　　　935
　Wyche be owrselff neuer may be amendyde

912 s.d. horrybyll] soull *canc. before* horrybyll　seven] *MS. F* vj　924 hatyst]
has *canc. before* hatyst　929 Wndyrstondynge] Wnst *changed to* Wndyrstondynge　schew] *MS. F* sew　933 WNDYRSTONDYNGE] Wyll *changed to*
Wndyrstondynge　935 dysyrvynge] *MS.* dysyrynge. *F* dysyrvynge

Wythowt Gode, in whom all ys comprehendyde.
   Therfor to hym let vs resort.
He lefte vp them þat be descendyde.
He ys resurreccyon and lywe; to hem, Wyll, resort.   940

WYLL. My wyll was full yowe to syne,
   By wyche þe Soule ys so abhomynable.
I wyll retorne to Gode and new begynne
Ande in hym gronde my wyll stable,
   þat of hys mercy he wyll me able   945
      To haue þe yiffte of hys specyall grace,
   How hys seke Soule may be recurable
      At þe jugment before hys face.

ANIMA. Than wyth yow thre þe Soule dothe crye,
   'Mercy, Gode!' Why change I nowte,   950
I þat thus horryble in synne lye,
   Sythe Mynde, Wyll, and Wndyrstondynge be brought
   To haue knowynge þey ill wrought?
      What ys þat xall make me clene?
   Put yt, Lorde, into my thowte!   955
      Thi olde mercy let me remene.

WYSDOM. Thow þe Soule mynde take
   Ande wndyrstondynge of hys synnys allwey,
Beynge in wyll, yt forsake,
   Yit thes do not only synnys awey,   f. 117ᵛ
   But very contrycyon, who þat haue may,   961
      þat ys purger and clenser of synne.
   A tere of þe ey, wyth sorow veray,
      þat rubbyt and waschyt þe Soule wythin.

All þe penance þat may be wrought,   965
   Ne all þe preyer þat seyde be kan,
Wythowt sorowe of hert relesyt nought;
   That in especyall reformyth man
   Ande makyt hym as clene as when he begane.
      Go seke þis medsyne, Soull! þat beseke   970

946 of hys specyall *written twice*   957 Thow] *F* Then [xall]   959 yt]
F yt [to]   963 veray] wery *canc. before* veray

Wyth veray feythe, and be ye sekyr than
The vengeaunce of Gode ys made full meke.

By wndyrstondynge haue very contrycyon,
 Wyth mynde of your synne confessyon make,
Wyth wyll yeldynge du satysfaccyon;   975
 þan yowr soule be clene, I wndyrtake.
   ANIMA. I wepe for sorow, Lorde! I begyn awake,
   I that þis longe hath slumberyde in syne.
                                    Hic recedunt demones.
   WYSDOM. Lo, how contrycyon avoydyth þe deullys blake!
   Dedly synne ys non yow wythin.   980

For Gode ye haue offendyde hyghly
 Ande yowr modyr, Holy Chyrche so mylde,
þerfor Gode ye must aske mercy,
 By Holy Chyrch to be reconsylyde,
 Trustynge verely ye xall neuer be revylyde   985
   Yff ye haue yowr charter of pardon by confessyon.
 Now haue ye foryeffnes þat were fylyde.   f. 118
   Go prey yowr modyr Chyrche of her proteccyon.

ANIMA. O Fadyr of mercy ande of comfort,
 Wyth wepynge ey and hert contryte   990
To owr modyr, Holy Chyrche, I wyll resort,
 My lyff pleyn schewenge to here syght.
 Wyth Mynde, Vndyrstondynge, and Wyll ryght,
   Wyche of my Sowll þe partyes be,
 To þe domys of þe Chyrche we xall vs dyght,   995
   Wyth veray contricyon thus compleynnyng we.

Here þey go owt, and in þe goynge þe SOULE syngyth in þe
most lamentabull wyse, wyth drawte notys as yt ys songyn in
þe passyon wyke:
ANIMA. Magna velud mare contricio, contricio tua: quis consoletur
tui? Plorans plorauit in nocte, et lacrime ejus in maxillis ejus.

---

975 Wyth] MS. Wyt   980 non] F now   981 hyghly] MS. hygly
988 Go] F To   989 comfort] MS. mercy. F comfort   996 compleyn-
nyng] MS. copleynnyng   996 s.d. lamentabull] MS. lametabull

WYSDOM. Thus seth Gode mankynde tyll
  The nyne poyntys ples hym all other before.
'Gyff a peny in thy lyve wyth goode wyll
  To þe pore, and þat plesythe Gode more   1000
  þan mowyntenys into golde tramposyde wore
    Ande aftyr thy dethe for the dysposyde.'
  Ande all þe goodys þou hast in store
    Xulde not profyght so moche wan þi body ys closyde.

The secunde poynt, Gode sethe thus: 1005
  'Wepe on tere for my loue hertyly,
Or for þe passyon of me, Jhesus,
  Ande þat plesyt me more specyally
  Than yff þou wepte for þi frendys or goodys worldly
    As moche water as þe se conteynys.'   f. 118ᵛ
  Lo, contrycyon ys a soueren remedy.   1011
    That dystroythe synnys, þat relessyt peynys.

The thyrde, Gode sethe: 'Suffyr pacyenly for my loue
  Off þi neybure a worde of repreve,
Ande þat to mercy mor dothe me move   1015
  Than þou dyscyplynyde þi body wyth peynys grewe
  Wyth as many roddys as myght grow or þrywe
    In þe space of a days jornye.'
  Lo, who suffyryth most for Gode ys most lewe,
    Slandyr, repreve, ony aduersyte.   1020

The fourte, Gode sethe: 'Wake on owyr for þe loue of me,
  And þat to me ys more plesaunce
Than yff þou sent twelve kyngys free
  To my sepulkyr wyth grett puysschaunce
  For my dethe to take vengeaunce.'   1025
    Lo, wakynge ys a holy thynge.
  þer yt ys hade wyth goode vsance,
    Many gracys of yt doth sprynge.

The fyfte, Gode sethe: 'Haue pyte and compassyon
  Off þi neybur wyche ys seke and nedy,   1030

998 The] *F* Thes   1001 þan] *MS.* þat. *F* þan   1014 repreve] reprove
canc. before repreve   1016 Than] *F* than [yf]   1017 on *changed to* or
þrywe] *MS.* prywe. *F* þrywe   1018 a days] *MS.* days. *F* [a] days
1020 ony] *MS. F* only   1021 owyr] *F* awyr

And þat to me ys more dylectacyon
   Than þou fastyde forty yer by and by,
   Thre days in þe weke, as streytly
     As þou cowdys in water and brede.'
   Lo, pyte Gode plesyth grettly,   1035
     Ande yt ys a vertu soueren, as clerkys rede.

The sixte, Gode seth on þis wyse:
   'Refreyn thy speche for my reuerens,
Lett not thy tonge thy evyn-Crysten dyspyse,   f. 119
   Ande þan plesyst þou more myn excellens   1040
   Than yff þou laberyde wyth grett dylygens
     Wpon thy nakyde feet and bare
   Tyll þe blode folwude for peyn and vyolens
     Ande aftyr eche stepe yt sene were.'

The sevente, Cryst seth in þis maner: 1045
   'Thy neybur to ewyll ne sterre not thou,
But all thynge torne into wertu chere,
   And than more plesyst þou me now
   Then yf a thowsende tymys þou renne thorow
     A busche of thornys þat scharpe were   1050
   Tyll þi nakyde body were all rough
     Ande evyn rent to þe bonys bare.'

The eyghte, Gode sethe þis man tyll:
   'Oftyn pray and aske of me,
Ande þat plesythe me more onto my wyll   1055
   Than yf my modyr and all sentys preyde for þe.'

The nynte, Gode sethe: 'Lowe me souerenly,
   Ande þat to me more plesant ys
Than yf þou went wpon a pyler of tre
   þat wer sett full of scharpe prykkys   1060
   So þat þou cut þi flesche into þe smale partys.'
     Lo, Gode ys plesyde more wyth þe dedys of charyte
    Than all þe peynys man may suffer iwys.
     Remembyr thes poyntys, man, in þi felycite!

1032 Than] *F* than [yff]   1040, 1048 plesyst þou] *MS.* plesyst
1048 And] *MS.* Ad   1051 rough] *MS.* rought

Here entrethe ANIMA, wyth þe Fyve Wyttys goynge before,
MYNDE on þe on syde and WNDYRSTONDYNGE on þe other syde
and WYLL folowyng, all in here fyrst clothynge, her chapplettys
and crestys, and all hauyng [f. 119ᵛ] on crownys, syngynge in here
commynge in: 'Quid retribuam Domino pro omnibus que retribuit
mihi? Calicem salutaris accipiam et nomen Domini inuocabo.'

ANIMA. O meke Jhesu, to þe I crye!   1065
   O swet Jhesu, my delectacyon!
O Jhesu, þe sune of Vyrgyne Marye,
   Full of mercy and compassyon!
My soule ys waschede be thy passyon
     Fro þe synnys cummynge by sensualyte.   1070
A, be the I haue a new resurreccyon.
   The lyght of grace I fele in me.

In tweyn myghtys of my soule I the offendyde:
   The on by my inwarde wyttys, thow ben gostly;
þe other by my outwarde wyttys comprehendyde,   1075
   Tho be þe fyve wyttys bodyly;
Wyth þe wyche tweyn myghtys mercy I crye.
     My modyr, Holy Chyrche, hath yowe me grace,
Whom ye fyrst toke to yowr mercy,
     Yet of myselff I may not satysfye my trespas.   1080

Magna est misericordia tua!
   Wyth full feyth of foryewenes to þe, Lorde, I come.
WYSDOM. Vulnerasti cor meum, soror mea, sponsa,
   In vno ictu oculorum tuorum.

Ye haue wondyde my hert, syster, spowse dere,   1085
   In þe tweyn syghtys of yowr ey:
By þe recognycyon ye haue clere,
   Ande by þe hye lowe ye haue godly.
It perrysschyt my hert to here yow crye,
     Now ye haue forsake synne and be contryte.   1090
Ye were neuer so leve to me verelye.   f. 120
   Now be ye reformyde to yowr bewtys bryght.

1064 s.d. commynge in] *MS. F* commynge I   1073 tweyn] te *canc. before*
tweyn

Ande ther yowr fyve wyttys offendyde has,
    Ande to mak asythe be impotent,
My fyve wyttys, þat neuer dyde trespas,   1095
    Hathe made asythe to þe Father suffycyent.
Wyth my syght I se þe people vyolent,
    I herde hem vengeaunce onto me call,
I smelte þe stenche of caren here present,
    I tastyde þe drynke mengylde wyth gall,   1100

By towchynge I felte peyns smerte.
    My handys sprede abrode to halse þi swyre;
My fete naylyde to abyde wyth þe, swet herte;
    My hert clowyn for þi loue most dere;
    Myn hede bowhede down to kys þe here;   1105
    My body full of holys, as a dovehows.
In thys ye be reformyde, Soule, my plesere,
    Ande now ye be þe very temple of Jhesus.

Fyrst ye were reformyde by baptyme of ygnorans
    And clensyde from þe synnys orygynall,   1110
Ande now ye be reformyde by þe sakyrment of penance
    Ande clensyde from þe synnys actuall.
Now ye be fayrest, Crystys own specyall;
    Dysfygure yow neuer to þe lyknes of þe fende.
Now ye haue receyuyde þe crownnys victoryall   1115
    To regne in blys wythowtyn ende.

MYNDE. Haue mynde, Soule, wat Gode hath do,
    Reformyde yow in feyth veryly.   f. 120ᵛ
Nolite conformari huic seculo
    Sed reformamini in nouitate spiritus sensus vestri: 1120
    Conforme yow not to þis pompyus glory
    But reforme in gostly felynge.
Ye þat were dammyde by synn endelesly,
    Mercy hathe reformyde yow ande crownyde as a kynge.

WNDYRSTONDYNGE. Take vndyrstondynge, Soule, now ye   1125
    Wyth contynuall hope in Godys behest.

1094 be] *MS.* by   1099 smelte] *MS.* selte. *F* felte   1102 þi] *MS.*
F þe   1107 plesere] *MS. F* plesynge   1119 conformari] *MS. F* confirmare

O than gre sonow wysdam my roy xp̄o
howlw oyth̄e & ōth̄e oyedtuȝ
yotde yow yowōvo for grace pleyntuȝ
yᵈ yoff to mu on to puduyr
now w̄ sent powle wo may soy thuo
yᵗ be reformyde thorow feyth̄e in yᵉ yḡoft
No hano pede & a wyde botwyx gode & wo
Justificati ex fide pacem ḡo mȝ ad don
now to Salamonyo cōclusyow ȝ cum
timor dn̄ micō̄ sapiēcio

Dobio qui truũtȝ don
Oriēt² sol justrow
tho tyn sow of Neffufuo
Byth̄e yᵗ yo ow loyde ȳu
Xall spruge in hem yᵗ eyede ḡo mobueo
Rowe yo muut owȝ sowle penowo
Ju grace & vȳ to ofchew
Ande so to ende wᵗ p̄ffecion
that yᵉ doctyno of wysdom wo may sow
Sapiencia pr̄o eruũt ȝ for ḡo passeid

Wysdom ——
Skill v wytt ——
Scyuce ——
Vndeistodynge ——
Snowbr ——

                    O liber siq̄ cm wōst
                    hrueffut q̄ monotacȝ

Renouamini spiritu mentis vestre
  Et induite nouum hominem, qui secundúm Deum creatus est:
  Ye be reformyde in felynge, not only as a best,
    But also in þe ouer parte of yowr reasun,   1130
  Be wyche ye haue lyknes of Gode mest
    Ande of þat mercyfull very congnycyon.

WYLL. Now þe Soule yn charyte reformyde ys,
  Wyche charyte ys Gode verely.
Exspoliantem veterem hominem cum actibus suis: 1135
  Spoyll yow of yowr olde synnys and foly
    Ande be renuyde in Godys knowynge ageyn,
  That enduyde wyth grace so specyally,
    Conseruynge in peyn, euer in blys for to reyn.

ANIMA. Then wyth yow thre I may sey this   1140
  Of Owr Lorde, soueren person, Jhesus:
Suavis est Dominus vniuersis,
  Et miseraciones ejus super omnia opera ejus.
  O thou hye soueren Wysdam, my joy, Cristus,   f. 121
    Hewyn, erthe, and eche creature   1145
  Yelde yow reuerens, for grace pleyntuus
    Ye yeff to man, euer to induyr.

Now wyth Sent Powle we may sey thus
  þat be reformyde thorow feythe in Jhesum:
We haue peas and acorde betwyx Gode and ws,   1150
  Justificati ex fide pacem habemus ad Deum.
  Now to Salamonys conclusyon I com:
    Timor Domini inicium sapiencie.
  Vobis qui timetis Deum
    Orietur sol justicie: 1155

The tru son of ryghtusnes,
  Wyche þat ys Owr Lorde Jhesu,
Xall sprynge in hem þat drede hys meknes.
  Nowe ye mut euery soule renewe

1129 only *added above the line*   1134 Wyche] *MS. F* Wyth   1137 Godys]
MS. gode. *F* Gode   1140 this] *MS. F* thus   1143 opera] *MS.* oper
1149 Jhesum] Je *canc. before* Jhesum   1157 Owr] *MS.* on. *F* one

In grace, and vycys to eschew, 1160
 Ande so to ende wyth perfeccyon.
That þe doctryne of Wysdom we may sew,
 Sapiencia Patris, grawnt þat for hys passyon!
AMEN!

Wysdom.
Anima, Fyve Wyttys.
Mynde.
Wndyrstondynge.
Lucyfer.

MANKIND

THE NAMES OF THE PLAYERS

MERCY

MISCHIEF

NOUGHT, NEW GUISE, NOWADAYS

MANKIND

TITIVILLUS

The title, the list of persons, and the scene divisions are not in the MS.

SCENE I

MERCY. The very fownder and begynner of owr fyrst creacyon
    Amonge ws synfull wrechys he oweth to be magnyfyede,
þat for owr dysobedyenc he hade non indygnacyon
    To sende hys own son to be torn and crucyfyede.
    Owr obsequyouse seruyce to hym xulde be aplyede,   5
      Where he was lorde of all and made all thynge of nought,
    For þe synnfull synnere to hade hym revyuyde
    And for hys redempcyon sett hys own son at nought.

Yt may be seyde and veryfyede, mankynde was dere bought.
    By þe pytuose deth of Jhesu he hade hys remedye.   10
He was purgyde of hys defawte þat wrechydly hade wrought
    By hys gloryus passyon, þat blyssyde lauatorye.
    O souerence, I beseche yow yowr condycyons to rectyfye
      Ande wyth humylite and reuerence to haue a remocyon
    To þis blyssyde prynce þat owr nature doth gloryfye,   15
      þat ȝe may be partycypable of hys retribucyon.

I haue be þe very mene for yowr restytucyon.
    Mercy ys my name, þat mornyth for yowr offence.
Dyverte not yowrsylffe in tyme of temtacyon,
    þat ȝe may be acceptable to Gode at yowr goyng hence.   20
    þe grett mercy of Gode, þat ys of most preemmynence,
      Be medyacyon of Owr Lady þat ys euer habundante
    To þe synfull creature þat wyll repent hys neclygence.
      I prey Gode at yowr most nede þat mercy be yowr
        defendawnte.

In goode werkys I awyse yow, souerence, to be perseuerante   25
    To puryfye yowr sowlys, þat þei be not corupte;
For yowr gostly enmy wyll make hys avaunte,
    Yowr goode condycyons yf he may interrupte.

Editions collated are Manly (M), *Brandl* (B), *Furnivall* (F), *and Adams* (A).
   7 hade] *M* late. *B* haue   9 Yt] *MBF* þat   21 þe] To *canc. before* þe
22 medyacyon] medytacyon *changed to* medyacyon   27 avaunte] *MS. B*
avaunce. *MF* avaunte

O 3e souerens þat sytt and 3e brothern þat stonde ryght wppe,
   Pryke not yowr felycytes in thyngys transytorye.   30
Beholde not þe erth, but lyfte yowr ey wppe.
   Se how þe hede þe members dayly do magnyfye.
   Who ys þe hede forsoth I xall yow certyfye:
      I mene Owr Sauyowr, þat was lykynnyde to a lambe;
   Ande hys sayntys be þe members þat daylyhe doth satysfye f.122ᵛ
      Wyth þe precyose reuer þat runnyth from hys wombe.   36

Ther ys non such foode, be water nor by londe,
   So precyouse, so gloryouse, so nedefull to owr entent,
For yt hath dyssoluyde mankynde from þe bytter bonde
   Of þe mortall enmye, þat vemynousse serpente,   40
   From þe wyche Gode preserue yow all at þe last jugement!
      For sekyrly þer xall be a streyt examynacyon,
   The corn xall be sauyde, þe chaffe xall be brente.
   I besech yow hertyly, haue þis premedytacyon.

MYSCHEFFE. I beseche yow hertyly, leue yowr calcacyon.   45
Leue yowr chaffe, leue yowr corn, leue yowr dalyacyon.
Yowr wytt ys lytyll, yowr hede ys mekyll, 3e are full of predy-
     cacyon.
   But, ser, I prey þis questyon to claryfye:
Mysse-masche, dryff-draff,
Sume was corn and sume was chaffe,   50
My dame seyde my name was Raffe;
   Onschett yowr lokke and take an halpenye.

MERCY. Why com 3e hethyr, broþer? 3e were not dysyryde.
MYSCHEFF. For a wynter corn-threscher, ser, I haue hyryde,
Ande 3e sayde þe corn xulde be sauyde and þe chaff xulde be
     feryde,   55
   Ande he prouyth nay, as yt schewth be þis werse:
      'Corn seruit bredibus, chaffe horsibus, straw fyrybusque.'
Thys ys as moche to say, to yowr leude wndyrstondynge,
As þe corn xall serue to brede at þe nexte bakynge.

---

42 þer] MS. þe   streyt] MS. F strerat. M streat   48 prey] F prey [yow]
49 Mysse-masche, dryff-draff] MS. dryff draff mysse masche

'Chaff horsybus et reliqua,'   60
The chaff to horse xall be goode provente,
When a man ys forcolde þe straw may be brent,
    And so forth, et cetera.

MERCY. Avoyde, goode broþer! 3e ben culpable
To interrupte thus my talkyng delectable.   65
MYSCHEFF. Ser, I haue noþer horse nor sadyll,
    Therfor I may not ryde.
MERCY. Hye yow forth on fote, brother, in Godys name!
MYSCHEFF. I say, ser, I am cumme hedyr to make yow game.
3et bade 3e me not go out in þe Deullys name   70
    Ande I wyll abyde.

          *   *   *   *   *   *   *   *

NEW GYSE. Ande how, mynstrellys, pley þe comyn trace!   f. 123
    Ley on wyth þi ballys tyll hys bely breste!

NOUGHT. I putt case I breke my neke: how than?
NEW GYSE. I gyff no force, by Sent Tanne!   75
NOWADAYS. Leppe about lyuely! þou art a wyght man.
    Lett ws be mery wyll we be here!
NOUGHT. Xall I breke my neke to schew yow sporte?
NOWADAYS. Therfor euer be ware of þi reporte.
NOUGHT. I beschrew ye all! Her ys a schrewde sorte.   80
    Haue þeratt þen wyth a mery chere!
                          Her þei daunce. MERCY seyth:
Do wey, do wey þis reull, sers! do wey!
NOWADAYS. Do wey, goode Adam? do wey?
Thys ys no parte of þi pley.
    NOUGHT. 3ys, mary, I prey yow, for I loue not þis rewelynge. 85
Cum forth, goode fader, I yow prey!
Be a lytyll 3e may assay.
Anon of wyth yowr clothes, yf 3e wyll play.
    Go to! for I haue hade a praty scottlynge.

60 reliqua] MF reliquid. B reliquia   61 provente] MBF produce
70 not added above the line   name] man canc. before name   71 A speech-
heading Mercy follows. One leaf is missing, for the first leaf of the play is numbered
i in a contemporary hand and the next leaf is numbered iij   72 NEW GYSE MF
not in MS.   73 ballys] M bowys   81 þen] MBF þem   s.d. daunce]
MS. daunc   88 play] MS. MBF pray

MERCY. Nay, brother, I wyll not daunce.   90
NEW GYSE. Yf ʒe wyll, ser, my brother wyll make yow to prawnce.
NOWADAYS. Wyth all my herte, ser, yf I may yow avaunce.
 ʒe may assay be a lytyll trace.
NOUGHT. ʒe, ser, wyll ʒe do well,
Trace not wyth þem, be my cownsell,   95
For I haue tracyed sumwhat to fell;
 I tell yt ys a narow space.

But, ser, I trow of ws thre I herde yow speke.
NEW GYSE. Crystys curse hade þerfor, for I was in slepe.
NOWADAYS. And I hade þe cuppe in my honde, redy to goo to
      met.   100
 Therfor, ser, curtly, grett yow well.
MERCY. Few wordys, few and well sett!
NEW GYSE. Ser, yt ys þe new gyse and þe new jett.
Many wordys and schortely sett,
 Thys ys þe new gyse, euery-dele.   105

MERCY. Lady, helpe! how wrechys delyte in þer synfull weys!
NOWADAYS. Say not ageyn þe new gyse nowadays!   f. 123ᵛ
þou xall fynde ws schrewys at all assays.
 Be ware! ʒe may son lyke a bofett.
MERCY. He was well occupyede þat browte yow brethern.   110
NOUGHT. I harde yow call 'New Gyse, Nowadays, Nought,' all
      þes thre togethere.
Yf ʒe sey þat I lye, I xall make yow to slyther.
 Lo, take yow here a trepett!

MERCY. Say me yowr namys, I know yow not.
NEW GYSE. New Gyse, I.
            NOWADAYS. I, Nowadays.
                        NOUGHT. I, Nought.   115
MERCY. Be Jhesu Cryst þat me dere bowte
 ʒe betray many men.

96 fell] fylde *canc. before* fell. *BF* fylde fell   97 tell] *MF* tell [yow]
99 hade] *M* haue ʒe. *B* haue. *F* had [ʒ]e   100 And] *MS.* A   cuppe] *MS.*
BF cuppe redy. *M* cuppe   106 synfull] *MS. BF* sympull. *M* synnfull
107 not] *M* nought   108 schrewys] *MS.* schewys   109 lyke] k
canc. before lyke   110 brethern] *M* hether *or* brether   115 NOWADAYS,
NOUGHT *not in MS.*   117 men] a man *canc. before* men

NEW GYSE. Betray! nay, nay, ser, nay, nay!
We make them both fresch and gay.
But of yowr name, ser, I yow prey, 120
That we may yow ken.

MERCY. Mercy ys my name by denomynacyon.
I conseyue ʒe haue but a lytyll fauour in my communycacyon.
NEW GYSE. Ey, ey! yowr body ys full of Englysch Laten.
I am aferde yt wyll brest. 125
'Prauo te', quod þe bocher onto me
When I stale a leg a motun.
ʒe are a stronge cunnyng clerke.
NOWADAYS. I prey yow hertyly, worschyppull clerke,
To haue þis Englysch mad in Laten: 130

'I haue etun a dyschfull of curdys,
Ande I haue schetun yowr mowth full of turdys.'
Now opyn yowr sachell wyth Laten wordys
Ande sey me þis in clerycall manere!
Also I haue a wyf, her name ys Rachell; 135
Betuyx her and me was a gret batell;
Ande fayn of yow I wolde here tell
Who was þe most master.

NOUGHT. Thy wyf Rachell, I dare ley twenti lyse.
NOWADAYS. Who spake to þe, foll? þou art not wyse! 140
Go and do þat longyth to þin offyce:
Osculare fundamentum!
NOUGHT. Lo, master, lo, here ys a pardon bely-mett.
Yt ys grawntyde of Pope Pokett,
Yf ʒe wyll putt yowr nose in hys wyffys sokett, 145
ʒe xall haue forty days of pardon.

MERCY. Thys ydyll language ʒe xall repent.
Out of þis place I wolde ʒe went.
NEW GYSE. Goo we hens all thre wyth on assent. f. 124
My fadyr ys yrke of owr eloquence. 150

122 by] and my *canc.*, by *above line*   123 fauour] *M* fors. *BF* faus
125–8 *added in margin, followed by* I prey cetera, *indicating that these lines belong
before 129.* Nowadays *is inserted in the left margin before 129*   126 Prauo
te] *M* I rausch. *B* I ranoch. *F* It ram be   130 Laten] *MS.* la... *This line
is added in margin before 125–8. MBFA omit all five lines from the text*

þerfor I wyll no lenger tary.
Gode brynge yow, master, and blyssyde Mary
To þe number of þe demonycall frayry!

NOWADAYS. Cum wynde, cum reyn,
Thow I cumme neuer ageyn!   155
þe Deull put out both yowr eyn!
  Felouse, go we hens tyght.
NOUGHT. Go we hens, a deull wey!
Here ys þe dore, her ys þe wey.
Farwell, jentyll Jaffrey,   160
  I prey Gode gyf yow goode nyght!
                                    Exiant simul. Cantent

MERCY. Thankyde be Gode, we haue a fayer dylyuerance
  Of þes thre onthryfty gestys.
They know full lytyll what ys þer ordynance.
  I preue by reson þei be wers þen bestys: 165

A best doth after hys naturall instytucyon;
  3e may conseyue by there dysporte and behauour,
Þer joy ande delyte ys in derysyon
  Of her owyn Cryste to hys dyshonur.

Thys condycyon of leuyng, yt ys prejudycyall;   170
  Be ware þerof, yt ys wers þan ony felony or treson.
How may yt be excusyde befor þe Justyce of all
  When for euery ydyll worde we must 3elde a reson?

They haue grett ease, þerfor þei wyll take no thought.
  But how þen when þe angell of hewyn xall blow þe trumpe 175
Ande sey to þe transgressors þat wykkydly hath wrought,
  'Cum forth onto yowr Juge and 3elde yowr acownte'?

Then xall I, Mercy, begyn sore to wepe;
  Noþer comfort nor cownsell þer xall non be hade;
But such as þei haue sowyn, such xall þei repe.   180
  þei be wanton now, but þen xall þei be sade.

154 *another hand adds* Novadeis *in margin*   161 s.d. simul] *F* silentio.
MB omit   Cantent *added in different ink*

The goode new gyse nowadays I wyll not dysalow.

I dyscomende þe vycyouse gyse; I prey haue me excusyde,
I nede not to speke of yt, yowr reson wyll tell it yow.

Take þat ys to be takyn and leue þat ys to be refusyde.   185

MANKYNDE. Of þe erth and of þe cley we haue owr propagacyon.

By þc prouydens of Gode þus be we deryvatt,
To whos mercy I recomende þis holl congrygacyon:

I hope onto hys blysse ye be all predestynatt.   f. 124ᵛ

Euery man for hys degre I trust xall be partycypatt,   190

Yf we wyll mortyfye owr carnall condycyon
Ande owr voluntarye dysyres, þat euer be pervercyonatt,

To renunce þem and yelde ws wnder Godys provycyon.

My name ys Mankynde. I haue my composycyon

Of a body and of a soull, of condycyon contrarye.   195
Betwyx þem tweyn ys a grett dyvisyon;

He þat xulde be subjecte, now he hath þe victory.

Thys ys to me a lamentable story

To se my flesch of my soull to haue gouernance.
Wher þe goodewyff ys master, þe goodeman may be sory.   200

I may both syth and sobbe, þis ys a pytuose remembrance.

O thou my soull, so sotyll in thy substance,
Alasse, what was þi fortune and þi chaunce

To be assocyat wyth my flesch, þat stynkyng dungehyll?

Lady, helpe! Souerens, yt doth my soull myche yll   205

To se þe flesch prosperouse and þe soull trodyn wnder fote.
I xall go to yondyr man and asay hym I wyll.

I trust of gostly solace he wyll be my bote.

All heyll, semely father! 3e be welcom to þis house.

Of þe very wysdam 3e haue partycypacyon.   210
My body wyth my soull ys euer querulose.

I prey yow, for sent charyte, of yowr supportacyon.

193 þem] *MBF* þes   196 þem] *MBF* þe   201–2 *added in margin.*
MBFA omit from the text   206 trodyn] drod *canc. before* trodyn

I beseche yow hertyly of yowr gostly comforte.
  I am onstedfast in lywynge; my name ys Mankynde.
My gostly enmy þe Deull wyll haue a grett dysporte   215
  In synfull gydynge yf he may se me ende.

MERCY. Cryst sende yow goode comforte! 3e be welcum, my
    frende.
  Stonde wppe on yowr fete, I prey yow aryse.
My name ys Mercy; 3e be to me full hende.
  To eschew vyce I wyll yow avyse.   220

MANKYNDE. O Mercy, of all grace and vertu 3e are þe well,
  I haue herde tell of ryght worschyppfull clerkys.
3e be aproxymatt to Gode and nere of hys consell.
  He hat instytut you aboue all hys werkys.

O, yowr louely wordys to my soull are swetere þen hony.   225
  MERCY. The temptacyon of þe flesch 3e must resyst lyke a man,
For þer ys euer a batell betwyx þe soull and þe body:
  'Vita hominis est milicia super terram.'

Oppresse yowr gostly enmy and be Crystys own knyght.
  Be neuer a cowarde ageyn yowr aduersary.   f. 125
Yf 3e wyll be crownyde, 3e must nedys fyght.   231
  Intende well and Gode wyll be yow adjutory.

Remember, my frende, þe tyme of contynuance.
  So helpe me Gode, yt ys but a chery tyme.
Spende yt well; serue Gode wyth hertys affyance.   235
  Dystempure not yowr brayn wyth goode ale nor wyth wyn.

Mesure ys tresure. Y forbyde yow not þe vse.
  Mesure yowrsylf euer; be ware of excesse.
þe superfluouse gyse I wyll þat 3e refuse,
  When nature ys suffysyde, anon þat 3e sese.   240

Yf a man haue an hors and kepe hym not to hye,
  He may then reull hym at hys own dysyere.
Yf he be fede ouerwell he wyll dysobey
  Ande in happe cast his master in þe myre.

216 synfull] MS. sympull but yn synfull is an early correction on f. 125
220 I changed to To   221 and vertu added above the line   225 wordys]
MBF workes   228 milicia] MS. nnilicia   238 line added in margin
C 4343   M

NEW GYSE. ʒe sey trew, ser, ʒe are no faytour.   245
I haue fede my wyff so well tyll sche ys my master.
I haue a grett wonde on my hede, lo! and þeron leyth a playster,
    Ande anoþer þer I pysse my peson.
Ande my wyf were yowr hors, sche wolde yow all to-banne.
ʒe fede yowr hors in mesure, ʒe are a wyse man.   250
I trow, and ʒe were þe kyngys palfreyman,
    A goode horse xulde be gesunne.

MANKYNDE. Wher spekys þis felow? Wyll he not com nere?
    MERCY. All to son, my brother, I fere me, for yow.
He was here ryght now, by hym þat bowte me dere,   255
    Wyth oþer of hys felouse; þei kan moche sorow.

They wyll be here ryght son, yf I owt departe.
    Thynke on my doctryne; yt xall be yowr defence.
Lerne wyll I am here, sett my wordys in herte.
    Wythin a schorte space I must nedys hens.   260

NOWADAYS. þe sonner þe leuer, and yt be ewyn anon!
I trow yowr name ys Do Lytyll, ʒe be so long fro hom.
Yf ʒe wolde go hens, we xall cum euerychon,
    Mo þen a goode sorte.
ʒe haue leve, I dare well say.   265
When ʒe wyll, go forth yowr wey.
Men haue lytyll deynte of yowr pley
    Because ʒe make no sporte.

NOUGHT. Yowr potage xall be forcolde, ser; when wyll ʒe go dyn?
I haue sen a man lost twenti noblys in as lytyll tyme;   270
ʒet yt was not I, be Sent Qwyntyn,
    For I was neuer worth a pottfull a wortys sythyn I was born.
My name ys Nought. I loue well to make mery.   f. 125ᵛ
I haue be sethen wyth þe comyn tapster of Bury
And pleyde so longe þe foll þat I am ewyn wery.   275
    ʒyt xall I be þer ageyn to-morn.

249 to-banne] *M ?* to-lam. *BF* to-samne   252 gesunne] *MS. BF*
gesumme. *M* geson   255 hym] us *canc. before* hym   261 *another hand
adds* Novadays *in margin*   266 When] *M* to them. *BF* to hem   271 Qwyn-
tyn] *M* Gis, certeyn. *B* Qwentyne. *F* Qisyntyn   275 And] *MS.* A. *MBF* I
wery] *MS. BF* wery wery. *M* very wery   276 to-morn] *MS. BF* to morow.
M to-morne

MERCY. I haue moche care for yow, my own frende.
Yowr enmys wyll be here anon, þei make þer avaunte.
Thynke well in yowr hert, yowr name ys Mankynde;
Be not wnkynde to Gode, I prey yow be hys seruante.　　　280

Be stedefast in condycyon; se 3e be not varyant.
Lose not thorow foly þat ys bowte so dere.
Gode wyll proue yow son; ande yf þat 3e be constant,
Of hys blysse perpetuall 3e xall be partener.

3e may not haue yowr intent at yowr fyrst dysyere.　　　285
Se þe grett pacyence of Job in tribulacyon;
Lyke as þe smyth trieth ern in þe feere,
So was he triede by Godys vysytacyon.

He was of yowr nature and of yowr fragylyte;
Folow þe steppys of hym, my own swete son,　　　290
Ande sey as he seyde in yowr trobyll and aduersyte:
'Dominus dedit, Dominus abstulit; sicut sibi placuit, ita factum
　est; nomen Domini benedictum!'

Moreouer, in specyall I gyue yow in charge,
Be ware of New Gyse, Nowadays, and Nought.
Nyse in þer aray, in language þei be large;　　　295
To peruerte yowr condycyons all þe menys xall be sowte.

Gode son, intromytt not yowrsylff in þer cumpeny.
þei harde not a masse þis twelmonyth, I dare well say.
Gyff them non audyence; þei wyll tell yow many a lye.
Do truly yowr labure and kepe yowr halyday.　　　300

Be ware of Tytivillus, for he lesyth no wey,
þat goth invysybull and wyll not be sen.
He wyll ronde in yowr ere and cast a nett befor yowr ey.
He ys worst of þem all; Gode lett hym neuer then!

278 make] MBF made　　282 bowte] F sowte　　286 in] MS. BF and.
M in　　292 ita factum est added in different hand in margin opposite 290 to
replace ita cancelled above placuit　　296 yowr] MS. þer　þe] MS. þer
297 intromytt not yowrsylff] intyrmyse yowr sylff not changed to intromytt not
yowr sylff　298 þis] MS. þi　301 for] MS. fo　303 ey] MS. BF eyn.
M ey

Yf ȝe dysples Gode, aske mercy anon,   305
  Ellys Myscheff wyll be redy to brace yow in hys brydyll.
Kysse me now, my dere darlynge. Gode schelde yow from yowr
    fon!
  Do truly yowr labure and be neuer ydyll.
The blyssynge of Gode be wyth yow and wyth all þes worschyp-
    pull men!
MANKYNDE. Amen, for sent charyte, amen!   310

Now blyssyde be Jhesu! my soull ys well sacyatt
  Wyth þe mellyfluose doctryne of þis worschyppfull man.
The rebellyn of my flesch now yt ys superatt,   f. 126
  Thankynge be Gode of þe commynge þat I kam.

Her wyll I sytt and tytyll in þis papyr   315
  The incomparable astat of my promycyon.
Worschypfull souerence, I haue wretyn here
  The gloryuse remembrance of my nobyll condycyon.

To haue remos and memory of mysylff þus wretyn yt ys,
  To defende me from all superstycyus charmys: 320
'Memento, homo, quod cinis es et in cinerem reuerteris.'
  Lo, I ber on my bryst þe bagge of myn armys.

NEW GYSE. The wether ys colde, Gode sende ws goode ferys!
'Cum sancto sanctus eris et cum peruerso peruerteris.'
'Ecce quam bonum et quam jocundum,' quod þe Deull to þe
    frerys,   325
  'Habitare fratres in vnum.'
MANKYNDE. I her a felow speke; wyth hym I wyll not mell.
Thys erth wyth my spade I xall assay to delffe.
To eschew ydullnes, I do yt myn own selffe.
  I prey Gode sende yt hys fusyon!   330

NOWADAYS. Make rom, sers, for we haue be longe!
We wyll cum gyf yow a Crystemes songe.

NOUGHT. Now I prey all þe yemandry þat ys here
To synge wyth ws wyth a mery chere:

---

307 schelde] *MS.* schede   314 Thankynge be] *M* Thankyd be. *F*
Thankynge be [to]   commynge þat I kam] *MBF* connynge þat I kan
319 remos] *MBF* remors   323 goode] god *canc. before* goode   327 hym]
hym hym *changed to* hym   328 erth] erth erth *changed to* erth

Yt ys wretyn wyth a coll, yt ys wretyn wyth a cole,   335
NEW GYSE and NOWADAYS. Yt ys wretyn wyth a colle, yt ys
 wretyn wyth a colle,
NOUGHT. He þat schytyth wyth hys hoyll, he þat schytyth wyth
 hys hoyll,
NEW GYSE, NOWADAYS. He þat schytyth wyth hys hoyll, he þat
 schytyth with his hoyll,
NOUGHT. But he wyppe hys ars clen, but he wyppe hys ars clen,
NEW GYSE, NOWADAYS. But he wype hys ars clen, but he wype
 his ars clen,   340
NOUGHT. On hys breche yt xall be sen, on hys breche yt xall be
 sen.
NEW GYSE, NOWADAYS. On hys breche yt xall be sen, on hys
 breche yt xall be sen.
Cantant OMNES. Hoylyke, holyke, holyke! holyke, holyke, holyke!

NEW GYSE. Ey, Mankynde, Gode spede yow wyth yowr spade!
I xall tell yow of a maryage: 345
I wolde yowr mowth and hys ars þat þis made
 Wer maryede junctly together.
MANKYNDE. Hey yow hens, felouse, wyth bredynge.
Leue yowr derysyon and yowr japyng.
I must nedys labure, yt ys my lyvynge.   350
 NOWADAYS. What, ser, we cam but lat hethyr.   f. 126ᵛ

Xall all þis corn grow here
þat ȝe xall haue þe nexte ȝer?
Yf yt be so, corn hade nede be dere,
 Ellys ȝe xall haue a pore lyffe.   355
NOUGHT. Alasse, goode fadere, þis labor fretyth yow to þe bon.
But for yowr croppe I take grett mone.
Ȝe xall neuer spende yt alonne;
 I xall assay to geett yow a wyffe.

How many acres suppose ȝe here by estymacyon?   360
NEW GYSE. Ey, how ȝe turne þe erth wppe and down!
I haue be in my days in many goode town
 Ȝett saw I neuer such another tyllynge.

---

336 wyth a colle] *MS.* cetera *and so for other words repeated.* M *omits 336–42,*
A *337–42*. 346 þis] *MS.* þs *or* ys

MANKYNDE. Why stonde ye ydyll? Yt ys pety þat ʒe were born!
NOWADAYS. We xall bargen wyth yow and noþer moke nor
    scorne.   365
Take a goode carte in herwest and lode yt wyth yowr corne,
    Ande what xall we gyf yow for þe levynge?

NOUGHT. He ys a goode starke laburrer, he wolde fayn do well.
He hath mett wyth þe goode man Mercy in a schroude sell.
For all þis he may haue many a hungry mele.   370
    Ʒyt woll ʒe se he ys polytyke.
Here xall be goode corn, he may not mysse yt;
Yf he wyll haue reyn he may ouerpysse yt;
Ande yf he wyll haue compasse he may ouerblysse yt
    A lytyll wyth hys ars lyke.   375

MANKYNDE. Go and do yowr labur! Gode lett yow neuer the!
Or wyth my spade I xall yow dynge, by þe Holy Trinyte!
Haue ʒe non other man to moke, but euer me?
    Ʒe wolde haue me of yowr sett?
Hye yow forth lyuely, for hens I wyll yow dryffe.   380
NEW GYSE. Alas, my jewellys! I xall be schent of my wyff!
NOWADAYS. Alasse! and I am lyke neuer for to thryue,
    I haue such a buffett.

MANKYNDE. Hens I sey, New Gyse, Nowadays, and Nowte!
Yt was seyde beforn, all þe menys xuld be sought   385
To perverte my condycyons and brynge me to nought.
    Hens, thevys! Ʒe haue made many a lesynge.
NOUGHT. Marryde I was for colde, but now am I warme.   f. 127
Ʒe are ewyll avysyde, ser, for ʒe haue don harme.
By cokkys body sakyrde, I haue such a peyn in my arme   390
    I may not chonge a man a ferthynge.

MANKYNDE. Now I thanke Gode, knelynge on my kne.
Blyssyde be hys name! he ys of hye degre.
By þe subsyde of hys grace þat he hath sente me
    Thre of myn enmys I haue putt to flyght.   395
    Ʒyt þis instrument, souerens, ys not made to defende.
Dauide seyth, 'Nec in hasta nec in gladio saluat Dominus.'

---

374 compasse] MB compost. F compasste   385 xuld] MS. BF xull. M
xulde. A xulld   394 þe subsyde] M this spade. B þe fisyke. F þe syde or
ayde   397 hasta] MS. hastu

NOUGHT. No, mary, I beschrew yow, yt ys in spadibus.
Therfor Crystys curse cum on yowr hedybus
   To sende yow lesse myght!   Exiant   400

MANKYNDE. I promytt yow þes felouse wyll no more cum here,
For summe of þem, certenly, were summewhat to nere.
My fadyr Mercy avysyde me to be of a goode chere
   Ande agayn my enmys manly for to fyght.

I xall convycte þem, I hope, euerychon.   405
3et I say amysse, I do yt not alon.
Wyth þe helpe of þe grace of Gode I resyst my fon
   Ande þer malycyuse herte.
Wyth my spade I wyll departe, my worschyppull souerence,
Ande lyue euer wyth labure to corecte my insolence.   410
I xall go fett corn for my londe; I prey yow of pacyence;
   Ryght son I xall reverte.

SCENE II

MYSCHEFF. Alas, alasse, þat euer I was wrought!
Alasse þe whyll, I wers þen nought!
Sythyn I was here, by hym þat me bought,   415
   I am wtterly ondon!
I, Myscheff, was here at þe begynnynge of þe game
Ande arguyde wyth Mercy, Gode gyff hym schame!
He hath taught Mankynde, wyll I haue be vane,
   To fyght manly ageyn hys fon.   420

For wyth hys spade, þat was hys wepyn,
Neu Gyse, Nowadays, Nought hath all to-beton.
I haue grett pyte to se þem wepyn.
   Wyll 3e lyst? I here þem crye.   Clamant
Alasse, alasse! cum hether, I xall be yowr borow.   425
Alac, alac! ven, ven! cum hethere wyth sorowe!   f. 127ᵛ
Pesse, fayer babys, 3e xall haue a nappyll to-morow!
   Why grete 3e so, why?

404 Ande] Ad *canc. before* Ande   414 I] *MF* I [am]   422 hath] *F*
hath [he]

NEU GYSE. Alasse, master, alasse, my privyte!
MYSCHEFF. A, wher? alake! fayer babe, ba me!   430
Abyde! to son I xall yt se.
   NOWADAYS. Here, here, se my hede, goode master!
MYSCHEFF. Lady, helpe! sely darlynge, ven, ven!
I xall helpe þe of þi peyn;
I xall smytt of þi hede and sett yt on agayn.   435
   NOUGHT. By owr Lady, ser, a fayer playster!

Wyll ȝe of wyth hys hede! Yt ys a schreude charme!
As for me, I haue non harme.
I were loth to forbere myn arme.
   ȝe pley in nomine patris, choppe!   440
NEU GYSE. ȝe xall not choppe my jewellys, and I may.
NOWADAYS. ȝe, Cristys crose, wyll ȝe smyght my hede awey?
Ther wer on and on! Oute! ȝe xall not assay.
   I myght well be callyde a foppe.

MYSCHEFF. I kan choppe yt of and make yt agayn.   445
NEW GYSE. I hade a schreude recumbentibus but I fele no peyn.
NOWADAYS. Ande my hede ys all saue and holl agayn.
   Now towchynge þe mater of Mankynde,
Lett ws haue an interleccyon, sythen ȝe be cum hethere.
   Yt were goode to haue an ende.   450

MYSCHEFF. How, how, a mynstrell! Know ȝe ony out?
NOUGHT. I kan pype in a Walsyngham wystyll, I, Nought,
   Nought.
MYSCHEFF. Blow apase, and þou xall bryng hym in wyth a flewte.
   TYTIVILLUS. I com wyth my leggys wnder me.
MYSCHEFF. How, Neu Gyse, Nowadays, herke or I goo!   455
When owr hedys wer togethere I spake of si dedero.
NEU GYSE. ȝe, go þi wey! We xall gaþer mony onto,   f. 128
   Ellys þer xall no man hym se.

Now gostly to owr purpos, worschypfull souerence,
We intende to gather mony, yf yt plesse yowr neclygence,   460
For a man wyth a hede þat ys of grett omnipotens.

442 Cristys] *MS.* crastys   443 Ther wer on and on! Oute!] *MS.* Ther
wher on & on oute. *M* Ther wer on anon! Oute! *B* Ther, wher one but one
outh. *F* Ther, wher, on & on. Oute!   453 MYSCHEFF] *MS.* Myschef . . .
457 ȝe] *MS. F* ȝo. *B* ȝe *or* Go. *M* ȝe   461 þat ys] *MS. M* þat. *BF* þat ys

NOWADAYS. Kepe yowr tayll, in goodnes I prey yow, goode broþer!

He ys a worschyppull man, sers, sauyng yowr reuerens.

He louyth no grotys, nor pens of to pens.

Gyf ws rede reyallys yf ȝe wyll se hys abhomynabull presens.   465

NEW GYSE. Not so! ȝe þat mow not pay þe ton, pay þe toþer.

At þe goodeman of þis house fyrst we wyll assay.

Gode blysse yow, master! ȝe say as yll, ȝet ȝe wyll not sey nay.

Lett ws go by and by and do þem pay.

ȝe pay all alyke; well mut ȝe fare!   470

NOUGHT. I sey, New Gyse, Nowadays: 'Estis vos pecuniatus?'

I haue cryede a fayer wyll, I beschrew yowr patus!

NOWADAYS. Ita vere, magister. Cumme forth now yowr gatus!

He ys a goodly man, sers; make space and be ware!

TITIVILLUS. Ego sum dominancium dominus and my name ys Titivillus.   475

ȝe þat haue goode hors, to yow I sey caueatis!

Here ys an abyll felyschyppe to tryse hem out at yowr gatys.

Loquitur ad NEW GYSE:

Ego probo sic: ser New Gys, lende me a peny!

NEW GYSE. I haue a grett purse, ser, but I haue no monay.

By þe masse, I fayll to farthyngys of an halpeny;   480

ȝyt hade I ten pound þis nyght þat was.

TITYUILLUS loquitur ad NOWADAYS. What ys in þi purse? þou art a stout felow.

NOWADAYS. þe Deull haue the qwytt! I am a clen jentyllman.

I prey Gode I be neuer wers storyde þen I am.

Yt xall be otherwyse, I hope, or þis nyght passe.   485

TYTIVILLUS loquitur ad NOUGHT. Herke now! I say þou hast many a peny.

NOUGHT. Non nobis, domine, non nobis, by Sent Deny!

þe Deull may daunce in my purse for ony peny;

Yt ys as clen as a byrdys ars.

464 of] *MBF* or   477 hem] *MS*. hym   481 ten pound] *MS*. x^{li}
482 þi] þis *canc. before* þi   felow] *MB ?* man   483 the qwytt] *A ?* [the]
qwytt. *MS. B* qwyll. *MF* [the] qwyll   487 Non] *MS*. No

TITIVILLUS. Now I say ʒet ageyn, caueatis!   490
Her ys an abyll felyschyppe to tryse hem out of yowr gatys.

Now I sey, New Gyse, Nowadays, and Nought,
Go and serche þe contre, anon yt be sowʒte,
Summe here, summe þer; what yf ʒe may cache owʒte?

Yf ʒe fayll of hors, take what ʒe may ellys.   495
NEW GYSE. Then speke to Mankynde for þe recumbentibus of
     my jewellys.
NOWADAYS. Remember my brokyn hede in þe worschyppe   f. 128ᵛ
     of þe fyve vowellys.
     NOUGHT. Ʒe, goode ser, and þe sytyca in my arme.
TITYUILLUS. I know full well what Mankynde dyde to yow.
Myschyff hat informyde of all þe matere thorow.   500
I xall venge yowr quarell, I make Gode avow.
     Forth, and espye were ʒe may do harme.
     Take William Fyde, yf ʒe wyll haue ony mo.
     I sey, New Gyse, wethere art þou avysyde to go?

NEW GYSE. Fyrst I xall begyn at Master Huntyngton of Saus-
     ton,   505
Fro thens I xall go to Wylliam Thurlay of Hauston,
Ande so forth to Pycharde of Trumpyngton.
     I wyll kepe me to þes thre.
NOWADAYS. I xall goo to Wyllyham Baker of Waltom,
To Rycherde Bollman of Gayton;   510
I xall spare Master Woode of Fullburn,
     He ys a noli me tangere.

NOUGHT. I xall goo to Wyllyam Patryke of Massyngham,
I xall spare Master Alyngton of Botysam
Ande Hamonde of Soffeham,   515
     For drede of in manus tuas qweke.
Felous, cum forth, and go we hens togethyr.

---

490 *The scribe repeated and then crossed out* Now I sey ageyn caueatis
493 yt] *MF* þat [yt]. *B* þat   497 fyve vowellys] *MS. F* .v. vowellys. *M*
vij (*or* xx) devellys. *B* dewellys   500 informyde] *BF* informyde [me]
501 make] *F* made   503 William] *MS.* W. *F* William. *MB* w[ith yow]
505 Master] *MS.* M.   512 ys a] va. *canc.*, ys a *above line*   516–17 *lines
transposed in MS. and F, corrected by M and B*

NEU GYSE. Syth we xall go, lett ws be well ware wethere.
If we may be take, we com no more hethyr.
   Lett ws con well owr neke-verse, þat we haue not a cheke. 520

TITYVILLUS. Goo yowr wey, a deull wey, go yowr wey all!
I blysse yow wyth my lyfte honde: foull yow befall!
Com agayn, I werne, as son as I yow call,
   And brynge yowr avantage into þis place.
To speke wyth Mankynde I wyll tary here þis tyde   525
Ande assay hys goode purpose for to sett asyde.
þe goode man Mercy xall no lenger be hys gyde.
   I xall make hym to dawnce anoþer trace.

Euer I go invysybull, yt ys my jett,
Ande befor hys ey þus I wyll hange my nett   530
To blench hys syght; I hope to haue hys fote-mett.
   To yrke hym of hys labur I xall make a frame.
Thys borde xall be hyde wnder þe erth preuely;
Hys spade xall enter, I hope, onredyly;
Be þen he hath assayde, he xall be very angry   535
   Ande lose hys pacyens, peyn of schame.
I xall menge hys corne wyth drawke and wyth durnell;
Yt xall not be lyke to sow nor to sell.
Yondyr he commyth; I prey of cownsell.
   He xall wene grace were wane.   540

MANKYND. Now Gode of hys mercy sende ws of hys sonde! f. 129
I haue brought sede here to sow wyth my londe.
Qwyll I ouerdylew yt, here yt xall stonde.
   In nomine Patris et Filii et Spiritus Sancti now I wyll begyn.
Thys londe ys so harde yt makyth wnlusty and yrke.   545
I xall sow my corn at wynter and lett Gode werke.
Alasse, my corn ys lost! here ys a foull werke!
   I se well by tyllynge lytyll xall I wyn.

---

518 be well ware] *MS. F* be well ware &. *MB* se well ware &   520 con]
MS. com. *MBF* con   þat *added later*   522 lyfte] ryght *canc. before* lyfte
524 And] *MS.* A   525 tary] be *canc. before* tary   534 onredyly] *F* ouer
redyly   537 durnell] *B ?* darnell   540 wane] *MS.* wane *canc. before*
cum. *MBF* wane   543 Qwyll I ouerdylew yt] *M* I wyll ron dylewer,
that. *B* I wyll rone, dylewer yt. *F* qwyll I ouer dylew yt

Here I gyff wppe my spade for now and for euer.

                Here TITIVILLUS goth out wyth þe spade

To occupye my body I wyll not put me in deuer.   550
I wyll here my ewynsonge here or I dysseuer.
   Thys place I assyng as for my kyrke.
Here in my kerkc I kňell on my kneys.
Pater noster qui es in celis.

TYTYVILLUS. I promes yow I haue no lede on my helys.   555
   I am here ageyn to make þis felow yrke.

Qwyst! pesse! I xall go to hys ere and tytyll þerin.
A schorte preyere thyrlyth hewyn; of þi preyere blyn.
þou art holyer þen euer was ony of þi kyn.
   Aryse and avent þe! nature compellys.   560

MANKYND. I wyll into þi ȝerde, souerens, and cum ageyn son.
For drede of þe colyke and eke of þe ston
I wyll go do þat nedys must be don.
   My bedys xall be here for whosummeuer wyll ellys.   Exiat

TITYUILLUS. Mankynde was besy in hys prayere, ȝet I dyde hym
    aryse.   565
He ys conveyde, be Cryst, from hys dyvyn seruyce.
Wethere ys he, trow ȝe? Iwysse I am wonder wyse;
   I haue sent hym forth to schyte lesynges.
Yff ȝe haue ony syluer, in happe pure brasse,
Take a lytyll powder of Parysch and cast ouer hys face,   570
Ande ewyn in þe howll-flyght let hym passe.
   Titivillus kan lerne yow many praty thyngys.

I trow Mankynde wyll cum ageyn son,
Or ellys I fere me ewynsonge wyll be don.
Hys bedys xall be trysyde asyde, and þat anon.   575
   Ȝe xall a goode sport yf ȝe wyll abyde.
Mankynde cummyth ageyn, well fare he!
I xall answere hym ad omnia quare.
Ther xall be sett abroche a clerycall mater.
   I hope of hys purpose to sett hym asyde.   580

---

555 TYTYVILLUS] Tytyvillus *and in margin farther down* nev gyse   561 þi]
MF þi[s]. *B* þe   562 *The scribe first wrote and then crossed out line* 564
564 ellys] *MS.* cumme *but* ellys *when line first written at* 562   565 TITYUIL-
LUS] *MS.* Tityui . . . nevgyse   576 a] *MF* [se] a   578 I] A *changed to* I

MANKYND. Ewynsong hath be in þe saynge, I trow, a fayer wyll.
I am yrke of yt; yt ys to longe be on myle.
Do wey! I wyll no more so oft ouer þe chyrche-style.
    Be as be may, I xall do anoþer.
Of labure and preyer, I am nere yrke of both;   585
I wyll no more of yt, thow Mercy be wroth.
My hede ys very heuy, I tell yow forsoth.
    I xall slepe full my bely and he wore my broþer.

TITYVILLUS. Ande euer ʒe dyde, for me kepe now yowr   f. 129ᵛ
    sylence.
Not a worde, I charge yow, peyn of forty pens.   590
A praty game xall be scheude yow or ʒe go hens.
    ʒe may here hym snore; he ys sade aslepe.
Qwyst! pesse! þe Deull ys dede! I xall goo ronde in hys ere.
Alasse, Mankynde, alasse! Mercy stown a mere!
He ys runn away fro hys master, þer wot no man where;   595
    Moreouer, he stale both a hors and a nete.

But ʒet I herde sey he brake hys neke as he rode in Fraunce;
But I thynke he rydyth on þe galouse, to lern for to daunce,
Bycause of hys theft, þat ys hys gouernance.
    Trust no more on hym, he ys a marryde man.   600
Mekyll sorow wyth þi spade beforn þou hast wrought.
Aryse and aske mercy of Neu Gyse, Nowadays, and Nought.
þei cun avyse þe for þe best; lett þer goode wyll be sought.
    Ande þi own wyff brethell, and take þe a lemman.

Farwell, euerychon! for I haue don my game,   605
For I haue brought Mankynde to myscheff and to schame.

MANKYND. Whope who! Mercy hath brokyn hys neke-kycher,
    avows,
Or he hangyth by þe neke hye wppon þe gallouse.
Adew, fayer masters! I wyll hast me to þe ale-house
    Ande speke wyth New Gyse, Nowadays and Nought   610

583 ouer] MF on. B one   584–6 added at foot of the leaf   589 TITY-
VILLUS] MS. Tityvillus nevgyse   593 ys] yd canc. before ys   594 stown]
B has stolen   597 as] MS. ab   598 on] MBF ouer   galouse] galouf
changed to galouse   603 cun] MBF cum   604 leve added in margin
in another hand   brethell] F [be] brethell or ? be left   605 Farwell] MS.
For well   609 masters] MBF mastere

And geett me a lemman wyth a smattrynge face.
NEW GYSE. Make space, for cokkys body sakyrde, make space!
A ha! well ouerron! Gode gyff hym ewyll grace!
  We were nere Sent Patrykes wey, by hym þat me bought.

I was twychyde by þe neke; þe game was begunne.   615
A grace was, þe halter brast asonder: ecce signum!
The halff ys abowte my neke; we hade a nere rune!
  'Beware,' quod þe goodewyff when sche smot of here
    husbondys hede, 'beware!'
Myscheff ys a convicte, for he coude hys neke-verse.
My body gaff a swynge when I hynge wppon þe casse.   620
Alasse, he wyll hange such a lyghly man, and a fers,
  For stelynge of an horse, I prey Gode gyf hym care!

Do wey þis halter! What deull doth Mankynde here, wyth sorow!
Alasse, how my neke ys sore, I make avowe!
MANKYND. 3e be welcom, Neu Gyse! Ser, what chere wyth yow?
  NEW GYSE. Well ser, I haue no cause to morn.   626
MANKYND. What was þat abowte yowr neke, so Gode yow
  amende?
NEU GYSE. In feyth, Sent Audrys holy bende.   f. 130
I haue a lytyll dyshes, as yt plesse Gode to sende,
  Wyth a runnynge ryngeworme.   630

NOWADAYS. Stonde arom, I prey þe, broþer myn!
I haue laburryde all þis nyght; wen xall we go dyn?
A chyrche her besyde xall pay for ale, brede, and wyn.
  Lo, here ys stoff wyll serue.
NEU GYSE. Now by þe holy Mary, þou art better marchande
  þen I!   635
NOUGHT. Avante, knawys, lett me go by!
  I kan not geet and I xulde sterue.

MYSCHEFF. Here cummyth a man of armys! Why stonde 3e so styll?
Of murder and manslawter I haue my bely-fyll.
NOWADAYS. What, Myscheff, haue 3e ben in presun? And yt
  be yowr wyll,   640
  Me semyth 3e haue scoryde a peyr of fetters.

611 And] *MS.* A   613 well ouerron] *MF* well! on! ron! *B* well one, rone
621 he] *B ?* ho   lyghly] *MF* lyghtly. *B* hyghly   627 þat] *MBF* þer

MYSCHEFF. I was chenyde by þe armys: lo, I haue þem here.
The chenys I brast asundyr and kyllyde þe jaylere,
3e, ande hys fayer wyff halsyde in a cornere;
   A, how swetly I kyssyde þe swete mowth of hers! 645

When I hade do, I was myn ow3n bottler;
I brought awey wyth me both dysch and dublere.
Here ys anow for me; be of goode chere!
   3et well fare þe new chesance!
MANKYNDE. I aske mercy of New Gyse, Nowadays, and Nought.
Onys wyth my spade I remember þat I faught. 651
I wyll make yow amendys yf I hurt yow ought
   Or dyde ony grevaunce.

NEW GYSE. What a deull lykyth þe to be of þis dysposycyon?
MANKYNDE. I drempt Mercy was hange, þis was my vysyon, 655
Ande þat to yow thre I xulde haue recors and remocyon.
   Now I prey yow hertyly of yowr goode wyll.
I crye yow mercy of all þat I dyde amysse.
NOWADAYS. I sey, New Gys, Nought, Tytivillus made all þis:
As sekyr as Gode ys in hewyn, so yt ys. 660
   NOUGHT. Stonde wppe on yowr feet! why stonde 3e so styll?

NEU GYSE. Master Myscheff, we wyll yow exort
Mankyndys name in yowr bok for to report.
MYSCHEFF. I wyll not so; I wyll sett a corte.
   Nowadays, mak proclamacyon, 665
   And do yt sub forma jurys, dasarde!
NOWADAYS. Oyyt! Oy3yt! Oyet! All manere of men and   f. 130ᵛ
   comun women
To þe cort of Myschyff othere cum or sen!
Mankynde xall retorn; he ys on of owr men.
   MYSCHEFF. Nought, cum forth, þou xall be stewerde. 670

NEW GYSE. Master Myscheff, hys syde gown may be tolde.
He may haue a jakett þerof, and mony tolde.

---

642 MYSCHEFF] *after* Myscheff *a later hand added* novadays   645 þe]
M that. *F* þo   664 MYSCHEFF] *a later hand added* nowadays   a] yt *canc.*
before a   665 *MBFA print this line as s.d.*   mak] p *canc· before* mak
666 And do yt sub] *MS.* A do yt sub. *M* A[nde] do yt in. *B* And do yt be. *F* A!
do yt   670 MYSCHEFF] *a later hand added* novadays   671 tolde] *MBF* solde

NOUGHT scribit

MANKYNDE. I wyll do for þe best, so I haue no colde.
　Holde, I prey yow, and take yt wyth yow.
Ande let me haue yt ageyn in ony wyse.　　　　　　675
NEW GYSE. I promytt yow a fresch jakett after þe new gyse.
MANKYNDE. Go and do þat longyth to yowr offyce,
　And spare þat ȝe mow!

NOUGHT. Holde, master Myscheff, and rede þis.
MYSCHEFF. Here ys blottybus in blottis,　　　　　680
Blottorum blottibus istis.
　I beschrew yowr erys, a fayer hande!
NOWADAYS. Ȝe, yt ys a goode rennynge fyst.
Such an hande may not be myst.
NOUGHT. I xulde haue don better, hade I wyst.　　685
　MYSCHEFF. Take hede, sers, yt stoude you on hande.

Carici tenta generalis
In a place þer goode ale ys
Anno regni regitalis
　Edwardi nullateni　　　　　　　　　　　　690
On ȝestern day in Feuerere—þe ȝere passyth fully,
As Nought hath wrytyn; here ys owr Tulli,
Anno regni regis nulli!

NOWADAYS. What how, Neu Gyse! þou makyst moche taryynge.
þat jakett xall not be worth a ferthynge.　　　　695
NEW GYSE. Out of my wey, sers, for drede of fyghtynge!
　Lo, here ys a feet tayll, lyght to leppe abowte!
NOUGHT. Yt ys not schapyn worth a morsell of brede;
Ther ys to moche cloth, yt weys as ony lede.
I xall goo and mende yt, ellys I wyll lose my hede.　　700
　Make space, sers, lett me go owte.

MYSCHEFF. Mankynde, cum hethere! God sende yow þe gowte!
Ȝe xall goo to all þe goode felouse in þe cuntre aboute;

　678 And] MS. A　　mow] MS. F may. MB mow　　680 MYSCHEFF] a
later hand added novght　　683 rennynge] MS. rennyge　　686 stoude]
MF stonde. B stondes　　687 Carici] M Garici. B ? Garricio. F Curia
690 nullateni] M millatene. B ? nullatenus. F millateni　　692 Tulli] MS.
BF tulli. M Tulli　　694 moche taryynge] MS. moche. B moche [troublynge].
MF moche [taryynge]

Onto þe goodewyff when þe goodeman ys owte.
  'I wyll,' say ȝe.
MANKYNDE. I wyll, ser.   705

NEW GYSE. There arn but sex dedly synnys, lechery ys non, f. 131
As yt may be verefyede be ws brethellys euerychon.
Ȝe xall goo robbe, stell, and kyll, as fast as ye may gon.
  'I wyll,' sey ȝe.
MANKYNDE. I wyll, ser.

NOWADAYS. On Sundays on þe morow erly betyme   710
Ȝe xall wyth ws to þe all-house erly to go dyn
And forbere masse and matens, owres and prime.
  'I wyll,' sey ȝe.
MANKYNDE. I wyll, ser.

MYSCHEFF. Ȝe must haue be yowr syde a longe da pacem,
As trew men ryde be þe wey for to onbrace þem,   715
Take þer monay, kytt þer throtys, thus ouerface þem.
  'I wyll,' sey ȝe.
MANKYNDE. I wyll, ser.

NOUGHT. Here ys a joly jakett! How sey ȝe?
NEW GYSE. Yt ys a goode jake of fence for a mannys body.
Hay, doog, hay! whoppe whoo! Go yowr wey lyghtly!   720
  Ȝe are well made for to ren.
MYSCHEFF. Tydyngys, tydyngys! I haue aspyede on!
Hens wyth yowr stuff, fast we were gon!
I beschrew þe last xall com to hys hom.
  Dicant OMNES. Amen!   725

MERCY. What how, Mankynde! Fle þat felyschyppe, I yow prey!
MANKYNDE. I xall speke wyth þe anoþer tyme, to-morn, or þe
    next day.
We xall goo forth together to kepe my faders ȝer-day.
  A tapster, a tapster! Stow, statt, stow!
MYSCHEFF. A myscheff go wyth! here I haue a foull fall.   730
Hens, awey fro me, or I xall beschyte yow all.
NEW GYSE. What how, ostlere, hostlere! Lende ws a football!
  Whoppe whow! Anow, anow, anow, anow!

712 And] *MS.* A   727 wyth þe] *MS.* wyth. *MBF* with [the]   730 wyth!
here] *MF* with here. *B* wyth; here

SCENE III

MERCY. My mynde ys dyspersyde, my body trymmelyth as þe
aspen leffe.
The terys xuld trekyll down by my chekys, were not yowr
reuerrence.   735
Yt were to me solace, þe cruell vysytacyon of deth.
Wythout rude behauer I kan not expresse þis inconvenyens.
Wepynge, sythynge, and sobbynge were my suffycyens;
All naturall nutriment to me as caren ys odybull.
My inwarde afflixcyon ȝeldyth me tedyouse wnto yowr presens.
I kan not bere yt ewynly þat Mankynde ys so flexybull.   741

Man onkynde, whereuer þou be! for all þis world was not apre-
hensyble
To dyscharge þin orygynall offence, thraldam and captyuyte,
Tyll Godys own welbelouyde son was obedient and passyble.
Euery droppe of hys bloode was schede to purge þin iniquite. 745
I dyscomende and dysalow þin oftyn mutabylyte.   f. 131ᵛ
To euery creature þou art dyspectuose and odyble.
Why art þou so oncurtess, so inconsyderatt? Alasse, who ys me!
As þe fane þat turnyth wyth þe wynde, so þou art conuertyble.

In trust ys treson; þi promes ys not credyble;   750
Thy peruersyose ingratytude I can not rehers.
To God and to all þe holy corte of hewyn þou art despectyble,
As a nobyll versyfyer makyth mencyon in þis verse:
'Lex et natura, Cristus et omnia jura
Damnant ingratum, lugent eum fore natum.'   755

O goode Lady and Moþer of mercy, haue pety and compassyon
Of þe wrechydnes of Mankynde, þat ys so wanton and so frayll!
Lett mercy excede justyce, dere Moþer, amytt þis supplycacyon,
Equyte to be leyde onparty and mercy to prevayll.

---

734 trymmelyth] tri *canc. before* trymmelyth   736 solace] *MS.* solalace
737 kan not] *MS.* kan. *MBF* kan [not]   746 þin] *MS. MBF* þis   muta-
bylyte] *MS. BF* imutabylyte. *M* mutabylyte   750 þi] *MS. F* þis.
MB þi   751 Thy] *MS. F* Thys. *MB* Thy   752 God and to] *MS.* go
on to. *MB* go ouer. *F* go ouer to   754 et omnia] *MS.* sit omnia. *MF* et
omnia.   758 amytt] *MF* a[d]mytt   759 onparty] *M* ouer, pety. *B* ouer
pety. *F* ouer party

To sensuall lyvynge ys reprouable, þat ys nowadays,   760
  As be þe comprehence of þis mater yt may be specyfyede.
New Gyse, Nowadays, Nought wyth þer allectuose ways
  They haue pervertyde Mankynde, my swet sun, I haue well
  espyede.

A, wyth þes cursyde caytyfs, and I may, he xall not long indure.
  I, Mercy, hys father gostly, wyll procede forth and do my
  propyrte.   765
Lady, helpe! þis maner of lyuynge ys a detestabull plesure.
  Vanitas vanitatum, all ys but a vanyte.

Mercy xall neuer be convicte of hys oncurtes condycyon.
  Wyth wepynge terys be ny3te and be day I wyll goo and neuer
  sesse.
Xall I not fynde hym? Yes, I hope. Now Gode be my protec-
  cyon!   770
  My predylecte son, where be ye? Mankynde, vbi es?

MYSCHEFF. My prepotent fader, when 3e sowpe, sowpe owt
  yowr messe.
3e are all to-gloryede in yowr termys; 3e make many a lesse.
Wyll 3e here? He cryeth euer 'Mankynde, vbi es?'
NEW GYSE. Hic hyc, hic hic, hic hic, hic hic!   775
þat ys to sey, here, here, here! ny dede in þe cryke.
Yf 3e wyll haue hym, goo and syke, syke, syke!
  Syke not ouerlong, for losynge of yowr mynde!

NOWADAYS. Yf 3e wyll haue Mankynde, how domine, domine,
  dominus!
3e must speke to þe schryue for a cape corpus,   780
Ellys 3e must be fayn to retorn wyth non est inventus.
  How sey 3e, ser? My bolte ys schett.
NOUGHT. I am doynge of my nedyngys; be ware how 3e schott!
Fy, fy, fy! I haue fowll arayde my fote.   f. 132
Be wyse for schotynge wyth yowr takyllys, for Gode wott   785
  My fote ys fowly ouerschett.

762 ways] ve *canc. before* ways   764 caytyfs] MS. cayftys. MBF caytyfs
773 to-gloryede] MS. B to gloryede. M to-glosyede. F to-gloryede   776 ny]
MS. my. MBF ny   779 dominus] MBF domine   780 cape corpus]
MS. cepe corpus. M cape corpus. B? cope coppus. F cepe coppus   782 schett]
M schotte. BF schott

MYSCHEFF. A parlement, a parlement! Cum forth, Nought,
  behynde.
A cownsell belyue! I am aferde Mercy wyll hym fynde.
How sey ȝe, and what sey ȝe? How xall we do wyth Mankynde?
  NEU GYSE. Tysche! a flyes weyng! Wyll ȝe do well?   790
He wenyth Mercy were honge for stelyng of a mere.
Myscheff, go sey to hym þat Mercy sekyth euerywere.
He wyll honge hymselff, I wndyrtake, for fere.
  MYSCHEFF. I assent þerto; yt ys wyttyly seyde and well.

NOWADAYS. Qwyppe yt in þi cote; anon yt were don.   795
Now Sent Gabryellys modyr saue þe cloþes of þi schon!
All þe bokys in þe worlde, yf þei hade be wndon,
  Kowde not a cownselde ws bett.   Hic exit MYSCHEFF
MYSCHEFF. How, Mankynde! Cumm and speke wyth Mercy, he
  is here fast by.
MANKYNDE. A roppe, a rope, a rope! I am not worthy.   800
MYSCHEFF. Anon, anon, anon! I haue yt here redy,
  Wyth a tre also þat I haue gett.

Holde þe tre, Nowadays, Nought! Take hede and be wyse!
NEU GYSE. Lo, Mankynde! do as I do; þis ys þi new gyse.
Gyff þe roppe just to þy neke; þis ys myn avyse.   805
  MYSCHEFF. Helpe þisylff, Nought! Lo, Mercy ys here!
He skaryth ws wyth a bales; we may no lengere tary.
NEU GYSE. Qweke, qweke, qweke! Alass, my thrott! I beschrew
  yow, mary!
A, Mercy, Crystys coppyde curse go wyth yow, and Sent Dauy!
  Alasse, my wesant! Ȝe were sumwhat to nere.   810
                              Exiant

MERCY. Aryse, my precyose redempt son! Ȝe be to me full dere.
  He ys so tymerouse, me semyth hys vytall spryt doth exspyre.
MANKYNDE. Alasse, I haue be so bestyally dysposyde, I dare not
  apere.
  To se yowr solaycyose face I am not worthy to dysyere.

795 Qwyppe] *M* I! Wyppe. *B* I wyppe. *F* I-wyppe   796 cloþes] *MS*.
cloþes *or* cloyes. *M* clowtes. *B* ? cleftes. *F* cloþes   798 s.d. *MF add* [and
re-enters with MANKIND.]   804 þi] *MB* þe   805 þy] *MS*. pye. *MBF* þy
807 bales] *M* balef. *B* bale   812 ys] *MS*. ys ys   814 solaycyose] a
added above the line

MERCY. Yowr crymynose compleynt wondyth my hert as a
    lance.   815
    Dyspose yowrsylff mekly to aske mercy, and I wyll assent.
Зelde me nethyr golde nor tresure, but yowr humbyll obeysyance,
    The voluntary subjeccyon of yowr hert, and I am content.

MANKYNDE. What, aske mercy зet onys agayn? Alas, yt f. 132ᵛ
    were a wyle petycyun.
    Ewyr to offend and euer to aske mercy, yt ys a puerilite.   820
Yt ys so abhominabyll to rehers my iterat transgrescion,
    I am not worthy to hawe mercy be no possibilite.

MERCY. O Mankend, my singler solas, þis is a lamentabyll
    excuse.
    The dolorus terys of my hert, how þei begyn to amownt!
O pirssid Jhesu, help þou þis synfull synner to redouce!   825
    Nam hec est mutacio dextre Excelsi; vertit impios et non sunt.

Aryse and aske mercy, Mankend, and be associat to me.
    Thy deth schall be my hewynesse; alas, tys pety yt schwld be
    þus.
Thy obstinacy wyll exclude the fro þe glorius perpetuite.
Зet for my lofe ope thy lyppys and sey 'Miserere mei, Deus!' 830

MANKEND. The egall justyse of God wyll not permytte sych a
    synfull wrech
    To be rewyvyd and restoryd ageyn; yt were impossibyll.
MERCY. The justyce of God wyll as I wyll, as hymsylfe doth
    precyse:
    Nolo mortem peccatoris, inquit, yff he wyll be redusyble.

MANKEND. þan mercy, good Mercy! What ys a man wythowte
    mercy?   835
    Lytyll ys our parte of paradyse were mercy ne were.

819 *The last four pages are in the hand of a second scribe*   wyle] *MBF* wyld
820 yt] *MBF* þat   821 iterat] *M* wekit. *B* wernt. *F* werst   822 not]
nto *canc. before* not   824 terys] *MF* feres. *B ?* sores   825 pirssid] *MS.*
pirssie. *MBF* blyssed   redouce] *MB* reduce. *F* redeme   829 exclude the]
MS. exclude. *MBF* exclude [the]   833 precyse] *M* preche *or* precysely
teche. *B* preche   834 yff] *F & yff   be redusyble] *MS.* reducylle *changed in
another hand to* re redusyble. *MBF* [be] reducyble   835 ys] hy *canc. before*
ys   836 were mercy] *M* where Mercy

Good Mercy, excuse þe ineuytabyll objeccion of my gostly enmy.
The prowerbe seyth 'þe trewth tryith þe sylfe.' Alas, I hawe
mech care.

MERCY. God wyll not make ȝow preuy onto hys last jugement.
Justyce and Equite xall be fortyfyid, I wyll not denye.   840
Trowthe may not so cruelly procede in hys streyt argument
But þat Mercy schall rewle þe mater wythowte contrauersye.

Aryse now and go wyth me in thys deambulatorye.
Inclyne yowyr capacite; my doctrine ys conuenient.
Synne not in hope of mercy; þat ys a cryme notary.   f. 133
To truste ouermoche in a prince yt ys not expedient.   846

In hope when ȝe syn ȝe thynke to hawe mercy, be ware of þat
awenture.
The good Lord seyd to þe lecherus woman of Chanane,
The holy gospell ys þe awtorite, as we rede in scrypture,
'Vade et jam amplius noli peccare.'   850

Cryst preserwyd þis synfull woman takeyn in awowtry;
He seyde to here þeis wordys, 'Go and syn no more.'
So to ȝow, go and syn no more. Be ware of weyn confidens of
mercy;
Offend not a prince on trust of hys fauour, as I seyd before.

Yf ȝe fele ȝoursylfe trappyd in þe snare of your gostly enmy,   855
Aske mercy anon; be ware of þe contynuance.
Whyll a wond ys fresch yt ys prowyd curabyll be surgery,
þat yf yt procede ouyrlong, yt ys cawse of gret grewans.

MANKEND. To aske mercy and to hawe, þis ys a lyberall pos-
sescion.
Schall þis expedycius petycion euer be alowyd, as ȝe hawe
insyght?   860
MERCY. In þis present lyfe mercy ys plente, tyll deth makyth hys
dywysion;
But whan ȝe be go, vsque ad minimum quadrantem ȝe schall
rekyn ȝour ryght.

844 so for rhyme MBF] MS. My doctrine ys conuenient Inclyne yowyr
capacite   847 ȝe syn ȝe thynke] M ȝe syn   854 I] MS. he. MBF I
858 grewans] grewang changed to grewans   860 insyght] MB in-syght. F in
syght   862 schall] MS. scha   ȝour] MBF þis

Aske mercy and hawe, whyll þe body wyth þe sowle hath hys
annexion;
Yf ye tary tyll your dyscesse, ȝe may hap of your desyre to mysse.
Be repentant here, trust not þe owr of deth; thynke on þis lessun:
'Ecce nunc tempus acceptabile, ecce nunc dies salutis.'   866

All þe wertu in þe word yf ȝe myght comprehend
Your merytys were not premyabyll to þe blys abowe,
Not to the lest joy of hewyn, of ȝour propyr efforte to ascend.
Wyth mercy ȝe may; I tell ȝow no fabyll, scrypture doth
prowe.   870

MANKEND. O Mercy, my suavius solas and synguler recreatory,
My predilecte spesyall, ȝe are worthy to hawe my lowe;   f. 133ᵛ
For wythowte deserte and menys supplicatorie
ȝe be compacient to my inexcusabyll reprowe.

A, yt swemyth my hert to thynk how onwysely I hawe wroght.   875
Tytiuillus, þat goth invisibele, hyng hys nett before my eye
And by hys fantasticall visionys sediciusly sowght,
To New Gyse, Nowadayis, Nowght causyd me to obey.

MERCY. Mankend, ȝe were obliuyows of my doctrine monytorye.
I seyd before, Titiuillus wold asay ȝow a bronte.   880
Be ware fro hensforth of hys fablys delusory.
þe prowerbe seyth, 'Jacula prestita minus ledunt.'

ȝe hawe thre aduersaryis and he ys mayster of hem all:
That ys to sey, the Dewell, þe World, þe Flesch and þe Fell.
The New Gyse, Nowadayis, Nowgth, þe World we may hem call;
And propyrly Titiuillus syngnyfyth the Fend of helle;   886

The Flesch, þat ys þe vnclene concupissens of ȝour body.
These be ȝour thre gostly enmyis, in whom ȝe hawe put ȝour
confidens.

863 sowle] MS. sowe   hys] MS. yys. MBF hys   865 thynke] y canc.
before thynke   867 word] MBF wor[l]d   869 lest] h canc. before lest
870 prowe] MS. F prewe. M prove. B prowe   871 suavius] M solatius. F
suatius   876 my] y canc. before my   877 sediciusly] M sedulously.
B seducively. F sedociusly   878 To] M He. BF Be   879 monytorye]
MS. manyterge. F manyterye. M marytorye. B monytorye   883 and he]
MBF he   884 þe Fell] MB [I] the tell   885 The] M That   Nowgth]
MB and Nought   886 propyrly] MS. propylly

þei browt ȝow to Myscheffe to conclude ȝour temporall glory,
   As yt hath be schewyd before þis worcheppyll audiens.   890

Remembyr how redy I was to help ȝow; fro swheche I was not
   dangerus;
   Wherfore, goode sunne, absteyne fro syn cuermore after þis.
Ȝe may both saue and spyll ȝowr sowle þat ys so precyus.
   Libere welle, libere nolle God may not deny iwys.

Be ware of Titiuillus wyth his net and of all enmys will,   895
   Of ȝour synfull delectacion þat grewyth ȝour gostly substans.
Ȝour body ys ȝour enmy; let hym not haue hys wyll.
   Take ȝour lewe whan ȝe wyll. God send ȝow good perseuerans!

MANKEND. Syth I schall departe, blyse me, fader, her f. 134
   þen I go.
   God send ws all plente of hys gret mercy!   900
MERCY. Dominus custodit te ab omni malo
   In nomine Patris et Filii et Spiritus Sancti. Amen!

                             Hic exit MANKEND

Wyrschepyll sofereyns, I hawe do my propirte:
   Mankynd ys deliueryd by my fauerall patrocynye.
God preserue hym fro all wyckyd captiuite   905
   And send hym grace hys sensuall condicions to mortifye!

Now for hys lowe þat for vs receywyd hys humanite,
   Serge ȝour condicyons wyth dew examinacion.
Thynke and remembyr þe world ys but a wanite,
   As yt ys prowyd daly by diuerse transmutacyon.   910

Mankend ys wrechyd, he hath sufficyent prowe.
   Therefore God grant ȝow all per suam misericordiam
þat ye may be pleyferys wyth þe angellys abowe
   And hawe to ȝour porcyon vitam eternam. Amen!

                        Fynis.

890 before] among *canc.*, before *above line. M* omits   892 fro] syro *canc.*
before fro   894 libere nolle] *MS.* liebere nolle. *M* libere velle. *F* libere welle.
B libere nolle   895 enmys]? his impyse *changed to?* enmys. *M* enmys *or*
enuius. *B* enuiys. *F* enuyus   901 custodit] *MBF* custodi[a]t   904 fauerall]
M sunerall *or* special. *B* seuerall. *F* suuerall   906 condicions] *MS.* condo-
cions   910 diuerse] *MS.* duerse   912 God grant] *MS* god. *MF* God
[kepe]. *B* god ȝive   913 pleyferys] *M* pleseres. *B* plesered. *F* pleyseris
angellys] *MS. B* angell. *MF* angellis

NOTES

A list of abbreviations used in the Notes is printed on p. 228.

THE CASTLE OF PERSEVERANCE

Stage plan. *stytelerys*: 'marshals', the only example quoted in *OED*. under *stightler*, from *stightle* 'to arrange, set in order'. *Stickler* 'umpire, moderator' is first recorded in 1538, and *styffeler* in 1473 from *Paston Letters*, ed. Gairdner, iii. 98.

gunnepowdyr: the word is first recorded by *OED*. in 1414 and by *MED*. in 1400, but gunpowder was described by Roger Bacon and used at Crecy: T. F. Tout, 'Firearms in England in the Fourteenth Century', *English Historical Review*, xxvi (1911), 666–702; J. R. Partington, *A History of Greek Fire and Gunpowder*, 1960.

Righteousness or Justicia is all in red like a judge in scarlet, Peace in black because she mourns for man: S. C. Chew, *The Virtues Reconciled*, pp. 44–45. White is a symbol of Mercy and dark green suggests that Truth is everlasting, 'For þe greneschipe lasteþ euere' (*Castel off Loue*, ed. Weymouth, line 709).

18 The Good and Bad Angels vying for man's soul appear in early English drama only here and in Marlowe's *Dr. Faustus*. The differences are discussed by Douglas Cole, *Suffering and Evil in the Plays of Christopher Marlowe*, 1962, pp. 236–8.

25 As E. N. S. Thompson observes in 'The English Moral Plays', *Transactions of the Connecticut Academy*, xiv (1910), 358, 'without a moral struggle based on the doctrine of freedom of the will there was no true moral play'. Discussing *The Castle* on pp. 312–20, he calls it 'a "sermo corporeus"', 'the most typical specimen of the morality play'.

28 On the three enemies of man see the *Meditations* attributed to St. Bernard, *Patrologia Latina*, clxxxiv. 503–5, translated in *Minor Poems of the Vernon MS*. ii. 511–22, and in an edition printed by Wynkyn de Worde in 1496.

31 Pride is here associated with the World, as in *Mary Magdalene* in *The Digby Plays*. Elsewhere in *The Castle* Covetise is treasurer to the World, Pride, Wrath, and Envy serve the Devil, and Gluttony, Lechery, and Sloth serve the Flesh. The seven sins are so assigned in *Ancrene Riwle*, Part IV, and in most later English works, though Grosseteste assigns to the World Envy in *Le Chasteau d'Amour* and both Envy and Wrath in *Templum Domini*. See M. W. Bloomfield, *The Seven Deadly Sins*, 1952, pp. 141, 149–50.

39 More than seven sins are often listed, as in *The Assembly of Gods*, 635–65, *Jacob's Well*, i. 294–6, *Speculum Christiani*, pp. 76–100, and

English Writings of Richard Rolle, ed. Allen, pp. 97–99, 155; the last three lists are translated from *Compendium Theologicae Veritatis*.

44 The role of Conscience has been cut, since he appears neither in the text nor among the names of the players. Conscience reclaims Manhood from Folly in *Mundus et Infans* (1522).

52 *þe Castel of Good Persoucraunce*: the name is explained by the text quoted after line 1705. It is also called the Castle of Goodness (1708, 1757, 2355), the Castle of Virtue (1896), and the Castle of Virtue and of Goodness (2019). Roberta D. Cornelius, *The Figurative Castle*, 1930, discusses medieval allegories of castles and sieges, as in works attributed to Bernard of Clairvaux and Hugh of St. Victor, in *Le Chasteau d'Amour* by Robert Grosseteste, and in *Piers Plowman*, B. ix and xx. She considers it 'not improbable that Grosseteste's allegory influenced *The Castell*' but doubts whether such an influence can be definitely established. The Castle of Love is the Virgin, in whom man's soul takes refuge against assaults by the Devil, the World, the Flesh, and the Seven Sins. See also Owst, pp. 77–85.

54 Cf. Isaiah lix. 17; Wisdom of Solomon v. 18–24; Ephesians vi. 11–17.

91 Cf. *The Prick of Conscience*, 790, an old man 'es covatous and hard haldand', and Chaucer, *Troilus and Criseyde*, iv. 1369, 'elde is ful of coveytise'.

108 *scyfftyd*: 'distributed'. *OED.* quotes this line under both *skift* from ON. and *shift* from OE., but the spelling points to *skift*; cf. *Lincoln Diocese Documents*, EETS., pp. 56, 342–3, 'to skift euyne emong yam' in a Lincolnshire will of 1451.

124 E. K. Chambers comments in *English Literature at the Close of the Middle Ages*, p. 55: 'The prologue does not quite square with the play itself and may be a later addition. It anticipates a conclusion by grace of "oure lofly lady", the Virgin, who does not in fact appear.' The banns do not actually say that she will appear, but it is true that they do not mention the debate in heaven. As Ramsay suggests, 'this method of salvation seems to be described as the intervention of "oure lofly lady", who does not actually appear in the play at all; and we have a precisely similar reference to "oure lady mylde" in the prologue to the *Pride of Life* (ll. 97–108)': introduction to Skelton, *Magnyfycence*, p. clxiv. Mary is 'Moþer of mercy', as in *M.* 756 and in Caesarius of Heisterbach, and in *The Castle* she is represented by Mercy.

132 *propyrtes*: the first example in *OED.* of the theatrical sense, 'appurtenances used in acting a play'.

138 *we schul be onward be vnderne of þe day*: *vnderne* is ambiguous, since it may mean mid-morning, midday, or mid-afternoon. It refers to both *hora tertia* and *hora sexta* in Wyclif, to noon in *Prompt.*, and to *hora nona* in *Early English Carols*, ed. Greene, p. 18. This line is less likely to mean 'we must be on with the play by mid-morning' than 'we must be moving on by noon' or 'by afternoon'. *Ludus Coventriae* began at 6 a.m. on tour.

144 *Os*: 'as'. F. prints D*eus*, but the *O* is clear. Although Morris called *os* a sign of West Midland dialect, it is common in the East Midland *Speculum Christiani*, in some works in *Rolle* (i. 83–91, 157–72), and in *The Earl of Toulouse* and other romances, and it occurs in *York*, viii. 66, 140; *Towneley*, x. 37, xxxii. 67; *The Fire of Love*, p. 42; Malory, ed. Vinaver, i. 160, ii. 988: *Secular Lyrics of the XIVth and XVth Centuries*, ed. Robbins, pp. 32, 137, 145, 187; *Paston Letters*, ed. Davis, 1958, pp. 30 (*os, osse*), 104 (*osse*); and *Catholicon Anglicum*, p. 262.

154 *lende*: emended to the infinitive. For the rhyme cf. 2760–4.

158 *weye-went*: '? pathway'; F. 'road-turn, cross-road'; *OED*. '? a turn of the road'.

160 *þis propyr pleyn place*: 'this fine open space'; cf. *Ludus Cov.*, Banns, 399, 'we purpose to shewe in oure pleyn place'.

170 The World boasts like Herod in the miracle plays. Lists of place-names are often alliterated; cf. 224 *Fluundris and Freslonde*; *Towneley*, xvi. 42–49; *Ludus Cov.* xxiii. 161–75; *Croxton Play of the Sacrament*, 15–35; *Mundus et Infans*, 245–8; *Hickscorner*, 309–25.

176 Mandeville mentions 'Pynceras' in Thrace and 'la terre des Pigmains' (Pigmies) in Cathay (*Travels*, ed. Letts, i. 5, ii. 247). 'Pyncenarde' is in *Kyng Alisaunder*, 1693.

177 The Dry Tree in Eden withered when Adam fell; see *Cursor Mundi*, 1319–52; Rose Peebles, 'The Dry Tree: Symbol of Death', *Vassar Mediaeval Studies*, 1923, pp. 59–79; Mary Lascelles in *Medium Ævum*, v (1936), 173–88; *Kyng Alisaunder*, ed. Smithers, ii. 146–7. The Hereford Map places it near India, Marco Polo in Persia (ed. Yule, i. 127–39). Another, Abraham's oak of Mamre, withered when Christ died, according to Friar Odoric and Mandeville; cf. Lydgate, *Minor Poems*, ii. 696.

181 Greed is treasurer of the Devil's castle in Bromyard's fourteenth-century *Summa Predicantium*; see Owst, p. 82.

184 *Per is no wythe*: the sense requires a negative; cf. 3642, 'þer is no wyth in þis werld þat may skape þis'.

188 *I dawnse doun as a doo*: cf. *Pearl*, 345, 'þoȝ þou daunce as any do'; *Two Coventry Corpus Christi Plays*, p. 28, 'trypp lyke a doo'.

189 *boy*: 'fellow'. E. J. Dobson, 'The Etymology and Meaning of *Boy*', *Medium Ævum*, ix (1940), 121–54, shows that *boy* in this play is usually a term of contempt or abuse or a term of address to an inferior. It never means 'child', but it may mean 'servant', as in 1750, 1971, 2895.

199 *Belyal*: here identified with Satan, though usually distinct, as in *York*, xxxvii. 139, *Towneley*, xxv. 109, *Ludus Cov.* xxiii. 5, and *The Conversion of St. Paul* (*Digby Plays*, p. 43), 'Nexte vnto lucyfer I am in magestye'. Belial is also called *Belsabub* in 2114.

201 *fro Carlylle into Kent*: cf. Skelton, i. 369, 'they ryde and rinne from Carlyll to Kente', and i. 257, 'Frome Tyne to Trent, From Stroude to Kent'.

235 *brustun-gutte*: 'burst-belly', a compound like *burstengutted* (1661 in *OED*.). In Yorkshire and N. Lincs. dialect *brussen-guts* means 'a glutton, very corpulent person' (*Eng. Dialect Dict.*).

247 *I ӡeue not a myth*: see *geue* in Glossary for variations with *a hawe*, *a louse*, *a gres*.

285 In *Mundus et Infans* (Manly, *Specimens of the Pre-Shaksperean Drama*, i. 355) the child enters 'Poore and naked as ye may se'. Cf. Job i. 21; *The Prick of Conscience*, 508, 'Naked we come hider, and bare'; *Hymns to the Virgin and Christ*, p. 58, 'I saw a child modir nakid, New born þe modir fro. Al aloone, as god him makid, In wildirnesse he dide goo, Til two in gouernaunce it takid, An aungil freende, an aungil foo.'

307–9 Cf. Chaucer, *Parson's Tale*, 643, 'the devel, that evere is aboute to maken discord'; Owst, *Preaching in Medieval England*, p. 201, 'the devylls and other wyckyd spryritis are moste besy a bowte for to drawe a man in to synne and wrechednes'.

329–30 Cf. *The Prick of Conscience*, 468–9, 'þan has a man les myght þan a beste When he es born, and es sene leste'.

353 *be strete and stye*: 'by road and path'. *OED*. under *sty* quotes Layamon, 16366, and this play, 363; see also *York*, xxviii. 229; *Towneley*, ii. 365; *Chester Plays*, xxiv. 24.

361a Prov. xxx. 8, 'mendicitatem et divitias ne dederis mihi'. This is an instance of the frequent differences from the Vulgate text approved in 1592.

410a Varied from Ecclesiasticus vii. 40, 'memorare novissima tua, et in aeternum non peccabis'. Cf. 3648 and *M.* 321.

425 *sompe*: 'swamp', the first instance in *OED*. (*sump*), as the first record of *swamp* is in Captain John Smith from Lincs. dialect.

446 *Of God ne of good man*: On this proverbial phrase, repeated in 460 and 479, see C. T. Onions, '"God and Good Men"', *T.L.S.*, 13 Aug. 1931 (cf. 20 Aug., 17 Sept.).

457 *trotte and tremle*: not for fear but for joy, like the devil in *Mary Magdalene*, 555, 'how I tremyl and trott'.

469 E. K. Chambers, *English Literature at the Close of the Middle Ages*, p. 59, thinks that 'Lust (*Voluptas*) is a little difficult to differentiate from Lust (*Luxuria*)', but *Voluptas* or Pleasure serves the World while *Luxuria* or Lechery serves the Flesh. *Voluptas* is variously called *Lust* (539, 726), *Lykynge* (623), *Lust, Lykyng* (469, 526), *Lust and Lykynge* (519), or *Lykynge and Luste* (522). *Detraccio* also calls himself by two names, *Bakbytynge and Detracion* (777). In *Mundus et Infans* the World tells the child when he is fourteen, 'Loue, Lust, Lykynge, in-fere, These thy names they shall be' and the child says, 'now Lust and Lykyng is my name'.

479 *not a hawe*: again in 1166; cf. *Ludus Cov*. iii. 22, 'I ȝyf not þer of An hawe', and xxi. 27, xxix. 13; *Oxford Proverbs*, p. 283; Tilley, H 221.

503a Quoted in a commonplace book, *Reliquiae Antiquae*, i. 289; cf. *C*. 2638a and *Dives and Pauper* (1493), f. 8, 'The niggard has never enough'. Cf. also H. Walther, *Sprichwörter*, iii (1965), no. 17645.

516a Cf. Ecclesiasticus i. 1, 'Omnis sapientia a Domino Deo est'.

604 *jentyl justyse*: cf. preface to Rolle, *Psalter*, ed. Bramley, p. 2, 'ihu gentil iust iustice'.

659 *My namo is Bacbytere*: cf. *Ludus Cov.*, xiv. 29–30, Secundus Detractor, 'I am bakbytere þat spyllyth all game Buthe kyd and knowyn in many a place'.

664 Cf. Chaucer, *Parson's Tale*, 644, 'swiche as speken faire byforn folk, and wikkedly bihynde'; *Towneley*, xxx. 157–8; Lydgate, *Minor Poems*, ii. 798; *Jacob's Well*, i. 87; *Nature*, ii. 1193–7; Skelton, i. 386, 'That speke fayre before the and shrewdly behynde'.

676 *thyrde*: the rhyme with *hyd* suggests *thryd*, but *thyrde* is possible.

691 *For to spye a preuy pley*: Robert Withington in *Philological Quarterly*, xiv (1935), 270, suggests the emendation *prey*.

772 *swetter þanne mede*: cf. *York*, xxxix. 89; *Towneley*, xxviii. 111; *C*. 799, 2025 'swetter þanne sens'; *M*. 225 'swetere þen hony'.

775 *Flepyrgebet*: cf. 1724 'Flypyrgebet, Bakbytere' and 1733 'Flepyrgebet'. *OED*. quotes the first use from Latimer in 1549. *MED*. compares a translation of Cato *c*. 1400, 'flipers and alle fals flaters'. The meanings here and in *King Lear* are discussed by I. B. Cauthen, Jr. in *Notes and Queries*, cciii (1958), 98–99.

794 *bonde*: the rhyme with *wende* suggests *bende*, as in 2629, but cf. 924 and 974 *bonde* rhyming with *londe*: *wende*: *schende*.

798 *ponndys*: the MS. may be read either *poundys* (cf. 767, 816) or *ponndys* 'ponds', mentioned with *parkys* in 2728, 2935, 2974.

802 Cf. *Towneley*, ii. 84, 'Let furth youre geyse, the fox will preche'; *Modern Philology*, xxxviii (1940), 125, 'Whan þe wox prechyth be-ware the gese'; *Oxford Proverbs*, p. 223; Tilley, F 656. For carvings of the fox preaching see Owst, *Preaching in Medieval England*, p. 86, and M. D. Anderson, *The Medieval Carver*, pp. 44, 114.

811 *in dethys dow*: Furnivall conjectured 'in death's grip' and *MED*. 'at the time of death', taking *dow* as a variant of *day*. But the usual sense of *dow* is 'dough', so that the phrase means 'in the earth of the grave', as again in 2639 *closyd in dethes dow*.

849–53 On deceit in merchants see Owst, pp. 352–61.

866 *Catonis Disticha*, ii. 17.

879 *si dedero*: not 'I'll pay you back with profit' (F.) but 'If I give, I expect money in return'. With the same phrase in *M*. 456 Smart (*Modern Philology*, xiv. 296–7) compares Lydgate's '*Si dedero* ys now so mery a song' (*Minor Poems*, ii. 577), Gower's *Vox Clamantis* (iii. 233–4), and five other instances. See also D'Evelyn, *Peter Idley's Instructions to His Son*, p. 216, and H. Walther, *Sprichwörter*, iv (1966), nos. 28415–9.

890 *lyth as leuene*: 'bright as lightning' (not as in F. 'light as yeast'). Cf. 191 and 3498; *York*, xlv. 175, 'aungellis . . . lighter þan þe levene'; *Mary Magdalene*, 2043, 'angylles brygth as þe lewyn'.

913 *fogge*: 'jog along'; cf. *fodge* in Lyly, *Endimion* (1588), IV. ii. 27; *OED*. *fadge*, v. 6, 'jog along, trudge'; and n. on 3098, *dagge* 'jog'.

999 *dowtyr*: in *Mary Magdalene*, 347, she is 'my fayer spowse lechery'.

1035 *pynyngys stol*: cf. *Piers Plowman*, B. iii. 78, 'To punyschen on pillories and pynynge stoles Brewesteres and bakesteres bocheres and cokes'.

1057 *new jettys*: 'new fashions'; cf. *M*. 103, 'þe new jett'; *Canterbury Tales*, Prologue, 682; Hoccleve, *Regiment of Princes*, 449; *Towneley*, xxx. 287; *Ludus Cov*. xxxi. 885.

1059 *crakows*: 'pointed toes'. *MED*. quotes six instances of the noun or the verb from it: *Eulogium Historiarum* under 1362 (probably written later), Rolls Series, IX. iii. 231, 'sotulares rostratas in unius digiti longitudine quae "crakowes" vocantur; potius judicantur ungulae daemonum quam ornamenta hominum'; 'Of Antecrist and His Meynee' (written by a follower of Wyclif) in *Three Treatises of John Wycliffe*, ed. Todd, 1851, p. cxxviii, 'tagged cloþes & crakowe pykis'; 'The Eight Blessings of Christ' (written before 1400), *Reliquiae Antiquae*, i. 41, 'longe crakowis'; *The Lanterne of Liȝt* (1409–10), EETS., p. 132, 'cracowen'; *Political and Other Poems* (1400–21), ed. Kail, EETS., p. 93, 'dagged cloþes, And longe pyked crakowed shon'; and a continuation of *Polychronicon* (written before 1425), Rolls Series, XLI. viii. 467, a man in 1384 'compellede to eite the crawcows and leder of his schoone'. I find three more examples, one in a MS. sermon quoted by Owst, p. 410, 'crakowes of half a fote longe', and two in *Historia Vitae et Regni Ricardi II*, ed. Hearne, 1729, pp. 53, 126, where a monk of Evesham mentions the eating of 'Cracowys' in 1384 and says of Queen Anne, 'Cum ista Regina venit de Boëmia in Angliam abusiones illae execrabiles, sotulares sil. [i.e. scilicet] cum longis rostris (Anglice *Cracowys* vel *Pykys*)'. So far as the examples of *crakow* can be dated, the word seems to have been current only from about 1382 to about 1425.

1060 *Jagge*: 'slash for ornament'. See Smart in *Manly Anniversary Studies*, pp. 42–53; *MED.*, citing *dagges* in a Wardrobe Account for 1394; *Morte Arthur*, 905, 'jaggede in schredez'; *Towneley*, xxx. 552, 'iaggid hode'; Margery Kempe, pp. 9, 109, 223 'daggyd', 'daggys'; *Prompt.*, '*Iaggyd*, or *daggyd, fractillosus*'; *Peter Idley's Instructions to His Son*, i. 106, 'cuttyng and Iaggyng of clothis', ii B. 184, 'all to-Iagged'; and *Paston Letters*, i. 476, 'iagged huke' (1459).

1067 *schelfe*: F. 'shelve, shove aside'; *OED*. '? to ruin', 'Origin and meaning obscure; cf. OE. *scelfan* to shake ... Perh. an arbitrary formation for rhyme: cf. *Shelve v.*' See note on 2575.

1084 MS. has *I þi bowre* here, *I my cunte* at 1190, and *I þe sawter* at 2985. These may indicate pronunciation or they may be scribal errors. Cf. *W.* 24 *I wysdom* (Digby MS. *In Wysdam*), 133 *I a sowle* (Digby *In A soule*), and 1064 s.d. *commynge I* for *commynge in*. In *W.* 613 Digby has wrongly *In reioyse* for *I reioys*.

1124 *Kyll ... wythowtyn knyve*: cf. 1617; *Ludus Cov.* ii. 401; *Conversion of St. Paul* (*Digby Plays*), p. 48; *Secular Lyrics*, p. 167.

1140 *reynynge*: 'flourishing', like *reynande* in *W.* 679.

1212–16 Cf. *Handlyng Synne*, 4253–9:

> how sey þese men þat are þus slogh,
> þat oute of mesure slepe a throwe?
> whan he heryþ a bel ryng,
> To holy cherche men kallyng,
> þan may he nat hys bedde lete
> But þan behoueþ hym to lygge and swete,
> And take þe mery mornyng slepe.

1275 *a ballyd resun*: 'a bald, paltry argument' (*OED*.) rather than 'a glib or crafty argument' (*MED*.). Cf. *Piers Plowman*, B. x. 54; *Mum and the Sothsegger*, iv. 70.

1291 *saggyd*: 'sunk'. *OED.* quotes this as the earliest use of the verb *sag*.

1346 *benote*, or *be note*, is unexplained; it seems to mean 'known' (*notus*).

1349 Sister Philippa Coogan, *An Interpretation of the Moral Play, Mankind*, pp. 32–37, quotes warnings against putting off confession 'nygh tyl lentyn be al gone' in *Handlyng Synne*, 4783–8; Bromyard, *Summa Praedicantium*, I. VIII. xxiii; and *Speculum Sacerdotale*, pp. 67–68, which says that the sinful come to confession 'noȝt in the first weke comenly, ne in the secounde, ne in the þridde, but in the vi. weke and in Good Friday and on Paske Day'.

1350 *to sone*: *OED*. cites *too soon* first from Skelton, but Chaucer uses it in *Troilus and Criseyde*, ii. 1291, *Physician's Tale*, 68 and 70, and *Manciple's Tale*, 285.

1369 *We haue etyn garlek euerychone*: a pungent saying, not listed in collections of proverbs.

1528 John v. 14, viii. 11.

1577 *Sare and Sysse*: cf. *Elinor Rumming*, Skelton, i. 99, 'Thyther cometh Kate, Cysly, and Sare', and *Chester Plays*, vii. 419–22, 'will you heare how he sang "Celsis"? . . . nether sang "Sar" nor so well "sis" / ner "pax" "mery mawd when she had met him"'.

1601 The missing leaf must have included speeches by Meekness and Patience, whom Mankind answers in 1671–5. Seven women Virtues conquer seven Vices in Prudentius, *Psychomachia*, Grosseteste, *Chasteau d'Amour*, and Rutebeuf, *La Bataille des Vices contre les Vertues*; see Bloomfield, *The Seven Deadly Sins*, pp. 64–67, 134, 141. *Piers Plowman*, ed. Skeat, i. 190–1, ii. 71–72, names the seven sisters as in *The Castle* except that *Solicitudo* is *Pees* for alliteration. They were pictured as armed maidens, each trampling on an opposing Vice, in the Painted Chamber at Westminster: E. W. Tristram, *English Medieval Wall Painting*, 1950, pp. 105–6 and plates. See also Émile Mâle, *L'art religieux de la fin du moyen âge en France*, pp. 262–7, Adolf Katzenellenbogen, *Allegories of the Virtues and Vices in Mediaeval Art*, 1939, and *Die Psychomachie in der Kunst des Mittelalters*, 1933, and M. D. Anderson, *Drama and Imagery in English Medieval Churches*, 1963, pp. 80–84. In Medwall's *Nature*, ii. 1076–1375, the Seven Virtues are men, not women, and are called Mekenes or Humylyte, Pacyence, Charyte, Lyberalyte, Good Occupacyon or Good Besynes, Abstynence, and Chastyte or Contynence.

1610 A favourite image, discussed by Greene in *Early English Carols*, p. 406.

1611 I Corinthians xiii. 1–3.

1631a Freely quoted from Romans viii. 8, 'Qui autem in carne sunt Deo placere non possunt'.

1638 *in bankys brymmne*: 'on the brink of a slope'; cf. *Ludus Cov.* xviii. 42, 'by bankys and brymmys browne'.

1644a *Osiositas parit omne malum*: A fuller form, 'Omne malum pertulit ociositas e[t] pro ocio deuenit omne malum', is quoted by Meech in *Modern*

Philology, xxxviii. 125, 132, with other instances. *Jacob's Well*, i. 235, 285, and *Speculum Christiani*, p. 64, quote Jerome, 'Do thou alwey somwhate of gude werkes that the deuyl fynde the wele occupyede'. Cf. Ecclesiasticus xxxiii. 29; Chaucer, *Second Nun's Prologue*; *Oxford Proverbs*, p. 313; Tilley, I 13.

1660 Cf. *Piers Plowman*, B. xv. 128, and xx. 288–91, where executors 'make hem-self myrye' with other men's goods; Greene, *Early English Carols*, pp. 246, 255, 'Secuters be oft onekynd'; *Handlyng Synne*, 1180–8, 1219–26, 6233–6508; *Peter Idley's Instructions to His Son*, pp. 185–8, 235, 'They lieve merily by othir mannes laboure—No force if the soule goo daunce with a taboure'; Owst, p. 529.

1662 *owle*: not in *OED*.; F. 'accumulate'. Cf. Agnes Paston *c.* 1451 in *Paston Letters*, ed. Davis, 1958, pp. 21, 131, 'that I sett men to werke to owle money' (to gather money).

1668 On the lily as the flower of virgins see *Vitis Mystica*, *P.L.* clxxxiv. 672–708.

1696a Psalm xvii. 26; again in *M.* 324.

1705a Matthew x. 22; cf. xxiv. 13.

1705 s.d. A hymn still sung in matins from Ascension to Pentecost; see Dreves, *Analecta Hymnica Medii Aevi*, ii. 48.

1711 *with dyen dos*: F. '? dying', '? dose of vinegar and gall . . . or text corrupt'; Gollancz suggested *drery dos*. *MED.* finds *dose* used only for 'the giving of medicine in a specified amount or at a stated time', as in 'þe dose is . . .'.

1712 *clos*: either 'fortified' (*MED.*) or the noun 'stronghold, enclosed area, wall around a castle'; cf. *castel cage* 2703, *castel town* 2015, 2157.

1726 *Blythe*: 'quickly'. *MED.* gives three meanings for *blithe* adv., 'joyfully', 'kindly', or 'quickly', but all four instances of the meaning 'quickly' are scribal variants for *blive*, and so probably here. Cf. 2974 *blyfe*, probably for *blyþe* a.

1731 *moderys*: first explained by Henry Bradley in Furnivall, p. 188a. *OED.* describes *mauther*, a young girl, as 'Chiefly current in East Anglia and the adjoining counties', citing *Prompt.*, '*Moder*, servaunte, or wenche', Tusser, 'moether', 'mother', Fraunce, 'Modder', Jonson, 'Mauther', and Dickens, 'mawther'. Cf. Richard Brome, *The English Moor* (1658), iii. 1:

> O th'art a Norfolk woman (cry thee mercy)
> Where maids are mothers, and mothers are maids.

1733 *rasche*: 'rush', not in *OED.*, but cf. *rash* v. and *rush* sb.[2] and *Mary Magdalene*, 1331, 'with a rage' ('in haste').

1744 Smart in *Manly Anniversary Studies*, pp. 48–49, sees an allusion to the rebellion of Glendower and the Percies, but *Walys* is merely a useful rhyme, like *tales*: *Wales* in Skelton, i. 106, Bale, *King Johan* 563–4.

1748 *lowe in helle*: cf. Lucifer in *W*. 336, 'I am lowest in hell', and Skelton, i. 127, 'Lucifer lowest in helle'.

1751 *hothe*: 'heath'; see *Kyng Allsaunder*, ed. Smithers, ii. 43 and *Sir Launfal*, ed. Bliss, line 250 and pp. 9, 89.

1760 *Hathe*: 'he hath', as in 3040 and *M*. 422.

1766 s.d. The MS. has 'vocau*i*t', not '*vertunt*' as in F. See A. Henry in *Notes and Queries*, ccx (1965), 448.

1777 *abeye*: *MED*. assigns this to *abeien* 'bow, submit (oneself)', but it is certainly a variant of *abien* 'pay the penalty', as in *W*. 768. Cf. 1822.

1821 *ne had*: F. *nad*, but cf. *ne had* in 3323 and 3340.

1848 *lake*: 'fine linen'; cf. Lydgate, *Minor Poems*, i. 257, Our Lady 'white as ony lake'.

1853 *bowde*: F. 'malt-worm, drunkard'; *Prompt.*, '*Bowde*, malte-worme'. *MED*. says of the word here and in 2337, 'Used contemptuously of a person, either with ref. to the dung beetle or the malt weevil'.

1880 Smart in *Manly Anniversary Studies*, pp. 49–53, compares two similar attacks by the Deadly Sins. In *Piers Plowman*, B. xx, Antichrist attacks the fortress of Holy Church with Pride bearing his banner (as in *Castle*, 1928 ff.) and Fortune sends Lechery with a bow, Covetise with wiles (as in *C*. 2427 ff.), and Sloth with a sling. In the *Reply of Friar Daw Topias*, 1402 (*Political Poems and Songs*, ed. Wright, ii. 57–58), 'The devel is 30ur duke, / and pride berith the banner; / wraththe is 30ure gunner [cf. *C*. 2111–12], / envie is 30ur archer [*C*. 2159], / 30ur coveitise castith fer, / 30ur leccherie brennith [*C*. 2289 ff.], / glotony giderith stickes therto [*C*. 1961], / and sleuthe myneth the wallis [*C*. 2326]'. Smart concludes that these are parallels, not sources for this play, but that all three authors may have used a common source. Chambers suggests that 'the Sins perhaps wielded pitchforks', but lines 1944 ff. mention shot and sling, shafts, a lance, and *many a vyre* or cross-bow bolt.

1941 *as a gogmagog*: like the British giant described by Geoffrey of Monmouth. *OED*. first records the word as a common noun from *c*. 1565.

1966 *powdyr*: *OED*. does not record *pother* in the sense 'choking smoke' until 1627. This spelling suggests that it is the same as *powder* 'dust'.

2000 *a careful kaue*: 'a cavern full of grief', hell, as again in 3049; not, as explained in *MED*., 'A warning' from L. *cave* 'beware'.

2007a James i. 2, 'Omne gaudium existimate, fratres mei, cum in tentationes varias incideritis'.

2020a Psalm xxxvi. 4.

2022 *Prymrose pleyeth parlasent*: unexplained; cf. 1013 *par asent* 'willingly'.

2026 *Rode*: 'ruddy', as in *Mary Magdalene*, 959, 'rody as þe rose'.

2037 *helpynge honde*: the first instance in *OED*. is from *Imitation of Christ, c.* 1450.

2094a Luke i. 52.

2107a Luke xiv. 11, xviii. 14.

2120 *motyhole*: '? dusty hole'; F. 'moth-hole?'; cf. 1974 *mote* 'speck of dust' and *OED. motty, motey* 'containing motes'.

2124a James i. 20.

2145 *rosys*: so MS., though F. misread as *rolys*. Wrath laments in 2219–20, 'I am al betyn blak and blo Wyth a rose þat on rode was rent', and Envy in 2211 complains that Charity 'Wyth fayre rosys myn hed gan breke'. Roses are symbols of charity and of Christ's passion: *Vitis Mystica, P.L.* clxxxiv. 708–15.

2163a Matthew xviii. 7.

2165 Cf. Chaucer, *Canon's Yeoman's Tale*, 1047, 'Bileveth this as siker as your Crede'; Gower, *Confessio Amantis*, v. 2912, 'also siker as the crede'.

2169 *gres*: as in 821 and 2737; in 1907 *grese* rhymes with *ese*, but here *gres* rhymes with *wers: vers*. A better rhyme would be *gers*, but the rhyme may not be exact.

2180 Cf. *Rolle*, i. 71, 'Synful man, on þe I cry, / alanly for þi lufe I dy'.

2228 *fall on bord*: 'attack'. *OED., aboard*, records *fall aboard* first in 1604.

2239 *wynnyth a scho*: imperative, 'gain renown'.

2259 Cf. *Opera S. Bonaventurae*, ed. 1864–71, xii. 159, 'Si gulam non viceris . . . statim advocat sororem suam, id est, luxuriam'.

2277a Matthew iv. 2, 'cum jejunasset quadraginta diebus et quadraginta noctibus'.

2295, 2299 *bondys, londys* should perhaps read *bendys, lendys* ('loins'), but see note on 794. Cf. ON. *lundir* 'loins'.

2303a *Mater et Virgo, extingue carnales concupiscentias!*: not found elsewhere. M. D. Anderson, *Drama and Imagery in English Medieval Churches*, 1963, pp. 81–82, suggests that 'Chastity's invocation to the

Blessed Virgin to quench the fires of lust may have been accompanied by a well-aimed bowlful of water', since Lechery says in 2388, 'Sche hathe me dayschyd and so drenchyd'.

2335 *Thre mens songys*: first instance in *OED.*; cf. *Prompt.*, 'Thre mannys songe'.

2340 *Slugge*: the earliest instance in *OED. Slugnesse* or laziness is the first of eighteen kinds of Sloth in *Jacob's Well*, i. 103.

2341 Cf. *Handlyng Synne*, 1470, 'bytterer þan galle'; *Mary Magdalene*, 997, 'Thys sorow is beytterar þan ony galle'.

2347 *myskaryed*: 'led astray', the earliest transitive use in *OED.*

2364a *Nunc lege nunc ora nunc disce nuncque labora*: Tags like this were common. See H. Walther, *Sprichwörter*, iii (1965), nos. 19348–50.

2381 *þe deuelys dyrt*: the earliest use of this phrase; cf. *Towneley*, xxi. 170.

2385 *cowche qwayl*: 'crouch like a quail'. Cf. Chaucer, *Clerk's Tale*, 1206, 'thou shalt make hym couche as doth a quaille'; Skelton, ii. 21, 'to play cowche quale'; *Thersites*, sig. A iv, 'I haue made the knaues for to play cowch quaile'.

2395 *irchoun*: originally 'hedgehog', but here 'little child, brat', a sense first recorded in *OED.*, urchin, from *Calisto and Melibea*, c. 1530. A boy is also an *vrchyn* in *Nature* (before 1500), i. 787.

2402 *lurkynge lathe*: '? secret by-path'; F. 'hidden path?' *OED.* does not record *lathe*, but cf. *lade*, variant of *lode* 'way', in the *Ormulum* and in Scots c. 1400 (*Dictionary of the Older Scottish Tongue*).

2409 *loke lyke an howle*: 'stare like an owl'; cf. *York*, xxix. 117–19, 'he lokis . . . like an nowele in a stok'; Bale, *King Johan*, 198, 'loke lyke an owle'; *Common Conditions*, 419, 'The slaue lookes like an owle in a tree'.

2414 J. W. McCutchan, 'Covetousness in *The Castle of Perseverance*', *Univ. of Virginia Studies*, iv (1951), 175–91, comments that 'Covetousness is the strategic reserve, held in abeyance until the outcome of the struggle is at its most crucial point; he is thrown into the conflict as the last resort; he receives full credit from Mundus when the victory is won'. Bernard Spivack, *Shakespeare and the Allegory of Evil*, p. 85, compares Prudentius, *Psychomachia*, where Avarice, disguised as Thrift, deceives her victims through guile.

2421 *þe galows of Canwyke*: Smart in *Manly Anniversary Studies*, pp. 42–53, points out that the gallows stood on Canwick Hill near Lincoln and that Jews were hanged there for the murder of Hugh of Lincoln in 1255, 'A coste de Canevic, sur halt mont U la gent pendu sunt'. See also J. W. F. Hill, *Medieval Lincoln*, 1948, p. 231. A similar bit of gallows humour is in *Chester Plays*, vi. 287–8, where Octavian says to his messenger, 'the highe horse besides Boughton / take thou for thy travayle'.

2452a *Maledicti sunt auariciosi huius temporis*: not traced.

2465 1 Timothy vi. 10.

2482 *waxyn hory and olde*: emended from MS. *colde* by E. K. Chambers, *English Literature at the Close of the Middle Ages*, p. 57. Cf. Medwall, *Nature*, i. 1243–5, 'whan hys hed waxeth hore / than shalbe good season / To folow couetyse and hys way'.

2484 *crulle*: *MED*. places this under *croulen* 'tremble', but see the quotations under *craulen* 'crawl, walk slowly, drag oneself', especially 'crepe or creule' in *St. Robert of Knaresborough*, EETS., 878.

2497 *parage*: '? partnership'; the nearest meaning in *OED*. is 'tenure in equality, as of brothers'.

2513 *þe bok of kendys*: *De Naturis Rerum* by Alexander Nequam contains three books of commentary on *Ecclesiasticus*, as yet unedited.

2537 *Aforn mele men mete schul tyle*: not in *Oxford Proverbs* or Tilley.

2541 *whouso þe wynde blowe*: F. *whon-so* led to misinterpretation in *OED*., *wind* sb. 15, where *wind* is taken 'in unfavourable sense'. The idea is repeated in 2543, *what happe so-euere betyde*.

2571 *MED., axe*, takes 'holden the axe bi the helve' to mean 'be in control of a situation, be well off'. But this line means rather 'He acted of his own free will'.

2573 Cf. the refrain in *Rel. Lyrics XVth C.*, p. 270, 'he may wytyn hym-self his owyn woo', and *Jacob's Well*, i. 111, 'ȝif þou chese to be dampnyd, wyte it þiself and noȝt god!'

2575 *schelue*: F. 'shield, protect'; *OED., shelve* v.¹ '? To shield, defend', 'perh. an arbitrary alteration of *shelde* Shield *v.* for the sake of rhyme. Cf. Shelf v.¹'

2599a 1 John ii. 17.

2612a Psalm xlviii. 11, 'et relinquent alienis divitias suas'.

2615 Cf. Rastell, *The Four Elements*, sigs. A vi, A vii^v, 'I account hym neuer better than a best'.

2625a Psalm xlviii. 18.

2628 'It shall weigh thee down like a weight in a balance'. *OED*. finds *pounder* sb.¹ used only in 1429, 1439, and 1440; cf. the verb in Norfolk dialect, '*punder*, to be exactly on an equipoise' (*Eng. Dialect Dict.*).

2638a Ecclesiastes v. 9, 'Avarus non implebitur pecunia'.

2649–51 Cf. *Bulletin of the John Rylands Library*, xiv (1930), 100, 'Ther ben women, þer ben wordis, Ther ben gese, ther ben toordes'; Douce MS. 52 in *Oxford Proverbs*, p. 406; Tilley, W 686–7.

2652 *rakle*: 'haste', not in *OED.*, but cf. *rackle* 'hasty' and *rake* sb.³, sense 3, 'a run, rush; speed', citing *Towneley*, xvi. 65, 'Fast afore wyll I hy radly on a rake'.

2665 Cf. the song, 'Peny is an hardy knyȝt, / peny is mekyl of myȝt', and another on 'Sir Peny', 'so mekill es he of myght', both in *Latin Poems Commonly Attributed to Walter Mapes*, ed. Wright, Camden Soc., 1841, pp. 359–61, and in *Secular Lyrics*, pp. 50–55.

2709 Cf. 'Store is no sore' in *Oxford Proverbs*, p. 623; Tilley, S 903.

2711 *more and more*: Margery Kempe as a young wife 'euyr desyryd more & mor' (p. 9). Owst, p. 318, quotes from Bromyard, 'Ever the more thei have, the more thei nedeth'. Cf. *Rel. Lyrics XVth C.*, p. 275, on Avarice, 'ffor evyr he covetith more and more', where the line should end with a full stop.

2726 Here Covetousness takes gold nobles from his 'copbord be þe beddys feet'.

2778 Death appeared also in the lost part of *The Pride of Life*. In *Ludus Cov.* xx. 168 ff. Death, dressed as a skeleton, suddenly kills Herod and his knights as they feast. Miss Block, pp. liv–v, compares Death in the *Castle*: 'the entry of this character has not the quality of dramatic irony that makes the entry in the *Death of Herod* play so impressive . . . but the general effect is similar as are (naturally) the two speeches of Death'; for example,

> I am sent fro god deth is my name
> All thynge þat is on grownd I welde at
>   my wylle . . .
> what man þat I wrastele with he xal ryght
>   sone haue schame
> I ȝeve hym such a trepett · he xal evyr more
>   ly stylle . . .
> Ow se how prowdely ȝon kaytyff sytt at mete
> of deth hath he no dowte he wenyth to
>   leve evyr-more
> to hym wyl I go and ȝeve hym such An hete
> þat all þe lechis of þe londe hys lyf xul
>   nevyr restore
> A-ȝens my dredful dentys it vaylyth nevyr to
>   plete . . .
> Ffor now I go to sle hym with strokys sad
>   and sore . . .
> with my spere sle hem I xall.
>   and so cast down his pride.

See also Owst, 527–36.

2778 *it is tyme hye*: *OED*., *high* a., 11, quotes 'it is high time' first from 1581. Cf. *Paston Letters*, ed. Davis, 1958, p. 26, 'It is hey tyme'; *Ludus Cov.* xxxv. 1552, 'it was hy3 tyme'.

2785 *geyn-went*: 'return road'; not in *OED*., but cf. *gainchare* 'way of returning', *gaincome*, *gainturn*, and *Prick of Conscience*, 1718, 'Of bodily ded es no gayn-turnyng'.

2793 *downbrynge*: probably a compound verb, as in *Towneley*, xxii. 54, 'oure lawes to downe bryng' (cf. 109, 182; xxi. 92; and *Ludus Cov.* xxx. 247). Not in *OED*. or *MED*., but the latter quotes, under the adverb, *doun broght* from *Prick of Conscience*, 1467. Cf. *forth browth* in *C*. 326 and *In-browth* in *Mary Magdalene*, 1025.

2815 *In þe grete pestelens*: the Black Death struck England in 1348–9, 1361–2, 1369, 1375–6, and in later years.

2820 *þe grete fyschys ete þe smale*: cf. *Pride of Life* in *Non-Cycle Mystery Plays*, 361–2: 'þai farit as fiscis in a pol / þe gret eteit þe smal'; Lydgate, *Minor Poems*, ii. 564, 575, 588. Tilley, F 311, cites many instances, including Shakespeare's *Pericles*, II. i. 31.

2879 *tottys*: *toot* is a Lincolnshire word for 'the devil', according to Halliwell, *Dictionary of Archaic and Provincial Words*. *OED*. quotes this line under *tot* sb.[1] 'fool', but 'devils' makes better sense.

2900 *Forbrostyn*: 'burst in pieces', as in *Towneley*, xxiii. 589, 'ffor brestyn is his gall'.

2908 *Garcio*: 'servant' as in *Towneley*, ii and xii. Cf. *Prompt*., '*Ladde*, or knave, *garcio*'. 'Boy', 'ladde', and 'knaue' all meant 'servant', and he is old enough to inherit. See note on 189.

2958 *jeste*: '? entertainment': see *OED*., *gist* sb.[1] 'a stopping-place or lodging', '? refreshment'. *MED*. interprets the word here as *geste* 'action, way of acting'.

2969 *welaway*: cf. 3020 *So welaway þe whyle* and 3069 *Weleaway*.

2974 *blyfe*: probably for *blyþe* 'joyful' rather than for *blyve* 'quickly'; see note on 1726.

2985a Psalm xxxviii. 7.

3008 ff. For poems of the Soul reproaching the Body see *Latin Poems Commonly Attributed to Walter Mapes*, ed. Wright, Camden Soc., 1841, pp. 95–106, 321–49; W. Linow in *Erlanger Beiträge zur englischen Philologie*, i (1889); *A Worcestershire Miscellany*, ed. N. S. Baugh, 1956, pp. 42–50, 107–21; R. W. Ackerman in *Speculum*, xxxvii (1962), 541–65. Tempe E. Allison, 'On the Body and Soul Legend', *Modern Language Notes*, xlii (1927), 102–6, suggests that the Body may have replied in the missing leaf; but Mankind says in 3006, 'A word may I speke no more'.

3063 Psalm cxliv. 9, quoted in 3456*a*; cf. *Minor Poems of the Vernon MS.* ii. 658, and *Hymns to the Virgin and Christ*, pp. 95–100.

3096–7 'Quia in inferno nulla est redemptio' is from the Office of the Dead, *Breviarium ad Usum Sarum*, ii. 278. Lucifer quotes it as 'þis tyxt of holde' in *Ludus Cov.* xxvi, prologue, 48, and it is attributed to Job in *Prick of Conscience*, 2832–3 and 7248–50, *Piers Plowman,* B. xviii. 149, *York*, xxxvii. 285–8, *Towneley*, xxv. 299–302, and *Hickscorner*, 785–6. Sir John Harington, *The Metamorphosis of Ajax*, ed. Donno, 1962, p. 138, says that he has heard the text 'oft alleadged by great clerkes, but I thinke it is in the Epistle of S. Paule to the Laodiceans, or in Nicodemus Gospel: for I never yet could find it in the Bible'. The source is Job vii. 9, 'qui descenderit ad inferos, non ascendet'. See also Tilley, R 60.

3099 *dagge*: 'jog', the only instance in *MED.*, which compares Mod. E. *tag* 'trail'. But *Eng. Dialect Dict.* gives instances of *dadge* 'saunter' from 1747 and later Northern dialect, and of *dodge* 'to go at a slow pace, to jog or trudge along' from Scots and Northern dialect. *Dagge* may have been pronounced with the /dʒ/ sound, like *loggyth* in 99, *bagge* in M. 322, and *fogge* 'jog along' in 913.

3117 *kewe*: 'mew', not in *OED.*, but cf. *Prompt.*, '*Kewtyn*, as cattes' and '*Kewtynge* of cattys'.

3129 The four daughters of God appear in Psalm lxxxiv. 11 (A.V. lxxxv. 10): 'Misericordia et veritas obviaverunt sibi, iustitia et pax osculatae sunt', quoted in 3521*a*. Their debate before God is presented in Hugh of St. Victor, *P.L.* clxxvii. 623–5; St. Bernard, *P.L.* clxxxiii. 385–90; Grosseteste, *Le Chasteau d'Amour*, followed in *Cursor Mundi*, 9517–9752; and the *Meditationes Vitae Christi* formerly ascribed to Bonaventura. Hope Traver, *The Four Daughters of God*, pp. 125–40, suggests that the *Meditationes* or some work based upon them influenced *The Castle*, *The Charter of the Abbey of the Holy Ghost* (Rolle, i. 349–52), and the later *Ludus Cov.* xi. See also R. A. Klinefelter, 'The Four Daughters of God, a New Version', *Journal of English and Germanic Philology*, lii (1953), 90–95. *The Castle* changes the traditional time of the debate, before the Incarnation, to the judgement of the soul after death, as in Caesarius of Heisterbach and *Processus Belial*, and adds the debate of the sisters before they appeal to God. For the four daughters in art see S. C. Chew, *The Virtues Reconciled, An Iconographic Study*, 1947.

3151 Justice is here first personified in English drama; cf. J. W. McCutchan, 'Justice and Equity in the English Morality Play', *Journal of the History of Ideas*, xix (1958), 405–10.

3162 *As he hath browyn, lete hym drynke*: Truth uses the same proverb in 3274 and in 3299–3300. Cf. Skeat, *Early English Proverbs*, pp. 49–50; *Oxford Proverbs*, p. 64.

3163a Galatians vi. 5.

3167a Matthew vii. 21, 'Non omnis qui dicit mihi: Domine Domine, intrabit in regnum caelorum'.

3252a Psalm l. 8.

3265a *Aurum sititi, aurum bibisti*: not traced.

3281 Matthew xii. 31–32.

3284 Psalm cxvi. 2, 'veritas Domini manet in aeternum'.

3313a 2 Corinthians i. 3–4. Cf. *Ludus Cov.* xi. 73, 'O Ffadyr of mercy and god of comforte', and *Rolle*, ii. 377–80, where a meditation ascribed to Augustine quotes this and other texts on mercy also found in *C*.

3339a Cf. Gregory, *P.L.* lxxix. 222, 'nisi Adam peccaret, Redemptorem nostrum carnem suscipere nostram non oporteret'; Lydgate, *Minor Poems*, i. 298; *Ludus Cov.* xi. 139; 'Adam lay I-bowndyn' in *Rel. Lyrics XVth C.*, p. 120, 'Ne hadde þe appil take ben, þe appil taken ben, ne hadde neuer our lady a ben heuene qwen'; A. O. Lovejoy, 'Milton and the Paradox of the Fortunate Fall', *ELH.*, iv (1937), 161 ff., reprinted in his *Essays in the History of Ideas*, 1948.

3341 *offent*: 'sinned against', a form not mentioned in *OED.* but used in *Sir Ferumbras*, line 1916, by analogy with such past participles as *shent*, *spent*. See A. H. Marckwardt in *Univ. of Michigan Publications, Language and Literature*, xiii (1935), 286–95, and *discent* in Hardyng's *Chronicle* (*OED.*, *descend*, 8 b.).

3351–2 John xix. 28, 'Jesus . . . dixit: Sitio'. Cf. *Rel. Lyrics XVth C.*, p. 143, ' "I thrist", The heill of saulis'; *Jacob's Well*, i. 185, ' "I haue thryst", þat is, for helth of mannys soule'.

3354–6 John xix. 29–30: 'illi autem spongiam plenam aceto hysopo circumponentes obtulerunt ori ejus. Cum ergo accepisset Jesus acetum, dixit: Consummatum est.'

3357 John xix. 34, 'unus militum lancea latus ejus aperuit'. Longinus in the *Gospel of Nicodemus* is called Longius in Chaucer, *ABC*, 163, and Longeus in *York, Towneley, Chester Plays*, and *Ludus Cov.* See Rose J. Peebles, *The Legend of Longinus*, 1911.

3361–4 *Aqua baptismatis et sanguis redempcionis . . . est causa saluacionis*: not traced.

3374 Psalm lxxxviii. 29, 'In aeternum servabo illi misericordiam meam'.

3378 Psalm lxxxviii. 2.

3382a Psalm x. 8, 'Quoniam justus Dominus et justitias dilexit'.

3391a, 3404 Deuteronomy xxxii. 18, 'Deum, qui te genuit, dereliquisti, et oblitus es Domini creatoris tui'.

3443a Psalm lvii. 11.

3456a Psalm cxliv. 9, 'Et miserationes ejus super omnia opera ejus'.

3469a Luke i. 50; cf. Psalm cii. 17.

3470 *non*: 'not at all', a sense which *OED*. first records from 1651. Cf. Margery Kempe, 176, 'þei wil non oþerwyse þan I wil'; *Minor Poems of the Vernon MS*. i. 414, 'Mercy ne pite is non worthi'.

3478 Matthew xxv. 41–46.

3521a Psalm lxxxiv. 11.

3529 Cf. John xvi. 24, 'ut gaudium vestrum sit plenum'.

3531–2 Cf. *The Prick of Conscience*, 7817–44:

> þare es rest ay, with-outen trauayle;
> þare es all gudes þat neuer sal fayle;
> þare es pese ay, with-outen stryf; . . .
> And parfyte luf and charyte,

and Lydgate, *Minor Poems*, i. 295, 'Where euer is Ioye, and pes withoute werre'.

3534a Cf. *Meditations of Bernard*, *P.L.* clxxxiv. 492, 'Est ibi pax, pietas, bonitas, lux, virtus, honestas'.

3547a Cf. *Prick of Conscience*, 9129–32:

> And þarfor haly kyrk, þat oft prays
> Ffor þe saules in purgatory, þus says:

Tuam Deus deposcimus pietatem, ut eis tribueris [*read* tribuere] digneris lucidas et quietas mansiones.

3552 Acts viii. 32.

3560a Jeremiah xxix. 11, 'Ego enim scio cogitationes, quas ego cogito super vos, ait Dominus, cogitationes pacis et non afflictionis'. Cf. *Ludus Cov*. xi. 137, 'I thynke þe thoughtys of pes and nowth of wykkydnes'.

3573a Psalm xxxii. 5.

3595 Cf. *Piers Plowman*, B. i. 154; Chaucer, *Clerk's Tale*, 1211; *Towneley*, x. 368; Tilley, L 139.

3597a 'Sicut scintilla ignis in medio maris, ita omnis impietas viri ad misericordiam dei' is quoted from Augustine in *Prick of Conscience*, 6316–17, and *Piers Plowman*, B. v. 291*a*, and translated in *Rel. Lyrics XVth C*., p. 224, and *Speculum Christiani*, pp. 72, 114.

3610a Deuteronomy xxxii. 39, 'Ego occidam et ego vivere faciam; percutiam et ego sanabo; et non est qui de manu mea possit eruere'.

3623a Ezekiel xxxiv. 10, 'Ecce ego ipse super pastores; requiram gregem meum de manu eorum'; *Prick of Conscience*, 5288–9, 'Ecce! ego requiram gregem meam de manu pastoris'.

3628 *þe seuene dedys of mercy*: Six deeds are mentioned in Matthew xxv. 31–46. The seventh deed is to bury the dead, as Tobias did. Cf. *Speculum Christiani*, p. 40: '1. I visette the seke. 2. I ȝeue drynke the thursty. 3. I fede the hungry. 4. I bye the presoner oute of thraldom. 5. I couer the nakede. 6. I herbere the pore man housles. 7. I bery the ded body.' The works of mercy were often pictured, as at Bury Abbey: E. W. Tristram, *English Medieval Wall Painting*, 1950, p. 517.

3636a From the Athanasian Creed; cf. Matthew xxv. 46, 'Et ibunt hi in supplicium aeternum, justi autem in vitam aeternam'; *Piers Plowman*, B. vii. 111*a*; *Wisdom*, 877–8.

3647–8 Cf. 410*a*, 'Homo, memento finis'; *Everyman*, 10–11, 'Man, in the begynnynge / Loke well and take good heed to the endynge'; *Mundus et Infans*, 485, 'Alwaye, or ye begyn, thynke on the endynge'.

WISDOM

First stage direction. Wisdom appears as Christ the King, wearing an imperial crown and carrying in his right hand a sceptre and in his left hand an orb. This is the only instance in *MED.* of *balle* for 'orb as emblem of rule'. The Smiths' Company of Coventry bought 'a cheverel gyld' for Christ in 1490: *Two Coventry Corpus Christi Plays*, p. 85.

W 1–65 Smart showed that these lines are from Suso, *Orologium Sapientiae*, and that they follow the English version edited by Horstmann in *Anglia*, x (1888), 323–89. *Wisdom* adds such words and phrases as 'imperyall', 'egalle', 'eternall', 'and wery patrone', 'yt ys myrable', and 'no creature can specyfye', and new sentences in 24–26, 39–40, and 47–48.

W 4 *nobley*: 'nobleness', as again in 576; cf. *Orologium*, 'þe whiche name is most conuenient and best acordynge to myne nobleye'.

W 9–10 Cf. 1 Corinthians i. 24; Augustine, *De Trinitate*; Sister Mary Frances Smith, *Wisdom and Personification of Wisdom Occurring in Middle English Literature before 1500*, 1935; and J. J. Molloy, *A Theological Interpretation of the Moral Play, Wisdom, Who is Christ*, 1952.

W 16 *Thus Wysdom begane*: not 'Wisdom began to speak thus' but 'This was the origin of the name Wisdom'. Smart thought the words irrelevant; E. K. Chambers, *English Literature at the Close of the Middle Ages*, p. 59, wrote that the speech ends oddly, as if it were meant for a prologue; Molloy suggested that the expression was used 'to have the speaker, Christ, add emphasis to the fact that He is Wisdom' and 'to signify that He has finished stating his genealogy and function'.

W 16 s.d. *gysely*: 'handsomely', an emendation which seems to me more likely than *gyntely* or *goodly*. *OED.*, *guisily*, quotes *Sir Orfeo*, 297, 'In queynt atire gisely'. See also *Peter Idley's Instructions to His Son*, ii. B, 182, 'To be arraied giselie'.

W 17–20 Wisdom of Solomon viii. 2, 'Hanc amavi, et exquisivi a juventute mea, et quaesivi sponsam mihi cam assumere, et amator factus sum formae illius.'

W 21–23 Wisdom of Solomon vii. 10, 11.

W 27–29 Wisdom of Solomon vii. 29 and *Orologium* both read *speciosior*.

W 30–32 Wisdom of Solomon vii. 26.

W 33–37 Proverbs iii. 15–16 and viii. 11.

W 47 Proverbs viii. 17, 'ego diligentes me diligo'.

W 56 Cf. *Orologium*, 'hit ȝeviþ fredam to hem þat beþ parfyte'.

W 63 The Digby reading is closer to *Orologium*, 'hit maye be in experience felt'.

W 69–70 From *Orologium*, 'souereynlye fayre and worþi spowse . . . þi amyke or loue'. *MED.* quotes only three examples of *amyke*, this from *Wisdom* and two from *Orologium*, but five instances from *Orologium* are cited by Schleich in *Archiv*, clvi (1929), 184–94.

W 79 Proverbs xxiii. 26, with *mihi*; *Orologium*, with *mi*; cf. Margery Kempe, pp. 90, 302, 'I aske no mor of þe but þin hert for to louyn me'.

W 86–90 *Orologium* describes 'þe scole (of) soþfaste diuinyte'. The disciple enters the school and asks, 'teche me in schort manere þat heuenelye diuinite'. Wisdom answers: 'Mye dere sone, wille þou noht sauere in kunynge to hye, but drede! . . . takynge owre biginnynge of helefulle disciplyne at þe drede of godde, þe wheche is þe beginnynge of wisdam'. Cf. Proverbs xv. 33, 'Timor Domini disciplina sapientiae', ix. 10, 'Principium sapientiae timor Domini', and Ecclesiasticus iii. 22, 'Altiora te ne quaesieris . . . ne fueris curiosus'.

W 91–92 Cf. *Mary Magdalene*, 1081–3, 'mannys hartt is my gardyn here; / þer-In I sow sedys of vertu all þe ȝere; / þe fowle wedes and wycys, I reynd vp be þe rote'.

W 95–98 Smart, pp. 28–31, compares the *Meditations* attributed to St. Bernard, *P.L.* clxxxiv. 485 ff.: 'per cognitionem mei valeam pervenire ad cognitionem Dei. Quanto namque in cognitione mei proficio, tanto ad cognitionem Dei accedo. Hilton, *The Scale of Perfection*, i. xl, quotes Augustine, 'By the knowing of myself, I shall get the knowing of God'.

W 103–70 Smart shows that these lines follow, freely at first and closely in 135–70, Hilton's *Scale of Perfection* (Book II, chapters i, ii, vi, xiii, and

xii). Smart quotes an edition of 1507; see also the partly modernized
edition by Evelyn Underhill, 1923. Hilton says that every soul 'is the
ymage of god' (1 Corinthians xi. 7) 'and made to the ymage and to the
lyknes of hym', 'wonderly fayre', 'but thorough synne of the fyrst man
adam it was dysfygured'. 'A soule of a chylde that is borne and is un-
crystenyd by cause of orygynal synne . . . is nought but an ymage of the
fende & a bronde of helle'. Since Christ made amends, man's soul is now
'reformed & restored to the fyrst lyknes', by the sacrament of baptism.
Sensuality, 'that is flesshly felynge by the fyve outwarde wyttes', 'whan
it is unskylfully and unordynatly ruled is made the ymage of synne'.
Reason has two parts: 'The over partye . . . is propyrly the ymage of god /
For by that only the soule knowyth god and lovyth him', and 'the neyther
. . . lyeth in knowynge and rulynge of erthly thynges: for to use hem
dyscretly after nede. and for to refuse hem whan it is no nede'. 'Fayr is
mannes soule & fowle is a mannes soule', 'Foule without as it were a
beest / fayre within lyke to an angel'. The two texts quoted from the
Song of Solomon mean: 'ye angels of heven that arne doughters of the
hye Jerusalem wonder not on me ne dyspyse me not for my blacke
shadowe / For though I be blacke without by cause of my flesshly kynde
as is a tabernacle of cedar / Nevertheles I am ful fayre within as the
skynne of salomon'. *Cedar* is interpreted, not as Kedar, but as cedar
wood: 'By cedar is understood murkness, and that is the devil', while
'By the skynne of salomon is understood a blessed angel'.

W 135 *sensualyte*: 'the part of the soul concerned with the senses'; cf.
Rolle, *Psalter*, ed. Bramley, 1884, p. 23, 'the nether party of my saule.
that is cald the sensualite'; Hilton, *Scale of Perfection*, ii. xiii; Lydgate,
Reson and Sensuallyte; *The Assembly of Gods*; and Reason and Sensuality
in *Mary Magdalene*, 394, and in Medwall, *Nature*.

W 159 *a angell*: as in *a angell* 333, *a ordenance* 786; wills of 1450 and
1465 in *Lincoln Diocese Documents*, EETS., cxlix, p. 288; Capgrave,
Chronicle, Rolls Series, i. 123, 124; Bokenham, *Legendys*, 1106.

W 162 *fyve prudent vyrgyns*: Matthew xxv. 2; here the five senses (cf. 173,
1075–6, and Molloy, p. 29).

W 164 Song of Songs i. 4 (*filiae*); *Scale of Perfection* (*filie*, but translated
as 'ye doughter of Jherusalem' in the 1507 edn.).

W 169–70 Song of Songs i. 5, 'Nolite me considerare quod fusca sim,
quia decoloravit me sol'. *Jouis* is added for rhyme.

W 177 *Thre myghtys*: The faculties of the soul, Mind, Understanding,
and Will, are associated in 279–82 with the Father, the Son, and the Holy
Ghost respectively, as in Augustine, *De Trinitate*, xv. 23, where they are
memoria, *intelligentia*, and *voluntas* (*amor*). Smart compares 185–90 with
Meditations of Bernard, 'Cum Dei reminiscor, in memoria mea eum in-
venio', and shows that 245–64 and 275 are translated from the *Meditations*.

Will comes before Understanding in 180–278, 324 s.d., and 358, but elsewhere the order is Mind, Understanding, Will (cf. Molloy, pp. 48–49).

W 213–18 Smart, p. 32, compares *Tractatus de Interiori Domo, P.L.* clxxxiv. 511: 'bona voluntas . . . per quam imago similitudinis Dei in nobis reparatur. . . . Sine bona voluntate omnino salvari quispiam non potest: cum bona voluntate nemo perire potest. . . . Fac igitur magnam bonam voluntatem tuam, si vis habere magnum meritum.' *Speculum Christiani*, p. 213, quotes Augustine, 'Cum bona uoluntate omnino perire non potes, & sine bona uoluntate saluari non potes'.

W 221 *Wyll for dede oft ys take*: cf. Augustine, quoted in *Speculum Christiani*, p. 213, 'Bona uoluntas sufficit, si desit operacionis facultas'; *Alphabet of Tales*, EETS., cxxvii, p. 520, 'Voluntas pro facto reputatur'; Margery Kempe, pp. 212, 339–40, 'I receyue euery good wyl as for dede'; *Oxford Proverbs*, p. 709; Tilley, W 393.

W 227 *lybrary*: 'collected learning', as in *Ludus Cov.* ix. 234, 'we xal lerne ȝow þe lyberary of oure lordys lawe lyght'.

W 231 From *Scale of Perfection*, I. xii, 'The knyttynge & ye fastynge of Jhesu to a mannes soule: is by good wyl'.

W 247–8 Cf. Revelations i. 8, 'Ego sum Alpha et Omega, principium et finis'.

W 265 *make reporture*: 'declare'; cf. 355, *Mary Magdalene*, 2084, and Medwall, *Nature*, ii. 364.

W 270–2 1 John iv. 15, 16.

W 276 Ecclesiasticus xxiv. 12.

W 288 1 Corinthians xiii. 13; cf. *W.* 1117–39. Smart, pp. 43–44, quotes homily in Harleian MS. 2373, f. 12ᵛ: 'Be ye refourmede wiþ virtewes. þe mynde wiþ belefe. þe reson wiþ hope. and þe wylle wiþ charite. and so ye bene lyche to þe holy trinite.'

W 293 *thre enmyes*: see note on *Castle*, 28.

W 301–3 The three steps of temptation, mentioned again in 365–7 and 497–9, are described by St. Bernard, *P.L.* clxxxiii. 669, and in Smart, p. 45: *memoria, ratio*, and *voluntas* fall 'per suggestionem, delectationem, consensum', and rise again through faith, hope, and charity. See also Bede on St. James, *P.L.* xciii. 11.

W 307 Cf. 1 Timothy vi. 12, 1 Peter v. 4, James i. 12, and *M.* 231.

W 310–20 Smart, pp. 33–34, suggests that these lines are translated from Bonaventura, *Soliloquium de Quatuor Mentalibus Exercitiis*, or a similar source, in a passage based on Hugh of St. Victor. *Wisdom* adds mainly rhyme-words such as *gloryus, Cristus, Jhesus, truthe, ruthe*. See also the

translations of St. Edmund's *Speculum* in *Minor Poems of the Vernon MS.*
i. 228–9, and in *Rolle*, i. 243.

W 319 *go wyll*: 'go astray', as in Margery Kempe, pp. 1–2, 'þis creatur
whych many ȝerys had gon wyl & euyr ben vnstable'.

W 321 *þe oyll of mercy*: promised to Adam and brought to man by
Christ, according to the *Gospel of Nicodemus, Vita Adae et Evae*, and
Cursor Mundi, 1237 ff. See Esther C. Quinn, *The Quest of Seth for the
Oil of Life*, 1962.

W 324 s.d. '*Tota pulcra es*': Song of Songs iv. 7, 'Tota pulchra es, amica
mea, et macula non est in te', sung as an antiphon for the procession on
Trinity Sunday (*Sarum Missal*, ed. Legg, p. 173). *Lucyfer*: his fall is
presented in York, Towneley, and Chester plays and in *Ludus Cov.* The
disguise of Lucifer as a proud gallant is like his disguise in *Ludus Cov.*
xxvi, prologue, 65 ff., and the disguise of Pride as a gallant called Curiosity
in *Mary Magdalene*, 550.

W 325 *Owt, harow!*: the cry of Lucifer in *York*, i. 97 and of Satan in xxx.
159, xxxvii. 185, 343, as of devils in *Towneley*, xxv. 116, 185, 207;
Chester Plays, i. 245; *Ludus Cov.* xxiii. 187, xxxiii. 1002; *Mary Magdalene*,
722, 963; but also of the widow and her daughters in Chaucer, *The Nun's
Priest's Tale, C.T.* vii. 3380.

W 327–8 Cf. *York*, vii. 23–24, 'þanne made he manne to his liknes,
That place of price for to restore'; *Towneley*, iii. 28–29, 'to his liknes
maide man, That place to be restord'; and *Ludus Cov.* xi. 48, 'of locyfere
to restore þe place'.

W 338 Cf. *Mary Magdalene*, 366, 'for at hem [man] I haue dysspyte'.

W 343–5 Smart compares *Rolle*, ii. 109: 'as Leo the pope sayth: The
fende our ghostly enemy aspyeth in euery man what wyse he is dysposed
by his compleccyon / and by that disposicyon he tempteth hym'.

W 394 Matthew xx. 6.

W 401 Ecclesiastes iii. 1, 'Omnia tempus habent'; cf. 'alle thyng hath
tyme' in Chaucer, *Friar's Tale*, 1475, and Skelton, i. 137.

W 405–29 Walter Hilton, *Epistle on Mixed Life*, says that men 'bounde
to þe world be children & seruauns' should not utterly 'leue ocupacions &
bisynes of þe world' for prayer; they should be like both Martha and
Mary, for Christ gave example to 'sum men to vse þis medled lyf' (*Rolle*,
i. 264–9; Smart, pp. 26–28).

W 413–14 *Mertha, Maria*: Luke x, 38–42, 'Maria optimam partem
elegit'.

W 415–16 Cf. *Scale of Perfection*, II. xviii, 'For they saye that it is
ynough to hem for to be saaf and have the leest degre in heven'.

W 417 See *The Form of Perfect Living, Rolle*, i. 46–9; *The Fire of Love*, p. 48; *The Mending of Life*, p. 130.

W 437–9 Cf. *Scale of Perfection*, II. xxii: vain dreads and spirits with wiles shall say that it is perilous to leave the world, 'thou shalt falle in to sykenes or in to fantasyes or in to frenesyes as thou seest that som don'.

W 442 *nesesse*: *OED*. quotes this with one other use of the adjective, in 1456, and one use of the noun *necesse* in *Play of the Sacrament* (*Non-Cycle Plays*, line 694).

W 444 Cf. *Proverbs of Hendyng*, 'Clymb not to hye, lest þou falle'; *Ludus Cov.* xli. 32, 'Whoso clyme ouer hie· he hath a foule fall'; Lydgate, *Minor Poems*, ii. 477, 565, 813; Greene, *Early English Carols*, p. 236; *Rel. Lyrics XVth C.*, p. 237; *Oxford Proverbs*, pp. 282, 295; Tilley, C 414.

W 469 Molloy argues that Lucifer says to Understanding, 'I advise you to bend Will towards the choice of this delectable good'; but Lucifer is probably speaking to Will.

W 470 *þow*: 'those'. F.'s emendation *þow* [*þey*] is not needed; cf. 1074 *thow ben gostly*.

W 471 Cf. Matthew vi. 16, 'Cum autem jejunatis, nolite fieri sicut hypocritae tristes'; *Scale of Perfection* II. xx and lix.

W 490 Matthew vii. 15; *Oxford Proverbs*, p. 723; Tilley, W 614. Molloy suggests an allusion to the black cloak and white habit of a Dominican preacher.

W 491 Cf. Ecclesiasticus iv. 32; *Proverbs of Alfred*, 123–4, 'Sorwe hit is to rowen aȝen þe se-flode'; Gower, *Confessio*, iv. 1781, 'rowe ayein the stremes stronge'; *Oxford Proverbs*, p. 627; Tilley, S 927.

W 492 Cf. Chaucer, *Merchant's Tale*, 1516; *Nature*, i. 865, 1084; *Oxford Proverbs*, p. 421; Tilley, P 335.

W 510 *syde aray*: 'long clothing'. Cf. *M.* 671 where New Guise urges that Mankind's long gown be cut short, and *Nature*, i. 768–71:

> Than haue I suche a short gown
> Wyth wyde sleues that hang a down
> They wold make some lad in thys town
> a doublet and a cote.

Smart in *Modern Philology*, xiv. 304–5, quotes statutes of 1463 and 1482 forbidding short gowns.

W 511 *hanip la plu joly!*: the meaning is uncertain; cf. *hanap* 'wine-cup' in *OED*. and Godefroy and *hanapus* in Du Cange, with variant *hannipa*.

W 515–16 Cf. 767; *Handlyng Synne*, 4149–52, 'þat Frenshe men synne yn lecherye'; Lydgate, *Minor Poems*, ii. 519; *Ludus Cov.* xii. 56, 'after þe frensche gyse'.

W 521 *clumme*: 'silent'; cf. *clom* in Chaucer, *Miller's Tale*, 3638 and 3639.

W 529–34 Smart compares the *Myroure of Oure Ladye*, p. 99, 'Pryde. Couetyse. and flesshely synne, in whiche ar vnderstonde all synnes. as saynte Iohn sayeth' (1 John ii. 16). Bloomfield cites also *Speculum Sacerdotale*, ed. Weatherly, p. 22. Pride is the chief sin according to Augustine and Gregory, who writes in *Moralia* (*P.L.* lxxvi. 620), 'Exercitus diaboli dux superbia'.

W 533 *rende*: '? tear' or '? render, hand over'.

W 550 s.d. *boy*: an early use of *boy* in the modern sense, as in 912 s.d. *small boys*. Cf. a proverb in Rawlinson MS. D. 328 (*Modern Philology*, xxxviii. 123), 'Of a scrod boey (*prauo puero*) comyt a good man', and Dobson's article cited in the note on *C*. 189.

W 552 *wyrre*: 'hurry!'; cf. the shepherd's call in *Towneley*, xii. 117, 119, 'Tup, I say, whyr! . . . Whop!'; *Ralph Roister Doister*, I. iii. 11–12, 'No haste but good, Madge Mumblecrust; for whip and whurre The olde prouerbe doth say, neuer made good furre'.

W 552 *care awey!*: familiar in songs, as in *Secular Lyrics*, pp. 4, 34, 39. Cf. *Prompt.*, '*Care-awey*, sorowles'; Lydgate, *Minor Poems*, ii. 704, 'Care away is a good medycyne'; and Jenkin Careaway in *Jack Juggler*.

W 555 In *Mary Magdalene*, 506, Pride, called Curiosity, says, 'I do it for no pryde', and in *Nature*, i. 772–3, Pride says, 'Som men wold thynk that this were pryde / But yt ys not so'. Cf. *W*. 604, where covetous falseness 'ys clepyde wysdom'; *Ludus Cov.* xxvi, prologue, 111–12, 'ʒe xal kalle pride oneste and naterall kend lechory / And covetyse wysdam'; *Nature*, i. 1209–17, Pride is called Worship and Covetise 'calleth hym selfe worldly polycy'. Owst, p. 314, quotes from a sermon: 'A prowde man is callyd an honest man. ffor now a dayes, thowʒe a man be never so prowde of hert . . . is that pride? Nay, forthe, he seythe it is clenlynes and honestye.'

W 567 Cf. Skelton, *Magnificence*, 839–40, 'Me seme I flye, I am so lyght'.

W 575 Cf. Chaucer, *Parson's Tale*, 450, on pride, 'Somtyme it spryngeth of the goodes of nature, and somtyme of the goodes of fortune, and somtyme of the goodes of grace', and Owst, p. 308, quoting from a sermon: 'The ʒiftis of kynde are theis, noblei of kynrede, gentilnes of blood. . . . The ʒiftis of fortune arn. . . lordschipe, worchep and frenschip. ʒiftis of grace arn . . . eloquense in speking, coriouste in craft, in reding, or such othir.'

W 577 *soleyn*: 'aloof, apart from others'; F. 'solitary ?'; *OED.* 'unique, singular'; *Prompt.*, 'he þat lovythe no cumpany'. In *Piers Plowman*, C. vii. 36, Pride is 'so synguler by my-self as to sight of the puple, Was non suche as my-self'.

W 594 *affyable*: 'affable, agreeable', rather than 'one's betrothed' (F. and *MED.*). Cf. *Mary Magdalene*, 548, 'fayer and afyabylle', and *Hugues Capet* (Paris, 1864), 5741, 'Le roy va acoller par maniere affiable'.

W 604 *Ser Wyly*: cf. *Wyly-man* in *Piers Plowman*, C. v. 27; *Syr gyle* in *Towneley*, xiii. 408; and *Geffrey Gyle* in *Ludus Cov.* xiv, prologue, 9. Sir John Paston in 1473 writes 'Ware that, quod Perse' 1 N. Davis, 'The Language of the Pastons', *Proc. Brit. Academy*, xl (1954), 136.

W 614 *ewell joy me wrynge!*: cf. *York*, xxxvi. 76, 'Ille joie hym wring!'

W 617 *tenowr*: the shepherds sing *tenory*, *tryble*, and *meyne* in *Towneley*, xiii. 186–8, and the devils *trebill* and *meyn* in xxx. 537–8. Cf. *thre-mens songys* in *C.* 2335, and Lydgate, *Minor Poems*, ii. 448.

W 623 Cf. 'I am als light as birde on bowe', *York*, xxv. 388; *Secular Lyrics*, p. 62.

W 638 *Enbrace questys*: 'bribe juries'; cf. Lydgate, *Dance of Death*, 481–2, 'Maister ioroure, whiche that atte assise / And atte shires questes doste embrace', and Arnold Williams, *The Characterization of Pilate in the Towneley Plays*, 1950, pp. 45–53. Stow records that in 1468 'diuerse persons being common Iurors, such as at assises were forsworne for rewards, or fauour of parties, were iudged to ride from Newgate to the pillorie in Cornehill, with Miters of paper on their heads' (*Survey of London*, ed. Kingsford, i. 191).

W 652 *comun as þe way*: cf. *Piers Plowman*, B. iii. 131, where Mede is 'As comune as a cartwey to eche a knaue that walketh'.

W 653 Cf. a sermon in Owst, p. 329, 'lawe goys as lordshipp biddeth hym'.

W 666 Cf. *Piers Plowman*, B. iii. 160–1, 'Lawe is so lordeliche and loth to make ende, With-oute presentz or pens she pleseth wel fewe'; *Ludus Cov.* xiv. 25–26, 'And loke 3e rynge wele in 3our purs For ellys 3our cawse may spede þe wurs'.

W 667 *malewrye*: 'misfortune', not in *OED.*, which, however, records uses of *mal(h)eur* and *maleurtee* by Caxton in 1471.

W 680 Cf. *Minor Poems of the Vernon MS.* ii. 685, 'Seþþe þe tyme þat god was boren, þis world was neuer so vntrewe'; *Peter Idley's Instructions to His Son*, ii. B, 22–23, 'I reporte me yf now vsed be pride inordinate; Neuer more I trowe sith God was born'.

W 687 *by contenance*: 'by gestures, in dumb show'; the eighteen dancers do not speak. Cf. *Towneley*, xxvi. 114; stage directions in *Ludus Cov.* xxvii. 669a, and xxviii. 972a 'be contenawns'; and a document of 1468 in *Archaeologia*, xxxi. 328, 'The pageantes wer so obscure . . . because all was cuntenaunce, and no wordes'.

W 693 Mind plays the role of Maintenance and calls in his six retainers who 'wolde ber wp falsnes Ande maynten yt at þe best'. Their 'sute' or livery, not described, would be appropriate to Pride, Wrath, and Envy, like their red beards and the lions rampant on their crests. Molloy compares the red beard of Judas in the cycle plays. Wrathful men are 'rede as blode' in *Handlyng Synne*, 10229–30. The lions need not refer to the badges of the Dukes of Suffolk and Norfolk (Smart, pp. 88–89), since they were familiar symbols of pride: Jeremiah v. 6; Dante, *Inferno*, I; *Scale of Perfection*, II. xiv; Bloomfield, *The Seven Deadly Sins*, appendix I. Many treatises on sins discuss Disdain and Stubbornness (*Indignacyon* and *Sturdynes*) under Pride, Malice and Discord under Envy, and Hastiness and Vengeance (*Wreche*) under Wrath. In *Jacob's Well*, i. 70, one branch of Pride is 'meyntenauns of pletynges & of strives'.

W 694 *Hastynes*: 'rash anger'; cf. Margery Kempe, p. 55, 'For a lytil hastynes, hym-self defendyng . . . he smet a man or ellys tweyn, wher-thorw, as he seyde, [they] wer ded or ellys lyche for to be ded'.

W 697 Cf. *York*, xliv. 7–11, where the eleven disciples choose a twelfth:

> Or we begynne vs muste be even,
> Ellis are owre werkis noght to warande.
> For parfite noumbre it is none,
> Off elleuen for to lere,
> Twelue may be a-soundir tone . . .

W 698 See Josephine W. Bennett, 'The Mediaeval Loveday', *Speculum*, xxxiii (1958), 351–70.

W 699 *Ande þe Deule hade swore yt*: 'even if the Devil had sworn to oppose it'; cf. Herod in *York*, xix. 63–64, 'This gadlyng schall agayne Yf þat þe deuyll had sworne', and Caesar in *Towneley*, ix. 83–84.

W 700 *þe Deullys dance*: cf. Dunbar, *Dance of the Seven Deadly Sins*. Arthur Brown in *Folk-Lore*, lxiii. 70, compares Stubbes, *Anatomy of Abuses*, ed. Furnivall, p. 147, on the Lord of Misrule dancing through the church with pipers and drummers 'to strike vp the deuils daunce withall'.

W 707 *Madam Regent*: apparently the name of a dance tune. Cf. Jonson, *Bartholomew Fair*, I. v. 18–19, 'you thinke, you are Madam *Regent* still, Mistris *Ouer-doo*; when I am in place?'

W 718 Cf. Lydgate, *Minor Poems*, i. 69, ii. 450, 455, 758, 775; *Peter Idley's Instructions to His Son*, pp. 85, 215; *Oxford Proverbs*, p. 679; Tilley, F 20.

W 721 F. assumes (*Digby Plays*, p. 168) that the quest of Holborn was a wardmote quest, but that was a jury of inquiry which only presented suspected offenders and did not try them: *Liber Albus*, ed. Riley, pp. 36–39, 257–60. The Holborn quest was probably a jury presided over by the sheriff and justices of Middlesex, who met in High Holborn, where a new Quest House was built about 1590 in Middle Row opposite Grays Inn Lane: E. Williams, *Early Holborn and the Legal Quarter of London*, ii. 1232; Jeaffreson, *Middlesex County Records*, ii. 70, 77–78.

W 722 *rechases*: *OED*. suggests that this may be a transferred use of *rechase* 'chase back', suggested by the hunting sense of *quest*, cf. Chaucer, *Book of the Duchess*, 379. *The Master of Game* uses *rechase* for 'recheat, blow the horn to call together the hounds'; cf. the noun *rechace* in *W*. 908.

W 724 s.d. Their visors or masks suggest the two faces of perjured jurors. Understanding plays the role of Perjury. In the *Psychomachia* of Prudentius Perjuries and Falsehood are among the ten followers of Avarice. Molloy compares St. Gregory, *Moralia*, xxxi. 45, who names seven daughters of Covetousness, including *perjurium, fraus, proditio, fallacia*, and *violentia*. See *W*. 744, 'For þe fadyr of vs, Covetyse'.

W 724 s.d. *hattys of meyntenance*: the Commons petitioned in 1377 against the giving of hats by way of livery for maintenance (*Rotuli Parl.* iii. 23).

W 731 *entyrecte*: this word, rhyming with *streytt* and *beyght*, is spelled *Entret* in 796 and means 'salve, plaster', from OF. *entrait, entret* (MED. and Godefroy). A jury should remedy wrongs, but this jury is an evil plaster or ointment which takes bribes to plaster wrongs and oil its own palms. Cf. *Hickscorner*, 267, 'And with an oyntment the iuges hande I can grece'.

W 741–2 Cf. Whetstone, *Promos and Cassandra* (1578), sig. K iii, 'He that is rytch, as my dame sayth, goes away with the Hare', and the proverb 'There be more ways to the wood than one', in *Oxford Proverbs*, p. 696, and Tilley, W 179.

W 752 s.d. The three women disguised as gallants seem to be *Rekleshede* (Heedlessness), *Idyllnes*, and *Surfet and Gredynes*, perhaps a double name for one character (unless seven women enter, four disguised as gallants). They represent Sloth and Gluttony, as Lechery is represented by the three matrons Adultery, Mistress, and Fornication. Will does not give himself a new name, as Mind and Understanding did, but he calls the dance 'a sprynge of Lechery', the corruption of the Will as Love. MS. *conregent*, found nowhere else, does not fit the sense as well as *congruent* or *convenyent* (which occurs in lines 6, 701); cf. Skelton, i. 83, 'ryght conuenyently And full congruently'.

W 757 The hornpipe with its mouthpiece of horn is appropriate to the horns of cuckolds.

W 759 Cf. Skelton, i. 386, 'Furdrers of loue, with baudry aqueinted'. Bette is a nickname for Bartholomew in *Piers Plowman*, B. ii. 109, v. 32, 330, and in *Ludus Cov.* xiv, prologue, 24. Bet for Elizabeth is later (Besse in Skelton), but Beatrice is *Bete* or *Betune* in *Prompt.* and *Beto(u)n* in *Piers Plowman*, B. v. 33, 306.

W 775 *Dompe*: not 'Master' (F.) but 'dumb'. Apparently Will wants the mummers (the 'dumb device') to remain quiet (*dare*).

W 783–4 Cf. *Towneley*, xiii. 64–108, on wives, 'wo is hym that is bun', 'wo is hym that has many'. See F. L. Utley, *The Crooked Rib*, 1944.

W 789 *At Westmyster*: the courts of King's Bench, Common Pleas, and Chancery were all held in Westminster Hall: Stow, *Survey of London*, ed. Kingsford, ii. 118. The four law terms were Hilary, Easter, Trinity, and Michaelmas terms.

W 793–4 *at þe parvyse* . . . *A Powlys*: at the enclosure in front of St. Paul's, where lawyers met their clients. See Robinson's note in *The Works of Chaucer*, ed. 1957, p. 659; *Secular Lyrics*, p. 56; *Paston Letters*, ed. Gairdner, iii. 156, 'at the parvyse' (1476). *OED.* finds the earliest use of *a* for *of* in 1480, but see also *M.* 127 and 272, *Minor Poems of the Vernon MS.* i. 407, 'Robert, Bisschope a lycoln', and *Cursor Mundi*, 1367, 'þe quilk a þe appel tre he nam'.

W 796 *Entret* seems to mean 'bribery' (see note on *W.* 731), *juge-partynge* 'sharing with judges', and *to-supporte* 'giving backing (or financial support) to' a litigant.

W 800 The common stews or brothels were on the Bankside; cf. *Nature*, ii. 180–4, 'at the tother syde of the water . . . le stewys'; *Mundus et Infans*, 592–3, 'ouer London-brydge I ran, And the streyght waye to the stewes I came'; *Cock Lorel's Boat*, 'By syde London brydge in a holy grounde Late called the stewes banke'.

W 824 Whiting, *Proverbs in the Earlier English Drama*, p. 76, compares the proverb 'Spend and God will send'; see Greene, *Early English Carols*, p. 429; *Oxford Proverbs*, p. 613; Tilley, G 247; and *C.* 1655.

W 828 Cf. *Nature*, ii. 200–3, 'at a banket or a rere supper . . . yet wolde I spende xx. shylling'.

W 832 *Sent Audre*: St. Etheldreda in Bede and other Latin writers, *Audre* here and *Audrys* in *M.* 628 are earlier examples of the English form than any mentioned in Withycombe, *Oxford Dictionary of English Christian Names*, but *Audre* is also in *Handlyng Synne*, 10526, 10689, and *Altenglischer Legenden*, ed. Horstmann, pp. 291–307.

W 834 *Jenet N.*: 'Nomen', any name, as in the services of baptism and marriage, Margery Kempe, pp. 9, 10, and the Banns of *Ludus Cov.*, 'N. town'.

W 840 *in þe wyrry*: 'seized by the throat' as dogs worry an animal. *OED.* does not record the noun *worry* until 1804.

W 850 *Arest hym fyrst to þes for fyght*: 'first have him bound over to keep the peace for fear of fighting'. Cf. Skelton, *Magnificence*, 814, 'Ye, for surety ofte peas is taken for frayes', which editors misprint because they have missed the reference to taking surety of the peace (*securitatem pacis*).

W 851 *in another schere hym endyght*: the Church excommunicated all who 'do clepyn here aduersaryis in straunge schyres þere þe trespas is noȝt knowyn, tyl þei bcn owtlawyd or banyssched out of þe reem': *Jacob's Well*, i. 26. Men often complained in Chancery that they had been convicted in another shire without their knowledge.

W 853 *þe Marschalsi*: the court held before the steward and the knight-marshal of the king's household. Brinklow, *Complaynt of Roderyck Mors*, EETS., p. 26, attacks the 'unreasonable chargys of that court'. Pollard, p. xxii, confuses the court with the prison of the Marshalsea, mentioned in Skelton, ii. 40.

W 854 *þe Amralte*: the court of the Lord Admiral: see *Select Pleas in the Court of Admiralty*, Selden Society, vi, xi.

W 855 *A preuenire facias*: OED. explains *preuenire* as an error for *praemunire*, a writ bidding the sheriff 'cause to warn' or summon a person accused of prosecuting in a foreign country a suit cognizable by the law of England. Statutes of Praemunire were enacted from 1353 to 1393.

W 858 'I shall conceal it by money, the head and tail of a coin'; cf. Lydgate, *Minor Poems*, ii. 667, 'cros nor pyl'; *Rel. Lyrics XVth C.*, p. 291, 'here-In of al wynnyng lyth crosse & pile'; Tilley, C 835.

W 864 *seyer*: 'speaker'; '? assayer, trier' (Bradley in F.) and thus defined in *OED.*, *sayer* sb.², but see *sayer* sb.¹, 2 b., 'One who speaks', quoting More in 1533, 'shrewd sayers'.

W 872 Cf. *Cristys curs* in *C.* 2163 and *M.* 99, 399, 809.

W 902 s.d. Since Furnivall's side-notes from this point to the end of the play refer to the soul as masculine, Theodore Spencer, *Shakespeare and the Nature of Man*, 1942, p. 56, thinks that Anima has 'apparently changed sex since the beginning of the play'. This is not so, for in 1085 Wisdom calls her 'syster'.

W 912 s.d. MS. *vj* should be *vij*, as in Luke viii. 2; *Ludus Cov.* xxvii. 502, 'Now þese vij ffendys be fro me fflytt'; *Mary Magdalene*, 691 s.d., 'vij dyllys xall dewoyde frome þe woman'. This emendation was suggested by Molloy, p. 136.

W 913–24 For appeals of Christ to man, based on the Good Friday service, see 'Goddis Owne Complaynt' in *Political, Religious, and Love Poems*, ed. Furnivall, pp. 190–232; *Rolle*, i. 71, 156, ii. 457; *Rel. Lyrics XIVth C.*, pp. 17, 86–93; *Rel. Lyrics XVth C.*, pp. 151–75, where a typical poem asks, 'Why wratthis þu me þat am þy frende? . . . Quid vltra debui facere?'

W 932 *þis*: 'to this extent'; quoted in *OED.*, with *þis longe* in *W*. 978, as the earliest uses in this sense.

W 940 John xi. 25.

W 965–7 Cf. *Scale of Perfection*, II. vii: God 'abydeth not grete penaunce doynge ne paynful flesshly sufferyng or he foryeve it / But he askyth a lothynge of synne & a ful forsakynge in wyl' (cf. *W*. 959).

W 986 Cf. *Scale of Perfection*, II. vii: 'It is not ynough to hym to ful sykernesse for to have foryevenes of god oonly by contrycyon betwene god and hym. but yf he have a charter made by holy chyrche yf he may come therto. And that is the sacrament of penaunce the whiche is his charter & his token of foryevenes.' See also *W*. 1078–80.

W 989 See note on *C*. 3313*a*.

W 996 s.d. Lamentations ii. 13, 'Magna est enim velut mare contritio tua: quis medebitur tui?' The next sentence is from i. 2. Both verses are sung on Holy Thursday.

W 997–1064 These lines are translated from *Novem Virtutes*, formerly attributed to Richard Rolle (*Rolle*, i. 110–12, and ii. 455–6; Smart, pp. 34–37). The main additions are 1003–4, 1011–12, 1018–20, 1026–8, 1035–6, 1049–52, and 1062–4. Cf. 1 Corinthians xiii. 2, 'si habuero omnem fidem ita ut montes transferam, charitatem autem non habuero, nihil sum'.

W 1020 Perhaps *ony* should read *or*.

W 1021 Cf. Matthew xxvi. 40, Mark xiv. 37, 'vna hora vigilare'.

W 1023 *kyngys* should probably be *knyghtys*, since *Novem Virtutes* reads 'quam si mitteres vltra mare duodecim milites sepulcrum meum Vindicaturos', and a version in *Rolle*, i. 112, 'twell armed knyghtes'.

W 1065 s.d. Psalm cxv. 12, 13. Molloy notes that these verses have been spoken by the celebrant of the mass since the ninth century.

W 1081 Psalms lxxxv. 13, cvii. 5.

W 1083–4 Song of Songs iv. 9. *W*. adds *ictu*.

W 1086 *In þe tweyn syghtys of yowur ey*: Smart suggests a reference to the two eyes of the soul, understanding and love. Molloy interprets: 'the "tweyn syghtys" are the concomitant glances of each eye which fuse into one glance or *"uno ictu oculorum"*; secondly, "ey" is plural, being used for the rhyme instead of "eyen"'.

W 1097–1106 Smart, pp. 31–32, 37, compares *Meditations on the Passion* (*Rolle*, i. 87–88, 100–1) with 1097–1101 and quotes a passage attributed to St. Bernard in Bonaventura, *Soliloquium*: 'O Anima, Christus in Cruce te expectans, habet caput inclinatum, ad te . . . deosculandam, habet brachia extensa, ad amplexandam . . . pedes affixos, ad tecum commanendum:

latus apertum, ad te in illud intromittendum. Esto ergo, O Anima, iam columba nidificans in foraminibus petrae.' A similar appeal is in *Rel. Lyrics XVth C.*, p. 218, 'Thyne hede þu bowdist all a-downe. . .'. The comparison to a dove-house is found in *Ayenbite of Inwyt*, Rolle's *Meditations on the Passion, Orologium*, and Margery Kempe, p. 70.

W 1107 *plesere*: the rhyme with *here* suggests *plesere*, a form of *pleasure*.

W 1119–20 Romans xii. 2. *Wisdom* miswrites *confirmare* for *conformari* and adds *spiritus*, changes not found in *Scale of Perfection*, II. xxxi, where three texts from St. Paul are quoted in the same order as in *Wisdom*.

W 1127–8 Ephesians iv. 23, 24. *Wisdom* follows the comment in *Scale of Perfection*: 'ye shall be refourmed not in bodily felynge ne in ymaginacion but in the over partye of your reason'.

W 1134 1 John iv. 8, 16, as in *W*. 270.

W 1135 Colossians iii. 9, 'exspoliantes vos veterem hominem cum actibus suis, et induentes novum, eum qui renovatur in agnitionem. . .'. The second half of this text, which F. inserts, does not rhyme with *foly*. The line omitted in the MS. after 1135 probably followed the wording in *Scale of Perfection*, 'induite novum qui renovatur in agnicionem dei. . .'. 'Godys knowynge' is also from the *Scale*, 'ye shal be renewed in ye knowynge of god'.

W 1142–3 Psalm cxliv. 9.

W 1151 Romans v. 1 reads *habeamus*. *Wisdom* follows *Scale of Perfection*, II. ix: 'As saynt poul sayth / Justificati ex fide pacem habemus ad deum / That is: we that arn ryghted & refourmed thorugh faythe in cryst hathe pees & accorde made betwyx god & us'.

W 1153 Proverbs i. 7; cf. Psalm cx. 10; Ecclesiasticus i. 16.

W 1154–5 Malachi iv. 2, 'Et orietur vobis timentibus nomen meum Sol justitiae'. *Wisdom* uses the version in *Scale of Perfection*, II. xxvi, and the explanation, 'ye true sonne of rightwysnes that is our lorde Jhesu shal sprynge to you that dreden hym / that is to meke soules . . .'. *Wisdom* changes this only in 1158.

MANKIND

M 12 *lauatorye*: 'cleansing place'; cf. *waschynge well* in *C*. 3145 and these lines from the hymn 'Hostis Herodes impie', 'Lavachra puri gurgitis Cælestis Agnus attigit', *Breviarium ad Usum Sarum*, i. 319; Augustine, *P.L.* xxxv. 1953; Douglas Gray in *Notes and Queries*, ccviii (1963), 83, 131–3.

M 24 *defendawnte*: this is the only instance in *MED*. of the sense 'defender, protector'.

M 29 As T. W. Craik observes in *The Tudor Interlude*, p. 20, 'a social distinction appears to be drawn between the "sovereigns" who sit and the "brethren" who stand up'. Robert Reynes of Accle, Norfolk, a church-warden who presented parish plays in 1474, preserved an epilogue which thanks for their 'laudabyl lystenyng' the 'wursheppful souereyns þat syttyn here in syth, / lordys and ladyes and frankelens in fay': Iris G. Calderhead, 'Morality Fragments from Norfolk', *Modern Philology*, xiv (1916), 1–9.

M 32 Colossians i. 18; 1 Corinthians xii. 27. In 'Some Notes on *Mankind*', *Modern Philology*, xiv (1916), 45–58, 293–313, Smart compares Hilton's *Epistle on Mixed Life* (*Rolle*, i. 272).

M 43 Matthew iii. 12; Luke iii. 17.

M 45 *calcacyon*: 'trampling'; not in *MED*.; *OED*. cites the first use from 1656.

M 47 Cf. 'Mickle head, little wit', *Oxford Proverbs*, p. 422; Tilley, H 245.

M 49 *mysse-masche*: *OED*. cites this as the earliest use of *mish-mash*; cf. German *mischmasch*. It may be formed from *mys*, wrong, and *mash*, the mixture of malt and water used in brewing. The rhyme-word *dryff-draff* reduplicates *draff* 'refuse'; cf. *riff and raff*, *riff-raff*.

M 51 *Raffe*: Smart suggests a pun on the noun *raff* 'refuse'.

M 52 *Onschett yowur lokke*: Smart interprets as 'speak', comparing 133, 'Now opyn yowr sachell wyth Laten wordys'. The line may mean 'Open your locked door and give a halfpenny'.

M 57 Mischief mocks the manner of a preacher by quoting a mock-Latin text and explaining it for his unlearned hearers. Nought uses the same Latin ending in *spadibus* and *hedybus*, 398–9.

M 73 *ballys*: Smart interprets as 'bellows' used as a slang term for the bagpipe and suggests that the line means either 'Blow till your bagpipe bursts' or 'Play till the dancer's belly bursts'. But *ballys* may be the same word as *bales* in *M*. 807, 'a rod or switch for flogging' (*MED*., *baleis*). Either New Guise or Nowadays tells his companion, not the minstrels (since he says *þi*, not *yowr*), to apply the rod to make Nought dance.

M 75 *Sent Tanne*: 'St. Anne', as in *The Cely Papers*, pp. 186–7, 'Sent Tannys mony' and 'Sent Annys lyght'.

M 83 *goode Adam*: 'good old man'.

M 85 Sister Philippa Coogan, *An Interpretation of the Moral Play, Mankind*, p. 107, thinks that Mercy should speak this line; but Nought, who had no wish to break his neck, may mean that he has danced enough and that Mercy may take his place.

M 88 *play*: reasons for the emendation are given by Smart and by Sister Philippa, p. 7 n.

M 100 *And*: The first scribe wrote *a* or *A* for *and* here and in 275, 524, 611, 678, 712. *MED*. quotes nine instances of *a* as a weak form of *and*, but they may be scribal errors; cf. *OED*., *a* conj. The reduced form was printed by Caxton, *Paris and Vienne* (EETS.) 7/30. In *W*. 821 the scribe wrote *A* and then corrected it to *And*.

M 101 *curtly*: 'briefly', the only instance in *MED*.

M 103 *þe new jett*: see note on *C*. 1057.

M 109 *lyke*: 'taste', as in *Towneley*, iii. 378, 'Ye shal lik on the whyp'.

M 116 Even Cain and Herod swear 'bi hym that me dere boght' in *Towneley*, ii. 114 and 461, xiv. 444.

M 124 *Englysch Laten*: see J. C. Mendenhall, *Aureate Terms*, 1919.

M 125–6 The scribe's omissions leave no lines rhyming with *brest* or *me*. Earlier editors give 125–8 and 130 in their notes but not in the text, so that their line-numbers differ from this edition after 124. *Prauo te* seems to mean 'I shrew thee, I curse thee'. *Prauo* is defined as 'to shrewe' in *Ortus Vocabulorum* in 1500 (see Skelton, ii. 296, and *Prompt*. III. liv–lxiv); cf. *deprave* 'revile'.

M 134 *clerycall*: 'clerkly, learned'. *OED*. found no instance before 1592. *MED*. cites only this use, but see also *M*. 579, where *a clerycall mater* may mean 'a subtle matter'.

M 143 *bely-mett*: to the measure of the belly, full and satisfying; cf. *bely-fyll* 639, *fote-mett* 531, and *mowþis met(te)* in *C*. 758, 1243.

M 153 *þe demonycall frayry*: 'the brotherhood of devils'. An allusion to Dominican friars is seen by L. W. Cushman, *The Devil and the Vice in the English Dramatic Literature before Shakespeare*, 1900, p. 85, and by Sister Philippa, pp. 4–6, 116–18. Cf. *The Image of Hypocrisy* in Skelton, ii. 442, 'ffryer Domynike And ffryer Demonyke'.

M 154–5 Smart compares *Mundus et Infans*, 491–2, 'come wynde and rayne, God let hym neuer come here agayne!' Meech prints the proverb from Rawlinson MS. D. 328 in *Modern Philology*, xxxviii, 124, 'Come wynde, come reyne, come he neuer agayne'.

M 159–60 Tilley, D 556 and G 81, cites Heywood, *Proverbs* (1546), 'Nowe here is the doore, and there is the wey, And so (quoth hee) fare-well, gentill Geffrey'; *The Bugbears* (1565), 1. i. 70, 'now farewell gentell gefferye'; and *Look about You* (1600), 'gentle Ieffrey'. Cf. Smart, p. 293; *Oxford Proverbs*, p. 191.

M 180 Galatians vi. 7; *Proverbs of Alfred*; *Oxford Proverbs*, p. 608.

M 200 Cf. the Scottish proverb, 'It is a sour reek, where the good wife dings the good man', *Oxford Proverbs*, 1935 edn. only, p. 228. This proverb, like another in Tilley, S 573, is based on a story which explains a carol in Greene, *Early English Carols*, pp. 274–5. Cf. Greene, pp. 272–3, 'The most mayster of the hows weryth no brych'.

M 201–2 Earlier editors have omitted these lines from the text. A lost line presumably rhymed with *dungehyll*: *yll*: *wyll*.

M 211 *querulose*: *OED.* quotes this under *querulous* but suggests that it may be for *querelous* 'quarrelsome', which makes better sense.

M 228 Job vii. 1.

M 229 Cf. *Mary Magdalene*, 1952, 'now ar ȝe be-cum goddes own knygth'.

M 234 *a chery tyme*: 'the brief time of a cherry-harvest festival'; cf. Gower, *Confessio Amantis*, prologue, 454, 'Al is bot a chirie feire', and vi. 891, 'as it were a cherie feste'; Skelton, ii. 85–86. *MED.* quotes twelve instances of the comparison, usually in the form 'þis world nis but a chirie feire'.

M 237 *Mesure ys tresure*: cf. Lydgate, *Minor Poems*, ii. 773, 776; *Secular Lyrics*, p. 111; Smart, p. 294; *Oxford Proverbs*, p. 415; Tilley, M 805.

M 241 Smart, p. 294, compares *A Treatise of Ghostly Battle* (*Rolle*, ii. 421–2), where the body is a horse to be restrained by the bridle of Abstinence. Sister Philippa cites *Speculum Sacerdotale*, pp. 56–57.

M 251 *palfreyman*: 'officer of the stable'. *OED.* has a ghost-word under *palfrey* from Brandl's misreading 'palfrey mare'.

M 252 *gesunne*: 'scarce' (not 'plentiful' as glossed by F. nor 'treasure' as explained by *MED.* under *gersume*).

M 261 'The soner the better' is first quoted by *OED.* from *Paston Letters*, iii. 194 (1477); cf. Tilley, S 641.

M 262 *Do Lytyll*: found as a surname since 1204: Reaney, *Dictionary of British Surnames*, 1958.

M 271 Deceit swears 'by saynte Quyntyne' in Skelton, i. 49, and Merry Report in Heywood, *The Weather*, 834–5.

M 274 *þe comyn tapster of Bury*: Smart, p. 294, quotes an order at Lynn in 1465 to expel 'eny common Tapster . . . whiche is knowen for a mis-governed woman'.

M 287 Job xxiii. 10 refers to gold: 'et probavit me quasi aurum quod per ignem transit'. Smart, pp. 294–5, compares a translation of *Duodecim Utilitates Tribulationis*: 'as gold with fire, & ierne with file'.

M 292 Job i. 21 (*sibi* for *Domino*).

M 301 *Tytivillus*: explained in 886, 'propyrly Titiuillus syngnyfyth the Fend of helle'. Only in *Mankind* is he more than a minor devil. Tutivillus is 'chefe tollare' for the Devil in *Towneley*, xxx. 206 ff., where he quotes the traditional verses describing his function, 'ffragmina verborum / tutiullus colligit horum'. See Gower, *Vox Clamantis*, iv. 864, 'Qui magis est blanduo quam Titiuillus'; Owst, pp. 512–14; *Mirror of Our Lady*, p. 54, 'I am a poure dyuel, and my name ys Tytyuyllus'; *Rel. Lyrics XVth C.*, p. 277, 'Tutiuillus, þe deuyl of hell'; *OED.*, *titivil*; and M. D. Anderson, *Drama and Imagery in English Medieval Churches*, 1963, pp. 173–7.

M 303 *ey*: emended for rhyme; cf. 876, 'Tytiuillus, þat goth invisibele, hyng hys nett before my eye'.

M 319 *remos*: so pronounced, like *mossel* in *C.* 1171.

M 321 Job xxxiv. 15, 'homo in cinerem revertetur'.

M 322 Smart, p. 295, explains the badge as the sign of the cross written on the paper hung about Mankind's neck. Cf. *Mary Magdalene*, 992 s.d., 'Here xall enter þe iij maries . . . with sygnis ofe þe passion pryntyde vpone þer breste'.

M 324 Psalm xvii. 26, 27; also in *C.* 1696a. Sister Philippa cites discussions of this text in *Ayenbite of Inwit*, p. 205, and Bromyard, *Summa Praedicantium*, I. III. v.

M 325–6 Psalm cxxxii. 1.

M 332 *a Crystemes songe*: this is not 'a carol' (*MED.*) since it is not in stanzas. It has only four lines, repeated, and a line sung in chorus. Owst, pp. 483–4, cites Thomas Gascoigne, *Loci e Libro Veritatum*, p. 144, 'cavete et fugite in hoc sacro festo viciosa et turpia, et praecipue cantus inhonestos et turpes', and another preacher who wrote, 'be well ware that ʒe syng not the songes of fowle rebawdry and of unclennes' at Christmas. Cf. Bale, *King Johan*, 564, 'crystmes songes are mery tales'.

M 343 *Hoylyke*: a pun on *holy*, with possible meanings 'hole-like', 'hole-lick', or a leek called *holleke*.

M 348 *wyth bredynge*: not 'with politeness' (F.) nor 'in haste, instantly' (*MED.*, *breidinge* from *breiden* 'move quickly') but 'with upbraiding, reproach' (from *breiden* 'reproach'): see *OED.*, *braiding* sb.², and *Nature*, ii. 525–30, 'Let hym stand wyth a foule euyll . . . Let hym stande on hys fete wyth bredyng.'

M 363 Cf. *W.* 394.

M 374 *compasse*: *MED.* overlooks *compost* in this sense, 'a mixture for fertilizing land'. *OED.* records it first in 1587.

M 390 *By cokkys body sakyrde*: 'by the sacrament'; cf. 612 and *Nature*, i. 1174, 'by cokkys precyouse body'.

M 397 1 Samuel (1 Regum) xvii. 47, 'non in gladio nec in hasta salvat Dominus'.

M 435 Smart compares the bringing to life again in the mumming plays (*Modern Language Notes*, xxxii [1917], 21–25). See also Arthur Brown in *Folk-Lore*, lxiii (1952), 65–78.

M 443 *on and on*: 'one and one, one after another' (*OED.*, *one* 16 b).

M 452 A *Walsyngham wystyll* may have been used by pilgrims to the shrine of Our Lady of Walsingham in Norfolk (Smart, p. 296), or it may have been sold to the pilgrims at Walsingham. Brooches and ampoules from the shrine are illustrated in J. C. Dickinson, *The Shrine of Our Lady of Walsingham*, 1956.

M 453 *flewte*: the rhyme calls for *flowte*; cf. *Prompt.*, '*Flowte*, pype'.

M 456 *si dedero*: see the note on *C.* 879.

M 460 *yowr neclygence*: instead of *yowr reverence*, like *neglygence* used instead of *diligence* in *Nature*, i. 1265.

M 461 Titivillus probably wore a grotesque mask; cf. Smart in *Modern Language Notes*, xxxii. 23, and Brown in *Folk-Lore*, lxiii. 69.

M 462 *Kepe yowr tayll*: 'keep your reckoning' (of the money gathered).

M 464 *pens of topens*: 'coins worth twopence', the earliest mention in *OED.* of this phrase; cf. 'Pens of two Pens' in the *Rolls of Parliament* (iii. 183) for 1477, 'a peny of twa pens' in *Catholicon Anglicum* (1483), and 'half grotes or pence of ijd.' in a statute of 1503–4.

M 465 *reyallys*: the rial, royal, or rose noble, a gold coin worth 10s., was first coined in England in 1465 : *OED.*; Smart, *Sources for Wisdom*, p. 89 n; R. L. Kenyon, *The Gold Coins of England*, pp. 57–58; D. C. Baker, 'The Date of *Mankind*', *Philological Quarterly*, xlii (1963), 90–91. Margaret Paston sent her son half a 'riale' in 1471: *Paston Letters*, iii. 24. Coins listed in a sixteenth-century hand on f. 121ᵛ between *Wisdom* and *Mankind* are *sofferens*, *dobyll ducketts*, *angelys*, and *ii olde Ryallys*.

M 467 *þe goodeman of þis house*: 'the head of this household' or 'the host of this inn'.

M 468 *Ʒe say as yll*: F. suggests that *as* is for *ws*.

M 471 *I sey new gyse*: 'I speak in the new fashion'.

M 475 *Ego sum dominancium dominus*: cf. Deuteronomy x. 17, 'Dominus dominantium'; Revelation xix. 16, 'Rex regum, et Dominus dominantium'; and Pilate in *Towneley*, xxiv. 10, 'sum dominus dominorum'. Pilate and Titivillus both say 'caueatis!'

M 482 *felow*: *velan* would rhyme with *jentyllman* and assonate with *am*.

M 483 'The Devil have the whit!' or 'Not a whit! My purse is empty'. *OED*. under *whit* quotes *Robert the Deuyll* (1480), 'The devyll have the whyt that he was soreye therfore'; *Rede Me and Be Nott Wrothe* (1528), 'The devil of the whit that I can'; *Celestina* (1631), 'The divell awhit'. But it is possible that the true reading was *a qwytt*, and that the scribe wrote *haue* in place of *a*.

M 487 Psalm cxiii. 9.

M 488 Smart, p. 297, compares Hoccleve, *Regiment of Princes*, 684–6, and Skelton, *The Bowge of Courte*, 364. See also *Oxford Proverbs*, p. 139; Tilley, D 233; Nashe, *Works*, i. 305, 'the Deuils dauncing schoole in the bottome of a mans purse that is emptie, hath beene a gray-beard Prouerbe two hundred yeares before Tarlton was borne'.

M 489 Tilley, B 391, quotes Sir Thomas More and Heywood, *Proverbs*, ii. viii, 'as bare as a byrdes arse'.

M 497 *þe fyve vowellys*: Smart, pp. 297–8, suggests 'þe v. wellys', a term for the five wounds of Christ, and quotes charms to be said 'in the worschep of the fyve woundys'. Nowadays may be varying this formula to refer to his cries of pain, 'A! e! i! o! u!' Cf. the refrains in *Rel. Lyrics XIVth C.*, p. 96, 'With I & E'; *Rel. Lyrics XVth C.*, pp. 141, 256, 289, 'Wiþ an O & an I', 'Wiþ an .v. & an I'; Greene, *Early English Carols*, pp. 367, 390, and his article in *Medium Ævum*, xxx (1961), 170–5.

M 505–15 The place-names are discussed by Brandl, p. xxvi, by F. and Pollard, pp. xi–xii, 19, and by Smart in *Modern Philology*, xiv. 48–55, 306–8. In Cambridgeshire are Sawston, Hauxton, and Trumpington, a group of villages just south of Cambridge, and Fulbourn, Bottisham, and Swaffham, to the east of Cambridge in the direction of Bury (mentioned in 274). East Walton, Gayton, Massingham, and another Swaffham are in Norfolk, a few miles to the east of Lynn. Swaffham and Soham in Cambridgeshire are mentioned in Skelton, i. 417. Smart cited documents for Huntingdons of Sawston in 1428, a John Thyrlowe of 'Hawkeston' (also spelled 'Hauston') in 1450, John and William Pychard of Trumpington (1450–89), William Baker of East Walton (d. 1491), Alexander Wood of Fulbourn (J.P. 1471, d. 1479), William Allington of Bottisham (J.P. 1457, speaker of the Commons in 1472, knighted in 1478, d. 1479), and Hamonds of Swaffham in Cambridgeshire and Swaffham in Norfolk. A John Fydde lived in 1450 at Waterbeach, near Cambridge. The rogues took care to avoid the two justices and 'Hamonde of Soffeham', probably, as Professor Bruce Dickins suggests, the William Hamond whose brass dated 6 Feb. 1481/2 was once at Swaffham Bulbeck, Cambs. For the Huntingdon family see T. F. Teversham, *A History of the Village of Sawston*, 1942–7, i. 52 f., 101–6. J. C. Wedgwood, *History of Parliament*, 1936, i. 9, records that William Allington, M.P., was exiled with Edward IV in September 1470, and is said to have been the king's standard bearer at Barnet in April 1471.

M 512 *a noli me tangere*: 'a touch-me-not' (John xx. 17). The first use of the phrase for a person in *OED.* is *c.* 1635. Smart, *Modern Philology*, xiv. 50–51, cites Gower, *Mirour de l'Omme*, line 1518, where Arrogance is named 'Le mal *Noli me tangere*', and Lydgate, *Pilgrimage of the Life of Man*, line 15607, where Wrath says his name is *Noli me tangere*. Cf. *Oxford Proverbs*, p. 460; Tilley, N 202.

M 516 *For drede of in manus tuas qweke*: 'for fear of hanging'; cf. 'In manus tuas commendo spiritum meum' in Psalm xxx. 6, Luke xxiii. 46, and the prayer said by the dying (Smart, p. 299; Sister Philippa, p. 119). *Qweke*, which rhymes with *cheke* (check), is used again in 808 for the sound of choking; cf. *Tale of Beryn*, 2944–6, 'pleying in the strete Att a gentill game þat clepid is the quek, A longe peny halter was cast about my nekk'; Skelton, i. 292, 'For by robbynge they rynne to in manus tuas quecke'; *Youth*, sig. A ii, 'I catche a quecke'; *Gammer Gurton's Needle*, iv. iii. 12, 'kecke'.

M 520 *neke-verse*: the first instance in *OED.* A man might escape hanging for his first offence if he could read a Latin verse, usually the third verse of the fiftieth Psalm, 'Miserere mei, Deus, secundum magnam misericordiam tuam; secundum multitudinem miserationum tuarum dele iniquitatem meam'. *Jacob's Well*, i. 236, calls this 'þe psalme of grace'. See L. C. Gabel, *Benefit of Clergy in England in the Later Middle Ages*, Smith College Studies in History, xiv (1928–9).

M 522 The left hand is the devil's, according to Dionysius the Areopagite and Rabanus; see V. F. Hopper, *Medieval Number Symbolism*, p. 169.

M 537 'Drawk' and 'darnel' are names for several different weeds that grow among grain; see Britten and Holland, *A Dictionary of English Plant-Names*, English Dialect Society (1886), and *Prompt.*, Camden Society, xxv. 119, 130.

M 552 The Lollards believed, according to the trial of William and Richard Sparke for heresy in 1457, that 'a prayer made in a field or other unconsecrated place is just as efficacious as if it were made in a church': *Lincoln Diocese Documents*, ed. Clark, EETS., 1914, p. 93.

M 555 Cf. Tilley, L 136.

M 558 Smart, p. 299, quotes 'Breuis oratio penetrat celum', *Piers Plowman*, C. xii. 296*a*, and two English versions.

M 570 *powder of Parysch*: Smart, p. 300, suggests that this was an arsenic compound (like the later 'Paris green'), which would make brass pass for silver in the dusk of evening. Skelton uses *owle flyght* in i. 247, and ii. 77.

M 576 *ʒe xall a goode sport*: ellipsis, 'Ye shall have a good sport'. This idiom occurs in *Paston Letters*, ed. Davis, 1958, p. 28, 'ye schall [have] anoder letter wretyn tomorow', and p. 52, 'he shall [have] Cristes curs'.

Brandl interpreted *a* in *a goode sport* as a reduced form of *have*, but *Mankind* uses that form only for an unstressed auxiliary, as in 798, *Kowde not a cownselde*. The emendation in Manly and Furnivall, *3e xall se a goode sport*, is unnecessary.

M 578 *ad omnia quare*: perhaps 'with a reason for everything'.

M 593 *þe Deull ys dede*: cf. Greene, *Early English Carols*, p. 318, 'The deuyll is dede, for there I was; Iwys, it is full trew'; Skelton, i. 312; *Oxford Proverbs*, p. 140; Tilley, D 244.

M 598 *he rydyth on the galous*: see note on *C.* 2421 and 'ryde the horse with foure eeres', *John the Evangelist*, Malone Soc., 509.

M 600 *marryde*: 'marred, ruined' (not 'married', as interpreted by F.).

M 604 *brethell*: possibly for *betell* 'deceive', as in *Towneley*, xxiii. 79, 'he shall . . . No longere vs be tell'.

M 607 *avows*: '[he] declares'.

M 611 *smattrynge*: '? pretty'; *OED*.'? Ready for smacking or kissing'. Cf. Rastell, *The Four Elements*, sig. B vii, 'And two or thre proper wenchis mo, Ryght feyr and smotter of face'.

M 614 *Sent Patrykes wey*: see T. Wright, *St. Patrick's Purgatory*, 1844, and G. P. Krapp, *The Legend of St. Patrick's Purgatory*, 1900.

M 617 *a nere rune*: 'a narrow escape'; the first instance in *OED*. of the noun *run*.

M 621 *he wyll hange such a lyghly man*: 'he who will hang such a handsome man'; cf. *W.* 554 and the spelling *lylly* for 'likely' in *Mary Magdalene*, 1265.

M 628 *Sent Audrys holy bende*: silk bands for the neck were hallowed at the shrine of St. Audrey in Ely Cathedral; see *OED.*, *tawdry lace*, and *Victoria History of Cambridgeshire*, iv. 50.

M 632 Cf. Luke v. 5, 'per totam noctem laborantes'.

M 641 *scoryde*: 'scoured, rubbed clean'; cf. *Prompt.*, 'Scowryn a-wey ruste', spelt '*scoryn*' in the Winchester MS. and the edition of 1499; and *skore* in *Ludus Cov.* xiii. 111.

M 649 *þe new chesance*: 'the new way of getting money', as in *Ludus Cov.* xxvi, prologue, 103, 'þe newe chevesauns'.

M 660 The earliest instance of this saying in Tilley, G 175.

M 666 These spellings of *oyez* are unusual; cf. the original pronunciation 'oyets'. The earliest spellings in English are: *York*, xxx. 369 'Oyas', xxxi. 319 'O3es! O3es! O3es!', 360 'O yes!'; *Towneley*, ii. 416, 'oyes, oyes, oy!'; *Ludus Cov.* x. 142, 'Oy'.

M 668 *sen*: *send* shortened for rhyme. Tenants were bound either to attend the manor court or to send excuses ('essoins').

M 671 *syde gown*: see note on *W*. 510.

M 671–2 The first *tolde* seems to mean 'taken toll of', the second 'counted out'.

M 683 *rennynge fyst*: 'cursive hand', the only instance of the phrase in *MED.* (*fist*).

M 685 *hade I wyst*: many uses are cited by Zupitza in *Archiv*, xc, 258; D'Evelyn in *Peter Idley's Instructions to His Son*, p. 213; *Oxford Proverbs*, p. 270; Tilley, H 8, 10.

M 687 *Carici*: Nought should have written *Curia*, but his Latin and his handwriting are both incorrigible. 'Curia tenta' was the usual heading for a manor roll: see *The Court Baron*, Selden Soc., iv, and N. J. Hone, *The Manor and Manorial Records*. Nought's lack of Latin is suggested by his dropping into English and by his writing *regitalis* for *regis* and *nullateni* for *nullatenus* ('by no means'). Cf. Lydgate, *Minor Poems*, ii. 454, 455, 'Nullatensis' and 'somme vnthryffty bysshop Nullatense'. A line rhyming with *nullateni* seems to have dropped out after 693.

M 690 Edward IV reigned from 1461 to October 1470, and from April 1471 to 1483. Smart, pp. 45, 301–2, takes *Edwardi nullateni* and *regis nulli* as allusions to Edward being 'no king' when the play was written, but Mischief may only be making fun of Nought for writing *nullateni* instead of setting down the regnal year. Smart gives an explanation by Manly for *þe ʒere passyth fully*: 'the year is entirely wanting—the year is unknown'. It seems to mean 'The year goes away completely'.

M 692 *Tulli*: interpreted as Cicero by Manly, Brandl (p. xxxi), and Sister Philippa (pp. 119–20), who suggests that 'Mischief is introducing Nought mockingly to the audience as his lawyer'. He may mean 'here is a fine writer of Latin!'

M 714 *da pacem*: a nickname for a sword or dagger, 'Give-peace, Put-to-rest' (*MED.*). The rhyme suggests that the author may have written *onbrace hem, ouerface hem*.

M 720 *Hay, doog, hay!*: also in Skelton, i. 100, 126, and ii. 69.

M 724 Cf. *Hickscorner*, 544, 'Beshrewe hym for me that is last out of this place!'

M 729 *Stow, statt, stow!*: 'Ho, woman, ho!'; cf. *Ludus Cov.* xxiv. 125, 145, 'Stow þat harlot' and 'Come forth þou stotte'. *Sto* is a call to hounds in *The Master of Game*, chaps. 35, 36, and *stow* is a call to hawks in Skelton, i. 157, 255, 257.

M 732 *football*: see F. P. Magoun, 'Football in Medieval England and in Middle English Literature', *American Historical Review*, xxxv (1929), 33–45, 'Shrove Tuesday Football', *Harvard Studies and Notes in Philology and Literature*, xiii (1931), 9–46, and 'History of Football from the Beginnings to 1871', *Kölner Anglistische Arbeiten*, xxxi (1938).

M 750 *In trust ys treson*: Smart, p. 302, cites several examples of this proverb, including *Ludus Cov.* xxvi, prologue, 58. See also *Rel. Lyrics XVth C.*, p. 236; *Oxford Proverbs*, p. 673; Tilley, T 549.

M 753–5 The versifier is unidentified, but Smart, p. 302, quotes similar verses in Latin and English from Gower, *Confessio Amantis*, v, sec. vii. Cf. Lydgate, *Minor Poems*, ii. 583, 'Lawe and nature pleynyn on folke vnkynde'. See H. Walther, *Sprichwörter*, ii (1964), no. 13700.

M 767 Ecclesiastes i. 2.

M 776 *cryke*: probably 'brook' rather than 'inlet of the sea'; cf. *Prompt.*, '*Cryke* of watyr. *Scatera*' (for *scatebra* 'spring-water').

M 780–1 *a cape corpus . . . non est inventus*: a capias or writ of arrest and the sheriff's answer in his return that the defendant has not been found in his jurisdiction (the first quotation in *OED.* for *non est inventus*).

M 782 *My bolte ys schett*: cf. 'A fool's bolt is soon shot', *Oxford Proverbs*, pp. 216, 585; Tilley, B 512, F 515.

M 784 *fowll arayde*: 'soiled'. Cf. *arrayde* with the meaning 'soiled' in Heywood, *Johan Johan* (1533), 256, 'And bycause it is arrayde at the skyrt, Whyle ye do nothyng, skrape of the dyrt', and Thomas Wilson, *Arte of Logyke* (1551), v. iv, 'His cote somwhat araied'.

M 790 *Tysche*: *OED.* cites this as the second quotation under *tush*, after *tussch* in *York*, xxxi. 121.

M 790 *a flyes weyng*: cf. *Towneley*, xxi. 94, 'he settys not a fle wyng bi sir cesar full euen'.

M 817–18 Smart, p. 303, compares *W.* 79–82.

M 825 *pirssid*: possibly *precyus* or *blyssid*, but neither is as close to MS. *pirssie*.

M 826 Psalm lxxvi. 11, and Proverbs xii. 7.

M 828 *tys*: the first instance of '*tis* in *OED.*, but an earlier example of *tys* occurs in a stage direction in *Ludus Cov.* xxviii. 998.

M 833 *precyse*: the rhyme suggests *preche* 'declare'.

M 834 Ezekiel xxxiii. 11, 'Nolo mortem impii, sed ut convertatur impius a via sua, et vivat'.

M 838 Not in *Oxford Proverbs* or Tilley; cf. *Rel. Lyrics XVth C.*, p. 267, 'The trewth In dede hyt-selff well preffe'.

M 840 Mercy names three of the Four Daughters of God; see note on *C.* 3129.

M 845 Cf. Ecclesiasticus v. 4–7; *Handlyng Synne*, 2693–6, 4791–2; *C.* 3164–76.

M 846 Cf. Psalm cxlv. 2.

M 850 John viii. 11.

M 857 Smart, p. 303, quotes *The Gouernaunce of Prynces* (1422), 'lyghtyre is a fressh wounde to hele, than a festrid'; cf. *Oxford Proverbs*, pp. 266–7.

M 862 Matthew v. 26, 'donec reddas novissimum quadrantem'.

M 863 *Aske mercy and hawe*: cf. Matthew vii. 7 and *Ludus Cov.* xxiv. 24, 'haske thou mercy and þou xalt haue'.

M 866 2 Corinthians vi. 2. Sister Philippa notes that this is read in the epistle for the first Sunday of Lent. It is also in Matins on Ash Wednesday: *Breviarium in Usum Sarum*, i. 555, 572, 575–6, 583.

M 882 *þe prowerbe*: Cf. H. Walther, *Sprichwörter*, ii (1964), no. 13019.

M 884 *þe Flesch and þe Fell*: F. glosses *fell* as 'devil' and Adams therefore omits *the Dewell* as a scribal error, but 'the Flesh and the Skin' is another name for the Flesh.

M 894 *Libere welle, libere nolle*: 'freely to will, freely not to will'.

M 899 *her þen I go*: 'before I go', like *or I go* in 455; *er þan* with a verb is frequent in Margery Kempe, pp. 3, 45, 165, 171, 203 ('er þan sche cam').

M 901 Psalm cxx. 7.

M 904 *patrocynye*: 'protection', the first instance in *OED*.

M 913 *pleyferys*: Henry Bradley, in Furnivall, p. 188a, pointed out that this should be *pleyferys* and compared 'aequales angelis' in Luke xx. 36. Cf. *Peter Idley's Instructions to His Son*, p. 142, 'In heuene who shal be my playefeeris'.

ABBREVIATIONS IN THE NOTES

EETS.	Early English Text Society.
F.	Furnivall in *The Macro Plays*, EETS., 1904.
Ludus Cov.	*Ludus Coventriae*, ed. Block, EETS., 1922.
Mary Magdalene	*Mary Magdalene* in *The Digby Plays*, EETS., 1896.
MED.	*Middle English Dictionary*, ed. Kurath and Kuhn, Ann Arbor, 1952–.
OED.	*Oxford English Dictionary*, Oxford, 1933.
Owst	G. R. Owst, *Literature and Pulpit in Medieval England*, Cambridge, 1933.
Oxford Proverbs	*The Oxford Dictionary of English Proverbs*, compiled by W. G. Smith, revised by Sir Paul Harvey, Oxford, 1948.
P.L.	*Patrologia Latina*, ed. Migne, Paris, 1844–64.
Prompt.	*Promptorium Parvulorum sive Clericorum*, ed. Way, Camden Society, nos. xxv, liv, lxxxix, 1843–65.
Rolle	*Yorkshire Writers, Richard Rolle of Hampole and His Followers*, ed. Horstmann, 2 vols., London, 1895–6.
Skelton	*The Poetical Works of John Skelton*, ed. Dyce, 2 vols., London, 1843.
Smart	W. K. Smart, *Some English and Latin Sources and Parallels for the Morality of Wisdom*, Menasha, Wisconsin, 1912.
Tilley	M. P. Tilley, *A Dictionary of the Proverbs in England in the Sixteenth and Seventeenth Centuries*, Ann Arbor, 1950.
Towneley	*The Towneley Plays*, ed. England and Pollard, EETS., 1897.
York	*York Plays*, ed. L. T. Smith, Oxford, 1885.

GLOSSARY

References are to *The Castle of Perseverance* unless a line-number or pair of line-numbers is marked W for *Wisdom* or M for *Mankind*. They are usually limited to two examples of a meaning in each play. An asterisk indicates a form restored by emendation. The letter þ follows *t* and ʒ follows *y*. Spelling variants do not usually include alternative spellings of the same sound: *c* or *k*, *c* or *s*, *i* or *y*, þ or *th*, *u* or *v* or *w*, ʒ or *y*.

a *interj.* O! 323, 349, W 39, 77, ah! M 613, 645.
a see **haue, of.**
abak *adv.* back: *putte* ~ set aside 3304.
abavyd *pp. adj.* amazed 3268.
abed *adv.* into the grave 2810.
ab(e)y(e), abyn *v. intr.* pay the penalty 1104, 1777, W 768, 846; *tr.* suffer for 3159.
able *v.* enable W 945.
about, abo(w)tyn *adv.* concerning it 516, in every direction 655, W 464, M 703, to and fro 1782, 1928, M 76, 697; *al* ~ on every side 30, in every direction 166, 683; *be* ~ be busy 307, 1270, be concerned with 3009; *prep.* around, p. 1, W 1 s.d., M 617, 627; see **loke.**
above, abovyn, *adv.* on high 235, 1139, in heaven 1656, W 63, 284, M 868, 913; *prep.* more than 3603, W 21, 290, surpassing W 29, higher than 2589, M 224.
abroche *adv.*: *sett* ~ opened up M 579.
abrode *adv.* wide W 453, 1102.
abyde, abydyn *v.* remain 161, 888, W 1103, wait 2925, M 431, 576.
acordance *n.* agreement W 689.
acorde *n.* harmony W 1150; *at myn* ~ in agreement with me 431; *at on* ~ in complete harmony 3537.
acorde *v.* agree 3514, W 495, 829; **acordyt** *pr. 3 sg.* is fitting W 5; **acordyd** *pp.* 3563.
actuall *adj.* done by one's own act W 1112.

acumberyde *pp.* overcome W 396.
adew *interj.* farewell! M 609.
adjutory *adj.* helping M 232.
adown *adv.* down 1490, 1570.
adred *pp. adj.* terrified 2804, 3093.
aferde *pp. adj.* afraid M 125, 788.
affyable *adj.* agreeable W 594.
affyance *n.* reliance W 83, 657, M 235; *of myn* ~ dependent on me W 690.
affye *n.* trust: *of myn* ~ trusted by me W 643.
affynyte *n.* companions W 799.
aforn *prep.* before 2537.
afrayed *pp. adj.* harassed 2444.
aftyr *adv.* afterwards 33; *prep.* subsequent to 261, W 1002, 1044, M 892, in accordance with 275, 685, W 228, M 166, 676, according to 860, 1262, in pursuit of 921; see **sende.**
aftyrward *adv.* later 103.
agaste *pp. adj.* frightened 854.
agayn, ageyn *adv.* back 60, 84, W 912 s.d., M 523, 675, in return W 73, 190, once more W 119, 1137, M 276, 435.
ageyn(s), aʒeyn(s) *prep.* against 63, 192, W 491, 722, M 107, 230, contrary to 3384, W 529.
agryse *v.* shudder with fear 793, 1012.
akale *pp. adj.* made cold 3014.
aknowe *pp. adj.*: *be* ~ confess 1328, 1472.
alholy *adv.* completely 218, 1446.
al(l)-day *adv.* all the time 1072, 2366, W 153.

allectuose *adj.* alluring M 762.

al(l)wey *adv.* always 336, 506, W 958.

allyede *pp. adj.* well-connected W 862.

alowyd *pp.* granted M 860.

also, als, as, os, *adv.* as much as 144, as 197, 213, like 197, 1970, M 734, 815, likewise 174, 851, W 426, 1130, M 135, 802; *correl. also, as . . . as* just as 1088, 1374, W 129, 623, *as . . . so* like . . . so M 749; *as for* to serve as M 552; *as make* may he make 2590; *as moche* the same M 58.

altogedyr *adv.* (in red) entirely p. 1, (in the place) all the time p. 1.

amendys *n.: make yow*~make reparation to you M 652; *take* ~ exact a fine W 802.

among(e) *adv.* also 1031, 1330; *euere* ~ all the time 436; *prep.* among 433, 533, M 2.

amongys *prep.* among 108, 665.

amownt *v.* ascend M 824.

amyable *adj.* worthy of love W 43, 590.

amyke *n.* beloved W 70.

amys(se) *adj.* wrong 1339, W 403; *adv.* sinfully 796, 1295, W 75, wrongly W 874, M 406, 658.

amytt *v.* grant M 758.

and(e) *conj.* if 1417, W 330, 451, M 249, 251.

anhangyn *v.* be hanged 3084.

annexion *n.* union M 863.

anon(e) *adv.* quickly 347, 392, at once 1097, 1113, M 88, 240.

anosyde *pp. adj.* harmed W 224.

anoþyr *pron.* another 305, 2872; *adj.* another 1461, 2162, W 851, M 727, different M 528; *adv.* differently M 584.

anow see inow(e).

anoyed *pp. adj.* offended 206.

any see ony.

a-party *adv.* somewhat 2701.

apase *adv.* quickly M 453.

aplye *v.* devote W 513; *refl. imp.* W 446; ap(p)lyede *pp.* W 178, M 5.

appeyere *v.* injure W 860.

apposyde *pp. adj.* examined W 225.

aprehensyble *adj.* able to perceive how M 742.

aproxymatt *adj.* close M 223.

aqueyntance *n.* familiarity 2865, W 658, 763.

aquite, aqwyt *v.* release 3383, W 811.

aray *n.* display 134, 274, condition 409, behaviour 2372, clothing W 150, 510, M 295; *of* ~ in warlike manner 2368.

arayed *pp. adj.* dressed 2488; *fowll arayde* soiled M 784.

arbritracion *n.: fre* ~ free choice 25.

are *adv.* before W 810; see or.

arest(e) *v.* seize 2956, arrest W 805, 850.

arme *n.* arm 1233, M 390, 439.

armys *n. pl.* heraldic insignia M 322; *as* ~ to arms! 1969, 2069; *man of* ~ soldier M 638.

arom(e) *adv.* at a distance W 524, M 631.

ars *n.* arse p. 1, 1931, M 339, 375, 489.

as *conj.* in the way that 280, 3274, W 516, M 692, 706, as though 803, 1088, W 130, 489, while M 715; ~ *I can* as much as I can 442, 2441.

aske *v.* demand 1387, W 80, require 1441, pray for 1492, 3154, W 983, M 305, ask for 2585, W 814, M 602, beg W 1054; askyth *pr. 3 sg.* 1387; askyd *pt. sg.* 2585.

askynge *n.* prayer 3486.

aslake *v.* to make less 2266.

asoly, asoyle *v.* absolve 1500, 1507.

asonder, asundyr *adv.* apart M 616, 643.

aspye, espye *v.* perceive W 395, M 763, spy out M 502; espyede *pp.* found out W 857, aspyede caught sight of M 722.

as(s)ay *v.* test 394, try M 87, 93, appeal to M 207; asayed *pp.* 3090.

assays *n. pl.: at all* ~ under any circumstances M 108.

as(s)ent *n.: par* ~ willingly 1013; *wyth on* ~ by agreement M 149.

assyduly *adv.* continually W 256.

assyng *v.* designate M 552; asynyd *pp.* appointed 301.

astat(e) *n.* condition M 316; *com to mans* ~ come of age 3401.

astore *v.* restore 1303, 1408.

asyse *n.* fashion 2889; *fals* ~ false measure 842.

asythe *n.* atonement W 1094, 1096.

at *prep.* subject to 179, 1018, at the time of 295, 330, W 822, in 580, W 789, 793, against 2110, 2368, from 2313, 2995, because of 3569, beginning with M 467, 505, by way of M 477; ~ *hert* taken to heart 801; ~ *honde* assiduously 629.

atastyde *pp.* tasted W 568.

atawnt *adv.* to excess W 606.

atenyde *pp. adj.* grieved 2427.

attende *v.* pay attention W 100, 748.

atwynne *adv.* in two 1293, 3186.

auctoure *n.* Creator W 99; **awtors** *pl.* authorities W 270.

a(u)ngel, aungyl *n.* angel 19, 41, W 62, 159, M 175, 913.

avale *v.* bring low 2822.

avantage *n.* profit M 524.

avante, avaunt *interj.* forward! 2061, 2414, away! M 636.

avaunce *v.* help 2532, 3423, M 92, benefit W 790; **avauncyd** *pp.* 1188.

avaunte *n.* boast: *make (his, þer)* ~ boast W 605, M 27, 278.

avaunt(e) *v.* boast W 586, 597.

avayle *v.* benefit 3560.

avent *imp. refl.* relieve M 560.

avow(e) *n.* oath: *I make (Gode)* ~ I swear 877, W 372, M 501, 624; *to God (I make)* ~ I swear 708, W 562, 622; *to Golyas I make* ~ I vow to Goliath 1929.

avows *pr. 3 sg.* declares M 607.

avoyde *imp. intr.* go away M 64; *tr.* **avoydyth** *pr. 3 sg.* drives out W 979.

avyse *n.* advice M 805; *at myn* ~ under my orders 179.

avyse *v.* consider 2582, counsel M 25, 220; *refl.* take thought M 603; **avysyde** *pp.* resolved M 504; *ewyll avysyde* unwise M 389.

awake *v.* be aroused 2692, W 977, arise 3297, 3637.

award *n.* keeping 1083.

awenture *n.* risk M 847.

awowtry *n.* adultery M 851.

awreke *v.* carry out 1719.

ay *adv.* always 726, 3377, W 554, 677.

ayer see **eyr.**

ay-whan *adv.* every time W 345.

ba *imp.* kiss M 430.

bace *adj.* low 2717.

bacheler *n.* young knight 161, 1050.

bagge *n.* badge M 322.

baggys *n. pl.* bagpipes 2198, sacks 2655, 2916.

bagpype *n.* bagpiper W 724 s.d.

bakbyte *v.* slander 1123.

bakbyter(e) *n.* slanderer 659, 676.

bakbytynge *n.* slander 34, 773.

bakyn *v.* bake 1590; **bake** *pp.* 3299.

bale *n.* torment 60, 220, suffering 683, 2338, pain 936, grief 1302, 1310.

bales, ballys *n.* rod, scourge M 73, 807.

balle *n.* orb, royal emblem W 1 s.d.

ballokys *n. pl.* testicles 2403.

ballyd *adj.* bald, bare 1275.

bane *n.*[1] summons 166, 1198.

bane *n.*[2] ruin 655, 1888.

banke *n.* slope, hillside 570, 744, shore 589, 1174.

baptem, baptomm, baptyme *n.* baptism W 126, 1109; *þe watyr of* ~ the water from the side of Christ on the cross 3362.

basnetys *n. pl.* helmets 162.

baston *n.* staff 923.

bat *n.* club 3119.

bat(a)yl(e), batell *n.* battle 2013, 2415, W 703, M 136, 227.

bate *n.: at* ~ in strife 3516.

be *n.* bee 898, 954.

be, by *prep.* by means of 125, 3236, W 134, 145, M 10, 12, by the time of 138, throughout 158, 188, by way of 403, 591, M 37, in the name of 548, 2435, W 487, 768, M 75, 116, beside 589, 1197, in accordance with 3258, 3564, according to W 422, M 95, concerning W 621, 645, during M 87, 769, at M 714, along M 715, 735; see **blod(e), reson(e), skyl(le), sonde** *n.*[2]

bede *n.* prayer 1491, 2618; *pl.* prayer beads 1649, 2358, M 564, 575.

bede *v.* offer 871, present 2080, 2498; ~ *batayl* challenge to fight 189, 1913; **bedyth** *pr. 3 sg.* 189.

bedene *adv.* immediately 329, one and all 991.

befall(e) *impers. v.* be fitting 820, 2422; *fayre þe* ~ good fortune to you 725, 1794; *foull yow* ~ bad luck to you M 522; **befelle** *pt. 3 sg.* 2564.

befor(e), beforn, byfor *prep.* in the presence of 8, 133, M 172, 890, in front of 1936, W 179, 948, M 303, 530; ~ *all* above all W 291, 998; *adv.* earlier 46, W 237, M 385, 601, to one's face 664, foremost W 324 s.d., 417.

begrete *v.* weep for 2578.

begyn(ne) *v. intr.* start 88, 1415, W 119, 161, M 178, 505, come into existence 2445, W 16; *is to* ~ is just starting 1393, 1639; *tr.* start 1148, M 615, create W 103, 347, originate W 306, 332; **begynnyt(h)** *pr. 3 sg.* 88, W 223; **began(e)** *pt. 3 sg.* 2445, W 16; **begunne** *pp.* M 615.

begynner *n.* originator W 236, M 1.

behende, behynde *adv.* in the rear 21, 103, W 16 s.d., M 787, to one's back 664; see **brynge, cast(e), go(ne).**

behest *n.* promise 3402, W 1126.

behete *v. tr.* promise 782, 2860; *intr.* 243, 393; **behyth** *pr. 1 sg.* 243, **behete** 1334; **behyth** *pr. 3 sg.* 782; **behott** *pt. 3 sg.* 2892; **behetyn** *pp.* 393, **behete** 2860.

behold(e) *pp. adj.*: *be* ~ be obliged 706, 2905.

behoue *n.* duty 1660.

behoueable *adj.* necessary W 238.

beleue *n.* belief: *bryngyth hym in* ~ convinces him 82.

beloke *pp. adj.* locked up 2871.

bely-fyll *n.* bellyful, enough to satisfy M 639.

bely-mett *n.* enough to satisfy M 143.

belyve, blyue, blythe, bylyue *adv.* at once 471, 1122, M 788, quickly 3291.

bemys *n. pl.* trumpets 617, 2376.

be(n) *v.* 17, 27, be 105, 137, W 36, M 2, exist W 3, 109, live W 442; am *pr. 1 sg.* 199; art *2 sg.* 540; is *3 sg.* 16, ys W 38; arn *pl.* 73, M 706, ar(e) 162, W 104, M 128, be 77, W 3, M 77, ben(e) 301, W 257, M 64, hetho W 178; bê *pr. subj. sg.* 241, 417, W 7, M 24; be *imp. sg.* 116; beth *imp. pl.* 898, be W 442; was *pt. 1 sg.* 276; were *2 sg.* 2096, was W 831; was *3 sg.* 1636; ware *pt. pl.* W 105, wer(e) W 107; were *pt. subj.* 108, M 723; wore W 330, M 588; beynge *pr. p.* W 959; be *pp.* 721, W 130, M 17, ben(e) 1521, 3524, W 109; see **let(e).**

bende *n.* captivity 2629, 2897, band of ribbon M 628.

bende *v.* stoop 160, 2483, submit 230, 1107; **bent** *pp.* 2199.

benome *pp.* numbed 81.

berd *n.* person of high birth 254, 974, lady 988, 1202.

ber(e) *v.* give birth 16, W 115, carry 120, 655, wear 2315, W 166, 718, M 322, support 3190, endure M 741; *refl.* behave 436, 1824; *intr.* go 1726; ~ *u . . . tonge* speak 2714, 2890; ~ *hym wele* be well off 2919; ~ *wpe* uphold W 669, 699; ~ *wytnesse* corroborate 361, support 781; **bere** *pr. 1 sg.* 655; **beryst** *2 sg.* 2714; **beryth** *3 sg.* 2315; **bare** *pt. 2 sg.* 2447; **born(e)** *pp.* 16, W 669, M 272, **bor(r)e** 3342, W 115, 419.

bereuyd *pp. adj.* taken away 2207.

besauntys *n. pl.* coins of gold or silver or ornaments like these coins 588, 701.

beschrew *v.* curse W 506, M 80, 398.

beschyte *v.* soil M 731.

beseke *v.* seek W 970.

beset *pp. adj.* surrounded 1241, besieged 2076.

best(e) *adj.* best 735, 3508, W 443; *sb.* 857, 1171; *at þe* ~ in the best way W 622, 700; *for þe* ~ 1601, M 603, 673; *to þe* ~ 3107; *adv.* 545, 2671, W 5, 825; see **do(ne).**

besy *adj.* diligent 268, W 406, occupied M 565.

besyde *prep.* against 3462; *adv.* nearby M 633.

besynes(se) *n.* diligence 1641, 1684, W 441.

bete *v.*[1] cure 367, 1311.

bete, bett, betyn *v.*[2] beat 924, 1052, W 771; **betyn** *pp.* adorned 588.

beteche *v.* entrust 3461; **betawth** *pp.* given 2278.

bett(e) *adv.* better 754, M 798.

bet(t)yr *adj.* better 1068, 2615, W 33, 477, M 635; *adv.* 190, 1184, W 849, M 685.

betyde *v.* occur 2543; *wel þe* ~ be fortunate 751; **betydde** *pp.* current 680.

betyme, bytyme *adv.* early 137, promptly W 691, on time M 710; *al* ~ all in good time 411, 1349.

bey(e), bye *v.* redeem 715, 3407, M 255, 415, suffer for 3015, W 108, buy W 665, 762; *absol.* buy 852, suffer 3096; *dere bought* dearly redeemed M 9, 116; **bowth** *pt. 2 sg.* 3407; **bowte** *3 sg.* M 255, **bought** M 415; **bowth** *pp.* 715, **bought** W 762, M 9.

beyght *n.* bait, enticement W 730.

blase *v.* shine brightly 1939.

ble *n.* condition 284, 2999, complexion 915, 1265.

blench *v.* deceive M 531.

bleryn *v.* stream at the eyes 1884.

bleykyn *v. tr.* make pale 1265, 1450; *intr.* turn pale 1965, 2999; **bleyke** *pr. 1 sg.* 2999; **bleykyn** *2 pl.* 1450.

blo *n.* blowing 617.

blo, bloo *adj.* dark 928, 2195, livid 1989; *betyn* ~ *and blak* (or *blak and* ~) beaten black and blue 2175, 2219.

blod(e) *n.* blood 356, 3147, M 745, kin 111, 2946; *be Goddys* ~ by Christ's blood 877.

blodyr *v.* blubber 1965.

blow(e) *v. tr.* blow (an instrument) 228, 254, M 175, speak 1058; *absol.* blow 813, W 702, 707, M 453, speak 2770; *whouso þe wynde* ~ however things go 2541; **blowyth** *pr. 3 sg.* 3617; **blowe** *pp.* proclaimed 166.

blynde *v.* make spiritually blind 531, 557; **blent** *pp.* 1287, **blendyd** 1294.

blyn(ne) *v.* refrain from 1292, 1440, W 549, cease M 558.

blys(se) *v.* make happy 2704, give a blessing to M 899; *refl.* bless 1649; *I* ~ *yow wyth my lyfte honde* I curse you M 522.

blys(se) *n.* happiness 60, 87, W 70, 192, M 189, 284.

blythe, blyue see **belyve**.

blyþe, blyfe *adj.* joyful 898, 2974.

bobaunce *n.* worldly pomp 1421.

bobbyd *pp.*[1] bounced up and down 1180.

bobbyd *pp.*[2] mocked 1287.

bocher *n.* butcher M 126.

bofett, buffett *n.* blow M 109, 383.

bok(e) *n.* book 382, 516, M 797, written record M 663.

bold(e) *adj.* courageous 161, 199, strong 923, shameless 1355; ~ *as a belle* brazen as a bell 3591.

bolne *v.* swell 2999; **bolnynge** *pr. p.* 1853, 3076; **bolnyd** *pp.* 2337.

bonde *n.* fetter 1259, 3076; ~ *of loue* tie of friendship 2873; *byttyr* ~ cruel domination 794, 974, 1891, M 39.

bonde *adj.* subject to another's will 3451; *sb.* 2798.

bon(e) *n.*[1] bone 936, 3333, W 1052, M 356; *be (for) Belyals bonys* 1715, 1798, 2186; *by þe* ~ W 784.

bone *n.*[2] petition 2585, 3387; *bydde a* ~ ask a prayer 315.

bord(e) *n.* table 2655, 3539, plank M 533; see **fall(e)**.

borow *n.* protector M 425.

bost(e) *n.* boasting 462, 1058.

bote *n.* remedy 1302, helper M 208; ~ *of bale* remedy for suffering 443, 2863.

bottler *n.* butler M 646.

boþe, boþyn *adj.* both 1208, W 617; *sb.* M 585; ~ *to* two together 3095; *correl.* ~ . . . *and* 38, 1744, W 157, M 119, 201.

bo(u)n *adj.* ready 474, 702.

bounte *n.* munificence 3638.

bowde *n.* (a term of scorn) 1853, 2337.

bowe, bowyn *v. intr.* be obedient 678, 702, submit 1100, 1669, stoop 2483; *tr.* obey 1055; **bowhede** *pp.* bent W 1105.

bowre *n.* inner room 254, 367; *pl.* dwelling 753, 1700, houses 2974; *balys* ~ hell 1541, 3042; ~ *of blys* heaven 1418, 1488; *in* ~ *and in hall* everywhere 151.

bowth see **bey(e)**.

boy *n.* fellow 189, 677, servant 1750, 1971, ruffian 2128, 2138, boy W 550, 912 s.d.

boystous *adj.* fierce 199, 2138.

boystowsly *adv.* violently 120.

brace *v.* tie up M 306.

brawle *v.* brag 462.

bred *pp. adj.* roasted 3091.

brede *n.* breadth 2763; *be bankys* ~ by the width of banks 589, 2331; *be bankys on* ~ by banks far and wide 1174; *on* ~ far and wide 953, 1915.

brede *v.* cause 936, make 988, 1211; **bre(y)de** *pr. 1 sg.* 936, 2212.

bredynge *n.*[1] propagation 994.

bredynge *n.*[2] reproach M 348.

breke *v. tr.* break 859, 1481, M 74, 78, destroy 1723, break open 2211, M 497; *intr.* break 2147, 3005; **brekyste** *pr. 2 sg.* 859; **brekyth** *3 sg.* 3005; **brake** *pt. 3 sg.* M 597; **brokyn** *pp.* 1481, M 607, **broke** 2873.

bren *n. pl.* eyebrows W 196.

brenne *n.* fire; *on* ~ into flame 202.

brenne *v. intr.* burn p. 1, W 281, burn in hell 2603, 3076; *tr.* burn 191, 2115, burn in hell 1855, 3640, M 43; **brennynge** *pr. p.* ardent W 281; **brent(e)** *pp.* 191, M 43.

brere *n.* briar 3246.

brest(yn) *v. tr.* break apart 1830, M 643; *intr.* M 73, 125; **brestyth** *pr. 3 sg.* breaks forth 202; **breste** *pr. subj.* M 73; **brast** *pt. sg.* M 616.

brethel(l) *n.* rascal 2346, M 707.

brethell *v.* ? M 604.

brewe *v.* prepare 950, 963, brew (drink) 3274, 3299; ~ *bale, balys* prepare pain(s) 683, 2338, 2419; ~ *bote of bale* prepare help for grief 1310, 2863; *þi bale* ~ relieve your grief 1302; **brewyth** *pr. 3 sg.* 3274; **brewyth** *imp. pl.* 950; **browyn** *pp.* 3019, **browne** 3299.

breyd *pr. 1 sg.* rouse 2925.

breydest *pr. 2 sg.* reproach W 763.

broche *v.* pierce 2836.

brodde *n.* spike 1971.

brode *n.* breadth: *on* ~ on every side 2001.

bronde *n.* firebrand W 114, 917.

bronte *n.* attack M 880.

brothel *n.* lecher 988, 1211.

broþyr *n.* brother 1786, 2614, comrade 1115, M 53, 64; **breþeryn** *pl.* 1019, **brothern** M 29, **brethern** M 110.

broun *adj.* dark 570.

browe *n.* brow, expression 2251; *pl.* artificial eyebrows W 1 s.d.

brustun-gutte *n.* greedy eater 235.

brymmne *n.* brink 1638.

brynge, bryngyn *v.* bring, cause to come 60, 1418, 3122, W 23, 197, M 110, 152; ~ *byhynde* mislead W 296; ~ *to mynde* remember W 925; *forth browth* born 326; **brynge** *pr. 1 sg.* 974; **bryngyst** *2 sg.* 1843; **bryngyt(h)** *3 sg.* 28, W 189; **brynge** *pr. subj.* W 296, M 152; **browtyst** *pt. 2 sg.* 3317; **browth** *3 sg.* 2267; **browt** *pt. pl.* M 889; **browt(h)** *pp.* 818, 2274, **brought(e)** W 23, M 542; see **beleue**.

bryst *n.* breast M 322.

bryth, bryght(e) *adj.* shining 162, 356, beautiful 915, 988, W 24, glorious 1005, 1271, W 1092; **bryther** *compar.* 3246.

bryth *adv.* brightly 3.

buffett see **bofett**.

bultyn *v.* fornicate 1159.

bunche *v.* beat 3119.

buske, buskyn *v. tr.* prepare 923; *refl.* 161, 474, bring quickly 2810; *intr.* hasten 71, 910; **buskyth** *pr. 3 sg.* 71.

buskys *n. pl.* groves 570.

but *conj.* but 36, 65, unless 72, 219, W 484, 619, M 339, yet 3513, except W 206, 572; ~ *if* unless 257, 879, W 363; ~ *þat* except that 2015, W 920; *adv.* merely 838, 1061, W 305, 555, M 234, 706; ~ *lat* just now M 351.

by see **be**.

by *adv*. closely W 495, nearby 2036, M 799; *by and by* continually W 751, 1032, one after another M 469; *go* ~ go past M 636; see **set(te)**.

bydde *v*. command 678, 819, M 70; **byd** *pr. 3 sg*. 3191; **bad** *pt. 3 sg*. 819, **bade** *pt. 2 pl*. M 70; see **bone** *n*.²

byddynge *n*. command 230, 236.

byde *v. intr*. remain 235, 883; *tr*. engage in (battle) 2063; **bydith** *pr. 3 sg*. awaits 784.

byggyngys *n. pl*. dwellings 589.

byght *v*. bite, be severe W 854.

byll(e) *v*. dwell 883; *þi bourys* ~ make your home 1700; **bylde** *pp*. built 744.

bynd(e) *v*. fetter 650, 951; **byndyth** *pr. 3 sg*. 1356; **bond** *pt. 2 sg*. ensnared 2099; **bownde** *pp*. wrapped 701, 2916, **bowndyn** 3345.

bynne *n*. stall 220.

bysytyth *pr. 3 sg*. assails 24.

byttyr *adj*. painful 126, 650, M 39, bitter-tasting 950, 1590; **byttyrer** *compar*. 2341; see **bonde**.

cacche, cache(n), cachyn *v*. drive 982, 1972, get 3495, W 507, M 494; **cawth** *pp*. 294, **kawt** 1205.

cage *n*. stronghold 2495, 2703, prison 2874.

cakle *v*. cackle, chatter 2648.

calcacyon *n*. trampling, threshing M 45.

call(e) *v. intr*. call out 320, 731, M 111; *tr*. summon 37, 47, M 523, describe as 2327, M 444, 885, demand W 1098; **callyth** *pr. 3 sg*. 58; **callyn** *pl*. 47, **callyth** 52; **callyd** *pt. 3 sg*. called upon 3427; **callyd** *pp*. named 1238.

can, con, cunne *v*. be able (to) 59, 718, W 62, 210, M 445, know 868, W 342, 841, M 256, 619, learn 1279, M 520, know how to W 848; ~ *(hys) wyt* be able to think 535, 2594; **can** *pr. I sg*. 2441; **canst** *2 sg*. 868; **can** *3 sg*. 2594; **canne** *pl*. 59, **cun(ne)** 1957, M 603; *pr. subj. I sg*. 1309; **coude** *pt. 3 sg*. M 619; **cowdys** *pt. subj. 2 sg*. W 1034; see **as, skyl(le)**.

care *n*. sorrow 205, 1043, W 500, 552, M 622, anxiety 384, W 737, M 277.

car(e)ful *adj*. harmful 791, 2085, miserable 1004, 1053.

caren *n*. dead flesh W 1099, M 739.

carpe, karpyn *v*. cry out 919, 1992, complain 2224, 2407; **carpyd** *pt. 3 sg*. 919.

carpynge *n*. rebuke 201, way of speaking 907.

caryth *pr. 3 sg*. feels concern 106.

cas(e) *n*. matter, theme 13, 14, cause in court 3219, 3319; *I putt* ~ supposing M 74; *in* ~ assuming 387, into question 3323.

cas(se) *n*. box; ? frame of a gallows M 630; *hert* ~ strongbox of the heart 1460.

cast(e) *v*. put 180, 2497, M 303, overthrow 977, throw 1053, M 244, shoot 1944, prepare 2000; *refl*. plunge 937, prepare 971, dispose 1643, place 2132, devote W 239, 339; ~ *behynde* reject 96; ~ *no dowte* have no fear W 502; **casten** *pr. 3 pl*. 2000; **castynge** *pr. p*. W 339; **caste** *pp*. 96, **castyn** 180.

catel *n*. property 106.

caue *n*. cavern, hell 2000, 3049, cave 2735.

caytyf(e) *n*. unhappy wretch 560, villain 1103, 1972, M 764*.

certys *adv*. certainly 296, 339.

chace, chasyn, chache *v*. follow 786, drive 1035, 2550, expel 2306.

chafe *v*. fume 198*.

champe *v*. gnash the teeth 198.

chappelet *n*. head-dress W 16 s.d.*, 164 s.d., 1064 s.d.

charge *n*. person for whom one is responsible W 407, 410; *gyue yow in* ~ command you M 293.

charge *v*. command 1122, M 590.

chaunce *n*. luck 1810, M 203, situation 2538, 2866.

cha(u)nge, chonge *v*. alter 2857, W 510, 950, buy or sell M 391; *refl*. W 375; see **choppe** *v*.¹

chefe, cheve *adj*. foremost 1132, 3133.

cheke *n*. disaster M 520.

cheke v. choke 2153.

chere n. behaviour 1741, spirit W 819, M 81, 334; *what* ~ how goes it M 625.

chere adj. precious W 1047.

chery n.: ~ *tyme* the brief time of a cherry-harvest festival M 234.

ches n. quarrelling 651.

chesance, chevesaunce n. device to get money W 787, M 649.

chese v. choose 696; chose pp. W 16.

chesun n. reason 1277, cause 2096.

cheueler n. wig W 1 s.d., 16 s.d.

cheve, scheue v. thrive 148, 3114, attain 3235.

cheveleryde pp. wearing a wig W 324 s.d.

chocke v. thrust 198.

choppe v.¹: ~ *and chonge* bargain and barter W 639.

choppe v.² cut M 440, 441.

chorle n. base fellow W 835, 848; cherlys pl. 1156.

chyld(e) n. child 2127, 3293; chyldryn pl. 894, chyldyr 956, 2976, chylderne W 406.

chyrch(e) n. church 2336, W 15, 995, M 633; *Holy Chyrche* W 982, 984.

chyrche-goynge n. attending church 1216.

chyrche-style n. steps over a churchyard wall M 583.

chyrcheward adv.: to ~ towards church 1225.

clad n. clod 241.

clappe n. stroke 2846.

clappyd pp. adj. thrust 241.

claryfye v. throw light on M 48.

clateryd pp. adj. shattered 1867.

clatyr v. rattle 1932.

clen(e) adj. clean 1383, M 339, pure 1910, 2005, W 45, 81, unmixed W 749, bare M 483, 489.

clene adv. chastely 1633, completely 1901; clenner compar. more splendidly 732.

clennes(se) n. purity 47, 2018, W 543.

clepe v. call W 692; clepyd(e) pp. W 3, 136.

clere adj. purifying 45, pure 1459, bright 2109, 2957.

clere adv. handsomely 692, with clear sight W 1087.

clerke n. learned man 866, W 1036, M 129, 222, cleric 2732.

clerycall adj. clerkly, learned M 134, subtle M 579.

cleue, clynyn v. split, wreck 1901, 1924; cleuyn pp. 2845, clowyn W 1104.

clos n. prison (of hell) 1004, ? stronghold 1712.

closyd(e) pp. adj. buried 408, 2639, W 1004.

clothynge n. dress 293, W 474, 1064 s.d., livery 501.

clott n. clod 2893.

cloþe v. give clothes to 873, 3473; clad pp. dressed p. 1, 564, cloþyd 692, 732.

cloþes n. pl. ? clouts, cleats M 796.

clourys n. pl. sod: *vndyr* ~ under the sod 241, 977.

clowte n. rag 2150; pl. pieces 1867.

clowte v. beat 1932.

cloyed pp. adj. hampered 205.

clumme adj. silent W 521.

clyfte n. gash 2845.

clynge v. moulder 2894, waste away 3052; clonge pp. 2718.

cokkys g. sg. God's: *by* ~ *body sakyrde* by the sacrament M 390, 612.

colde adj. chilling 1043, 2062, cold 2432, 2484, M 323.

coloryde pp. perverted W 673.

colo(u)rs n. pl. pretences W 379, 547.

comberaunce n. temptation 3421.

com(en) v. come 109, 2105, be derived 297, W 154, be descended W 112; cum pr. *1* sg. 1749; comyst *2* sg. 2927; comyth *3* sg. 99, cummyth W 153; com pl. 150, cum 3230; cum imp. sg. 345, com 2437; com pr. subj. 1735, cum(me) M 154, 155; cam pt. *1, 3* sg. 297, 304; pt. pl. W 112; cummynge pr. p. W 687; com pp. 2934, comne 903, cum(me) M 69, 449.

comfort(e), counfort(e) n. courage 1324, W 704, M 217, support 1571, 3319, W 205, M 213, consolation W 989*, M 179.

comly *adj.* noble 470, 993, becoming W 454*.

com(m)ynge *n.* coming 14, M 314, birth 330.

comowns *n. pl.* common people 8.

compacient *adj.* compassionate M 874.

compasse *n.* compost M 374.

complexion *n.* constitution 1618, temperament W 343, 557.

compleynt *n.* lament M 815.

comprehence *n.* contents M 761.

comprehend(e) *v.* contain W 715, 937, attain M 867; comprehendyde *pp.* W 937.

comun, comyn *adj.* ordinary W 472, 652, M 72, 274; *sb.* W 443; ~ *women* harlots M 667; *off þe ~* usually W 751.

con see can.

condescende *v.* give way, accede W 711.

condycyon *n.* habit W 626, M 13, 170, disposition M 191, 195.

co(n)gnycyon *n.* knowledge W 143, 1132.

congruent *adj.* corresponding W 752 s.d.*

conjecture *n.* scheming W 354.

conseruynge *pr. p.* preserving W 1139.

contena(u)nce *n.* bearing 1937; *by ~* with gestures, in dumb show W 687.

contynua(u)nce *n.* continuing 142, M 856, duration of life M 233.

conuertyble *adj.* changeable M 749.

convenyent *adj.* appropriate W 6, 701, M 844.

conversacyon *n.* familiarity W 425.

conversant *adj.* familiar W 607.

conveyde *pp.* taken M 566.

convicte *adj.* found guilty M 768; *sb.* a convicted man M 619.

convycte *v.* conquer M 405.

cope *n.* long cloak 805.

coppyde *pp. adj.*: ~ *curs* heaped-up curse M 809.

corn-threscher *n.* thresher of grain M 54.

cors *n.* person 590.

cort(e) *n.* manor court M 668; *sett*

a ~ appoint a session of a manor court M 664; *þe holy ~ of hewyn* the heavenly host M 752.

coryows see curyous.

cost *n.*[1] region 167, 2086, coast 2755.

cost(e) *n.*[2] manner 1060, 1990; *pl.* habits 1239.

cosyn *n.* relative 2945; mistress W 826, 834.

cote *n.*[1] dwelling 1348, 1958, cottage 2733.

cote *n.*[2] kirtle M 795.

coude see can.

coueyt *v.* desire eagerly 23, 350; coueytyst *pr. 2 sg.* 406; coueytyth *3 sg.* 66.

coue(y)tyse *n.* avarice 31, 119, W 531, 744.

co(u)nsel(l) *n.* counsel 1101, advice 1133, 3083, W 923, M 95, 179, secrecy M 539, conference M 788; *of (my, hys)* ~ in (my, his) confidence 1132, M 223.

count *n.* reckoning 3618.

coure *v.* crouch 2230, 2407.

cowche *v.* crouch: ~ *qwayl* crouch like a quail 2385.

crachen, crake *v.* crack 1852, 1945; crake *pr. 3 pl.* brag 1731.

craft(e) *n.* art 1788, 1990, subtle device W 861.

crakows *n. pl.* pointed toes 1059.

crase *v.* shatter 1945.

craue *v.* beg 1485; cravyd *pt. 3 sg.* 3266.

credyble *adj.* worthy of belief W 99, reliable M 750.

crepe *v.* creep, crawl 805, 2215.

Cresten, Crysten *adj.* Christian W 177; *sb.* Christians W 212.

crofte *n.* enclosure 1144, 2144; *helle* ~ the prison of hell 555.

cros(e), croys *n.* the cross of Christ 2132, 2268, M 442; *þe* ~ *and þe pyll* the head and tail of a coin W 858.

crowde *v.* jostle 2336.

croysyd *pp. adj.* crucified 2087.

crulle *v.* ? crawl 2484.

cry(e) *n.* call 1017, 1375, outcry 2085, 2232.

cry(e), criye v. beseech 300, 847,
W 1077, proclaim 471, W 323, speak
loudly 647, 2215, call 907, 919,
M 424, 774, call on God, pray 1434,
W 949, 1065, blow loudly on a
trumpet or flute 2197, M 472,
lament 2407, 2846; ~ wreche call
for vengeance 3443; ~ yow mercy
ask for pardon M 658; crie pr. 1
sg. 3443; cryeth 3 sg. M 774;
cryeth imp. pl. 2197; cryenge
pr. p. W 550 s.d.; cry(e)de pp.
996, M 472.

cryinge n. lamentation 651.

cryke n. brook M 776.

crymynose adj. acknowledging guilt
M 815.

crys(y)me n. cloth wrapped round
the head at baptism 294, 324.

cukke v. excrete 2230.

cunne see can.

cunnyng adj. crafty M 128.

cunte n. female private parts 1190.

cure n. care 3495, grief W 53; take
of ~ taken responsibility for W 240.

curs(e) n. curse (of God) 2389,
W 872; Crystys ~ 2163, M 99, 399;
þe grete ~ excommunication 854.

cursyd(e) adj. wicked 106, 2291,
M 764.

cursydhed n. wickedness 1592.

curs(s)ydnesse n. wickedness 1239,
1589.

cursyn v. excommunicate 857, in-
voke a curse (on) 2441, W 808.

curtely adj. courtly, courteous W 599.

curtly adv. briefly M 101.

curyous, curryus, coryows adj.
caring for man 320, exquisite W 579,
609.

cust, cyste see kys.

custummaly adv. according to
custom W 14.

da pacem n. weapon M 714.

dagge v. jog 3099.

daggys n. pl. shreds 2194.

dale n. valley 188, 462, grave 991,
2948; ~ of dol the valley of grief,
death 1247, 1591; ~ of dros the grave
1588, 1658.

dalyacyon n. chattering M 46.

dalya(u)nce n. conversation 140,
W 785.

dame n. lady 583, 2108, mother
W 115, M 51.

dampne v. condemn to hell 3430, 3566,
W 1123, condemn in court W 724;
dampnynge pr. p. 1042, 3011.

dangerus adj. reluctant M 891.

dapyrly adv. gracefully 1000.

dare v. remain quiet W 775.

dasarde n. blockhead M 665.

dasche v. shatter 2194, strike W 774;
dayschyd pp. 2388.

daunt(e) v. intr. be tame 2418; tr.
tame W 611.

day n. day 138, 2618, W 198, 810,
M 146, 727; endynge ~ day of
death 407, 2642; in my days in my
lifetime M 362; many a ~ for a
long time 422, 829; of dawe to
death 1687, 2961; þis ~ seuenenyt
a week from today 133; see haue.

dayl(e) v. have dealings 84, 2384.

deambulatorye n. covered walk,
cloister M 843.

debate n. combat 1111, quarrel 1785,
2453.

debatyth pr. 3 sg. combats 189.

ded n. death 2844, 3023.

dees, des(se) n. high platform 481,
649, judgement seat 3616; on ~ in a
place of honour 1000.

deface v. disfigure W 174.

defaute n. poverty 82, sin M 11.

defendawnte n. defender M 24.

def(f)ens n. resistance 2027, protection 2181, 2814, M 258; wythowtyn
any ~ without any remedy 3228.

defoule v. defile W 906; dyffowlyde
pp. W 130, defowlyde W 927.

degre n. quality 51, 508, way 307,
1449, condition 2281, M 190, position M 393; in all degres in every
way 1.

del(e), dol(e) n. grief 259, 1570,
anguish 2600; it is (were) gret ~ it is
(would be) great grief 299, 612, 1826.

dele v. intr. be concerned 373; tr.
deliver 2821, give away 2917; absol.
arrange 663.

delle n. pit of hell 1747, 3125;
dethys ~ the valley of death 3041.

delusory *adj.* deceiving M 881.
deluyn, delffe *v. tr.* pierce 1069, 2734, dig 2326, M 328; *intr.* be pierced 2577; doluen *pp.* 2679, delue buried 2948.
deme *v.* condemn 3206, judge 3219, 3441; dempte *pp.* 3258.
demonycall *adj.* of devils M 153.
dene *n.* den, lair 213, 901.
denne *n.* valley 208, 912.
denomynacyon *n.* designation M 122.
dent, dynt *n.* stroke 1862, 2218; *dethys* ~ the stroke of death 169, 663, 1069.
denteth *adj.* delicious 3294.
depravyd see dysprawe.
dere *n.* harm 3533.
dere *adj.* beloved 139, 483, W 1085, M 307, 758, costly M 354.
dere *adv.* in costly manner M 9, 282.
dere *v.* injure 1730, 3100.
derne *adj.* secluded 188, 1089, stealthy 2821.
derworthly *adv.* affectionately 829.
deryvatt *adj.* derived M 187.
descendyde *pp.* fallen down W 939.
deseruiture *n.* desert 3441.
despectyble *adj.* despicable M 752.
des(se) see dees.
desyderable *adj.* longed for W 253.
deth-drawth *n.* death-stroke 2791.
deth(e) *n.* death 99, 2790, W 123, 369, M 10, 736.
dett(e) *n.* debt of death, death-blow 2821, debt to God W 194.
deuer(e) *n.* duty; *doo my* ~ done my duty 1835, 2955; *put me in* ~ endeavour M 550.
deuyl, deull *n.* a devil 197, 213, W 324 s.d., 372, the Devil 266, 894, W 370, 508, M 70, 156; see wey(e), w(h)at.
deuys *n.* device W 775.
devnesse *n.* rights 3434.
dewoydyth *pr. 3 sg.* goes out W 380 s.d.
d(e)y(e), deyen, day *v.* die 546, 638, W 60, 882; *deye on* go ahead and die 2953; dye *pr. subj. 2 sg.* 1387; deydyst *pt. 2 sg.* 3370; d(e)yed

3 sg. 304, 1711; dyen *pr. p.* 1711; ded(e) *pp.* 2921, W 534, M 593.
deynte *n.*: *haue lytyll* ~ *of* take little pleasure in M 267
dobullnes *n.* duplicity W 726.
dogge, doog *n.* dog: *a dogge trot* at an easy pace 3099: *hay, doog* run, dog M 720.
dol(e) see del(e).
dolfully *adv.* grievously 99.
doluen see deluyn.
dom(e) *n.* judgement 3240, 3255, sentence 3437, the Last Judgement 3617, decision W 228, 995.
dompe, dumme *adj.* dumb W 523, 775.
domynacyon *n.* lordship W 31, 300.
do(ne) *v.* do 59, 1063, cause to 168, 471, W 685, M 469, 565, perform 1990, 2348, act 3384, W 230, M 673, finish M 574, 605; *refl.* make 1051, 1984; *auxil.* 2306, W 305, 884, M 15, 32; ~ *awey* take away W 960; ~ *ewyl* sin 312, 1373; ~ *here beste* do their utmost 857; ~ *mercy* perform deeds of mercy 3633; ~ *note* make profit 2729; ~ *of dawe* put to death 1687; ~ *trespas* sin W 1095; ~ *trewthe* keep one's word 3257; ~ *wey* stop M 82, 583, take off M 623; ~ *wronge* do harm 1027, 3433; *ellys to* ~ other things to do 1354; *haue do(n)* finish 1877, 2188, M 646; *wel* ~ act rightly 3637; dost *pr. 2 sg.* 830, doyst W 880; doth *3 sg.* 312, dos 1063; don *pl.* 1027, doth W 1028, do M 32; do *imp. sg.* 1984; *pl.* 471, dothe 2243; dedyst *pt. 2 sg.* 2944; dyd *3 sg.* 2306; dyde *pl.* 3134; doynge *pr. p.* M 783; don *pp.* 538, W 915, M 605, do 2955, W 913, M 646; see deuer(e), dyspyght, good(e).
doo *n.* doe 188.
dos *n.* ? potion 1711.
dote *v.* be witless 1970.
dow *n.* dough: *in dethys* ~ in the grave 811, 2639.
downbrynge *pr. 1 sg.* cast down 2793.
down(e) *n.* upland 439, 912.

down(ne), don *adv.* down 85, 2189, W 1105, M 361, 735.

dowte *n.* doubt 1820, 1841, danger 1869, fear 2119, 2293; *no* ~ doubtless W 468; see saun(z).

dowt(e) *v.* fear 912; *refl.* 3011; dowtyd *pp.* 1051.

dowty *adj.* valiant 197, 2193, worthy 901; dowtyest *superl.* 3613.

dowtyr, doughter *n.* daughter 999, 3230, woman W 165.

doynge *n.* action 291, 1604.

drad, dred(e), *pp. adj.* feared greatly 1051, 1089, terrible 3025, 3617.

draf *n.* filth 197.

drake *n.* dragon 197.

drawe, drawyn *v. intr.* come 217, go 419, 1573; *refl.* betake 342, 1344; *tr.* bring 308, 313, lead 1644, 1681; drawyth *pr. 3 sg.* 313; drow *pt. 2 sg.* 3109.

drawke *n.* a weed M 537.

drawte *pp. adj.*: ~ *notys* notes drawn out W 996 s.d.

drawth *n.* quantity of drink 965.

drede *v.* fear greatly 2787, W 632, stand in awe of 3607, W 88, 1158; *absol.* 2784; *refl.* 2043; dredys *pr. 3 sg.* W 632.

drenche *v.* drown 2561; drenchyd *pp.* 2388.

drenkelyd *pp. adj.* drowned 3079.

drepe *v. intr.*[1] droop 262; drepyn *pr. 3 pl.* 965.

drepe *v. tr.*[2] strike 1186; drepyn *pp.* 2759.

drery *adj.* dreadful 2309, 2790.

dresse *n.* (severe) treatment 3446.

dres(se) *v.* prepare 663, place 1759, 1820; *absol.* arrange W 698; *refl.* 902, 1000; dressyd *pp.* 3023.

dreye see dry(e).

dros(s) *n.* worthless matter 1604, 1665; see dale.

drulle *v.* ? stagger 2397.

dry(e) *adj.*[1] dry 528, 2331, unprofitable 1604; *þe Dreye Tre* the barren tree in the Earthly Paradise 177.

drye *adj.*[2] hard to endure 2843.

dryff-draff *n.* refuse, dregs M 49.

dryfte *n.* force 2843, taking by force 2915.

dryve, dryffe, droue *v. intr.* be forced to go 262, 1658, 2915, hasten 897, 1118, W 782; *tr.* force to go 1042, 2131, M 380; ~ *adoun* overthrow 1570, be overthrown 2378; drywe *pr. subj. 1 sg.* 262; dryuyth *imp. pl.* 897; dryuynge *pr. p.* forcible 1862, drywande W 782; dreuyn *pp.* 1042, dreue 1570, drewyn 2824.

dublere *n.* platter M 647.

duke *n.* duke 649, 902, Lord (Christ) 1995, powerful man 2672.

durke *v.* lie in wait 2793.

durnell *n.* darnel, a weed M 537.

dyche *n.* ditch 439, 733.

dye(n) see d(e)y(e).

dyfye *v.* renounce, scorn W 510.

dyght see dyth.

dygne, dyng(n)e *adj.* noble 213, 3616, worthy 483.

dyke *n.* ditch 208, 2352.

dylectable, delectable *adj.* giving delight W 255, 591, M 65.

dylectacyon, delectacyon *n.* pleasure W 366, 451, M 896.

dylyuerance *n.*: *a fayer* ~ good riddance M 162.

dynge *v.* beat 1781, W 774, M 377.

dynt see dent.

dyrke *adj.* black 3395, W 166.

dyrknes, derknes *n.* blackness of hell 3448, W 118.

dyrt *n.* excrement 2381.

dys *n. pl.* dice 806.

dysalow *v.* dispraise M 182, 746.

dyscheyit *n.* deceit W 727.

dyscorde *v.* disagree 3515.

dyscretly *adv.* discerningly W 145.

dyscrye *v.* perceive W 859; dyscrye *pr. 1 sg.* 1980.

dyscyplyne *n.* instruction W 89, chastisement in penance W 434.

dyscyplynyde *pt. subj.* chastised W 1016.

dyses(s)e, dyshes *n.* discomfort M 629, trouble 621, 2453.

dysgysynge *n.* symbolic clothing W 150, new-fangled dress W 590.

dyspectuose *adj.* contemptible M 747.

dyspent *pp. adj.* spent 1657.

dyspersyde *pp. adj.* distracted M 734.

dysporte *n.* sport W 688, conduct M 167, pleasure M 215.

dyspose *refl. imp.* prepare M 816; dysposyde *pp.* inclined W 222, 344, M 813, applied (for the good of the soul) W 1002.

dysposycyoun *n.* disposal 2753, ordering W 29, state of mind M 654.

dysprawe *v.* revile W 838; depravyd *pt. 3 sg.* disparaged 3264.

dyspyght, dyspyt(h) *n.* malice 1652; *do* ~ treat with insult and injury 2310, 2514, W 921; *haue in* ~ hate W 338.

dyspytuusly *adv.* insultingly W 842.

dysseuer *v.* depart M 551.

dystaunce *n.* discord 1437, 1551; *at* ~ in opposition 77, 3517; *wythoutyn* ~ undoubtedly 48, 1547.

dystresse *n.* anguish 71, 357.

dysvygure, dysfygure *v.* spoil the beauty of W 353; *refl.* W 1114; dysvyguryde *pp.* W 117, 901*.

dyth, dyght *v.* put 169, 259; *refl.* W 995; dyth *imp. sg.* remove 3025, prepare 1970; dyth *pr. subj. 2 sg.* perform 1605; dyth *pp.* 169, 213, deth 756, dyght ordained W 123.

dyverte *imp. pl. refl.* go astray M 19.

eche see iche.

egall(e) *adj.* equal in worth W 4, equitable M 831.

eke *adv.* also M 562.

elde *n.* old age 2529.

ell, ellys *adv.* otherwise 823, 1027, 1061, 3132, 3312, W 506, M 306, 355; *not* ~ nothing more 1578, W 80.

elmesdede *n.* act of charity 2009.

empryse, enprise *n.* power 600, 2835.

enbrace *v.* bribe W 638.

enbraces *n. pl.* briberies W 791.

enduyde *pt. 3 sg.* endowed W 382, 1138; endewyd *pp.* 2579.

endyght *v.* indict, prosecute W 810, 851.

endynge *n.* end 3467, 3648; *make* ~ end life 1392, 1806.

endytynge *n.* accusation 34.

engrose *v.* corner W 804*.

ensense *v.* arouse 1364.

entayle *n.*[1] disposition 2697.

entayle *n.*[2] settlement of inheritance 2993.

entende *v.* give attention 1676.

entent, intent *n.* attention 389, 527, heed 863, W 228, will 3220, M 285, purpose M 38; *in good* ~ well inclined 2028; *wyth good* ~ with good will 1507.

entret, entyrecte *n.* plaster, ointment W 731, 796.

erdyn *n.* petition 2498, errand 2896.

ern *n.* iron M 287.

erth(e) *n.* soil 297, 298, M 186, 328, ground 1490, 2626, M 31, 533, the world 3496, W 1145; *in* ~ on earth 351, W 3.

erys, herys *n. pl.* ears p. 1, 1516, W 758, M 303, 557.

erytage *n.* inheritance 111, 2872.

eryth *v.* inherit 111.

es(e), eas(e) *n.* comfort 244, 619, W 814, M 174; easy life W 411; *at* ~ satisfied 707, 1911, 2747, W 564.

espye see aspye.

ete *v.* eat 1154, 1619; *we haue etyn garlek euerychone* we have all sinned 1369; ete *pr. 3 pl.* 2820; *pr. subj. 3 sg.* 1619; *pt. 3 sg.* 2276; etyn *pp.* 1369, etun M 131.

euer(e) *adv.* always 24, 66, W 46, 67, M 22, 79, at any time 1261, W 21, 352, M 413, 559; *(for)* ~ *and ay* for ever 3377, 3391; see among(e).

euer(e)more *adv.* always 23, 503, W 415, 569, M 892.

euery *adj.* every 15, 158, W 109, 152, M 745, 747; *sb.* each one 71.

euerychon(e) *pron.* each one 1369, 2595, M 263, 405.

euery-dele *adv.* every bit M 105.

evyn *adv.* exactly W 538, M 261, 571, completely W 1052, M 275; ~ *to* all the way to 177; *ful* ~ completely 35, 3422, 3500.

evyn-Crysten *n.* fellow Christian W 1039.

ewynly *adv.* calmly M 741.

ex *n.* axe: *he helde þe ex be þe helue* he acted of his own free will 2571.

expedycius *adj.* quickly made M 860.

expedyent(e) *adj.* fit W 705, M 846.

expres *adv.* for certain W 396, 443, specifically W 695.

ey *interj.* what! 1572, 2365, M 124, 344.

ey(e) *n.* eye 1388, 2229, W 963, 990, M 31, 303*; **eyn(e), yne** *pl.* 1106, 1516, 2229, M 156; *haue un* ~ have regard 1602.

eylyth *pr. 3 sg.* ails 2466.

eyr, ayer, hayer *n.* heir 103, 2907, W 159, 244.

eysyl *n.* vinegar 3136, 3354.

fadyn *v.* vanish 354, 836, decline 2031, wither 3000; **fadyth** *pr. 3 sg.* 354.

fadyr, father *n.* father 917, 1054, M 728, heavenly Father 3252, 3314, W 122, 285, spiritual father M 209, 403, old man W 393, M 86.

fall *n.* accident M 730.

fall(e), fallyn *v.* sink to death 261, allot 314, sink 808, 1622, rush 1034, lapse 1704, decline 2031, W 438, light (upon) 2048, come down 2222, be fitting W 11, yield to temptation W 318, come down in the world W 582; ~ *in repentaunce* repent 1417; ~ *on bord* attack 2228; *fayre* ~ may good befall 149, 3561; *foule* ~ may evil befall 2227; **fallyt(h)** *pr. 3 sg.* 808, W 11; **fallyn** *pl.* 1034, W 438; **fell** *pr. subj. 1 sg.* 261; **fel** *pt. 3 sg.* 1622, **fyl** 2095; **fel** *pl.* 2222; **falle** *pp.* 314.

fame *n.* reputation 576, W 598; *fals* ~ false rumour 1128, 1829, 2160.

fane *n.* banner 1886, 2071, weathervane M 749.

fare *n.* eating and drinking 261, boasting 2107, condition 2412.

fare, faryn *v.* come 278, journey 482, 1566, thrive 613, 2903, W 809, go 2139; *euyl* ~ live poorly 2530; ~ *amys* live poorly 870, 2702; ~ *wel* eat and drink well 257, 372, prosper 334, 601, M 470, 577; **faryst** *pr. 2 sg.* 2921; **faryth** *3 pl.* 2903; **ferd** *pt. subj. 1 sg.* 870; **ferdyst** *2 sg.* 2702.

far(e)wel(l) *interj.* good-bye 153, 945, W 512, 563, M 160, 605.

fast(e) *adv.* vigorously 63, swiftly 224, 933, M 708, 723, earnestly 3512; *also* ~ at once 913; ~ *by* nearby M 799.

fauerall *adj.* benevolent M 904.

faunt *n.* child 2416.

fauour(e) *n.* comfort W 209, M 123, forgiveness M 854.

fawe, fayn(e) *adj.* joyful 212, 498, eager 1765, 2283, glad 2286, 2962, content M 781.

fawte *n.* fault 2039, 3183.

fay see **feyth(e)**.

fayer *n.* beauty W 69.

fayle *v. intr.* suffer want 82, fall short W 436, be lacking M 495; *tr.* prove wanting to 2599, 2698, lack M 480; **faylyt** *pr. 3 sg.* 2599.

fayn *adv.* gladly 378, M 137, 368, eagerly 3512.

fayn(e) see **fawe**.

fayr(e), fer *adj.* pleasant 237, 511, 1177, M 162, 436, beautiful 366, 2071, W 129, 151, M 682, favourable W 719; *a* ~ *wyll* a long time M 472, 581; **fayrest** *superl.* W 105.

fayre *adv.* favourably 664, 2892, pleasantly 1178, 2283.

faytour *n.* deceiver 212, 2071, M 245.

febyll *pr. 3 pl.* grow weak W 438.

fede *v.* feed 414, 587, M 243, 250; *refl.* W 459, nourish spiritually 3609; **fadde** *pp.* 187, 1523, **fed(d)e** 212, 1982, M 243.

fee *n.* property 572.

feet *adj.* handsome M 697.

feffe, feffyn *v.* endow 730, 1026; *refl.* 1151; **feffyst** *pr. 2 sg.* 740.

fekyl *adj.* untrustworthy 102.

felaw, felow *n.* comrade 520, 566, M 157, 256, fellow 804, 1574, M 253, 327; *good* ~ pleasant companion 2608, M 703.

feld(e) *n.* field 187, 740, field of battle 1914, 1960.

fele *adj.* many 225, 1885.

fell *n.* skin M 884.

felle *adj.* fierce 118, 1885; **feller** *compar.* craftier 668.

fell(e) *adv.* fiercely 68, violently M 96.

fell(e) *v.* strike down 930, 1378;
fellyd *pp.* 1165.

felynge *n.* perception W 95, 1122,
faculty of sense perception W 136,
emotion W 154, 158.

felyschyppe *n.* company M 477, 726;
felechepys *pl.* friendships 1304,
2861.

fence *n.* defence M 719.

fend(e) *n.* the Devil 29, 33, W 294,
M 886, a devil 3054, 3576, W 528,
904.

fende *v.* defend 1536, 1695; fendyd
pp. 1296.

fen(ne) *n.* marsh 740, 876.

fer see fayr(e) *adj.*

ferd *n.* fear: *for* ~ in terror 2391.

fere *n.*¹ comrade 539, 1745; *in* ~
together 943, 997, 3245.

fer(e), feer, fyre *n.*² fire 1961, 2289,
W 821, M 287, 323; *helle* ~ hell-
fire 1457, 3309; *on (a)* ~ afire 1961,
2260; *wyld* ~ wild-fire 2115.

fer(e) *n.*³ fear 1968, 3532, W 582,
844, M 793.

fere *v.* frighten 1093; *refl.* fear M 254,
574.

fer(e), farre *adv.* far 2959, W 881;
~ *and nere* everywhere 657, 688,
2959; ~ *or nye* anywhere 473.

ferne *adj.* distant 1093, 2139.

fers *adj.* bold M 621.

feryde *pp.* set on fire M 55.

fese *v.* stir up 964.

fesyl *v.* break wind with a hiss 2408.

feterel *n.* ? deceiver 1580.

fett(e) *v.* cause to come 3631, get
M 411.

feyth(e), fay(th) *n.* belief 1274,
W 127, 285, faithfulness 3254; *be
my (þi)* ~ indeed 429, 1351, W 556;
(in) ~ indeed 212, 261, M 628; *in
good* ~ in truth 3179.

feythly *adv.* devoutly 3394.

flappyn *v.* beat 225.

flappys *n. pl.* blows 1885.

flapyr *v.* flutter 1886.

fle *v.*¹ *tr.* avoid 506, 1630, M 726;
intr. depart 1447, W 91, run away
2286, W 870, escape W 875.

fle *v.*² hasten 482, 1914, move swiftly
933, fly through the air W 567;

~ *awey* vanish quietly 2641; flet
pr. 3 sg. 933, flyet 2641.

flene *v.* flay 225.

flete *v.* float down 2053.

fleterynge *n.* flitting about 669.

flexybull *adj.* easily bent M 741.

flod(e) *n.* stream 306, 354, current
W 491; *in* ~ with force 1946.

florchynge *pr. p.* flourishing 967;
florchyd *pp.* adorned 237.

flowe *v.* flow, run 224.

flyt *v.* depart 358, 2592.

fodyr, foþyr *n.* company 1116, 2612;
on a ~ all together 1034.

fogge *v.* jog along 913.

folde *n.*¹ enclosure 3054.

folde *n.*² earth: *in* ~ on earth 700.

folk(e) *n.* people 187, 200, W 632.

followd *pp.* christened 3394.

folw(e), folow *v.* follow 316, 573,
M 290, practise 3156; folwyth
pr. 3 sg. 933; folwude *pt. 3 sg.*
W 1043; folowynge *pr. p.* W 795;
folwyd *pp.* 1525.

fomen *n. pl.* enemies 3358.

fond *v.* founder, sink to the ground 964.

fonde, fonnyde *adj.* foolish W 393;
sb. fool 627.

fonde *v.* tempt 679, try 1169, 2143,
go 1566, seek 3112, 3447.

fondnes *n.* foolishness W 438.

fo(o) *n.* enemy 306, 395; fon(e) *pl.*
1695, 3396, M 307, 407.

fo(o)de *n.* nourishment 415, 1151,
M 37, nourisher, nurse 551, 1232,
3372.

fo(o)le, foll *n.* fool 523, 1033, M 140,
275.

football *n.* a football M 732.

foppe *n.* fool M 444.

for *conj.* because 104, 122, W 20, 109,
M 39, 42; *prep.* in order 34, 120,
concerning 106, M 357, because of
119, 1017, W 166, 977, M 516, 793,
for the sake of 337, 1304, W 230,
1006, M 830, 907, in exchange for
1101, W 1025, M 367, in order to
get 2375, M 780, instead of W 221,
fit for W 618, for fear of W 850,
M 778; ~ *God* by God 1778, 1799;
~ *to* to 19, 34, W 192, 243, M 382,
404.

forbere, forberyn v. give up 1582, M 439, 712.

forbete pp. beaten thoroughly 2200.

forbled pp. adj. bloody 3087.

forbrostyn pp. adj. burst in pieces 2900.

force, fors n. value: see ǥeue.

forcolde adj. chilled M 62, 269.

forǥeue imp. forgive 1484; forȝeue opt. 1498; forǥafe pt. 2 sg. 3358; forǥevyn pp. 3280.

forǥoo v. give up 2877; forǥon pp. 2878.

forlore, forlorn pp. destroyed 926, lost 1870.

forme n. manner W 749.

forme-faderys n. pl. forefathers 275.

fors v. regard W 606, 656.

forsake, forsakyn v. abandon 93, 2515; forsok(e) pt. sg. 3070, 3082, 3396; pt. subj, 359, 381; forsake pp. 93, W 1090; forsakyn 452.

forschent pp. put to shame 2201.

forsoþe adv. truly 15, 327, W 30, M 33, 587.

forth(e) adv. forward 412, 894, W 885, M 68, 86; and so ~ and so on M 63; see brynge.

fortherers n. pl. promoters W 759.

forþi adv. because of that 2784, 3476.

forþynkyth impers. pr. 3 sg. makes (me) repent 1486.

forȝete, forǥett v. forget 2817, 2967, W 449; forǥetyth pr. 3 sg. 3291; forȝete pr. subj. 2 sg. 2967; forǥate pt. 3 sg. 3402; forȝete pp. 2817, forgetyn 3405.

forȝevenesse n. forgiveness 3278, W 987, 1082.

fote n. foot 3551, M 784; fete, feet pl. W 1042, 1103, M 218; þe beddys feet p. 1; vndyr fete (fote) 1165, M 206; on ~ M 68.

fote-mett n.: haue hys ~ take his measure M 531.

foul see ful(l).

foul(e) adj. slanderous 2158, filthy 2241, 2254, W 151, 477, M 730, ugly W 758, bad M 547; fowler compar. uglier W 904; ~ fend wicked devil 1384, 2012; ~ Flesch wicked Flesh 29, 58, 1523.

foule adv. grievously 206, 2408, slanderously 664, 2151.

fowe v. clean out 2329.

fownder n. originator W 393, 733, M 1.

frame n. device M 532.

frawt(h) pp. fully provided 368, 514.

frayed pp. bruised 3086.

frayry n. fraternity M 153.

fre adv. willingly 1874, freely 3317.

fre(e) adj. untrammelled 25, 3464, W 300, noble 896, 917, W 1023, excellent W 187; sb. free man 2798; see wyl(le).

freellnes n. weakness W 200.

freelte n. frailty 2031, W 75.

frele, frayll adj. fragile 968, 1982, prone to sin M 757.

frely adj. noble 11; adv. generously 1982, whole-heartedly W 499, 502.

frenchepe, frendeschyppe n. friendship 11, W 633.

frerys n. pl. friars M 325.

fresch(e) adj. bright 1807, 1982, gaily dressed W 511, 558, M 119, gay W 590, M 676, new M 857; freshest superl. most gaily dressed W 556; adv. vigorously 1735.

frete v. gnaw 937; absol. vex 2408; fretyth pr. 3 sg. wears down M 356; frettyd pp. 3087.

freyne v. request 11.

fro prep. from 12, 86, M 731, 829, away from 2884, 3036, M 262, 595, since W 18.

from prep. from W 1110, M 39, out of M 36, away from W 68, M 566.

froskys n. pl. frogs 1361.

fryke adj. brisk 427.

ful(l), foul adv. completely 16, 99, W 941, very 18, 30, W 45, 972, M 164, 219; adj. complete W 26, 122, full 2638, 2720, W 168, 570, M 47, 124; at þe fulle to the full 2404; ~ my bely all I want M 588.

funte-ston n. baptismal font 3394.

fusyon n. plenty M 330.

fy interj. for shame! M 784.

fygure n. image W 184, 211.

fyle, n. wretch 1580.

fylle v. fill 3502, fulfill 3629; fyllyd pp. 1164.

fylyde *pp. adj.* defiled W 987.
fynde(n) *v.* discover 15, 1237, W 205, M 108, 770; fonde *pt. 1, 3 sg.* 2039, 3601; fyndende *pr. p.* 81; founde *pp.* 1255, foundon W 28.
fyst *n.* handwriting M 683.
fyth, fyght *n.* strife 3232, affray W 850.
fyth, fyght *v.* fight 63, 964, W 307, 704, M 231, 404; fytyth *pr. 3 sg.* 65; fytyn *pl.* 70, fyth 2374; faught *pt. 1 sg.* M 651.

gad(e)lyng(e), gedelynge *n.* base fellow 463, 1769, 2980.
gadyr, gaþer *v.* bring together 67, W 766, amass 95, 861, take up a collection of M 457, 460; *refl.* assemble 227; gaderyth *pr. 3 sg.* 67, accumulates, swells with infection 1620; gadryd *pp.* 2992, gederyde W 766.
gale *n.* speech 959.
galle *n.* gall-bladder 1732, 2900, bitter substance 3136, 3354, W 1100.
galont(e) *n.* man of fashion W 324 s.d., 598.
game *n.* game 838, 1148, M 417, pleasure 2696, W 40, sport W 603, 612, scheme M 591, 605; gamyn *pl.* 1331, gamys dramatic entertainments 3645; ~ *and gle* mirth and joy 183, 454, 1267, 1331; *make yow* ~ entertain you M 69.
gan see gynne.
gane *v.* overcome 2073.
gape *v.* open the mouth wide 1941; gapyn *pr. 3 pl.* 200.
gase *v.* stare 1941.
gast *v.* terrify 939; gastyd *pp.* 463.
gastful *adj.* dreadful 1463.
gate *n.*[1] way, course 1574.
gate *n.*[2] gate 2459, M 473, 477.
gay *adj.* joyous 705, 959, W 648, M 119, wanton 1160, rich 1248, bright 2975; *adv.* finely 1078.
gere *n.* weapons 939, 1957; *pl.* armour 1985.
gere *v.* equip 1985.
gerlys *n. pl.* young women 1160.

gesse, gees *v.* reckon 903, 1575, W 361.
gesunne *adj.* scarce M 252*.
get(e), getyn, geet(t) *v.* acquire (property) 95, 3018, W 560, 636, obtain 1322, 2965, M 359, 611, make (money) W 677, 801; getyst *pr. 2 sg.* 2319; gettys W 801; getyth *3 sg.* 2746; gete *pl.* 2819; gote *pp.* 2727, gotyn 2936, get(t) W 560, M 802.
geue, gyf, yeue, ȝeue, ȝyf(e) *v.* grant 18, 25, W 56, 550, M 161, deliver 762, give in alms 1486, 3474, W 999, offer W 73, 78, put M 805; *refl.* devote 720, 841, W 411; *absol.* make a gift W 647; ~ *in charge* bid M 293; ~ *neuere* (*no*) *tale* take no account 445, 460, 568; ~ *no force* care nothing 1002, M 75; ~ *not a myth* (*hawe, louse*) care nothing 247, 479, 489, 768; ~ *wppe* surrender M 549; *ne* ~ *a gres* care not a straw 2169; ȝeue *pr. 1 sg.* 247, ȝyf(e) 460, 762, yeff W 647, geve W 689, gyff M 75, gyue M 293; yewyst *2 sg.* W 922; ȝeuyth *3 sg.* 18, ȝeuyt 479, yewyt W 56; gyff *pl.* impart W 479, yeff W 1147; ȝeue *pr. subj. 2 sg.* 599; gyf(f) *opt.* W 550, M 161; yeue *imp. sg.* W 82, gyff W 999; gafe *pt. 1, 3 sg.* 1486, ȝafe 1497, gaff W 410; ȝeue *2 sg.* 3408; yevynge *pr. p.* furnishing W 704; govyn *pp.* 25*, ȝouyn 2560, ȝoue 2964, yewyn W 576, yowe devoted W 941.
geyn-went *n.* road to come back 2785.
gle *n.* joy; ~ *and game* joy and mirth 1045; see game.
glede *n.* live coal, fire 1463, 2603.
glemys *g. sg.* of bright light 2603.
gloto(u)n *n.* gluttony 1016, 1801, greedy person 1030.
gnawe *v.* suffer 1168.
gobet *n.* morsel 364.
God(e) *n.* God 1, 18, W 14, 90, M 20, 831; see cokkys, for.
Godhed(e) *n.* the Deity 3218, W 94, 214.
gogmagog *n.* a giant 1941.

go(ne), goo(n) v. go 323, 435, W 319, 501, M 100, 469, (with infin.) 2897, W 371, M 563, 632, (with *and* and infin.) M 141, 493, toll 1212, depart 2607, M 455, 723, turn out 2687, travel W 883, die M 862; ~ *away* depart 1756; ~ *behende* be defeated 21; ~ *hys* (*þi, yowr*) *wey* depart W 550 s.d., M 457, 521; ~ *out* depart M 70, 701; ~ *to* go to work 2235, M 89; *wel goo* well done 1778; gost *pr. 2 sg.* W 874; goth *3 sg.* 21; go(o) *pl.* 2799, W 883; *pr. subj.* 615, M 730; go we *hort.* 385, 434, W 868, M 149; goo *imp. sg.* 573; goth *pl.* 1002; goynge *pr. p.* W 1064 s.d.; gon *pp.* 1756, M 723, go(o) 1778, M 862.

gonge *n.* privy 2386.

good(e) *n.* property 83, 95, W 502, 792, virtue 302, 419, benefit 2944, 2949; *do* ~ profit 840, act virtuously 2184, 3168.

goodeman *n.* husband M 200, 704, head of household, host of an inn M 467.

goodewyff *n.* wife M 200, 618.

goos *n.* goose 802, 2651, fool 1061; gees, ges *pl.* 802, 2651.

gore *n.*¹ gown: *vndyr* ~ within the heart 1305.

gore *n.*² filthy person 1410.

gost(e) *n.* evil spirit 321, 3584, soul 793; *Holy* ~ Holy Spirit 3281, W 282, 287.

gostly *adj.* spiritual 1635, 2328, W 1074, 1122, M 29, 208; ~ *enmy* enemy of the soul 56, M 27, 215; *adv.* devoutly M 459.

gouerna(u)nce *n.* guidance 3419, control M 199, conduct M 599; *putte hys good in* ~ arrange the disposal of his property 107.

gouerne *v.* have control of 105; gouernyde *pp.* W 259.

govell *n.* usury W 602.

govyn see geue.

gowne *n.* robe 1248; gounse *pl.* 2073.

gownyde *pp. adj.* robed W 724 s.d.

goynge *n.* walking W 434, departing W 996 s.d., M 20.

gramercy *interj.* many thanks 566.

graspe *v.* grope 226.

grates *n. pl.* thanks W 190.

graue, grauyn *pp. adj.* buried 821, 2828.

graythyd *pp. adj.* dressed 1078.

grede, gredyn *v.* call loudly 958, 1992, call in prayer 1278.

grene *n.* grassy ground 227, 1892; *on þe* ~ on the green 134; *vndyr* ~ under the sod 2924.

grenne *v.* gnash the teeth 200, 3078.

gres(e) *n.* grass 821, 1907, blade of grass 2169; see geue.

gret(e), grett *adj.* great 38, 299, W 49, 76, M 21, 136, long 421, famous 579, 1007, especially devoted 1153, large 2820, M 247, 479, weighty W 448; see curs(e).

grete, grett *v.*¹ greet 1161, M 101.

grete *v.*² weep 1313, M 428.

gretynge *n.* weeping 1307.

greue *v.* cause pain 710, 3112; grewyth *pr. 3 sg.* M 896.

greuys, gryffys *n. pl.* groves 333, 2975.

grevaunce *n.* distress 3172, 3215, M 858, injury M 653.

greve *n.* harm 146.

grewe *adj.* severe, grievous W 1016.

grocchyn, grucche *v.* moan 321, 455, 2833.

grochynge *n.* lamentation 1305.

grom(e) *n.* man 939, 958.

gronde *v.* establish W 944.

grope *v.* grasp 200, 809.

gro(u)nd(e) *n.* surface of the earth 226, 2742, basis 2456, W 236; *on* (*upon*) ~ on earth 705, 1837, 3413.

grow(e) *v.* spring up 226, become 248, 1045, grow W 1017, M 352; growyth *pr. 3 sg.* 1882; growe *pl.* 183; growe *pp.* 248, growyn 1596.

gryffys see greuys.

grylle *adj.* fierce 3584.

grym *n.* cruelty 226.

grymly *adj.* cruel 3413.

grynde *v.* gnash 1278, torment 1732.

grype *v.* clutch 809.

gryse *v.* shudder 2833.

grysly *adj.* frightful 321, 939.

grysly(ch) *adv.* pitiably 449, 463.

guttys *n. pl.* bowels 1168.
gydynge *n.* conduct M 216.
gyf(f) see **geue.**
gyle *n.* deceit 3016.
gylyd *pp.* deceived 530.
gynne *n.* skill 1395, contrivance 1702, cunning W 547.
gynne *v. intr.* begin 376, 959; *auxil.* **gan** 224, 1662; *tr.* 1307; **gynnyst** *pr. 2 sg.* 1859; **gynnyth** *3 sg.* 932; **gunne** *subj.* 544; **gan(ne)** *pt. 1, 3 sg.* 63, 224; **gannyst** *2 sg.* 3013; **gun** *pl.* 37, **ganne** 1012; **gunne** *pp.* 1307.
gyse *n.* way of living 2887, M 183, custom W 516, behaviour W 767; *new* ~ latest fashion M 103, 676.
gysely *adv.* handsomely W 16 s.d.*

ha *interj.* ah! W 463, M 613.
habundance *n.* affluence, wealth W 654.
habundante *adj.* abounding M 22.
hakle *n.* feathers 2650.
ha(l)l(e) *n.* mansion 444, 458; *heuene* ~ the mansion of heaven 1334, 2343, a heavenly dwelling 1709; see **bowre.**
halpeny(e) *n.* halfpenny M 52, 480.
hals *n.* neck 430.
halse *v.* embrace W 594, 1102; **halsyde** *pt. 1 sg.* M 644; **halsyde** *pp.* W 44.
hande see **hond(e).**
hange, honge *v. tr.* put to death by hanging 430, 2745, M 621, 655, suspend M 530, 876; *intr.* quiver 2223, be crucified 2271, 3349, cling 2527, suffer death by hanging 2731, M 608, be suspended 3066, M 620, dangle W 16 s.d.; **hangyth** *pr. 3 sg.* 2223; **hynge** *pt. 1 sg.* M 620; **henge** *2 sg.* 3349; **hounge** *3 sg.* 2271, **hyng** M 876; **hangynge** *pr. p.* W 16 s.d.; **hangyn** *pp.* 190, **hange** M 655, **honge** M 791.
hanip *n.* ? wine-cup W 511.
hap(pe) *n.* fortune 1810, 1856, good fortune 3292; *pl.* successes 674; *in* ~ perhaps M 244, 569.

hard(e) *adj.* niggardly 92, harsh 2392, painful W 434, unyielding M 545; **harder** *compar.* 91; ~ *grace (happe)* harsh fortune 1769, 1810, W 723.
harlot *n.* evil man 1355, 1774, evil woman W 767.
harow *interj.* alas! W 325.
haryed *pp.* dragged, carried off 263.
hastynes *n.* rash anger W 694.
hatte *pr. 1 sg.* am named 2790, **hyght** W 334; **hyth** *pt. 3 sg.* promised 3398; **het** *pp.* promised 2054.
haue *v.* possess 89, 2934, W 177, M 241, keep 336, 787, W 48, enjoy 371, 2949, W 1150, bring 1428, 3031, suffer 1593, 3114, M 277, obtain 3131, 3166, M 19, M 179, 285, show 3327, 3415, wear W 1 s.d., M 714, hold M 100, receive M 186, 265, feel M 390, 423, engage in M 449; ~ *at* go to it W 615, 869; ~ *at yow* go to it W 627; ~ *good day* good-bye 917, 929, 3128; ~ *maystrye* dominate 1284; ~ *me excusyd* pardon me 2685, M 183; ~ *no dowte* feel no fear 2293; ~ *no gylt* be blameless 1318; ~ *þe victory* conquer 21, M 197; ~ *þou þat* take that! 3118; **han** *infin.* 2134, a (after **kowde, myth, schuld**) 1348, 2131, 2135, 3342, 3424, 3525, M 798; **hast(e)** *pr. 2 sg.* 393, 1412; **hath(e)** *3 sg.* 21, 25, **hat** 2801, W 401, M 224, **has(e)** W 177, 576; **han** *pl.* 216, 727, **hath(e)** 2293, M 176, **haue** W 48, M 180, **has** W 1093; **haue** *pr. subj.* 89, 400; **had(d)e** *pt.1, 3 sg.* 2945, 3266, M 100; *pp.* 2134, M 89, have had 3324; see **deynte, do(ne), dyspyght, ey(e), fote-mett, mende, nede, place, recors, reson(e), rest(e), skyl(le).**
ha(u)nte *v.* keep company with 1119, make a habit of wearing W 609; **hauntyth** *pr. 3 sg.* frequents 1709.
hawe *n.* hawthorn berry 479, 1166; see **geue.**
hay *n.* enclosed land 2973.
hay *interj.* M 720; see **dogge.**
hayer see **eyr.**

he *pron.* he 4, 15, he who M 621.
hedyr, hethyr, hydyr *adv.* in this
   direction 2475, to this place M 69,
   351; ~ *and thedyr* this way and that
   W 199, 732.
heelfull *adj.* salutary W 89.
hele *n.* well-being 371, 3292, W 21.
hele *v.* hide 1329.
helthe *n.* salvation 3351.
helue *n.* handle 2571.
hem *pron.* them; *obj.* 182, 650, W 331,
   599, M 477*, 491; *dat.* 7, 203; *after*
   prep. 652, 827, W 3, 56, M 883;
   refl. themselves 2013, 2349.
hem see **hym.**
hende *adj.* handsome 458, pleasant
   511, 736, M 219, gracious 3536,
   3574, W 45.
hendly *adv.* graciously 135.
hent *pp.* taken 864, 1246, struck 2851.
her *n.* hair 2491.
her see **or.**
herawd *n.* herald 1969*.
her(e), hyr(e) *pron.* her 1634, 1891,
   W 815, 838, M 136, 852; *refl.* her-
   self 1633.
her(e) *poss. adj.* their 649, 1225,
   W 634, 749, M 169.
here *v.* listen to 847, 1434, hear 906,
   3129, M 327, 424, listen M 774;
   heryth *pr. 3 sg.* 1434; **herd(e)**
   pt. 1 sg. 906, M 597; *2 pl.* 3134;
   harde *3 pl.* M 298; **herd** *pp.* 194;
   see **sey(ne), tell(e).**
her(e) *adv.* here 305, 461, W 101,
   405, M 77, 113.
here-at *adv.* by this 3643.
here-beforn *adv.* before this 2880,
   3340.
here-inne *adv.* within this 1347, 2551.
here-of *adv.* for this 1181, of this 2730.
herne *n.* nook 190, 1878.
hers *poss. pron.*: *of* ~ belonging to her
   M 645.
herys see **erys.**
hest(e) *n.* command 859, 1934.
hethe, hothe *n.* waste land 1751,
   2786.
hettys *n. pl.* rages W 716*.
heuene *n.* heaven 3, 889, W 116,
   122, M 175, 558; *gen.* 317, 318;
   ~ *and erthe* the universe 2, 3496;

~ *blys* heaven's joy 872, 3636;
   ~ *emperesse* empress of heaven
   2357; ~ *kynge* king of heaven 332;
   see **ha(l)l(e).**
heue(ne)ryche *n.* the kingdom of
   heaven 355; ~ *blys* heaven's joy
   3530.
heuy *adj.* heavy W 53, sad W 316,
   sleepy M 587; **heuyer** *compar.*
   2923.
hevynesse *n.* grief 3213, M 828.
hey see **hye, hy(3)e.**
heyl(e) *interj.* hail! 1746, 1791,
   M 209.
heynyd *pp.* exalted 3638.
hod(e), hoode *n.* hood 109, 2849,
   W 1 s.d., 718, coif of mail 1830.
hoke *n.* hook 512, 3066.
hold see **olde.**
holde *n.* fort 2428.
holde, holdyn *v. tr.* keep 78, 2860,
   consider 611, 1056, W 585, 832,
   continue to follow 2480, hold in the
   hand 2571, possess 3288, sustain
   W 317; *refl.* remain W 728; *absol.*
   have money W 723, take it! M 674,
   679; *intr.* remain 887, be faithful
   2527, remain opposed 3048; *be* ~
   be bound in obligation 825; ~
   excusyd regard as blameless 2569;
   ~ *hest(e)* obey command 194, 736;
   holdyste *pr. 2 sg.* W 317; **holdyth**
   3 sg. 78, halt 3288; **holde** *pl.*
   W 723; **helde** *pt. 3 sg.* 2571; *pt.*
   subj. 1 sg. 738; **holdyn** *pp.* 194,
   W 832, **holde** 825, W 585; see
   pes(e), tale.
hol(e), hoyll *n.* anus 1276, M 337,
   cavity W 1106.
hole, holl *adj.* complete W 187,
   entire M 188, unbroken M 447;
   haue ~ *hys hert* set all his heart
   2020, 2831.
holly *v.* hallow, honour as holy
   W 251.
holt(e) *n.* wood, grove 444, 690.
holy *adj.* holy 360, 803, W 348, 1026,
   M 377, 628; *sb.* righteous persons
   W 426; **holyer** *compar.* more
   devout M 559; ~ *Chyrche* Holy
   Church W 982, 984; ~ *Gost* the
   Holy Spirit 3281.

holy *adv.* entirely 182, 594.
homlyest *superl. adj.* most familiar 36.
hond(e), hande *n.* hand 4, 2475, W 1102, M 100, 522, pledge 597, authority 762, handwriting M 682, 684; *at ~* close by 629, 1560; *helpynge ~* assistance 2037; *in ~* in common use 2364, W 683; see lyfte, stond(e).
honest, oneste *adj.* virtuous 2363, decent W 555.
hoppe, hoppyn *v.* hop 458, 2650, leap 2489.
hordys *n. pl.* treasures 2653.
hore *n.* fornicator 1134.
hore *adj.* grey 2491.
hornepype *n.* player on a hornpipe W 752 s.d., a wind instrument with a horn mouthpiece W 757.
horryble, oreble *adj.* dreadful W 200, 926.
horryble *adv.* repulsively W 896, 951.
hors(e) *n.* horse 518, M 66, 241; *pl.* M 61, 476.
hory *adj.* grey-haired 2482.
hothe see hethe.
houte *v. tr.* shout 906, 1969; *intr.* 1926; howtyth *imp. pl.* call loudly with trumpets 1897.
how(e) *interj.* ho! 526, 1724, M 72, 451.
howle *n.* owl 2409.
howll-flyght *n.* twilight M 571.
howtys *n. pl.* shouts 906.
ho(y)lyke *adj.* hole-like (pun on holy) M 343.
hurde *v.* hoard W 582.
hurle *v.* drive W 767, harass W 856.
husbondry *n.* thrifty management 2739.
hy(e) *n.* haste: *in ~* in haste 892, 1022, 2741.
hye *imp. sg.* hasten M 68; *pl.* hyȝe 899, hey M 348, hye M 380.
hye see hy(ȝ)e.
hyen *v.* exalt 640.
hyght, hyth see hatte.
hy(l)l(e) *v.* shelter 887, 3055; *refl.* 2535.
hym, hem *pron.* him; *obj.* 3, 24, W 144, 251, M 241, 304; *dat.* 18, 190, M 418; *after prep.* 19, 1128,

W 11, 339, M 5, 255; *refl.* himself 185, 342, W 239, 411.
hymself, hymselue, hymsylfe *pron.* himself 15, 26, W 247, 758, M 793, he himself 1272, 2172, 2558, M 833, for himself 2576.
hyt(h) *n.* height: *in ~* to a high degree 135; *on ~* on a high place 1938.
hy(ȝ)e, hey *adj.* lofty 741, 2786, loud 906, exalted 2104, W 12, 61, M 393, deep 3077, proud 3292; *it is tyme ~* the time has come 2778; *on ~* above the earth 1386, 2034; *the ~ name* the name of God 1122.
hy(ȝ)e *adv.* high up 190, 518, W 444, M 608, deep 887, loudly 1897, 1969, lavishly M 241.

iche, eche *adj.*[1] every 329, 972, W 238, 262; *pron.* each one 1038, 2239, W 692 s.d.
iche *adj.*[2] same 1930, 2122, 2270.
ichon *pron.* each one 2046, 2596.
ifounde *pp. adj.* perceived 1838.
iknowe *pp. adj.* known 222, 1198.
ilent *pp. adj.* settled 238.
ilke *adj.*[1] each 1134.
ilke *adj.*[2] same 2288, 2912, 3081.
iment *pp. adj.* disposed 240.
in, i, yn *prep.* in 1, 3, W 3, 36, M 19, 25, into 82, 99, M 145, 244.
inclyne *v.* bend, submit W 469, 475, M 844.
inconsyderatt *adj.* thoughtless M 748.
inconvenyens *n.* trouble M 737.
indignacyon *n.* disdain W 693, M 3.
indwell *v.* remain in W 880.
ineuytabyll *adj.* unavoidable M 837.
inexcusabyll *adj.* unpardonable M 874.
informable *adj.* ready to accuse W 539.
informacyon *n.* instruction W 423, 449.
inne *adv.* within 78.
inow(e), anow *adj.* enough 837, 2724; *sb.* 812, 2637, W 416, 564, M 648, 733.
inowe *adv.* sufficiently 1196, W 368.
insolence *n.* pride M 410.
instytucyon *n.* ordained form M 166.

instytut *pp.* established M 224.
insuffycyens *n.* inability W 193.
insyght *n.* consideration W 189, understanding M 860.
interleccyon *n.* ? consultation M 449.
into *prep.* into 16, 120, M 561, unto, as far as 195, 201, until W 106.
intromytt *v. refl.* allow to enter M 297.
ipocryttys *n. pl.* hypocrites W 471.
ipyth *pp. adj.* adorned 209.
irchoun *n.* little child, brat 2395.
irent *pp. adj.* torn off 2026.
irke, yrke *v. intr.* grow weary 3399; *tr.* make weary M 532.
ispendyd *pp. adj.* spent 1295.
iterat *adj.* repeated M 821.
iwys(se) *adv.* certainly 58, 201, W 357, 1063, M 567, 894.

jagge *v.* slash, pierce for ornament 1060.
jake *n.* leather jacket M 719.
japyng *n.* jeering M 349.
jebet *n.* gallows 3085.
jent *adj.* beautiful 29.
jentyl(l), gentyl *adj.* noble 604, 3526, W 188, 756, generous W 832; ~ *Jaffrey* (term of mockery) M 160.
jeste *n.* ? entertainment 2958.
jett *n.* fashion 1057, M 103, custom M 529.
jette *v.* strut 743.
jewellys, juelys *n. pl.* costly ornaments 743, precious stones, testicles M 381, 441.
joly(e) *adj.* gay 29, W 566, handsome M 718.
jorours *n. pl.* jurymen W 718*, 724 s.d.
jorowry *n.* bribing of jurors W 637*.
jous *n.* juice 950, 3019.
juge-partynge *n.* sharing with judges W 796.
junctly *adv.* jointly M 347.
just *adv.*: ~ *to* right up to M 805.

k- see also **c-**.
kacke *v.* excrete 2407.
kakelynge *n.* chattering 2367.
kampyoun *n.* warrior in single combat 3611.
karke *n.* distress 2730.

kayser, caysere *n.* emperor 215, 343.
kelyn *v.* assuage 2526.
kempys *n. pl.* warriors 215.
ken, kenne *v.* recognize 907, direct 1546, be acquainted with M 121.
kende, kynde *n.* natural disposition 92, 786, W 927, manner 275, 648, W 297, race 1103, 1238, family 2901; *ageyn* ~ contrary to nature W 529; *þe bok of kendys* the book *De Naturis* 2513.
kendly *adv.* thoroughly 1028.
kene *adj.* bold 215, 746, mighty 2808, wild, untrained 2813.
kepe *n.*: *take* ~ take heed 1628.
kepe *v. tr.* guard 155, 802, retain 971, 1460, restrain 1675, observe 3399, 3606, M 300, 728, preserve W 174, 242, M 589, provide with food M 241, maintain properly M 462; *refl.* preserve 1534, 1633, limit M 508; *intr.* continue 2185; **kepyt(h)** *pr. 3 sg.* 1589, 1637; **kept(e)** *pt. 2, 3 sg.* 1633, W 312; **kept(e)** *pp.* 2744, W 242.
kettys *n. pl.* carrion 1053.
keuere *v.* recover 1954.
kewe *v.* mew 3117.
kloye *v.* hamper 970*.
knappe *n.* sharp blow 2840.
knaue *n.* fellow 548, 2931, M 636, servant 648, 817, base fellow W 835.
knett *v.* bind 560, 990, draw together W 196; **knytte** *pp.* 560, **knyth** 990, **knet(t)** 1239, W 231.
know(e), knowyn *v.* be acquainted with 13, 104, W 563, M 114, 451, recognize 167, 1990, be aware 2595, M 499, comprehend W 26, 98, M 164; **knowe** *pr. 3 sg.* 104, **knowyt** W 26; **knowe** *2 pl.* 2595, **knowyn** 2596; **know** *3 pl.* M 164; **knowe** *pp.* 167, **knowyn** 657.
knowynge *n.* understanding W 93, 155.
krake *n.*: *at a* ~ with a sudden loud noise 2197.
kyd *pp. adj.* renowned 2808.
kyll, kyllyn *v.* kill 1124, 1790, M 643, 708; **kyllyth** *pr. 3 sg.* 1617; **kylt** *pp.* 1316, **kyllyd(e)** 1360.
kynde *n.* see **kende**.

kynde *adj.* characteristic 853, grateful 1289.

kyn(ne) *n.* relatives 108, 2943, M 559; *al kynnys* of every sort 1151; *for no kynnys þynge* for anything 3098; *on* ~ akin 3207.

kynse *v.* ? wince 2813.

kyrke, kerke *n.* church M 552, 553; *Holy* ~ Holy Church 3146, 3393.

kys *v.* kiss 3519, W 594, 1105, M 307; **kyssyde** *pt. 1 sg.* M 645; **cust** *pp.* 400, **cyste** 1684, **kyssyde** W 44.

kyth *n.* belly, loins 971.

kyth *v.* show 1986, acknowledge 3295.

kythe *n.*: ~ *and kynne* friends and relatives 433.

kytt(e), cut *v.* cut 1768, W 1061, M 716.

lace *n.* cord: *louely in* ~ beautiful in dress 2548.

lace *v.* entwine W 578.

lache *v.* strike 1419, 2867; *refl.* take 1471; **lacchyd** *pp.* 653, **lawth** caught 717.

ladde *n.* serving-man 109, W 708.

lafte see leue *v.*³

lak *n.* poverty 2982; *wythowtyn* ~ free from flaw 2173.

lake *n.*¹ pit, grave 99, 2913; *be londe and (ne)* ~ by land and (nor) water 1081, 1256; *hell* ~ the pit of hell 3390, 3639.

lake *n.*² fine linen 1848.

lake *v.* find fault with W 165.

lante see len(d)e *v.*¹

lappe *v.* wrap 1214.

large *adj.* lavish W 640, licentious M 295.

largyte *n.* generosity 51, 1654.

lasche *v.* beat 2189.

last, leste *v.* continue 855, 1332.

late *adj.* delayed 3275; **last** *superl.* 922, 935, M 724; *at þe laste* in the end 113, 2171, W 526; *last ende, last endynge* death 17, 98, 3648, W 532.

late *v.* see let(e).

lat(e) *adv.* at a late hour 1110, W 798, not long since M 351; **latter** *compar.* later W 797; **last** *superl.*: *fyrst and last* from beginning to end 2936.

lathe *n.* by-path 2402.

lauatorye *n.* place of cleansing M 12.

laue, lawe see leue *v.*³

launcyth *pr. 3 sg.* springs 2290.

law(e) *n.* custom 216, 2963, law 480, 1398, W 387, justice by law W 666, 713.

lawnde *n.* glade 761.

lay, leye *n.* law 835, 2254, faith 2771.

lay, leye *adj.* fallow 687, 1587.

laykys *n. pl.* games 926.

leche *n.* physician 1668, 2476.

lede *n.*¹ people: *in any* ~ in any country 2800; *in londe or* ~ among men 2670; *londys and* ~ lands and vassals 2494.

led(e) *n.*² lead 2923, M 699; *I haue no* ~ *on my helys* I move quickly M 555.

lede *v.* bring, guide 30, 1587, carry on (life) 1176, 1615, W 420, 472; **ledyth** *pr. 3 sg.* 2343; **ledyn** *pl.* 30; **lede** *pt. 3 sg.* W 420; **lad** *pp.* 2584.

led(e)ro(u)n *n.* rascal 978, 989, 1953.

leeffull *adj.* permissible W 408.

leene *pr. 3 pl.* incline 989.

lefe, leve *adj.* dear 1189, 2502, W 1019, 1091, desirous 1613, 2344.

lef(f)e *n.* leaf 3595, M 734.

lefte see leue *v.*³, **lyfte**.

lely *adv.* truly 717, 908.

lelys *n. pl.* lilies, pure maidens 1668.

lemman *n.* lover 1189, mistress M 604, 611.

lende *n.* loin 279, 981; **londys** *pl.* 2299; *vndyr* ~ kept in store 662.

len(d)e *v.*¹ lend 19, 1379, M 478, 732; *absol.* give ear, consent 3575, W 299; *lystyn and* ~ listen 154, 2525; **lent** *pp.* 33, **lante** 335.

lende *v.*² remain 114, 281, be settled 250, 390, 533; **lent** *pp.* 250.

len(g)the *n.* length 2763; *the* ~ *of þe yerys* long life W 36.

lep(p)e *v.* leap 935, 2402, M 76, 697.

lere *n.* face: *on* ~ in face 592.

lere *v.* teach 541, 835, teach a lesson, punish 1963, W 848, learn 1624, 1788, W 303; **leryth** *pr. 3 sg.* 90.

lern(e) *v.* learn 186, 1095, M 259, 598, teach 1398, M 572; **lernyd** *pp.* 216.

les *n.* leash, control 653, 2471.
lese *v.* fail to attain 697; **lesyth**
pr. 3 sg. lets slip M 301; **lore** *pp.*
ruined 42, lost 838, **lorn** 2678.
les(se) *n.*[1] falsehood 3469, M 773;
wythout ~ truly 3550.
lesse *n.*[2] joy, comfort 998.
les(se) *adj.* smaller 3306, W 740,
inferior 3450, not so much M 400;
no ~ no fewer 904; see **mor(e)**.
les(s)e *v.* release 1497, 2862.
less(o)un *n.* subject of study 669,
teaching 1279, 2313, W 100, 303,
M 865; *a* ~ *tawth* punished 2795.
lest(e) *superl. adj.* very little 2609,
smallest 2613, 3368, W 50, 813,
M 869, inferior 3525; *adv.* in the
slightest degree 2905.
leste *v.* see **last**.
lesynge *n.* a lie 653, 662, M 387, 568;
wythowte ~ truly W 139.
let(e) *v.* consider 1061, 2615, permit
1771, 1803, W 565, M 376, 701,
abandon W 51, 452; *absol.* think
1167; *auxil.* let 156, 723, W 613,
M 77, cause to 624, W 453, M 758;
~ *be* cease from 370, 1375, 3446;
lete *imp.* 156, late 370; **letyst**
pt. 2 sg. 1857; **lete** *3 sg.* 2128;
let(e) *pl.* 1771, 1803.
let(t), **lettyn** *v. intr.* refrain 395,
delay 922; *tr.* hinder 987, 2344,
W 887; **let** *pp.* 1409.
lettynge *n.* obstructing p. 1.
leude, **lewyde** *adj.* base 1855*, un-
educated M 58; *lernyde and* ~
everyone W 682.
leue *v.*[1] believe 362, 3108.
leue, **leuyn**, **lyuyn** *v.*[2] live 399, 1081,
W 405, dwell 1557, 1564, remain
alive 2206, 3424; **leuyth** *pr. 3 sg.*
703, **lywyt** W 405; **levyd** *pp.*
3424.
leue *v.*[3] abandon 774, 3053, W 409,
M 45, 185; *be lafte* remain 1787,
2789; **laue** *pr. 1 sg.* deposit 2666;
lefe *imp.* 774, **lewe** W 441, **leue**
M 45; **lefte** *pt. 3 sg.* remained 3267;
lafte *pp.* 1787, **lefte** 2789.
leuene, **leuyn** *n.* lightning 191, 3498;
lyuys ~ light of eternal life 1471.
leuer(e) *compar. adv.*: *(had)* ~ *(had)*

rather 709, 2334, 2945; *þe* ~ the
more gladly W 797, M 261.
leve *n.* permission 3236, permission
to depart M 265; *take* ~ bid farewell 144, depart M 898.
leve see **lefe**.
levynge, **lywynge** *n.* manner of life
47, W 434, M 170, 214, means of
earning a living M 350, crop, produce M 367.
leye *n.* flame 2290.
leye see **lay**.
ley(e) *v.* place 1654, 1663, wager
M 139, set M 759; ~ *on* pour on
2396, deal blows M 73; ~ *lowe*
overthrow 2807; **leyth** *pr. 3 sg.*
is placed M 247; **leyd** *pt. 1 sg.*
2891; **leyd** *pp.* put to rest 1228.
leykyn *v.* play 2404; **leyke** *pr. 1 sg.*
461.
lofly, **louely**, **luf(fe)ly** *adj.* full of
love, 5, 124, M 225, beautiful 42,
W 43, noble 216, pleasing 415,
worthy of love W 43; *adv.* willingly
137, 154, pleasantly 525.
lofte *n.* sky: *of*, *on* ~ aloft 553, 1145.
loggyth *pr. 3 sg.* sends to lodging 99;
logyd *pp.* caused to lie down 1228.
loke *v.* see to it 137, 736, look 575,
stare 2251, 2409, keep the eyes open
W 894, see W 902; ~ *abowte* keep
watch 1821; **lokyd** *pp.* 1821.
lond(e), **land(e)** *n.* solid land 2,
country 6, 179, W 682, 732, landed
property 599, 761, ground M 411,
542; *be* ~ by land 164, M 37; *in* ~
on earth 344, 926; **londys lawe** the
law of the country 480; see **lede** *n.*[1]
longe *adj.* long 1059, 1963, W 770,
M 714, lengthy, tedious M 582;
~ *tyme* for a long time 864.
longe *adv.* long time 559, 855,
W 242, 978, M 262, 275, delaying
long 3060, M 331; **lenger** *compar.*
1172, 2431, M 151, 527.
longyth *pr. 3 sg.* pertains M 141, 677;
longe *pl.* belong W 686.
lopys *n. pl.* leaps 673.
lordeyn *n.* rascal 908, 1342, sluggard
2344.
lordlyche *adj.* like a lord 441.
lordlyche *adv.* in a lordly way 1081.

lordlyke *adj.* like a lord 426.
lore *n.* lesson 90, teaching 989, 1624, creed W 418.
lore *v.* scowl W 326.
lore, lorn see **lese.**
lose *v.* lose 1825, 3426, W 677, M 282, 536, be deprived of M 700; **loose** *pr. subj. 3 sg.* W 677; **lost(e)** *pt. 3 sg.* 3426, M 270; *pp.* ruined 2379, 3320, M 547.
losel *n.* good-for-nothing 1855, 1963.
losengerys *n. pl.* false flatterers 1217.
loth *adj.* hateful 935, 2554, reluctant 1282, M 439.
lot(h)ly *adj.* horrible 1095, 1342.
lot(t) *n.* destiny 2048, choice 2891; *in a ~* in turn 1228.
loue, lofe, luf *n.* love 390, 453, 3528. W 40, 65, M 830, 872.
loue *v.* love 144, 3250, W 47, 144, like 244, 1223, M 273, take pleasure in W 494, 924, M 85; **lovyste** *pr. 2 sg.* 3250, **louyst** W 924; **louyt(h)** *3 sg.* 661, W 66, 67, **louevyt** W 144; **loue** *pl.* 144, **lofe** 1223; **lovyd** *pp.* 972, **lowyde** W 261.
lou(gh)t(e) *v.* bow 32, W 503, submit 908, 3013.
lous(e) *n.* louse 489, 768; **lys(e)** *pl.* 804, M 139; see **geue.**
lowe *n.* flame: *on a ~* on fire 2253, 2298.
lowe *adj.* low 1748; **lowest** *superl.* W 336.
lowe *v. refl.* humble 2104.
lowe *adv.* low under ground 100, in a low position 250, to a humble state 2090, 3116, in a low voice 2635; see **ley(e).**
lowe-day *n.* day for settling disputes W 698.
luf, luf(fe)ly see **loue, lofly.**
lullyn *v.* put to sleep 1041, 1233; **lulle** *imp. sg.* 1233.
lurkynge *pr. p.* secret 2402.
lust *n.* sensual desire 37, W 460, pleasure 186, 238, W 51.
lusti *adj.* merry 926, cheerful 3575.
lustyly *adv.* pleasantly 30.
lybrary *n.* collected learning W 227.

lyche *adj.* equal 344, 388.
lyckely, lyghly *adj.* likely, apparently able 73, handsome W 554*, M 621.
ly(e), lyn *v.* remain 2612, 2743, W 951.
lyf(e), lyue *n.* life 112, 338, W 171, 812, M 861, way of living 238, 2970, W 417, 420, M 355, living person 2834; *on lyue* alive 114, 310, W 792; see **leuene.**
lyfte, le(y)fte *adj.* left: *~ honde, syde* 3627, W 1 s.d., 37, M 522.
lyfte *v.* exalt 1217, drive 1342, raise 2847, M 31, throw 2913; **lefte** *pr. 3 sg.* W 939.
lyghly see **lyckely.**
lyght, lyghtly see **lyth, lytly.**
lyke *adj.* similar (to) 2598, 3406, W 538, 928, likely M 382, fit M 538; *adv.* in the manner of 2409, M 226, in like manner M 375; *~ to (as)* in the same way as W 16 s.d., M 287.
lyke *v.* taste, feel M 109.
lykynge(e), lyckynge *n.* enjoyment 186, 238, W 51, sexual pleasure 250, W 460; *at hys ~* at his pleasure 1804.
lykynge *adj.* joyful 461, W 567, pleasant 553, 1668.
lykyth *pr. 3 sg.* pleases M 654.
lynde *n.* linden tree 949, 3595.
lyst *v.*1 desire 1682, W 837.
lyst *v.*2 listen M 424.
lyt, lyth *n.* little 2500, 2515.
lyth, lyght *n.* illumination of the soul 5, W 22, 30, brightness of heaven 698, 1409, W 333, 918.
lyt(h), lyghte *adj.*1 bright 191, 1667, W 28; **lyter** *compar.* 3498
lyth, lyght *adj.*2 nimble 673, merry W 569, 708, easy M 697; **lyter** *compar.* lighter in weight 3595; see **set(te).**
lyth *pt. 2 sg.* descended, alighted 3332; **lytyd** *3 sg.* 2089; **lytyd** *pp.* 112.
lyth *adv.* readily 137.
lythyr *adj.* good-for-nothing 109, 927.
lytly, lyghtly *adv.* quickly 949, nimbly M 720; **lyghtlyer** *compar.* W 792.

lytyl(l) *adj.* small 112, W 465, M 47, 836, short in time 397, 865, M 93, 270, scarcely any 1659, M 267, low in rank 3614, trifling M 629; *sb.* scarcely anything M 548; *a ∼* a short while M 87, a small amount of M 123, 570, somewhat M 375; *Do ∼* (nickname) M 262; *adv.* slightly W 816, M 164.

lywe, lywyt see **lyf(e), leue** *v.*²

make *n.* companion 2694.

mak(e), makyn *v.* create 2, 4, W 24, 328, M 6, cause 560, 3171, W 579, M 91, appoint 686, cause to be 705, 757, W 55, 616, M 545, fashion 2354, prepare 2954, utter 3350, M 387, render W 122, 1094, carry out W 371, translate M 130; *∼ confyrmacyon* confirm W 367; *∼ debate* fight 1111; *∼ ende* die 3029; *∼ mone* complain 459, 1689; *∼ mornynge* mourn 41; *∼ sorwe* grieve 1433; **makyt(h)** *pr. 3 sg.* 41, W 55, M 545, **mase** W 579; **makyn** *pl.* 459; **made** *pt. 2 sg.* 2, W 310, **madyste** 3350; **made** *3 sg.* 3029, M 6; **mad(e)** *pp.* 4, 686, W 24, **mayde** W 187; see **amendys, avaunte, avow(e), endynge, game, mery, mone** n.¹, **reporture, rom, space.**

malaundyr *n.* scab (in horses) 2212.

malewrye *n.* misfortune W 667.

mamerynge *pr. p.* muttering 1917.

maner(e) *n.* kind of 774, 2944, W 462, 466, M 667, way 1055, W 1045, M 766, style M 134.

manhod *n.* manly courage 32.

mankynd(e), mankende *n.* the human species 16, 287, W 44, 997, M 9, 194.

mankyn(ne) *n.* the human species 218, 2545, W 543.

mantyll *n.* cloak W 1 s.d., 912 s.d.; **mentelys** *pl.* p. 1.

manyfold(e) *adj.* of many kinds 1361; *adv.* in many ways 3281.

mare see **mor(e).**

marke, markys *n. pl.* sums of money, each worth two-thirds of a pound sterling 2494, 2726.

marre, merre *v.* hamper 1902, destroy 2074, perplex W 346; **marryde** *pp.* ruined M 388, 600.

mary *interj.* indeed 566, M 85, 398.

maskeryd *pp. adj.* bewildered 76, 101.

mastres *n.* mistress, wanton woman W 755.

masyd, mosyde *pp. adj.* crazed 1739, deceived W 348.

mat *n.* comrade 1576.

mawe *n.* stomach 1164.

may, moun, mow(e) *v.* be able 386, 509, W 34, 202, M 28, 67, be allowed 114, 373, W 116, have cause 325, 954, W 57, 161, be likely 420, 422, have opportunity W 892; *and I ∼* if I can help it M 441; *as I wel ∼* as I have good cause 2636; *myght well* could with good cause M 444; **may** *pr. 1 sg.* 375, **ma** W 625; **may** *2 sg.* 373, **mayst** 416; **may** *3 sg.* 15; *pl.* 325, **moun** 1849, **mow** M 466; **may** *pr. subj. 1 sg.* 316; **mown** *3 pl.* 2007; **myght** *pt. 1 sg.* W 915; **myth** *2 sg.* 3355; *pt. subj. 1 sg.* 425, **myght** M 444, **mytyst** *2 sg.* 1348, 2620, **myght** W 875; **myght** *3 sg.* W 919.

mayne *n.* power 174.

maynten(e), mayntein, meynten *v.* uphold 32, preserve 146, support 3644, W 700.

maynt(en)nance, meynt(e)nance *n.* unjust support (as of law-suits) W 634, 671, 696; *hattys of ∼* hats for retainers W 724 s.d.

maystry(e) *n.* dominion 1284, victory 2240; see **haue.**

mede *n.*¹ drink made with honey 772.

mede *n.*² recompense 1322, 1917, W 217, bribery W 672; *to ∼ (medys)* as recompense 599, 2163; *þe medys* as recompense 2420, 2776.

medelyth *pr. 3 sg.* mingles 1394.

mekyl(l), mykyl *adj.* great 41, 76, M 601, big M 47, high in rank 3614; *sb.* a great number 990, a great part 2781; *adv.* much 1222; *∼ þe bette* much the better 754; *neuere so ∼* no matter how much 89; *so ∼ þe werse* so much the worse 1260.

mekyt *pr. 3 sg.* makes meek W 85.

mel(e) *n.*¹ repast 616, 2537, M 370; *at mete and* (*at*) ~ at dinner and other meals 258, 372.

mele *n.*² ground grain 2918.

mell(e) *v.* concern oneself 72, 124, associate M 327.

men *indef. pron.* one 2537.

mende, mynde *n.* thought 94, 101, W 210, 381, inclination 240, 1281, W 199, sanity 2263, M 778, disposition W 42, the seat of thoughts and feelings W 55, M 734, the cognitive faculty W 183, 279, remembrance W 189, 197; *haue* ~ think, remember W 185, 208, 1117; *pl.* meyndys 1902.

mende, mendyn *v.* remedy 1693, 3644.

mendement *n.* reformation 46.

mene *n.* middle part (in singing) W 618, mediator M 17; *pl.* mediation 125, M 873, methods M 296, 385.

mene *v.* mean, have in mind 1381, 1890, M 34, say 2926; ment *pp.* spoken 165.

menge *v.* mix 3571, M 537; mengyth *pr. 3 sg.* troubles 107.

mengylde *pp. adj.* mixed W 1100.

menschepe *n.* honour 10.

meny(e), meynye *n.* disciples 351, retinue W 706, 795.

mere *n.* mare M 594, 791.

mery *adj.* joyful 148, 428, W 494, 623, M 77, 81; *make* ~ rejoice 55, 421, M 273; see pynne.

mes-crede *n.* the longer form of the Nicene Creed 2165.

meselynge *adj.* causing eruptions 2257.

messe *n.* portion M 772.

messe-belle *n.* bell for mass 1212.

mesure *n.* moderation M 237, 250.

mesure *v.* moderate M 238.

met(e) *n.* food 552, 1149, W 473, 814, a meal M 100; see mel(e).

mete *adj.* appropriate W 757.

met(te) *n.* measure: *at my* (*þyn owyn*) *mowþis* ~ to my (your) desire 758, 1243.

meve, mevyn, move *v. tr.* urge 46, control 174, stir up 1242, prompt W 1015; *refl.* apply (to) 1629, bestir 3494; *intr.* speak 3129; mevyn *pr. pl.* 46, mewythe 3494.

mevynge *n.* prompting W 226.

meyntement *n.* unjust support W 706*.

mo see mo(o).

moche see myche.

mod *n.* mind 107, anger 1094, frame of mind 1520.

mody *adj.* grieving 1464.

modyr, moþer *n.*¹ mother 276, 1054, W 982, 991, M 756, 796.

modyr *n.*² girl, wench 1731, 1763, 1890, 1917.

moke, moque *v. intr.* make sport W 822, jeer M 365; *tr.* deride M 378.

mold(e) *n.* earth: *on* ~ on earth 101, 428; *vndyr* ~ buried 1359, 2689.

mone *n.*¹ lament 1405, 1464, grief M 357; *make* (*my*) ~ lament 319, 447.

mone *n.*² moon 2589.

monytorye *adj.* warning M 879.

mo(o) *adj.* more in number 39, 884, M 264, additional 2888, 3040, M 503; *sb.* many others 1368, others 2881; *adv.* more 1196.

moque see moke.

mor(e), mare *compar. adj.* greater 1140, 2492, W 97, 740; *sb.* a greater amount 89, 2711; *adv.* in a greater degree W 98, 414, further, again 1301; *les and* ~ everyone W 740; ~ *and lesse* of all sorts 1761, 2359, every one 2511, 3614; *no* ~ nothing further 296, 1387, W 814, M 586, no longer 2799, W 491, M 583, not again M 401, 600; see mynne.

mornynge *n.* mourning 1301, 1394.

morow(e) *n.* morning 1224, M 710.

morsell, mossel *n.* choice dish 1171, small piece M 698.

most(e), mest *superl. adj.* greatest 1, 1948, W 78, M 21; *adv.* in the greatest degree 3411, W 6, 1131.

mosyde see masyd.

mote *n.* speck of dust 1974.

mote *v. auxil.*: must(e) *pr.* be
obliged to 431, 841, W 218, 433,
M 714, 780, be able to 2246, must
go 3037, 3043; *impers.* hym, us
must(e) 435, 2020; mote *opt.*
may 148, 828, mut W 1159, M 470.
motyhole *n.*? dusty hole 2120.
move see meve.
mowle *n.* ground 2406.
mowle *v.* ? grimace 2413.
mucke *n.* wealth 2706.
must(e) see mote.
mustyr *v.* call together 10.
myche, moche, mech *adj.* a great
amount of 1075, W 1010, M 205,
256, a great number of W 632; *adv.*
greatly 2444, W 414, 482; see also.
myddys *n.* middle p. 1.
mydylerd *n.* earth 4.
mykyl see mekyl(l).
mynde see mende.
mynne *compar. adj.* lesser: *more or*
~ greater or lesser 3188.
mynstrall, menstrell *n.* musician
W 692 s.d., 701, M 72, 451.
mynstralsye *n.* music 617.
myrable *adj.* wonderful W 41.
myrthe *n.* joy 146, 240, W 620.
mysbede *v.* ill-treat 1050.
myscha(u)nce *n.* disaster 1593, 3211,
W 766; ȝeue ~ overwhelm 1933.
myschef(f)e *n.* distress 1136, 2346,
poverty 2503, wickedness M 606,
889; *a ~ go wyth* Devil take it!
M 730.
mysdede *n.* sins 1467, 3152.
mysdyd *pt. 3 sg.* sinned 46.
mysdyspent *pp. adj.* spent wickedly
1513.
mysfare *v.* go wrong W 496.
mysgotyn *pp. adj.* ill-gotten 2627.
myskaryed *pt. 3 sg.* led astray 2347.
myspent *pp.* spent wrongly 2781.
mys(se) *n.* sins 3366, 3644, W 363*.
mys(se) *v. tr.* fail to get 57, M 372;
intr. fail 123, 3330, M 864, be lacking W 248; myssyd *pp.* 57, myst
done without M 684.
mysse-masche *n.* hodge-podge
M 49.
myth, myght *n.*¹ divine power 1,
3314, W 258, power 781, 3259,

faculty W 147, 177, strength of
body W 726, M 400; *to hys* ~ as
much as he can 3633; *wyth all hys*
(*my*) ~ as hard as he (I) can 62, 781.
myth *n.*² mite, a small coin 247.

name, nayme *n.* reputation 579,
1129, W 602, name 659, 2966, W 2,
M 18, 51.
nappyll *n.* apple M 427.
natur(e) *n.* inherent condition W 110,
M 15, 289, the vital functions
M 240, 560.
nay *adv.* not so 121, 402, W 830, 848,
M 56, 90; *no* ~ not at all W 555;
þis ys no ~ this is certain W 152.
ne *adv.* not 289, 375, M 836.
ne, nen, nyn *conj.* or 281, 282, nor
490, 714, 3475, W 64; *correl. ne . . .
ne* neither . . . nor W 852.
nede *n.* time of trouble 1321, 2698,
want W 458; *pl.* bodily necessities
1184; *at* ~ in distress 2599, 3475,
M 24; *hade* ~ would have to M 354;
have ~ require 2492, 2762, be in
want 869, 3632; *in* ~ in distress
2698; *is* ~ is necessary 1003,
W 504, 807.
nede *v.* need W 148, M 184; *nedyt
vs* is necessary to us W 662.
nedyngys *n. pl.* bodily needs M 783.
nedys *adv.*: *must* ~ must of necessity
502, 2661, W 867, M 231, 563.
neke-kycher *n.* neckerchief M 607.
neke-verse *n.* verse to save from
hanging M 520, 619.
nere *adj.* intimate M 223, close
M 617, 810; see rune.
ner(e) *adv.* close 1232, M 253, almost
2012, 2449, M 585; *prep.* close to
3248, M 614; see fer(e).
ner(e), nor *conj.* nor 395, 3474,
W 62, M 37; see noþer.
nerhand *adv.* almost 2443.
nesesse *adj.* necessary W 442.
nete *n.* ox, cow M 596.
neþer, neyther *adj.* lower 814,
W 145, 298.
neuer(e) *adv.* at no time 812, 2688,
W 68, M 155, 363, not at all 110,
111, M 230; ~ *so* no matter how 89,
W 641.

neueremore *adv.* never again 1317, 2940.

nevene *v.* mention 3502.

next(e), nex, nest *adj.* immediately following 1935, 2907, W 790, M 59, 353.

ney *v.* approach 2782.

neyther see neþer, noþer.

no *adj.* not any 388, 2730, 2834, W 297, 555, M 458, 555, not a M 245.

no *adv.* no indeed 1273, W 399, 831.

noble *n.* a coin worth 6*s.* 8*d.* (or 10*s.* after 1465) 2740, W 819, 828, M 270.

nobley *n.* nobleness W 4*, 576*.

nolde *pr. subj. 1 sg.* should not wish 2693.

noli me tangere *n.* person to be left alone M 512.

non *pron.* no one 596, 2663, no such thing M 706; *adj.* not any 412, 496, W 362, 658, M 3, 37; *adv.* not at all 3470.

nors *n.* nurse 860.

norysch *v.* feed 2283; norche *pr. 1 sg.* 2259; norchyst 2 *sg.* 2457.

not *pr. 1 sg.* know not 383, 451.

notary *adj.* notorious M 845.

note *n.* profit 2729.

note *v.* use 1957.

noþer, ne(y)thyr *conj.* neither: *correl.* ~ . . . *nor* 2746, 2823, M 66, 817.

noþynge *adv.* not at all 1263, 1586.

nou(gh)t, nowt(h), not *n.* nothing 2, 290, W 35, 194, M 6, 107, wickedness M 386; *adj.* worthless W 310, M 111, 273, wicked W 924; *adv.* not 104, 362, W 107, 950; see ell.

nowth *pr. 3 sg.* ought not 714.

ny(e) *adj.* nearly related 108; *adv.* near 473, 2105, almost M 776*.

nyfte *n.* nephew 2945.

nyn see ne.

nyse *adj.* foolish W 476, M 295.

nysyte *n.* trivial foible W 651.

nyth, nyght, nyȝte *n.* night 276, 284, M 485, 769; *day and* ~ continually 268, 497, 586; *þis* ~ *þat was* last night M 481.

obeys(y)ance *n.* obedience W 81, M 817.

objeccion *n.* assault M 837.

obsequyouse *adj.* obedient M 5.

occupye *v.* employ M 550; occupyede *pp.* M 110.

odde *adj.* uneven in number; *for* ~ *nor even* on any account 1469.

odyble, odybull *adj.* hateful M 739, 747.

of, off, a *prep.* from 2, 147, W 112, 803, M 186, 558, in 1, 279, of 5, 6, W 7, 25, M 1, 6, belonging to 7, 111, for 140, 491, W 2, 988, concerning 328, 409, W 40, because of 854, 1743, during 2276, on 3415, 3558, M 757, by W 44, 682, M 144, 222; see lofte, olde, out.

of *adv.* off 804, M 88, 435.

offend(e) *v. tr.* displease W 297, 436, M 854; *intr.* sin W 803, 1093, M 820; offendys *pr. 3 pl.* W 803; offendyde *pt. sg.* W 1073; offent *pp.* sinned against 3341, offendyde W 934.

olde, hold *adj.* of age 417, 1575, aged 1578, 2501, long-standing 2861, 2865, W 956, 1136; *sb.* old men 2066; *of* ~ for a long time 2430.

on *num.* one 1268, 2622, W 8, 135, M 582, 669, united M 149; *indef. pron.* a person W 562, 566, M 722; *at* ~ in unity W 780; *many* ~ many a man 2888, 3040, W 893; ~ *and* ~ one after another M 443; see as(s)ent.

on *prep.* upon 101, 134, W 381, in 225, 1850, M 600, in regard to 1326, against 1800, 2636; see d(e)y(e), lyf(e), mold(e), þynke *v.*1

onbrace *v.* carve up, take apart M 715.

onclennness *n.* unchastity W 650.

oncunnynge *n.* ignorance W 580.

oncurtes(s) *adj.* unkind M 748, 768.

ondon see vndo.

oneste see honest.

onethys *adv.* scarcely 2796.

onkynde see vnkynde.

onparty *adv.* apart: *leyde* ~ put aside M 759.

onredyly *adv.* not easily M 534.

onschett v. unlock M 52.
onthryfty adj. disreputable M 163.
onthryvande adj. wanton W 781.
onto, wnto prep. unto W 207, 391,
M 126, 740; adv. for the purpose
M 457.
onward adv. moving on 138.
onwysely adv. foolishly M 875.
ony, any adj. any 932, 1120, 1206,
3296, W 351, 618, M 171, 451.
onys adv. once 400, 2849, W 520, 840,
M 819, at one time in the past
M 651; al at ~ all together 1466,
2188; at ~ together 938, 1774.
ope v. open M 830.
op(p)resse v. overwhelm 73, M 229.
opyn adj. publicly declared 763.
opynly adv. publicly W 670.
or, her prep. before 559, 1360;
conj. before 2401, 2933, W 395,
M 455, 899; ~ þat before 1387,
2966, W 226.
ordena(u)nce n. decree 3521, plan
W 786, appointed place M 164.
ordeyn v. appoint 305, 1261, provide
1149, destine 3064, W 191, 475;
ordenyde pt. 3 sg. decreed W 475;
ordeynyd pp. 305, ordenyde
W 191.
ordynatly adv. properly W 138.
ore n. grace 300.
oreble, os see horryble, also.
ost n. multitude (of angels) 2088.
ostlere, hostlere n. innkeeper,
stableman M 732.
othere correl. adv.: ~ . . . or either
. . . or M 668.
oþyr, odyr adj. other 38, 93, W 141,
M 378; sb. pl. other persons 1117,
1740, W 709, M 256.
oþyrwhyle adv. sometimes 432,
1031.
ouer adj. higher W 300, 484.
ough see owe.
ought, owȝte, out n. anything
2585, M 494; adv. at all M 451,
652.
out, outhe, owt(e) adv. from within
78, 575, W 912 s.d., away 976,
M 70, 257, displaced W 524, away
from home M 704, completely
M 772; interj. alas! 2147, 2199,

W 325, 903; ~ of away from 60, 79,
M 148, 696, free from 2017,
beyond 2162, 2657, outside
W 659, M 491; ~ of mende insane
2263; ~ on a curse on 1411, 2387;
see put(te), sowpe.
outrage n. wrong 2876.
outwarde adj. external W 137, 1075;
adv. (go) away W 776.
ouyr prep. above, more than 502,
over 687, 897, M 570, 583.
ouerblysse v. consecrate M 374.
ouyrblyue adv. too eagerly 1619.
ouerdylew v. dig over M 543.
ouerface v. overcome M 716.
ouyrgoo v. overcome 642.
ouyrlate adv. too late 3427.
ouyrlede v. oppress 1098; ouyrlad
pp. 1049, 2014, ouyrled(de) 1988,
3089.
ouyrlonge adv. too long 65, M 778.
ouyrlyt adj. too little 3428.
ouyrmany adj. too many p. 1.
ouyrmekyl adj. too great 3200.
ouermoche adv. too much M 846.
ouerpysse v. urinate over M 373.
ouerron pp. outrun, escaped by running M 613.
ouerschett pp. covered with dung
M 786.
ouyrþynke v. make sorry 3161.
ouerwell adv. too well M 243.
ow(e) interj. oh! 828, 1221.
owe, ow(y)n adj. own 758, 2542,
W 131, 906, M 169, 744.
owe v. ought 1007, W 100, 212, M 2,
owe W 190*; pr. 1 sg. W 100,
ough W 190*; oweth 3 sg. M 2;
ow(e) pl. 1007, W 212.
owhere adv. anywhere 2539.
owle v. gather 1662.
owr, owyr n. hour W 1021, M 865;
owres pl. canonical hours M 712.
owse see vse.
owtwrynge v. squeeze out W 619;
outewronge pp. 2858.
oyet, oy(ȝ)yt interj. hear ye! M 666.

pace n. course 1594.
packe n. crew, set 2405.
page n. servant 780, 2938.
palfreyman n. horse-keeper M 251.

pall(e) *n.* rich cloth or robe 822, 1792.

par see as(s)ent.

parage *n.* ? partnership 2497.

paramoure *n.* mistress 582.

paramourys *adv.* for love, out of kindness 2025.

parcellys *n. pl.* parts, roles 132.

parde *adv.* certainly 2657.

parke *n.* enclosed land for hunting 761, 2728.

parlasent *adv.* willingly 2022.

parlement *n.* conference M 787.

part(e) *v. tr.* divide 1150; *intr.* separate 1293; partyn *pr. 3 pl.* 3186.

partycypable *adj.* able to share M 16.

partycypatt *adj.* sharing M 190.

partyes *n. pl.* parts W 135, 357.

parvyse *n.* enclosure in front of a church W 793.

passante *adj.* surpassing W 610.

pas(s)e, pace *v. intr.* depart 117, 156, be rendered 3223, come to an end M 485, be handed on M 571; *tr.* surpass 3063, 3453, spend more than W 830; pasyt *pr. 3 sg.* 3152, passyth ? is wanting M 691; past(e) *pp.* 117, 118.

passion *n.* suffering (of Christ) 3140, 3549, W 1007, 1069, M 12; *þe ∼ wyke* the week before Easter W 996 s.d.

passyble *adj.* able to feel emotion W 97, capable of suffering M 744.

pasture *n.* pastors 3624.

pate *n.* head 1112, M 472.

patrocynye *n.* protection M 904.

patrone *n.* protector, pattern W 15.

pawsacyon *n.* pause W 463.

pay *n.* satisfaction 833.

pay, pey *v.* pay 844, 2524, M 466, 469; payed *pp.* satisfied 2446.

pelourys *n. pl.* despoilers 2130.

pende *v.* limit 1244.

penne *n.* plume 909.

peny *n.* penny 856, 2524, W 870, 999, M 478; penys, pens *pl.* 767, 798, M 464; *pens of to pens* coins worth twopence M 464.

penyman *n.* money personified 2665, 2677.

perceyvable *adj.* recognizable W 595.

perseuerante *adj.* persevering M 25.

perseueraunce *n.* continuing steadfast 52, 1549, M 898.

person(e) *n.* person of the Trinity W 7, 1141, personage W 599.

pertly *adv.* quickly 1595.

peruersyose *adj.* perverse M 751.

pervercyonatt *adj.* perverse M 192.

perverse *v.* pervert W 379.

pervert(e) *v. intr.* be led astray W 292; *tr.* lead astray W 362, M 296, 386; pervertyde *pp.* M 763.

perysche *v. intr.* be ruined W 311, 395*; *tr.* ruin W 410, 1089; perrysschyt *pr. 3 sg.* W 1089; perysschede *pt. 1 sg.* W 311.

pes(e), peas *n.* silence 160, 3548, harmony 3143, 3214, W 1150; *agayn þe ∼* against law and order 647; *holde þi ∼* keep silence 2469; *to ∼* to find surety to keep the peace W 850; *wyth my ∼* silently 695.

peson *n. pl.* pease M 248.

pes(se) *imp.* be silent 340, 491, M 427, 557.

pesyble *adj.* peacefully disposed 3232, 3241.

petously *adv.* pitifully 3557.

pety, pyte *n.* pity 832, 3548, W 912, 1029, M 364, 423.

peyn(e) *n.* grief 260, W 193, torment 1245, 3043, W 935, 1012, painful sensation M 390, 434; *∼ of* on penalty of M 536, 590.

peyryth *pr. 3 sg.* injures 2162.

peys *n.* a weight 2628.

pirssid *adj.* pierced M 825*.

place, plas(e) *n.* place, locality 9, 126, M 148, 524, piece of land 160, 2935, dwelling-place W 132, 176, allotted space W 327; *have ∼* have an assigned position 3303, 3324.

placebo *n.* vespers for the dead 3124.

playn *n.* open space 1764.

playster *n.* plaster M 247, 436.

plesaunce *n.* pleasure W 78, 1022.

plese, plesyn *v.* gratify 620, 723, W 998, 1040; *refl.* satisfy 245; *impers.* seem good to M 460,

plese, plesyn (*cont.*)
629; **plesyst** *pr. 2 sg.* W 1040;
plesyt(he) *3 sg.* W 1000, 1008,
1035; **ples** *pl.* W 998; **plesse** *pr.
subj. 3 sg.* M 460; **plesyde** *pt.
3 sg.* W 413; **plesyde** *pp.* W 1062.

plesere *n.* pleasure W 1107*.

pley *n.* sport 691, W 887, method of
proceeding M 84, 267.

pley(e), play(e) *v. tr.* perform p. 1,
132, act the part of p. 1, play on an
instrument M 72, play in sport
M 440; *refl.* amuse oneself 1577,
1851, W 837; *intr.* act a play or part
p. 1, sport 396, 767, M 88*;
~ *þe foll* act foolishly M 275;
pleyeth *pr. 3 sg.* 2022; **pleyde**
pt. 1 sg. M 275; **pleyed** *pp.* 806.

pleyferys *n. pl.* companions in joy
M 913.

pleyn *adj.* open 160; *adv.* clearly
W 992.

pleynerly *adv.* fully W 404.

plyth *v.* pledge 3260; **plyth** *pp.* 827.

podys *n. pl.* toads 808, 1361.

pokett *n.* pocket, wallet M 144.

pokys *n. pl.* bags: **pyssynge** ~
private parts 2294.

polytyke *adj.* prudent M 371.

pompe *n.* vain display 3397.

pompyus *adj.* ostentatious W 1121.

pon(n)de *n.* pond 2728, 2935, 2974.

pose *v.* shove 2130.

pouert(e) *n.* poverty 81, 352, 1645,
W 667.

powdyr *n.* choking smoke 1966; ~
of Parysch a compound of arsenic
M 570.

pownde *n.* pound sterling 767, 2826;
poundys, pounde *pl.* 816, 2693.

poynt(e) *n.* item 832, W 998, 1005,
prick 1306, pointed weapon 1377,
2836; *in* ~ in danger 1314.

praty *adj.* pretty W 815, fine (ironic)
M 89, clever M 572, 591.

prawnce *v.* dance, caper M 91.

pray, prey(e) *v.* request 136, 142,
M 48, 86, pray W 1054, 1056,
M 24; **preyd** *pt. 1 sg.* 1357;
preyde *pt. subj. 3 pl.* W 1056.

preche *v.* exhort 1674, speak to per-
suade 3463; **prechyth** *pr. 3 sg.* 80.

prechors *n. pl.* preachers W 488.

precyse *v.* state definitely M 833.

predilecte *adj.* especially beloved
M 771, 872.

predycacyon *n.* preaching M 47.

prefe, prowe *n.* evidence from scripture 1611, evidence from experience
M 911.

prefe, preve, proue *v. tr.* make trial
of 150, 1975, M 283, demonstrate
2100, W 378, 399, M 165, 870, give
proof by action 2835, put to the
test 3233; *intr.* thrive 3110;
prouyth *pr. 3 sg.* M 56; **prewynge**
pr. p. W 541; **prowyd** *pp.* M 857.

premyabyll *adj.* deserving of reward M 868.

prene *n.* spike 1903.

prene *v.* pierce 1377.

prepotent *adj.* especially powerful
M 772.

pres *n.*: *in* ~ in a critical situation
3618; *putte me in* ~ exert myself
3240.

presse *v.* thrust 3438.

preue, preuy *adj.* secret 691, 1365,
sharing a secret M 839.

preuely *adv.* secretly M 533.

preve, prey(e) see **prefe, pray**.

pride, prede *n.* pride 31, 2079, splendid adornment 159, 757.

prime *n.* prayer at the first hour of
the day M 712.

privyte *n.* private parts M 429.

processe *n.* mandate in law 3384.

profyght *v.* benefit W 457, 1004;
profytyth *pr. 3 sg.* 1432.

promycyon *n.* promise M 316.

promytt *v.* promise M 401, 676.

propagacyon *n.* begetting M 186.

propyr, *adj.* goodly 160, own M 869.

propyrly *adv.* particularly W 9, 142,
M 886*.

propyrte *n.* stage property 132, special
attribute W 1, 182, M 765, 903.

proude *adv.* proudly 1792.

proue see **prefe**.

provente *n.* provender M 61.

provycyon *n.* providence M 193.

prow *n.* advantage 1927.

prycke *n.* torment 1646, 2183, spike
W 1060.

pryke *v.* fasten M 30; **prekyd** *pp.*
159, 1792, **pryckyd** attired 44.
prys *n.* worth 150, 808.
puerilite *n.* childish thing M 820.
punchyd *pp.* punished 3338.
pundyr *n.* a balance 2628.
purfyled *pp. adj.* bordered W 16 s.d.
purger *n.* purifier W 962.
put(te), **puttyn**, **pot** *v.* place 107,
822, M 145, impose 1128, apply
1138, remove 1458, affirm 1611,
drive 1645, 3434, M 395, subject
1809, put forth 2037, thrust 2109,
2118, W 524; *refl.* exert M 550;
~ *doun* overcome 2361; ~ *out* hang
out 1973, blind M 156; **puttys**
pr. 2 sg. 3434; **puttyth** *3 sg.* 1138,
put 1809; **put(te)** *pp.* 1245, W 524;
see **abak**, **cas(e)**, **deuer(e)**, **pres.**
puysschaunce *n.* armed force
W 1024.
pycke *n.* pitch 3078.
pyke *v.* pluck 804.
pyll see **cros(e).**
pylt *pp. adj.* thrust out 448.
pyne *n.* torment 1272, 3195.
pynne *n.* pin, peg 112; *on a mery* ~
in a joyful frame of mind W 492.
pynynge *pr. p.* tormenting 1306;
pynyd *pp.* 3557, 3596.
pynyngys *g. sg.:* ~ *stole* seat of
punishment 1035*.
pypys *n. pl.* tubes p. 1.
pystyl *n.* epistle 1611.
pyt(h), **pytte** *pp.* placed 31, 558,
adorned 909, 2070, set, fixed 1673.
pytyr-patyr *n.* repeated saying of the
Paternoster 2398.

querulose *adj.* quarrelsome M 211.
quest *n.* jury of inquiry W 638, 721.
quod *pt. sg.* said W 518, 604, 759,
M 126, 325.
qwak(e) *v.* tremble 3641, W 844, 898.
qwayl *n.* quail 2385; see **cowche.**
qwed *n.* evil 2927.
qweke *interj.* (sound of choking)
M 516, 808.
qwell *v.* destroy 66, W 542, 919.
qwenche *v.* put out 2303, 2764;
qwenchyd *pp.* 2390.
qwene *n.¹* queen 1632, 2315.

qwene *n.²* hussy 2390, 2648.
qweynt *adj.* ingenious 1702.
qweyntly *adv.* craftily 530.
qwyll see **whyl.**
qwyppe *imp. sg.* whip, put quickly
M 795.
qwyst *interj.* hush! M 557, 593.
qwyt(t)e, **qvyth** *v.* pay 3163,
reward 3635, pay back (for injury)
W 849.
qwytt see **whytt.**

rad *adv.* quickly 185.
rafte see **reue.**
raggyd *adj.* torn 1931.
raggys *n. pl.* shreds 1973.
rakle *n.* haste 2652.
rape, **rapyn** *v.* hasten 969, 2068;
refl. 185, 2741; **rapyth** *pr. 3 sg.* 185.
rapely *adv.* hastily 911, 1561.
rappe *n.* stroke 1783, 2841.
rappe *v.* strike 2154, 2368; **rappyth**
pr. 3 sg. 1828; **rappyd** *pp.* 1865.
rappokys *n. pl.* wretches 1894, 1943.
rasche *n.:* *upon* (*on*) *a* ~ in haste
1733, 1923.
rather *adv.* sooner 873, 1107.
raue, **rawyn** *v.* behave madly 168,
376, act passionately W 837.
raveyn *n.* robbery, violence W 727.
rayed *pp. adj.* dressed 2072.
rechace *n.* call to summon hounds
W 908.
rechases *pr. 3 pl.* ? chase back, call
hounds together W 722*.
reche *v. tr.* stretch out 2475, give
3022; *absol.* strike 1400; *intr.* proceed 2830.
recke, **rek(k)e** *v.* care 440, 1166,
W 808, 816, take heed 603; **rowt**
pt. 2 sg. 1512.
reclusyde *pp. adj.* shut up W 911.
recognycyon *n.* acknowledgement
W 1087.
recomaunde, **recomende** *v.* com-
mend M 188; *refl.* 916; **recomen-
dynge** *pr. p.* W 324.
recordaunce *n.* testifying (falsely)
W 791.
recorde *v.* recall 3471.
recors *n.:* *haue* ~ apply for help
M 656.

recreatory *n.* source of comfort M 871.

recumbentibus *n.* knock-down blow M 446, 496.

recurable *adj.* curable W 947.

recure *v.* obtain W 217; **recurythe** *pr. 3 sg.* obtains possession by law W 654.

red *n.* advice 1586, 3021.

reddere, reddure *n.* rigorous punishment 3565, W 76.

red(e) *adj.* red p. 1, W 692 s.d., golden M 465.

rede *v. tr.* advise 7, 722, find written 2167, M 849, read 2601, M 679; *absol.* read 1650; *intr.* give advice 370, 1096, W 469, 1036; **red** *pp.* decreed 2941.

redouce *v.* lead back to the right way M 825; **reducyde** *pt. 2 sg.* W 313.

redusyble *adj.* reclaimable M 834.

refeccyon *n.* refreshment 1616.

reforme *v. intr.* be renewed W 1122; *tr.* **reformyt(he)** *pr. 3 sg.* restores W 120, 127; **reformyde** *pt. 3 sg.* W 1118; *pp.* W 1092.

reformynge *n.* re-establishment W 337.

refreyn *v.* curb W 1038.

regne, reyn(ge) *v.* flourish 600, 1140, W 263, 1139; **reynynge** *pr. p.* 1140, **reynande** W 679.

regyn *n.* region W 760.

regystre *n.* written record 2601.

rekleshede, *n.* heedlessness W 753.

relacyon *n.* account W 422.

rele *n.* rushing about 1828.

reles *v. tr.* remit 3282; *absol.* set free W 967; **relessyt** *pr. 3 sg.* W 1012.

reme, revme *n.* realm 7, W 162.

remene *v.* recall to mind W 956.

remocyon *n.* inclination M 14, 656.

remos *n.* remorse M 319.

rende *v.* tear W 533; **rent** *pt. 3 sg.* 2126; *pp.* 2220, 2783, W 1052.

renew(e) *v. tr.* regenerate W 386; *intr.* be restored W 668, 1159; **renuyde** *pp.* W 1137.

rengne *n.* kingdom 185.

renne *v.* move rapidly 911, W 1049, M 721, hasten 1733, come to be 2260, flow 3364, M 36; ~ *upon a*

whele go on continuously 667; **rennyth** *pr. 3 sg.* 2260, **runnyth** M 36; **rennyt** *pl.* W 912 s.d.; **ronne** *imp.* 1733; **ran** *pt. 3 sg.* 3364; **rennynge** *pr. p.* 1073, cursive M 683*, **runnynge** spreading M 630; **runn** *pp.* M 595.

renoun(e) *n.* fame 470, 3253; *at myn* ~ subject to me 3615.

rent *n.* revenue 391; *pl.* sources of income 368, 2972.

repeyer *v.* resort W 71.

replicacyon *n.* reply, counter-argument W 447.

replyede *pp. adj.* replied to (by plaintiff answering defendant) W 863.

report *v. tr.* describe as W 603, write down M 663; *absol.* bring in a verdict W 730.

reporte *n.* talk M 79.

reporture *n.* declaration W 355; *make* ~ declare W 265.

reprefe, repreve, reprowe *n.* reproach 1138, 2501, W 1014, 1020, shame M 874.

reprouable *adj.* blameworthy W 537, M 760.

rere *adj.* partly raw 1461.

res(e) *n.*: *in (a)* ~ in haste 477, 969.

reson(e), re(a)sun *n.* argument 1275, rational faculty 2570, 3036, W 141, 145, M 184, explanation W 2, M 173; *by (ryth)* ~ in accord with reason 2100, 3043, W 10, M 165; *haue* ~ be right W 445; *of* ~ justly W 113.

resorte *n.* retinue W 692.

resort(e) *v.* go for help W 207, 938, proceed W 800.

rest(e) *n.* tranquillity 861, 1920, peace of mind 2296, freedom from care 3504, W 59; *so haue I* ~ as I wish to enjoy peace 1170, 1341.

reste *v.* remain 734, 1073, cease from effort W 380; *refl.* put to rest 1203; **restyd** *pt. 3 sg.* lay 2451; **restynge** *pr. p.* W 132, 176.

restore *v.* re-establish 88, W 239, 327, reinstate 1511, 1527; **restoryd** *pp.* M 832.

resythe see **reysyst.**

retenance *n.* retinue W 686.

retorn(e) *v.* go back W 912 s.d., 943, respond M 669, 781.

retornys *n. pl.* returning of writs W 791.

retribucyon *n.* reward (in heaven) M 16.

reue *v.* rob, deprive 1920; **rafte** *pp.* 1789.

reuell, reull *n.* loud merry-making W 505, M 82.

reuerens(e) *n.* due respect W 1038, M 735, veneration W 1146, M 14; *at þe* ~ *of* out of respect for 1631; *sauyng yowr* ~ with due respect to you M 463.

reull, rewlyn *v.* govern 581, 2580, control W 138, M 242, 842; **rewlyd(e)** *pp.* 484, W 138.

reverte *v.* return M 412.

revme see **reme**.

rewe *v. intr.* feel sorrow 562, 723; *tr.* grieve 1300, 2859, regret 3180.

rewelynge *n.* riotous merry-making M 85.

rewly *adj.* grievous 1114, 1865.

rewthe, ruthe *n.* pity 605, 3493, W 316, a thing to lament 823, W 720.

reyallys *n. pl.* gold coins worth 10*s.* each M 465.

reyn *n.* rain M 154, 373.

reyne *v.* fall like rain 2057.

reyn(ge) see **regne**.

reysyst *pr. 2 sg.* lift up W 318; **resythe** *3 sg.* W 231.

rode *n.* cross 304, 2220; *be þe* ~ indeed 1155, 1167.

rode *adj.* ruddy 2026.

rodyr, rothyr *n.* rudder 1114, 1738.

rom *n.*: *make* ~ give place M 331.

ronde *v.* whisper M 303, 593.

rop(p)e *n.* rope 2392, M 800.

ros *n.* boasting 1065.

rote *n.* root 2057, source 2342, 2465; *hert(e)* ~ heart's core 1400, 2842; ~ *and rynde* source 1135, altogether 2126.

rothyr see **rodyr**.

rouge *v.* handle roughly 3120.

rounde *adj.* hard 2068, spherical 2454, circular 2740, 2914.

rounde *adv.* on all sides 2072.

route *v.*[1] gad about 34, be riotous W 505.

route *v.*[2] roar 1783.

row, rough *adj.* harsh 710, rough, torn 1931, W 1051*.

row *v.* row: ~ *ageyn þe floode* strive against the stream W 491.

rowe *n.* line of persons 168; *on a* ~ in order 1470, 3120.

rowe *pr. opt. 1 sg.* repose 2296.

rowt see **recke**.

rowte *n.*[1] riot 911, 1973, retinue 1840.

rowte *n.*[2] violent blow 1865, 3015.

rowtynge *adj.* beating violently 1828.

ruble *v.* crush to pieces 1943.

ruggynge *pr. p.* tearing, eating away 1664.

rune *n.* act of running: *nere* ~ narrow escape M 617.

rust(e) *v.* rust, waste away 523, 636.

ryal(l), reyall *adj.* splendid 134, W 1 s.d., 585; *sb.* noble persons 7.

ryde, rydyn *v.* ride (a horse) 425, 518, M 67, be hanged 2392, M 598; **rydyth** *pr. 3 sg.* M 598; **rode** *pt. 3 sg.* M 597.

rynde *n.* bark 1135, 2126; see **rote**.

rynge *v. intr.* resound 1783, speak loudly 1796; *tr.* cause to resound 3094.

rys *n.* branch 2026.

rytfully *adv.* justly 3175.

ryth, ryght *n.* justice 750, 3522, W 668, 738, just claim 2375, due reward M 862; *be* ~ justly 3258; *þe* ~ the true course 7.

ryth, ryght *adj.* just 2100, 3043, proper 3022, right hand side 303, 3599, W 36; see **reson(e)**.

ryth, ryght *adv.* exactly 290, 834, W 628, 676, very 297, 322, W 486, M 222, 257, rightfully W 121; *ful* ~ to the full 64, 2072; ~ *now* just now M 255; ~ *wppe* upright M 29.

ryt(h)wys *adj.* righteous 3269, 3379.

ryt(h)wysnes(se), ryghtusnes *n.* justice 3048, 3133, W 1156.

ryve *v.* tear apart W 175.

ryve *adj.* ample 625.

sacyatt *adj.* satisfied M 311.

sad(e), sadde *adj.* dark p. 1, steadfast 196, 1162, lamentable 652, solid 1562, sorrowful M 181; *adv.* forcibly 1241, 2803, firmly 1527; ~ *aslepe* sound asleep M 592.

saf(e) see **saue, save.**

saggyd *pp. adj.* sunk 1291.

oakyrde *adj.* consecrated M 390, 612; see **cokkys.**

sale *n.* hall 456.

same *adv.* together 163.

sare see **sore.**

satysfaccion *n.* atonement 3149, 3429, W 975.

satysfye *v.* atone for W 1080, M 35.

saue, saf *adj.*: ~ *and holl* cured M 447; ~ *and sownde* with no danger of loss 2460, 2744.

saue *prep.* except 330.

saun(z) *prep.* without: ~ *dowte* without doubt 74; ~ *pere* without equal 3252.

sauour *v.* have understanding W 87.

save, safe *v.* protect 6, 12, M 796, deliver from sin 26, 129, W 311, keep from others 2827, preserve M 43; **sauyde** *pt. 2 sg.* W 311; **sauyd** *1 pl.* 2040; **sauyng** *pr. p.* M 463; **savyd** *pp.* 3184; see **reuerens(e).**

sawe *n.* speech 214, 492.

sawowre *n.* fragrance W 388.

sawter *n.* Psalter 2985.

say(n), saynt see **sey(ne), se(y)nt.**

saynge *n.* reciting (of prayers) M 581.

schade *v.* pour off 2328; **schede** *pp.* poured forth M 745.

schakle *n.* fetter 2654.

schal(l), xall *v.* be destined to 105, 109, M 42, 43, ought to 119, 424, W 146, 251, M 5, 197, must 138, 342, M 78, 703, will 333, 346, W 51, 52, M 108, 860, shall 401, 557, W 331, 356, M 33, 112, be determined to 608, W 586; *elliptic* shall go 121, 1572, shall be 2772, W 109, shall have M 576; **schalt** *pr. 2 sg.* 339, **schat** 1572; **schul** *1 pl.* 138, **schal** 401; **schulyn** *2 pl.* 2330; **schuld(e)** *pt. 1, 3 sg.,* pl. 42, 119, W 891, **sulde** 2480, **scholde**

3275, **xuld(e)** W 340, M 735; **schu(l)dyst** *2 sg.* 819, 1591.

schamely *adj.* shameful 2050.

schape, schapyn *v.* direct 677, 1827, fashion 1448, 2839, contrive 2360, 3445; *refl.* prepare 1362; **schapyn** *pr. 2 pl.* 1448; **schapyth** *imp. pl.* preparo 1905, **schapyn** *pp.* 280, M 698; see **scho.**

schappe *n.* appearance 2839, beauty W 20.

scharpe *adj.* prickly W 1050, 1060.

scharpe *adv.* piercingly 2222.

scharp(e)ly *adv.* fiercely 1722, 1952.

schawe *n.* thicket: *vndyr* ~ under the earth 221, 2285.

sche *pron.* she 124, 1578, W 816, 835, M 246, 249.

schelde, schylde *v.* defend 1457, 2049, M 307*, keep out 2459.

schelfe *v.* ? ruin 1067.

schelle *n.* ? covering 3039.

schelue *v.* ? defend 2575.

schende *v. tr.* disgrace 221, destroy 792, revile 1067, overthrow 2085, 2124, scold 2395, M 381; *intr.* be confounded 283; **schent** *pp.* injured 162.

schendeschyppe, schenchepe *n.* disgrace 12, shameful conduct W 634.

schene *adj.* bright 1905.

schenful *adj.* disgraceful 2839.

schere *n.* county W 851.

schere *v.* cut off 3102; **schorn** *pp.* fashioned 280, 2680.

schete *n.* under-linen 2209, winding-sheet 2919.

schete, schetyn *v.*[1] shoot, hit 1930, 1953, let fly from a bow 2157; *my bolte ys schett* I have finished M 782; **schete** *hort.* 1956; **schott** *pr. subj. pl.* M 783; **schett** *pp.* M 782.

schete *v.*[2] shut, make secure 2049; **schyttyth** *imp. pl.* 2551; **schet** *pp.* confined 2285.

scheue see **cheve.**

scheuere *v.* break into splinters 1952.

schew(e) *v.* demonstrate 2172, W 377, M 56, display 3318, W 726,

746, exhibit M 78, 591; **schewth**
pr. 3 sg. M 56; **schewynge** *pr. p.*
W 540; **schewyd(e)** *pp.* W 746,
M 890, **scheude** M 591.

scho *n.* shoe; **schos, schon** *pl.* 1059,
M 796; *schapyn a sory* ~ put
into a sad state 1448; *wynnyth a* ~
win fame by victory 2239.

schonde *n.* disgrace 677, 1887, ruin
3445.

schot(e) *n.* missile 1944, 1976; *all
at a* ~ all shooting at once 1956.

schotynge *n.* shooting M 785.

schrew *v.* curse W 759, 777.

schrewde, schroude *adj.* wicked
W 550 s.d.*, severe W 864, M 437,
446, mischievous M 80, bad, unlucky M 369.

schrewdnes *n.* malice 1743.

schrewe *n.* villain 1827, 2168,
M 108*.

schryfte *n.* confession 1219, 1326.

schryue *n.* sheriff M 780.

schryue, schryuyn *v.* hear confession 312, make confession 546,
1362; *refl.* 1333, 2345; **schrywe**
pp. 546, **schreue** 1569, **schreuyn**
beaten 2205.

schyfte *v.* move 2849.

schylle *adv.* shrilly 1813.

schyte, schytyn *v. intr.* void excrement 1968, 2209, M 337; *tr.* void
as excrement M 568; **schytyth**
pr. 3 sg. M 337; **schetun** *pp.*
befouled M 132.

sckyppe *v.* skip, jump W 561.

scolys *n. pl.* doctrines W 86.

scoryde *pp.* scoured, worn clean
M 641.

scottlynge *n.* scampering M 89.

scyfftyd *pp. adj.* distributed 108.

se see **se(ne).**

sed(e) *n.* semen 1192, 2320, seed
grain M 542.

se(e) *n.*¹ seat 834, dwelling-place
W 132.

se(e) *n.*² sea 2, 173, W 1010.

seke *adj.* ill 3634, W 1030, spiritually
ill W 947.

seke, sekyn *v. tr.* try to obtain 483,
W 18, 931, M 493, look for W 205,
M 385, ask for W 970, M 603;

intr. try 1540, search M 777, 792;
sekyth *pr. 3 sg.* M 792; **sek(e)**
imp. W 931, 970, **syke** M 777;
sowte *pp.* W 18, M 296, **sowght**
W 21, **sowȝte** M 493.

seker, sekyr *adj.* certain W 368,
534, secure W 886; *adv.* confidently
1562, assuredly M 660.

sek(k)atour *n.* executor 102, 1660.

sekyrly *adv.* assuredly M 42.

sekyrnes *n.* assurance W 60.

sel(e), sell *n.* time, moment 298,
M 369; *in euery* ~ at all times 1077.

selkowth *adj.* marvellous 1940.

selle *n.* seat, low stool 1746.

sely *adj.* miserable 263, 793, M 433,
insignificant 294.

seme *v. intr.* appear W 52, 590; *tr.*
think W 608, 743; *me* ~ it appears
to me W 445, 485; *me semyt(h)*
W 554, 597, M 641, 812; *yt semyth*
it appears W 480; **semyn** *pr. 3 pl.*
799.

sem(e)ly *adj.* well-appearing 163,
456, M 209.

semly *adv.* handsomely 249.

sen, syn *conj.* seeing that 314, 351,
W 377; from the time that 2445.

sende *v.* dispatch 44, 164, W 879,
M 4, cause to happen 652, cause to
go 1554, M 568, grant M 217;
absol. send help 3058, W 824, send
excuse M 668; ~ *afftyr* send for
102, 1011; **se(e)nde** *pr. 1 sg.* 652,
1554; **sendyth** *3 sg.* 44, 102; **sende**
pr. subj. M 217, **sent** W 1023; **sen**
imp. pl. M 668; **sent** *pp.* 164,
W 879, M 568.

sendel *n.* clothing of thin silk 369,
554.

se(ne) *v.* see 273, 303, W 818, 1097,
M 363, pay attention 492, perceive
1420, 2038, W 185, M 32, 199,
experience W 59, take care W 298;
seste *pr. 2 sg.* 2587; **se** *pl. pr.* 1420;
imp. sg. W 298; **seth(e)** *imp. pl.*
273, 492, **se** M 32; **sy** *pt. 1 sg.*
2038, **se** W 1097, **saw** M 363; **seyn**
pl. 2892, **sawe** 2567; **se(y)ne** *pp.*
327, shown by experience 1251,
sen 1516, seen W 818.

sens *n.* incense 799, 2025.

sensualyte *n.* the part of the soul concerned with the senses W 135, 154.

sensyble *adj.* capable of feeling W 96.

serche, serge *v.* explore M 493, examine M 908.

serdyn *v.* have intercourse with 1160.

serue, seruyn *v. tr.* do the will of 332, 338, W 144, 630, M 235, minister to 616, treat badly 1850, 2614; *intr.* be of use 1167, 1181, M 59, 634; **seruyt(h)** *pr. 3 sg.* 1167, 2614, W 144; **serwynge** *pr. p.* W 137; **seruyd** *pp.* 1850.

ses, ses(s)e *v. tr.* put an end to 2473, *intr.* cease 3144, 3554, M 240, 769.

sese *v.* take possession of 182, 246, endow 2751; **sesyd** *pp.* 182.

sesun *n.*¹ possession 763, 2102.

sesun *n.*² season: *in* ~ in fashion 1273.

sete *n.*¹ seat, place 369, 1315.

sete *n.*² plant, slip 1403.

seth, sethen see **syth(e), sythen.**

sethe *n.* atonement W 122.

sett *n.* sect, group M 379.

set(te), settyn *v.* place 752, 1039, M 259, 435, plant 1008, 1403, cause to be 2253, W 492, ornament W 1 s.d., establish W 786, lay out, spend W 819, put together M 102, 104, appoint M 664; ~ *at a thost* regard as worthless 1064; ~ *at nowth* value at nothing 3409, W 764, M 8; ~ *by* esteemed W 600; ~ *lyght by* value slightly W 923; ~ *on* kindle 1961; **settys** *pr. 2 sg.* W 923; **settyn** *1 pl.* 1008; **set** *pt. 3 sg.* 3409; **set** *pp.* settled in mind 561, **sette** 752, **sett** W 219, M 102; see **abroche, cort(e).**

seuenenyt *n.* week: *þis day* ~ a week from to-day 133.

sew(e), sue *v. intr.* result W 369, seek W 633, 664; *tr.* follow W 383, 429, seek W 665.

seyer *n.* speaker W 864.

sey(ne), say(n) *v.* say 214, 610, W 161, 997, M 9, 58, tell 1357, M 114, mention W 237, speak, plead W 853; *herde* ~ heard it said M 597; ~ *nay* speak in opposition 121, refuse 3141, M 468; **seyst(e)** *pr. 2 sg.* 610, 2081; **seyth** *3 sg.* 121, **seys** 3351, **seth** W 997; **seydyst** *pt. 2 sg.* 3115, **seyd** 3356; **seyde** *3 sg.* M 51; **seyenge** *pr. p.* W 1 s.d.; **seyd(e)** *pp.* 3141, W 237, M 9; see **skyl(le), soth(e).**

se(y)nt, saynt *adj.* holy 1487, W 487, 993, M 75, 212; *sb* blessed soul in heaven W 255, 1056, M 35.

skaf(f)old *n.* raised platform p. 1.

skallyd *adj.* scurvy 1814, 1906, scabby 2399.

skathe *n.* injury, damage 2401.

skerre *v.* frighten 1906; **skaryth** *pr. 3 sg.* drives off M 807.

skoute *n.* trull 1871, 1906, 1930.

skylful *adj.* reasonable, moderate 1616.

skylfully *adv.* reasonably 1626.

skyl(le) *n.* reason, argument 2531, 3050; *be* ~ according to reason 22; *can (no)* ~ be (not) able to judge 881, 3059; *haue no* ~ have no ability to judge 3312; *resun and* ~ reasonable and proper 3482, 3583; *seyst* ~ tell truth 1221.

slake *v.* abate 1435, 2473; **slakyth** *pr. 3 sg.* comes to an end 2889.

slaw, slow(e) *adj.* lazy, 1030, 1235, tardy in coming 2768; *Syr Slowe* Sir Slothful 2327.

slawth(e) *n.* sloth 37, 69.

sleper *adj.* deceitful 1685.

sley(gh)t *n.* trick 850, W 674, 865, skill 1944, trickery W 725.

slo *n.* muddy ground 2241, sink of evil 2756.

slo(o) *v.* slay, destroy 646, 1266; **sle** *imp.* 1987; **slow** *pt. 3 sg.* 3111.

sloppe *n.* gown 2488.

slugge, *n.* laziness 2340.

sly *adj.* crafty 2040, 2106.

slynge *n.*¹ noose 1205.

slynge *n.*² sling 1944.

slynge *v.* throw 2112, 2241.

slyther *v.* slip M 112.

smattrynge *adj.* ? pretty M 611.

smeke, smoke *n.* smoke 1967, 2248.

smert *v.* suffer pain for 797.

smert(e) *adj.* impudent 1389, sharp 2016, 3357, severe W 1101.

smete *pp. adj.* struck 1846.

smodyr *n.* suffocating smoke 1967.

snelle *adv.* vigorously 70.

snowre *v.* scowl 1866.

sobyrnesse *n.* temperance 50, 2279.

socoure *imp. pl.* help 2025.

socowre *n.* help 3046.

softe *adj.* soft, yielding 554, 2400.

softe *adv.* comfortably 1146.

sojet, subjecte *adj.* owing obedience 3625, subordinate M 197.

sokelys *n. pl.* sweet-tasting flowers 973.

sokett *n.* private part M 145.

solaycyose *adj.* consoling M 814.

soleyn *adj.* aloof W 577.

soloyen *v.* sully 2320; solwyd *pp.* 3420.

sompe *n.* swamp 425.

sonde *n.*[1] messenger 164, sending M 541.

sonde *n.*[2] sand, land 1562; *be se and ~ by* sea and land 760, 2035.

son(e), sun(ne) *n.* son 251, 2589, W 1067, Son of God W 10, 13, M 4, 8, spiritual son M 290, 811.

son(e) *adv.* quickly 348, 848, M 109, 257, readily W 595; *to ~* too early 1350, too quickly M 254, 431; sonner *compar.*: *þe ~* the more quickly M 261.

sore, sare *n.* misery 20, 40.

sore *adj.* sorrowful 1426, painful 2016, 2487, M 624.

sore *adv.* grievously W 331, with great grief 449, 1299, M 178, painfully 2803, greatly W 790.

sorte *n.* set of persons: *a good ~ a* great many M 264; *a schrewde ~* a bad lot M 80.

sorwe *n.* sorrow 652, 1381; *wyth ~* with bad luck M 426, 623; see mak(e).

sory *adj.* causing sorrow 1410, 1451, dismal 1741, full of grief 2970, 3337, M 200.

sotel, sotyll *adj.* wily 850, delicate M 202.

soth(e) *n.* truth 543, W 750; *~ to say(n)* to tell the truth 1763, 2003, 2520.

sothe *adj.* true 2165, 2171.

sothfastnesse *n.* truth 3302.

sothly *adv.* truly 1269.

soueren *adj.* supreme W 39, 77, most powerful W 1011.

souerenly *adv.* supremely W 254, 259.

souereyn *n.* supreme lord W 261; souerens, souerence, souereyngys, sofereyns *pl.* masters, gentlemen M 13, 29, 903, superiors W 588.

sowme *n.* sum 83.

sowpe *v.* sup M 772; *~ owt* drink up M 772.

space *n.* period of time 1557, 3620, M 260, opportunity 2719, 2996, room 3408, M 97, place W 719, distance W 1018; *make ~* give room 2304, M 474, 612, 701.

spar(e) *v.* refrain 1170, 1469, W 771, shun W 76, M 511, 514, save W 295, 736, M 678; *absol.* save W 584, refrain W 614, 769; sparyth *pr. 3 sg.* W 76.

specyal(l) *adj.* exceeding the usual 141, particular W 203; *in ~* particularly M 293; *adv.* particularly W 58*; *sb.* particular intimate W 131, 1113, M 872.

specyal(l)y *adv.* particularly 136, 3490, W 11, pre-eminently W 19, 390.

specyfye *v.* tell fully W 65, mention explicitly W 407; specyfyede *pp.* M 761.

spede *n.* profit W 636.

spede *v. intr.* fare 867, thrive 2671, succeed W 800; *tr.* hasten 1594; *refl.* make haste 1175, fare W 769; *Gode ~ yow* may God help you M 344; *so God me ~* may God help me 1320; *þe Deuyl ~ ʒou (me, hym)* may the Devil help you (me, him) 2405, W 508, 620; sped *pp.* satisfied 1184.

speke *v. intr.* talk 192, 519, M 140, 253, tell W 40, 41, M 184; *tr.* state in writing 2984, utter 3006, declare W 64; spekyth *pr. 3 sg.* 192, spekys M 253; spak(e) *pt. 1 3 sg.* 2468, 2984, M 140; spekynge *pr. p.* W 591; spoke *pp.* 2869, W 64.

spell(e) *v. intr.* speak 122; *tr.* tell 1535; **spellys** *pr. 3 sg.* utters W 275.

spense *n.* store-room 1365.

sperd *pp. adj.* shut up 193.

spete *n.* sharp point 1397.

spetously *adv.* shamefully 27.

spetows *adj.* shameful 2052.

spew *v.* vomit 1175.

sportaunce *n.* entertainment 141.

spot *n.* blot, disgrace 2052, 3101.

spousebreche *n.* adultery 1195, W 755.

spoyll *imp.* divest W 1136.

sprynge *n.* a lively dance W 747.

sprynge *v.* arise 886, 3123, W 1028, 1158, break out 1785, flow out 3067, grow up W 92, originate W. 124, leap W 561, 615; **spronge** *pt. 3 pl.* W 124; *pt. subj.* 886; *pp.* spread 681.

spud *n.* knife 1399.

spyll(e) *v. tr.* destroy 26*, 27, 2558, W 526, 713, M 893, shed 1092*, spill 2328; *intr.* be damned W 215, be destroyed W 292; **spylt** *pp.* 27, 450, 1314.

spynne *v.* move rapidly 1397; **spunne** *pp.* spun, wrought 2617.

sp(y)ryt *n.* soul 117, 121; *vytall* ~ breath of life M 812.

stage *n.* raised platform 784.

stakyr *v.* reel 961.

stale *v.* ? come to a stand 961.

stall(e) *n.* stable 147, 2749; *be strete* (*steppe*) *and* ~ by every place 316, 2896.

starke *adj.* sturdy M 368.

starre *v.* glare W 739; **staryste** *pr. 2 sg.* stare 934*.

stat(e) *n.* proper condition 1303, 1626, high position 3450, rank, class 3615, spiritual condition W 880.

statt *n.* term of contempt for a woman M 729.

staunche *adj.* firm 961.

stede *n.*: *stand in* ~ avail, be of service 776, 2619, 2947.

steke *v.* shut up 749.

stekyd *pp. adj.* slit in the throat 1108.

stele, stell *v.* carry off 1881, steal M 127, 594; **stale** *pt. 1, 3 sg.* M 127, 596; **stown** *pp.* has stolen M 594.

steppe *n.* step 2896, W 1044; *pl.* footsteps M 290; see **stall(e)**.

sterre *n.* star W 29; *vndyr* ~ under the sky 1904.

ster(r)e *v.* incite 1331, W 527, 1046; **steryste** *pr. 2 sg.* move, stir 934*.

sterue *v.* die 874, 2735, M 637.

sterynge *n.* prompting W 153, impulse W 304.

steuene *n.* cry, petition 2773.

stewerde *n.* recorder at a manor court M 670.

stew(y)s *n. pl.* brothels W 749, 800.

stodye *v.* be perplexed 292, 376.

stodyes *n. pl.* meditations W 470.

stoff, stuff *n.* furnishings M 634, 723.

stol(e) *n.* seat 1035, 1039, stool 2598; see **pynyngys**.

stomlynge *adj.* tripping up 1039.

stond(e), stande *v.* stand 8, 3626, M 29, 218, stand still 283, 2127, remain 298, 352, W 289, M 543, be of force 1531, W 678, stand firm 2148, W 172, 317, be fixed W 220; ~ *3ou at hert* concern you deeply 801; *yt stoude you on hande* it would behove you M 686; **stondyt(h)** *pr. 3 sg.* 801, W 220, **standyth** 776; **stonde** *pl.* 8, M 29, **stande** W 678; **stod** *pt. 3 sg.* 2127; **stode** *pl.* 352; **stod** *pt. subj.* 2947, **stoude** M 686; **stondynge** *pr. p.* W 172; see **stede**.

stonge *pt. 3 sg.* pierced 3359.

stoppyt *pr. 3 sg.* blocks legal action W 862.

store *n.* treasure 1427, 1451, possessions 2710; *in* ~ saved up W 1003.

store *v.* supply 837, restore 1868; **storyde** *pp.* provided M 484.

stounde *n.* moment 703, 2912; *styf in* ~ strong in attack 1836; *upon* ~ in a moment 960.

stout(e) *adj.* fierce 28, 1842, sturdy M 482; *adv.* resolutely 2148.

stow *interj.* ho! M 729.

stown see **stele**.

strayen *pr. 3 pl.* roam about 2051;
  strayed *pt. 3 sg.* 2305.
stresse *n.* hardship 1579; *in* ~ by
  force 3436.
strete *n.* road, street 353, 2051;
  see stall(e), stronde, stye, style.
streyne *v.* restrain 3436.
streyt(t) *adj.* strict W 729, M 42*,
  841; streight *adv.* close-fistedly
  W 584*.
streytly *adv.* strictly W 1033.
stronde *n.* shore: *be strete and* ~ in
  every place 537, 601, 628.
stroyed *pp. adj.* destroyed 207.
stryf, stryve *n.* toil 2972, conflict
  3171; *in* ~ in trouble 1621*, 1909.
stryke *v.* go 1904.
stryue *v.* contend 2581, W 661;
  strywyth *pr. 3 sg.* 64; stryvande
  pr. p. quarrelling W 779.
stuffe *v.* supply 1427.
sturdynes *n.* stubbornness W 693.
stye *n.* path: *be strete and* ~, *be
  and strete* everywhere 353, 363, 591.
styf(fe) *adj.* stalwart 1836, 1842,
  powerful 2111.
styfly *adv.* steadfastly 2011, 2041.
style *n.* stile: *be strete and* ~ by every
  way 403.
stylle *adj.* silent 2129, 3204.
styll(e) *adv.* continually 1696, 3310,
  motionless 345, 1697, M 638, 661,
  quietly 272, 1213, 1223.
stynt *v.* stop 960.
styrt(e) *v.* leap 960, escape 3355.
stytelerys *n. pl.* marshals p. 1.
suavius *adj.* sweet M 871.
subsyde *n.* help M 394.
suffre, suffyr *v. intr.* submit patiently
  1072, 1074, W 1019; *tr.* submit
  patiently to 2133, 2268, W 1013;
  suffyryth *pr. 3 sg.* W 1019;
  sufferyst *pt. 2 sg.* 3549; sufferyd
  3 sg. 2133.
suffycyens *n.* sustenance M 738.
suggestyon *n.* temptation W 301,
  365, proposal W 400, 497.
sumtyme *adv.* now and then 1649,
  1650, W 425, formerly W 516, 588.
sumwhat *pron.* something 1647; *adv.*
  somewhat M 96, 810.
sundyr *adj.*: *on* ~ asunder 2624.

sunne, son *n.* sun 1308, 2621, W 1156.
superatt *adj.* conquered M 313.
support *v.* maintain, uphold W
  635.
supportacyon *n.* assistance M 212.
sure *adv.* assuredly W 50.
sut(e) *n.* livery W 692 s.d., 724 s.d.;
  in ~ in the same dress W 324 s.d.,
  752 s.d.
swart *n.* swarthy person 2210.
swemyth *pr. 3 sg.* grieves M 875.
swet, swot *n.* sweating 1215, 1224.
swet(e) *adj.* beloved 251, W 70,
  1066, M 290, pleasant in taste 365,
  lovely 1020, M 645, precious 1266,
  1385, gracious 1312, 2047, fragrant
  2145, 2213, W 92, pleasant in
  sound W 758; ~ *herte* beloved
  W 1103; swet(t)er *compar.* 772,
  799, W 388, M 225.
swote *adj.* precious 1399, gracious
  2056.
s(w)ych(e), such(e) *adj.* such, of
  that kind 480, 1237, W 304, 848,
  M 684, 831; *non* ~ no similar
  M 37; ~ *another* another similar
  M 363; ~ *as* ... ~ *as* ... so M 180;
  ~ *to* two of that kind 310; swheche
  pron. matters of that kind M 891.
swyn(e) *n.* hog 1108, W 831.
swyre *n.* neck W 1102.
swythe *adv.* immediately 434, 624.
sy see se(ne).
syd(e) *n.* position to right or left 303,
  3626, W 36, 1064 s.d., side of the
  body 1085, M 714; *on* ~ aside 163,
  231, W 565.
syde *adj.* long W 16 s.d., 510, M
  671.
sye *v.* sigh 449, 1404*, 1866; syest *pr.
  2 sg.* 1299; syh *3 pl.* 1390.
syinge *n.* sighing 1308.
syke *n.* small stream 425.
syke *v.* see seke.
sylfe *n.*: *þe* ~ itself M 838.
symple *sb.* humble persons W 457.
syn see sen.
syne *n.* sign W 471.
synge, syngyn *v. tr.* sing 879, 2335;
  intr. W 613, 751, M 334; syngyth
  pr. 3 sg. W 996 s.d.; songe *pp.*
  880, songyn W 996 s.d.

sy(n)gnyficacyon *n.* meaning W 13, 182.

syng(u)ler *adj.* unusual W 441, 452, special W 574, M 823, 871.

synne-quenchand *adj.* extinguishing sin 3603.

sypres *n.* cloth of gold W 1 s.d.

syr(e), ser *n.* sir 764, 2327, W 397, 604, M 48, 66, father 2114.

syt(h), syght(e) *n.* the act of seeing p. 1, 1240, appearance 584, 984, thing to see 1940, W 573, power of vision W 68, 992, M 531, perception by seeing W 118, spiritual insight W 1086.

syth *v.* sigh M 201.

syth(e), seth *conj.* seeing that W 107, 952, M 518, 899, from the time that 1141, 2416, W 680.

sythen, sethen *conj.* from the time that 718, M 272, seeing that 721, M 449, after the time that M 415; *adv.* afterwards 2796, M 274.

sythynge *n.* sighing M 738.

syt(te), syttyn *v.* sit 196, 369, M 29, 315; **syttyth** *pr. 3 sg.* 249, **syt(t)** 783, 1656; **sytt** *2 pl.* M 29; **syttyn** *3 pl.* 2651; **sit** *imp. sg.* 834; **syth** *pl.* 492, **syttyth** 163.

sytyca *n.* sciatica M 498.

tafata *n.* glossy silk 239.

tak *n.*[1] spot 2177.

tak *n.*[2] endurance 2986.

tak(e), takyn *v.* take refuge in 53, take possession of 97, 1258, undergo 201, receive 295, 3329, W 1079, M 113, accept 389, 2623, W 221, 483, M 185, proceed to use 1037, M 366, 570, entrust 1082, take as nourishment 1616, 2262, feel 1640, M 357, carry 2179, M 674, derive W 111, marry W 476, give M 52, seize M 495, 716, take as companion M 503, catch M 519, 851; *refl.* commit oneself 380, 1691; ~ *example* learn 2995, 3643; ~ *hede* pay attention 1213, M 686, 803; ~ *to spowse* accept as husband W 57; ~ *venjaunce* inflict vengeance 1097, 1113, W 765, 1025; **takyst** *pr. 2 sg.* 2623; **takyt(h)** *3 sg.* 97, W 57,

taketh W 483; **take** *pl.* 201; *imp. sg.* 389; **takythe** *imp. pl.* 2995; **tok** *pt. 1 sg.* 295; **toke** *2 sg.* 3083; *3 sg.* 2179; **takande** *pr. p.* 144, **takynge** W 111; **tan** *pp.* 53, 3329, **take** 1258, W 221, M 519, **takyn** M 185; see **kepe, leve, þout(h)**.

takyllys *n. pl.* weapons M 785.

tale, tayll *n.* speech 654, 3008, reckoning M 462; *holde no* ~ care nothing 2818; *tellyn talys* spread stories 684, 1743, 1749; see **geue**.

tappyn *v.* strike 2110.

tapster *n.* woman keeper of an alehouse M 274, 729.

tapytys *n. pl.* tapestries 239.

targe *n.* shield 2155.

tary *v.* delay W 872, M 864, remain M 151, 525; **tarythe** *pr. 3 sg.* W 872; **taryed** *pp.* 2351.

taste *n.* liking 1640.

tayll *n.* shape, cut M 697.

teche, techyn *v.* teach 20, 1670, W 86, 314, M 419, give 366, guide 549; *absol.* give instruction 515; **techyth** *pr. 3 sg.* 20; **tawt** *pt. 2 sg.* W 314; **tawt(h)** *pp.* 366, 515, **taught** M 419; see **less(o)un**.

te(e) *v.* go 1561, 1916.

tell(e), tellyn *v. tr.* declare 543, 2904, W 626, M 97, 184, inform 2512, 2930, speak 3035, express in words W 62, 64, count W 583; *intr.* declare W 270; *here* ~ hear it said 1537, 3202, M 137, 222; **tellyth** *pr. 3 sg.* 684; **telle** *pl.* 2512, **tellys** W 270*; **told(e)** *pp.* 2904, W 64; see **tale**.

tende *v.* listen to W 355.

tender *adj.*: ~ *of age* young W 890.

tender *v.* value W 461.

tenderschyppe *n.* esteem W 631.

tene *n.* grief 331, 2633, pain 1773, 2292, anger 1899.

tene, tenyn *v.* harm 223, 253, vex 670; **tenynge** *pr. p.* 2890.

teneful *adj.* grievous 1754, painful 2602.

tenker *n.* tinker W 752.

tenowr *n.* tenor part W 617.

tente *v.* pay attention 1353.

ter *n.* tar 3078.

terage *n.* land, soil 2707.
tere *v.* rend 1877, 2155; **torn(e)** *pp.* 109, M 4, **tore** 2602.
tey(e) *v.* bind 1773, 2292.
th- see þ-.
to *prep.* to 19, 31, W 4, 71, so as to cause 24, in order to 32, W 19, till 143, for 582, W 6, 57, M 59, 914, into 2194; *elliptical* go to 121, 2508, 3037; see **for, go(ne), myth.**
to *adv.* too 1350, 3060, W 87, 482, M 96, 241.
to-banne *v.* curse thoroughly M 249.
to-begyle *v.* deceive thoroughly W 376.
to-beton *pp.* beaten soundly M 422.
to-dayschyd *pp.* shattered in pieces 2399.
to-gloryede *pp.* puffed up greatly M 773.
tokenynge *n.* sign 1396, meaning 1670.
tolde *pp. adj.*¹ taken toll of M 671.
tolde *pp. adj.*² counted out M 672.
tol(e) *n.* tool, instrument 1037, 2602.
tollyth *pr. 3 sg.* entices 85.
to-morn *adv.* tomorrow M 276*, 727.
ton *pron.*: þe ~ the one (of two) 21, 302, M 466; *adj.* one 2610.
too *n.* toe 611, 1985; see **top(pe).**
to(o) *num.* two 18, 1800, W 718, M 464.
top(pe) *n.* head: *fro ~ to þe too* from head to foot 611, 1985; *~ and tayl* all over the body 2383.
to-rase *v.* cut to pieces 1943.
tord *n.* turd 2226; **tordys, turdys** *pl.* 2651, M 132.
torne, turne *v.* change 1401, 1436, W 874, 1047, turn over M 361; *~ to* result in 3172; **turnyt(h)** *pr. 3 sg.* W 281, M 749.
to-schende *v.* destroy utterly 978; **to-schent** *pp.* 3345.
to-supporte *n.* giving backing to (a litigant) W 796.
tottys *n. pl.* devils 2879.
toþyr *pron.*: þe ~ the other (of two) 21, 313, 2610, M 466.
town(e) *n.* town 8, 177, village M 362; *castel ~* castle enclosure 2015, 2157.

towte *n.* rump 2289.
trace, trasche, trase *n.* course 1922, 3410, series of steps in dancing W 717, 746, M 93, music for a dance M 72.
trace *v.* dance M 95; **tracyed** *pp.* M 96.
tramposyde *pp. adj.* transformed W 1001.
trappyd *pt. 2 sg.* entrapped 2098; *pp.* 3045, M 855.
trat *n.* hag 1578.
trauest *n.* opposition 3523.
tre *n.* cross 1325, 2277, wood W 1059, gallows M 802, 803; see **dry(e).**
trebelen *v.* make a shrill sound 899.
trebull *n.* treble part W 619.
trecchyn *v.* deceive 253.
trem(b)le, trymbull *v.* tremble W 898, 903; **trymmelyth** *pr. 3 sg.* M 734; see **trotte.**
trepett *n.* tripping up M 113.
trespas(e) *n.* sins 1456, 3280, W 1080; see **do(ne).**
trew(e), tru *adj.* faithful 539, 563, truthful 882, 2714, reliable 2985, 3178, W 430, honest W 736, M 715, genuine W 1156; *sb.* the true God W 385; *adv.* faithfully 243, rightly M 245.
trewthe, truthe *n.* solemn promise 609, 827, truthfulness 3143, 3190, true doctrine W 314, honesty W 565, 724; *in ~* indeed W 869; see **do(ne).**
trone *n.* throne 317, 457.
trost, trust *n.* confident expectation 222, 3278, M 854, confidence 398, M 750.
trost *adj.* faithful 475, safe 2707.
trost, trust(e) *v. intr.* rely 524, M 600, have confidence W 824, 985, M 190, 208; *tr.* rely on W 488; **trustynge** *pr. p.* W 985.
trostyly *adv.* faithfully 631.
trotte *v.*: *~ and tremle* move quickly to and fro 457.
trow(e) *v.* believe, think 252, 401, W 621, 645, M 98, 251.
trowthe *n.* honesty W 654, truthfulness M 841; *be my ~* in good faith W 493.

trumpe *n.* trumpet 1898, W 702, M 175, trumpeter W 692 s.d.

trumpe *v.*: ~ *up* sound the trumpet 156, 574 s.d.

trussyd *pp. adj.* packed 1634.

try(e) *adj.* tried, tested 475, choice 552, 1181, good W 641; *good and* ~ excellent 355, 532.

trye *n.* attempt W 861; **trieth** *pr. 3 sg.* tests M 287, **tryith** proves M 838; **triede** *pp.* M 288.

tryse *v.* snatch M 477, 491; **trysyde** *pp.* M 575.

tryst *v.* trust 1680, 1686.

tweyn(e) *adj.* two 3212, 3214, W 135, 1073, M 196.

twychyde *pp.* jerked M 615.

tyde *n.* time 233, 253, W 317, M 525; *euery* ~ always 1087; ~ *nor tyme* season or time 2455.

tydynge *n.* news 1797, 3121; *pl.* 1753, M 722.

tyght(e), tyth *adv.* quickly M 157; *a(l)s, so* ~ immediately 3587, W 742, 855.

tyle *v.* obtain 2537.

tyl(l) *conj.* to the time that 99, 169, W 380, so that at length 1052, W 847, 1043, M 73, 246; ~ *þat* to the time that 723; **tyl(le)** *prep.* to 3207, 3526, W 997, 1053, until M 864.

tyllynge *n.* cultivating M 363, 548.

tyllyth *pr. 3 sg.* attracts 1032.

tymbyr *v.* build 239.

tyne *v.* lose 3197.

tyre *n.* accoutrements 223, head-dress 2110.

tys *phr.* it is M 828.

tysche *interj.* tush! M 790.

tysyd *pp.* enticed 536.

tytly *adv.* quickly 223.

tytyll *v.*¹ write down M 315.

tytyll *v.*² whisper M 557.

þan(ne), þen *adv.* then 28, 41, W 113, 119, M 74, 175; *be* ~ by the time that M 535; *her* ~ before M 899.

þat *dem. pron.* that 853, 880, W 82, 141, M 776, 884; *dem. adj.* that 556, 560, W 72, 267, M 12, 695;

rel. pron. who 2, 5, W 3, 48, M 11, 15, that which 59, 864, W 504, 662, M 141, 185, which 295, W 34, 89, M 394, he that 1279; *conj.* that 42, 108, W 59, seeing that 46, 56, so that 344, 542, W 945, M 16, 20; *so* ~ provided 569, 601, so that W 856; ~ *if* provided 84; see **haue, wyth.**

þe *def. art.* the 3, 6, etc.

þe *adv.* (with *compar.*) by so much 236, 754; *þe . . þe* by how much . . . by so much 91, 94, W 97, 797, M 261; see **wers.**

þe *pers. pron.* thyself 331, 436, W 917, M 560, 603, thee 366, 453, W 309, 323, M 140, 434.

þe, the(n) *v.* thrive 3104, W 866, M 304, 376.

thedom *n.* prosperity 2478.

þedyr *adv.* thither 1561, 1923, W 199, 732; see **hedyr.**

þedyrward *adv.* towards that place 135.

þei, þey, thay *pron.* they 30, 46, W 53, 878, M 26, 174.

þem *pron.* those (who, whom) W 810, 939, them W 811, M 95, 299.

þende *adj.* prosperous 788, 2659.

þer, there *poss. adj.* their W 48, M 167.

þerageyn *adv.* against that W 661.

þeratt *adv.* at it M 81.

þerby *adv.* because of that W 845.

þer(e), thore *adv.* there 55, 109, W 107, 650, M 276, where 356, 1547, W 667, 805, M 248, 688, to that place W 329, in that respect W 413; (expletive, introducing a wish) 145, 149.

þeretylle *adv.* to that 2562.

þerfor(e) *adv.* for that reason 123, 183, W 13, 222, M 67, 79, for that M 99.

þerfro *adv.* from that 3080.

þerin(ne) *adv.* in that 1439, 2899, W 302, 308, M 557.

þerof *adv.* of that 2096, 2949, W 50, M 171, 672.

þeron *adv.* on that 390, W 889, M 247.

þerto *adv.* to that 597, 1121, W 299, 499, M 794.

þerwyth *adv.* with that 2728, 2729.

þerwppon *adv.* about that W 450, over that W 724 s.d.

þis *dem. pron,* this 3501, W 18, 38, M 58, 84, **hym þis** (emphatic) 2348; **þese** *pl.* 466, 3476, **thes** W 402, 574, **thys** W 866, **these** M 888; *dem. adj.* this 6, 9, W 13, 166, M 44, 48; **þese** *pl.* 132, 179, **þis** 1775, W 721, **þes** W 488, M 163, **thes** W 709, **þeis** M 852, (with collective *n.*) W 706, 709.

þis, thys *adv.* in this way W 289, 812, to this extent W 932, 978.

þo, thow *dem. pron.* those 656, W 163, 686; *dem. adj.* those 308, 463.

þorwe, thorow *prep.* by means of 43, 3140, W 311, M 282, throughout 160, 224, W 760; *adv.* from beginning to end M 500.

thost *n.* turd 1064, 2412.

þou *pron.* thou 333, 339, W 310, 321, M 76, 140.

þou, though *conj.* though 241, 246, W 75, M 155.

þout(h), thought *n.* anxiety 292, 322, 2029, attention 577, 713, faculty of thinking 1510, W 236, what one thinks 1644, W 218; *take no ~* feel no anxiety W 624, 660, take no heed M 174.

þout see þynke *v.*[1]

thraldam *n.* bondage M 743.

þrall *adj.* servile 3358.

thre-fotyd *adj.* with three legs 2598.

thre-mens *n. phr.*: *~ songys* part songs for three men 2335.

þrowe *n.* space of time 397, 421, moment 1236, 2809; *many a ~* many times 1474.

þryfte *n.* prosperity 1344, 2478, W 644, acquired wealth 2911.

þryst *pt. 3 pl.* thrust 3555.

þryue *v.* prosper 387, 2380, W 662, M 382; **thryvande** *pr. p.* W 778.

thwyte *v.* whittle 1648.

þycke *adj.* abundant 309, 2182.

þynke *v.*[1] take thought 387, consider 409, 1226, W 195, M 279, intend 697, believe M 598; *~ on* reflect on 407, 715, M 258, 865; **þynkyth** *pr. 3 sg.* 1317; **þynkyn** *pl.* 1226,

thynke expect M 847; **thenke** *pr. subj. 2 sg.* 409; **thynkynge** *pr. p.* W 195; **þout** *pp.* supposed 2979.

þynke *v.*[2] seem 1583; *me þynkyth* it seems to me 2766, 2768; *me þynkyth it* I consider it 3157.

thyrlyth *pr. 3 sg.* pierces M 558.

vnabylythe *pr. 3 sg.* unfits W 893.

vnderne *n.* ? afternoon 138.

vndirstonde *v.* believe 535.

vndo *v.* ruin 1129; **vndone** *pp.* 1220, **ondon** M 416, **wndon** opened M 797.

vndyr, wndyr *prep.* under 221, 241, W 379, 912 s.d., M 193, 206.

vndyrfonge *pr. subj. 2 sg.* receive 884.

vnhende *adj.* unfitting 2029.

vnkynde, onkynde *adj.* ungrateful 1501, 3601, M 280, 742, uncharitable 3479, wicked W 905.

vnnethe *adv.* scarcely 3295.

vnquert *adj.* wicked 3353.

vnsayd *adj.* not spoken 689.

vnslye *adj.* unwise 2780.

vnstabullnes *n.* unsteadiness W 199*.

vnthende *adj.* feeble 287, 2485, unprosperous 507, unhealthy 1229, 2261.

vnthryfte *n.* dissoluteness 1218.

vnwolde *adj.* infirm 2486.

up *prep.* upon: *~ my powere* according to my power 1500.

upon *prep.* upon 667, W 1042, M 608.

up(pe) *adv.* up, upward 614, 831, W 669, M 31, 361.

vre *n.* habit 3442, 3628.

vsance *n.* habitual use W 655, method of use W 1027.

vse, owse *n.* function 770, 946, consumption M 237.

vse *v.* observe 1057, practise 1196, 1222, W 434, 637, use W 146; **vsyste** *pr. 2 sg.* carry on 849; **vsande** *pr. p.* customary W 681; **vsyde** *pp.* accustomed W 684.

vale *n.* valley, low place 3010.

vane see wane.

varyant *adj.* changeable M 281.

varya(u)nce *n.* dispute 76; *wythowt* ~ without question W 789.

vaunce *v.* lift up 1701.

vaunward, vaward *n.* vanguard 2060, 2191.

vayle *n.* benefit 86.

velony *n.* disgrace 2233.

vemynousse *adj.* venomous M 40.

ven *imp.* come M 426, 433.

verefyede *pp.* proved true M 9, 707.

ver(r)ay, very, wery *adj.* true 3367, W 15, 127, M 1, 210; *adv.* extremely M 535, 587.

vertu, wertu *n.* goodness 1556, 1896, W 378, 382, M 221, 867, a particular moral quality 1691, 1701, W 288, 1036, power 3140.

veryly, werely *adv.* truly W 57, 64, 546.

veyn, weyn *adj.* worthless W 195, M 853.

veynglory(e) *n.* undue pride 465, 745.

victoryall *adj.* of victory W 1115.

vowe, wou *v.* swear an oath 2249, 2255, W 625.

voys *n.* cry 3350.

vyle, wyle *adj.* vile 1816, M 819.

vyolence *n.* violation W 108, violence W 1043.

vyre *n.* bolt for a cross-bow 2112.

vyseryde *pp. adj.* masked W 724 s.d.

vysurs *n. pl.* masks W 752 s.d.

vysytacyon *n.* heavy affliction M 288, 736.

w- see also **u-**, **v-**.

wage *n.* payment 931, 2499.

wagge *v.* set in motion 1942.

wake *v.* be awake 1679, be stirred up W 223, stay awake for devotion W 433, 1021.

wakynge *n.* staying awake for devotion W 1026.

wall *v.* flow 3360.

walle *n.* wall 729, 2030.

waltyr *v.* float to and fro 2662.

wan *n.* ? woe W 346.

wane, vane *adj.* lacking 2075, M 540, absent M 419.

wan(ne) see w(h)an(ne).

wanton *adj.* unrestrained M 181, 757.

wappyd *pp. adj.* wrapped 1209.

wappyn *v.* strike 2837.

warder *n.* staff W 692 s.d.

ware *n.* goods 925.

war(e) *adj.* careful: *be* ~ be careful 2616, M 109, 171; *be* ~ *of* be on guard against 2004, 2339, W 293, M 895, be careful of 2700, W 291, M 79.

war(e) *imp.* look out! 2235, 2326, W 773; *tr.* look out for W 604.

warne see werne *v.*1

wasche *v.* plunge 1921, cleanse (the soul) 3395, W 125; waschyt(h) *pr. 3 sg.* 1383, W 964; waschede *pp.* W 1069, wesch 3395.

waschynge-well *n.* fountain of spiritual cleansing, 3145.

wat see w(h)at.

wave *v. intr.* waver 379, toss to and fro 2662, turn aside 3051; *tr.* cause to toss to and fro 2002.

wawe *v.* move, go 210.

waxyn *v.* grow, become 2482, 2484; waxit *pr. 3 sg.* 418, 2491; waxyn *pl.* 2848; *pp.* 2449.

waytyth *pr. 3 sg.* lies in wait for 1652.

weche, wyche *interr. pron.* which 383; *rel. pron.* 1512, W 178, 932, M 41; *rel. adj.* W 5, 124.

wede *n.* clothing 585, 1209, W 454.

weder, wedyr see w(h)edyr, wheþyr.

wedys *n. pl.* weeds W 91.

welde, wold *v.* possess 2906, use 742; *refl.* manage 1962, 2528.

wel(e) *n.* well-being 742, 1407, well-doing 3276.

wel(e), well *adj.* satisfied 1163, fortunate 1191, 2775; *adv.* thoroughly 54, 244, M 520, prosperously 148, 371, M 94, 470, clearly 297, 327, W 399, 440, M 499, 548, fittingly 610, 880, M 102, 721, heartily 1161, W 829, M 101, 246, with good reason 1353, 2636, uprightly W 877, M 110, 232; ~ *in age* advanced in years 2701; see do(ne), fare, go(ne).

weleaway *interj.* alas! 1264, 3069, alas for 3020.

wel(e)awo(o) *interj.* alas! 1260, 2217, 3034.

well(e) *n.* fountain 2302, 3067, M 221.

welle *v.* boil 3593.

wel(l)fare *n.* well-being W 625, good cheer W 735.

wel-ny *adv.* almost entirely 1285.

welthe *n.* riches 699, 3288, spiritual welfare 3637.

weltyr *v.* cause to roll 2002.

wen see w(h)an(ne).

wende, wendyn *v.* go 277, 942, W 531; went *pt. subj.* 242, M 148; *pp.* 31, 1661.

wene *v.* think 229, 322, M 540, 791, expect 545, 3424, W 57; wenyth *pr. 3 sg.* 545; wende *pt. 3 sg.* 3424.

wenne, wynne *n.* joy 204, 2725.

werd, werdly see werld, werldyly.

wer(e) see wer(r)e, w(h)er(e).

were *v.*[1] wear 476.

were *v.*[2] defend 2045; *refl.* 1728.

werely see veryly.

werke *n.* action 203, 264, W 250, creation M 224, deed, business M 547; *goode werkys* acts of piety 1231, M 25.

werke, wirke *v. tr.* cause 203, M 601, commit 1508, do 2190, 2196, create 3405, W 20, 251, M 413; *intr.* act 2424, 2885, W 953, M 11, 875; *lett Gode* ~ leave the rest to God M 546; werkyst *pr. 2 sg.* W 923; werkyn *3 pl.* 2264; werke *imp.* 2190, wyrke 2424; wrout(h) *pt. 3 sg.* 3276, 3405, wrought W 251, *pl.* 953; wrowth *pp.* 1508, wrowte W 20, wrought W 922, M 11, wroght M 875.

werld, werd, world(e), word *n.* earthly life 16, 288, W 464, 625, M 909, temporal affairs 29, 85, W 442, 486, M 885, the earth 184, 509, M 797, people on earth W 657, 660, M 742; werld(l)ys *g. sg.* 508, 835; *al þe (þis)* ~ the whole earth 157, 165, all the people on earth 229, W 670.

werldyly, werdly, wor(l)dly *adj.*

worldly 180, 1551, W 1009, earthly 824; *adv.* in worldly manner W 405.

werne, warne *v.*[1] forbid 184, 2141, stop 2829.

werne *v.*[2] defend 3080.

werne *v.*[3] command M 523.

wer(r)e *n.* battle 211, 1900, contention 3171, 3531.

wers *adj.* more wicked M 165, 171; *þe* ~ the less well off 858.

wers *adv.* less well 2161, 2170, W 809, M 484.

wery *adj.* weary M 275.

wery *v.* grow weary W 843.

wesant *n.* throat M 810.

wet(e) *adj.* moist (with tears) 1407, dripping (with blood) 2202.

wet(e), wetyn, wytte *v.* know 104, 375, W 440, M 595, be informed (of) 656, 1844, W 1, find out W 852; wot *pr. 1 sg.* 104, 110; wost(e) *2 sg.* 2084, 3316; wot(t) *3 sg.* 2939, W 560; wytte *2 pl.* 1021; wetyn *pr. subj. 2 pl.* 656; wyst(e) *pt. 1 sg.* 2717, M 685.

wethere see w(h)edyr.

wey *adv.* see do(ne).

weydyr see wheþyr.

wey(e), way *n.* road 693, 771, W 644, 652, journey 1585, manner 2007, way out M 159, device M 301, 762, habits W 874, M 106; *a deull* ~ in the devil's name M 158, 521; *go yowr* ~ go away W 509, M 266, 521; *Sent Patrykes* ~ the road to purgatory M 614.

weyen *v.* measure 925, weigh down 2628, M 699, balance 3187; weys *pr. 3 sg.* M 699.

weye-went *n.* ? pathway 158.

weyng *n.* wing M 790.

weytys see wyt.

w(h)an(ne), w(h)en *conj.* 21, 53, W 115, 310, M 62, 127; *interr. adv.* at what time M 632.

w(h)at *interr. pron.* what 1010, 1338, W 73, 78, M 203, 367, who 2926; *interr. adj.* what kind of W 190, 420, M 625; *rel. adj.* whatever 189, 200, W 217; *adv.* why 406, 606, how much 1568; *interj.* what! 1298, 1337, M 351, 640; ~ *a deull*

w(h)at (*cont.*)
why the devil M 654; ~ *deuyl* how
the devil 858, what the devil 1572,
M 623, why the devil 2431; ~ *how*
ho! M 694, 726.

whatso *rel. pron.* whatever 820, 1335.

w(h)edyr, wethere *interr. adv* to
what place 323, 790, M 504, 518,
in what place M 567; *rel. adv.* to
whatever place W 525.

w(h)er(e) *interr. adv.* in what place
1533, M 430, 502; *conj.* where 162,
226, W 305, M 836, wherever 1125,
1947, W 586; ~ *þat* wherever 591,
2667, W 46.

whereabowte, whereabowtyn
interr. adv. about what 2187, 2366.

whereof *interr. adv.* of what 384;
rel. adv. by which W 194.

whereso *rel. adv.* wherever 615, 876.

w(h)ereto *interr. adv.* for what purpose 288; *rel. adv.* to which W 344.

w(h)erfor(e) *adv.* wherefore W 323,
336, M 892.

wheþyr, we(y)dyr *pron.* which (of
two) 3188; *conj.* whether 281;
wheþyr . . . or whether . . . or 26,
wheydyr 2927, **wheyþyr** 3276.

w(h)o, whose, w(h)om *interr. pron.*
who 104, W 601, M 33, 138; *rel.
pron.* whoever W 50, 57, if any one
W 839*; *I wot not (neuere)* ~ some
person unknown 104, 2968.

who(o), whow see **whop(p)e, wo.**

whop(p)e *interj.*: ~ *who(o), whow*
hurrah! M 607, 720, 733.

w(h)oso *rel. pron.* whoever 192, 264,
W 412; **whomso** *obj.* 2795.

whosummeuer *rel. pron.* whoever
M 564.

whou, whow(e) *adv.* to what degree
287, in what way 1960; *interr. adv.*
how, in what way 16, 738, 1337,
W 763, 891.

whowso *adv.* however 1123, 3321.

whwtynge *n.* shouting 1938.

w(h)y *interr. adv.* for what reason 350,
1011, W 108, M 53, 428; *cause* ~ the
reason for that W 432; *sb.* cause 843.

whyl, wyll, qwyll *conj.* as long as
602, 608, W 543, 660, M 77, 543,
during the time that M 259, 419.

whyle, wyll *n.* length of time 405,
1577, M 472, 581; *þe* ~ the unlucky
time 3020, M 414; see **fayr(e).**

whylys *conj.* as long as 2528.

whylyst *conj.* during the time that
3054.

whyt, wyght, wyth *adj.* white 716,
1848, W 16 s.d., 151.

whytt *n.* bit 359, **qwytt** M 483*.

wndyrstondynge *n.* intellect W 180,
245, M 58.

wndyrtake *v.* venture: *I* ~ I venture
to say W 976, M 793.

wnlusty *adj.* dull M 545.

wo see **w(h)o, wo(o).**

wo, who(o) *adv.* wofully: ~ *ys hym*
it is sad for him W 347, 784; ~ *ys
me* I am sad M 748; see **worthe.**

wold see **welde, wyl(l).**

wolde *n.* ground 824.

woman *n.* woman W 573, M 848,
851; **wom(m)en, wymmen** *pl.*
2293, 2649, W 752 s.d., M 667.

wombe *n.* womb 3332, belly M 36.

wonde *n.*¹ rod 603.

wond(e) *n.*² wound 2202, M 247,
857.

wonde, wondyn *pp.* see **wo(u)nde.**

wondyr *adj.* extremely 325, 906,
W 616, M 567.

wondyrly *adj.* marvellous W 257.

wondyth *pr. 3 sg.* wounds M 815;
wondyde *pp.* W 1085.

wone *n.* wealth 2605.

wonne *v.* dwell 2725.

wonnynge *n.* dwelling 2549, 2906.

wonte *pp. adj.* accustomed 1444.

wonys *n. pl.* places 158, 755, dwellings 1717, 2190.

woo *n.* sorrow 95, 204.

wo(o) *adj.* sorrowful 325, 1949.

wo(o)de *n.* wood 255, 1962,
W 741.

wo(o)d(e) *adj.* mad 229, 404, W 330,
484, fierce 308, furious 920, 1883.

worchep, worschyp(p)e *n.* honour
1656, W 455, 513, M 497.

worchep *v.* adore 3506; **worchepyd**
pp. honoured 151.

wore see **be(n).**

world(e), wor(l)dly see **werld,
werldyly.**

worschypp(f)ull, worcheppyll, wyrschepyll *adj.* reverend M 129, 222, honourable M 890, 903.

worthe *v.*: ~ *wo* be cursed 2882.

wortys *n. pl.* vegetables M 272.

worþi, worthi, worthy *adj.* deserving 151, 485, M 800, 814, honourable 157, 585, W 69, virtuous 1642, 3026, merited W 935.

wo(u)nde, wondyn *pp.* wrapped 699, 1991, 2908.

wppe *adv.* stirring about W 518, on one's feet M 29, 218.

wrak(e) *n.*[1] ruin 2190, 2988.

wrake *n.*[2] pain 95, 203.

wre(c)ch(e) *n.* vile person 210, 920, W 66, M 2, 106.

wre(c)chyd *adj.* miserable 2123, 2553, M 911.

wreche *n.* vengeance 203, 3443, W 695.

wreke, wrekyn *v. tr.* avenge 748, 2135; *refl.* avenge oneself 925, 1106; *intr.* seek vengeance 2149; wreke *pp.* 748, wrokyn 2135, wroke 2875.

wrenchys *n. pl.* wiles 98, 2760.

wrethe *n.* twist 1962.

wrethe *v.* enrage 1090.

wretthe, wrath(e) *n.* wrath 210, 893, 925, W 716.

wronge *n.* wrong 61, 696, injustice 750, W 669, 725; see do(n)e.

wronge *adj.* incorrect 3062.

wronge *pp. adj.* wrenched, racked 2856.

wroth(e) *adj.* angry 870, 948, M 586.

wrought see werke.

wrye *v.* conceal W 858.

wryen *v. refl.* turn aside 1672.

wrynge, wryngyn *v.* wring (hands) 3449, pain W 614; *absol.* wring the hands 447; wryngyth *pr. 3 sg.* presses on 98.

wryt(te) *n.* scripture 360, 2167.

wulle *n.* wool 2400.

wy see w(h)y.

wy *interj.*: ~ *wyppe* why, quick W 517.

wyche see weche.

wyck(k)e *adj.* evil 1644, 2160; *sb.* wickedness 313, evil persons 2184.

wyde *adj.* spacious 157, 255.

wyd(e) *adv.* far 1198, 2448, W 549.

wyght *adj.* nimble M 76.

wyght see whyt.

wyldewode *n.* natural forest 158.

wyle see vyle.

wylfully *adv.* willingly W 230*.

wyl(l) *v.* wish to 13, 78, W 217, M 23, 231, choose to 26, W 894, desire 242, 380, M 239, 346, be willing to 3282, W 40, 102, M 88, will go W 741, M 561; *auxil.* intend to 394, 563, W 353, 491, M 327, will M 371, 840; wyl(l) *pr. 1 sg.* 394, W 353, woll W 491; wylt *2 sg.* 371, (with suffixed pron.) wytte = wilt thou 1767; wyl(l) *3 sg.* 79, W 217, wyle 2361; wyl(l) *pl.* 13, W 854, woll W 511, M 371; wold(e) *pt. 1, 3 sg.* 78, W 40, M 346; woldyst *2 sg.* 380, W 865, woldys 2321.

wyll *adv.* astray W 319.

wyll see whyl, whyle.

wyl(le) *n.* the faculty of choice 533, 1510, W 88, 213, desire 739, 3208, W 522, M 895, 897, divine purpose 3311, 3503; *at þynne owyn* ~ according to your choice 1694; *fre* ~ free choice 2560, W 290; *goode* ~ cheerful consent 273, W 999, favour M 603, 657, good intention W 468.

wyly *adj.* crafty W 341, 604.

wynke *v.* close the eyes W 894.

wynne *n.* see wenne.

wynne *v. tr.* entice 219, W 548, attain 1152, regain 1736, 1955, capture 2246, earn 3175, gain M 548; *intr.* get wealth 406, W 677, arrive 1550; wynnyth *imp. pl.* 2239; wynnande *pr. p.* W 677; wonne *pp.* 1717; see scho.

wynnynge *n.* getting wealth 862.

wynter *n.* winter M 54, 546; wyntyr *pl.* winters, years 417, 1575.

wyppe *interj.* quick! W 517, 552.

wyrre *interj.* hurry! W 552.

wyrry *n.*: *in þe* ~ worried, seized by the throat W 840.

wys *adv.* certainly 985.

wyse *n.* fashion 180, 602; *in ony* ~ in any way M 675; *on (in) no(n)* ~ in no way 846, W 116, 299; *on þis* ~ in this way 1850.

wys(e) *adj.* wise 340, 795, W 743, M 140, 250, clever M 567; *be* ~ be careful M 785, 803.
wysman *n.* wise man 515.
wystyll *n.* whistle, pipe M 452.
wyt *n.* weight (of a clock) 1942; **weytys** *pl.* scales 852.
wyte, wyth, wytyn *v.* blame 2504, 2573; ~ *it* blame it on 2647.
wyth *prep.* in the company of 30, 45, W 162, 398, M 274, 711, by 39, 61, W 224, 348, M 36, 601, with 54, 62, W 219, 260, M 14, 88, against 2581, M 211, 418; ~ *so þat* provided that 441; ~ *þat* at that instant 117; ~ *þys* with this purpose 3501.
wyth *adv.* quickly 211.
wyth(e), wythte *n.* person 184, 660, 1200; **wytys** *pl.* 157, 975; *foule* ~ wicked creature 3586.
wyt(h)ly *adv.* quickly 231, 3225.
wytholde *pp. adj.* kept as retainer 2065.
wythstonde *v.* withstand 2011.
wythsyt *v.* withstand 2593.
wyt(te) *n.* practical wisdom 184, 868, M 47, mind 795, 2856; *pl.* senses W 438; *wyttys fyue* five senses 311, 1513, W 163, 173; see **can.**
wytty *adj.* intelligent 1991.
wyttyly *adv.* cleverly M 794.
wyve *v.* marry W 663; **wywande** *pr. p.* W 783.

xall, xuld(e) see **schal(l).**

yemandry, yomandrye *n.* company of attendants W 698, yeomen M 333.

yeue, yne, ynowe see **ʒeue, ey(e), inowe.**
yrke *adj.* weary M 150, 545.

ʒa, ʒe, ya, ye *adv.* yes 150, 362, W 414, 891, M 94, 498.
ʒare *adj.* active 18.
ʒare *adv.* quickly 1977.
ʒe, ye *pron.* you (*pl.*) 135, 145, W 293, 395, M 29, 80, you (*sg.*) W 95, 98, M 47, 53.
ʒeld(e), yelde *v.* render 3619, W 391, 975, M 173, 177, pay W 194, 1146, M 817; *refl.* submit 704, 2078, M 193; ~ *up* surrender 1918, 2150; **ʒeldyth** *pr. 3 sg.* M 740; **yeldynge** *pr. p.* W 391, 975; **ʒolde** *pp.* 704, 2691.
ʒelpe, *v.* boast 2864.
ʒene, ʒone *dem. adj.* that 1552, 1772, those 1728, 1764.
ʒep *adj.* alert 18.
ʒer-day *n.* annual commemoration of death M 728.
ʒerde *n.*[1] rod 2324.
ʒerde *n.*[2] enclosure M 561.
ʒerne *adv.* quickly 1091, 1344.
ʒeue, ʒyf(e) see **ʒeue.**
ʒone see **ʒene.**
ʒonge, ʒynge *adj.* young 423, 520, 3242; *sb.* young men 2066.
ʒyfte, yiffte *n.* gift 2474, 2909, W 946; **yeftys** *pl.* W 640.
ʒys, yis, yes *adv.* yes 429, 438, W 399*, 802, M 85, 770.
ʒyt, ʒet, yit, yet *adv.* nevertheless 80, 89, W 415, 714, M 70, 276, still 754, W 342, 890, M 490, 819, hitherto 3488, by that time W 107*.

PROPER NAMES

Acaye Achaia 170.
Adam the first man 1622, W 106, 110, old man (nickname) M 83.
Almayne Germany 170.
Alyngton, Master M 514.
Amralte Admiralty court W 854.
Assarye Assyria 170.
Audre, Audry, Sent St. Audrey W 832, M 628.

Babyloyne Babylon (Cairo) 172.
Baker, Wyllyham M 509.
Belsabub(be), Beelzebub, the Devil 941, 2114.
Belyal Satan, the Devil 199, 915.
Bete Bartholomew W 759.
Bollman, Rycherde M 510.
Botysam Bottisham M 514.
Brabon Brabant 172.
Bretayne Brittany 172.
Burgoyne Burgundy 172.
Bury Bury St. Edmunds M 274.

Caluary Calvary 2087.
Cananee, Chanane Canaan 171, M 848.
Canwyke Canwick 2421.
Capadoyse Cappadocia 171.
Carlylle Carlisle 201.
Caton Cato 866.
Cauadoyse Calvados 171.
Cryst(e), Cristus Christ 12, 155, W 131, 312, M 116, 169.
Crystemes Christmas M 332.

Dauid(e) David 2984, 3468, M 397.
Dauy, Sent St. David M 809.
Deny, Sent St. Dennis M 487.

Ely Ely W 832.

Flaundrys Flanders 175, 224.
Flepergebet, Flypyrgebet, a name for Bakbyter 775, 1724, 1733.
Frauns France 175, 1553, W 516, 767, M 597.
Freslonde Friesland 175, 224.
Fullburn Fulbourn M 511.
Fyde, William M 503.

Gabryell, Sent the angel M 796.
Galys Galicia 173, 1742.
Gayton Gayton M 510.
Golyas Goliath 1929.
Grece Greece 173.
Gryckysch See Aegean Sea 173.
Gyle, Seynt St. Giles 2435.
Gylle Jill 1227.

Hamonde (surname) M 515.
Hauston Hauxton M 506.
Herry Harry 1227.
Holborn Holborn W 721, 731.
Huntyngton, Master, M 505.

Ingelond England 1744.

Jamys, Seynt St. James 1742.
Jenet (a form of Joan) W 834.
Jerusalem Jerusalem W 164, 165.
Jevys, Jves Jews 3136, 3554.
Jhesu, Jhesus Jesus 315, 318, W 286, 1141, M 10, 116.
Job Job M 286.
Jofferey, Jaffrey Geoffrey 1227, M 160.
Jone Joan 1227.

Kent Kent 201.

Lucyfe(e)r Lucifer 2095, W 324 s.d., 334.

Madam Regent name of a dance W 707.
Maria Mary of Bethany W 414.
Marschalsi court of the knight-marshal in London W 853.
Mary(e) the Virgin 147, 1629, W 1067, M 152, 635.
Masadoyne Macedonia 174.
Massyngham Massingham M 513.
Mertha Martha W 413.
Myhel St. Michael 3617.

Normande Normandy 175.

Parys(ch) Paris 176, M 570.
Patryke, Sent St. Patrick M 614.
Patryke, Wyllyam M 513.
Petyr St. Peter 1496, by St. Peter! 1368, 2492.

Powle St. Paul 1496, 1611, W 1148; *by Sent* ~ W 487, 903; **Powlys** St. Paul's Cathedral W 794.

Pycharde (surname) M 507.

Pygmayne land of the Pigmies 176.

Pyncecras land of the Pincenarii in Thrace 176.

Qwyntyn, Sent St. Quentin M 271.

Rachell Rachel M 135, 139.

Raffe Ralph M 51.

Rodys Rhodes 178.

Rome Rome 178.

Salamone Solomon W 168, 1152.

Sare Sarah 1577.

Satan(as) Satan 196, 548.

Sauston Sawston M 505.

Soffeham Swaffham M 515.

Sysse Cicely 1577.

Tanne, Sent St. Anne M 75.

Thurlay, Wylliam M 506.

Titivillus the Devil M 301, 475.

Trage ? Thrace 177.

Trumpyngton Trumpington M 507.

Tulli Cicero M 692.

Walsyngham Walsingham M 452.

Waltom East Walton M 509.

Walys Wales 1744.

Westmyster Westminster W 789.

Woode, Master M 511.

EARLY ENGLISH TEXT SOCIETY

THE Subscription to the Society, which constitutes full membership for private members and libraries, is £3. 3s. (U.S. and Canadian members $9.00) a year for the annual publications, due in advance on the 1st of JANUARY, and should be paid by Cheque, Postal Order, or Money Order made out to 'The Early English Text Society', to Dr. A. M. Hudson, Executive Secretary, Early English Text Society, Lady Margaret Hall, Oxford.

The payment of the annual subscription is the only prerequisite of membership.

Private members of the Society (but not libraries) may select other volumes of the Society's publications instead of those for the current year. The value of texts allowed against one annual subscription is 100s. (U.S. members 110s.), and all such transactions must be made through the Executive Secretary.

Members of the Society (including institutional members) may also, through the Executive Secretary, purchase copies of past E.E.T.S. publications and reprints for their own use at a discount of 4d. in the shilling.

The Society's texts are also available to non-members at listed prices through any bookseller.

The Society's texts are published by the Oxford University Press.

The Early English Text Society was founded in 1864 by Frederick James Furnivall, with the help of Richard Morris, Walter Skeat, and others, to bring the mass of unprinted Early English literature within the reach of students and provide sound texts from which the New English Dictionary could quote. In 1867 an Extra Series was started of texts already printed but not in satisfactory or readily obtainable editions.

In 1921 the Extra Series was discontinued and all the publications of 1921 and subsequent years have since been listed and numbered as part of the Original Series. Since 1921 just over a hundred new volumes have been issued; and since 1957 alone more than a hundred and thirty volumes have been reprinted at a cost of £65,000.

In this prospectus the Original Series and Extra Series for the years 1867–1920 are amalgamated, so as to show all the publications of the Society in a single list.

From 1 April 1969, since many of the old prices had become uneconomic in modern publishing conditions, a new price structure was introduced and the new prices are shown in this list. From the same date the discount allowed to members was increased from 2d. in the shilling to 4d. in the shilling.

LIST OF PUBLICATIONS

Original Series, 1864–1969. Extra Series, 1867–1920

O.S. 1. Early English Alliterative Poems, ed. R. Morris. (*Reprinted* 1965.) 54s.   1864
      2. Arthur, ed. F. J. Furnivall. (*Reprinted* 1965.) 10s.   ,,
      3. Lauder on the Dewtie of Kyngis, &c., 1556, ed. F. Hall. (*Reprinted* 1965.) 18s.   ,,
      4. Sir Gawayne and the Green Knight, ed. R. Morris. (*Out of print, see* O.S. 210.)   ,,
      5. Hume's Orthographie and Congruitie of the Britan Tongue, ed. H. B. Wheatley. (*Reprinted* 1965.)
         18s.   1865
      6. Lancelot of the Laik, ed. W. W. Skeat. (*Reprinted* 1965.) 42s.   ,,
      7. Genesis & Exodus, ed. R. Morris. (*Out of print.*)   ,,
      8. Morte Arthure, ed. E. Brock. (*Reprinted* 1967.) 25s.   ,,
      9. Thynne on Speght's ed. of Chaucer, A.D. 1599, ed. G. Kingsley and F. J. Furnivall. (*Reprinted*
         1965.) 55s.   ,,
     10. Merlin, Part I, ed. H. B. Wheatley. (*Out of print.*)   ,,
     11. Lyndesay's Monarche, &c., ed. J. Small. Part I. (*Out of print.*)   ,,
     12. The Wright's Chaste Wife, ed. F. J. Furnivall. (*Reprinted* 1965.) 10s.   ,,
     13. Seinte Marherete, ed. O. Cockayne. (*Out of print, see* O.S. 193.)   1866
     14. King Horn, Floriz and Blauncheflur, &c., ed. J. R. Lumby, re-ed. G. H. McKnight. (*Reprinted*
         1962.) 50s.   ,,
     15. Political, Religious, and Love Poems, ed. F. J. Furnivall. (*Reprinted* 1965.) 63s.   ,,
     16. The Book of Quinte Essence, ed. F. J. Furnivall. (*Reprinted* 1965.) 10s.   ,,
     17. Parallel Extracts from 45 MSS. of Piers the Plowman, ed. W. W. Skeat. (*Out of print.*)   ,,
     18. Hali Meidenhad, ed. O. Cockayne, re-ed. F. J. Furnivall. (*Out of print.*)   ,,
     19. Lyndesay's Monarche, &c., ed. J. Small. Part II. (*Out of print.*)   ,,
     20. Richard Rolle de Hampole, English Prose Treatises of, ed. G. G. Perry. (*Out of print.*)   ,,
     21. Merlin, ed. H. B. Wheatley. Part II. (*Out of print.*)   ,,
     22. Partenay or Lusignen, ed. W. W. Skeat. (*Out of print.*)   ,,
     23. Dan Michel's Ayenbite of Inwyt, ed. R. Morris and P. Gradon. Vol. I, Text. (*Reissued* 1965.)
         54s.   ,,
     24. Hymns to the Virgin and Christ ; The Parliament of Devils, &c., ed. F. J. Furnivall. (*Out of print.*)   1867
     25. The Stacions of Rome, the Pilgrims' Sea-voyage, with Clene Maydenhod, ed. F. J. Furnivall. (*Out
         of print.*)   ,,
     26. Religious Pieces in Prose and Verse, from R. Thornton's MS., ed. G. G. Perry. (*See under* 1913.)
         (*Out of print.*)   ,,
     27. Levins' Manipulus Vocabulorum, a rhyming Dictionary, ed. H. B. Wheatley. (*Out of print.*)   ,,
     28. William's Vision of Piers the Plowman, ed. W. W. Skeat. A-Text. (*Reprinted* 1968.) 35s.   ,,
     29. Old English Homilies (1220–30), ed. R. Morris. Series I, Part I. (*Out of print.*)   ,,
     30. Pierce the Ploughmans Crede, ed. W. W. Skeat. (*Out of print.*)   ,,
E.S. 1. William of Palerne or William and the Werwolf, re-ed. W. W. Skeat. (*Out of print.*)   ,,
      2. Early English Pronunciation, by A. J. Ellis. Part I. (*Out of print.*)   ,,
O.S. 31. Myrc's Duties of a Parish Priest, in Verse, ed. E. Peacock. (*Out of print.*)   1868
     32. Early English Meals and Manners : the Boke of Norture of John Russell, the Bokes of Keruynge,
         Curtasye, and Demeanor, the Babees Book, Urbanitatis, &c., ed. F. J. Furnivall. (*Out of print.*)   ,,
     33. The Book of the Knight of La Tour-Landry, ed. T. Wright. (*Out of print.*)   ,,
     34. Old English Homilies (before 1300), ed. R. Morris. Series I, Part II. (*Out of print.*)   ,,
     35. Lyndesay's Works, Part III: The Historie and Testament of Squyer Meldrum, ed. F. Hall.
         (*Reprinted* 1965.) 18s.   ,,
E.S. 3. Caxton's Book of Curtesye, in Three Versions, ed. F. J. Furnivall. (*Out of print.*)   ,,
      4. Havelok the Dane, re-ed. W. W. Skeat. (*Out of print.*)   ,,
      5. Chaucer's Boethius, ed. R. Morris. (*Reprinted* 1969.) 40s.   ,,
      6. Chevelere Assigne, re-ed. Lord Aldenham. (*Out of print.*)   ,,
O.S. 36. Merlin, ed. H. B. Wheatley. Part III. On Arthurian Localities, by J. S. Stuart Glennie. (*Out of
         print.*)   1869
     37. Sir David Lyndesay's Works, Part IV, Ane Satyre of the thrie Estaits, ed. F. Hall. (*Out of print.*)   ,,
     38. William's Vision of Piers the Plowman, ed. W. W. Skeat. Part II. Text B. (*Reprinted* 1964.) 42s.   ,,
39, 56. The Gest Hystoriale of the Destruction of Troy, ed. D. Donaldson and G. A. Panton.
         Parts I and II. (*Reprinted as one volume* 1968.) 110s.
E.S. 7. Early English Pronunciation, by A. J. Ellis. Part II. (*Out of print.*)
      8. Queene Elizabethes Achademy, &c., ed. F. J. Furnivall. Essays on early Italian and German
         Books of Courtesy, by W. M. Rossetti and E. Oswald. (*Out of print.*)   ,,
      9. Awdeley's Fraternitye of Vacabondes, Harman's Caveat, &c., ed. E. Viles and F. J. Furnivall.
         (*Out of print.*)   ,,
O.S. 40. English Gilds, their Statutes and Customs, A.D. 1389, ed. Toulmin Smith and Lucy T. Smith, with
         an Essay on Gilds and Trades-Unions, by L. Brentano. (*Reprinted* 1963.) 100s.   1870
     41. William Lauder's Minor Poems, ed. F. J. Furnivall. (*Out of print.*)   ,,
     42. Bernardus De Cura Rei Famuliaris, Early Scottish Prophecies, &c., ed. J. R. Lumby. (*Reprinted*
         1965.) 18s.   ,,
     43. Ratis Raving, and other Moral and Religious Pieces, ed. J. R. Lumby. (*Out of print.*)   ,,
E.S. 10. Andrew Boorde's Introduction of Knowledge, 1547, Dyetary of Helth, 1542, Barnes in Defence of
         the Berde, 1542–3, ed. F. J. Furnivall. (*Out of print.*)   ,,
11, 55. Barbour's Bruce, ed. W. W. Skeat. Parts I and IV. (*Reprinted as Volume I* 1968.) 63s.   ,,
O.S. 44. The Alliterative Romance of Joseph of Arimathie, or The Holy Grail: from the Vernon MS.;
         with W. de Worde's and Pynson's Lives of Joseph: ed. W. W. Skeat. (*Out of print.*)   1871

2

O.S. **45.** King Alfred's West-Saxon Version of Gregory's Pastoral Care, ed., with an English translation,
by Henry Sweet. Part I. (*Reprinted 1958.*) 55s. — 1871
  46. Legends of the Holy Rood, Symbols of the Passion and Cross Poems, ed. R. Morris. (*Out of print.*) „
  47. Sir David Lyndesay's Works, ed. J. A. H. Murray. Part V. (*Out of print.*) „
  48. The Times' Whistle, and other Poems, by R. C., 1616; ed. J. M. Cowper. (*Out of print.*) „
E.S. **12.** England in Henry VIII's Time: a Dialogue between Cardinal Pole and Lupset, by Thom.
Starkey, Chaplain to Henry VIII, ed. J. M. Cowper. Part II. (*Out of print, Part I is E.S. 32,*
1878.) „
  13. A Supplicacyon of the Beggers, by Simon Fish, A.D. 1528–9, ed. F. J. Furnivall, with A Supplication to our Moste Soueraigne Lorde, A Supplication of the Poore Commons, and The Decaye
of England by the Great Multitude of Sheep, ed. J. M. Cowper. (*Out of print.*) „
  14. Early English Pronunciation, by A. J. Ellis. Part III. (*Out of print.*) „
O.S. **49.** An Old English Miscellany, containing a Bestiary, Kentish Sermons, Proverbs of Alfred, and
Religious Poems of the 13th cent., ed. R. Morris. (*Out of print.*) — 1872
  50. King Alfred's West-Saxon Version of Gregory's Pastoral Care, ed. H. Sweet. Part II. (*Reprinted*
1958.) 50s. „
  51. Þe Liflade of St. Juliana, 2 versions, with translations, ed. O. Cockayne and E. Brock.
(*Reprinted 1957.*) 38s. „
  52. Palladius on Husbondrie, englisht, ed. Barton Lodge. Part I. (*Out of print.*) „
E.S. **15.** Robert Crowley's Thirty-One Epigrams, Voyce of the Last Trumpet, Way to Wealth, &c., ed.
J. M. Cowper. (*Out of print.*) „
  16. Chaucer's Treatise on the Astrolabe, ed. W. W. Skeat. (*Reprinted 1969.*) 40s. „
  17. The Complaynt of Scotlande, with 4 Tracts, ed. J. A. H. Murray. Part I. (*Out of print.*) „
O.S. **53.** Old-English Homilies, Series II, and three Hymns to the Virgin and God, 13th-century, with
the music to two of them, in old and modern notation, ed. R. Morris. (*Out of print.*) — 1873
  54. The Vision of Piers Plowman, ed. W. W. Skeat. Part III. Text C. (*Reprinted 1959.*) 55s. „
  55. Generydes, a Romance, ed. W. Aldis Wright. Part I. (*Out of print.*) „
E.S. **18.** The Complaynt of Scotlande, ed. J. A. H. Murray. Part II. (*Out of print.*) „
  19. The Myroure of oure Ladye, ed. J. H. Blunt. (*Out of print.*) „
O.S. **56.** The Gest Hystoriale of the Destruction of Troy, in alliterative verse, ed. D. Donaldson and
G. A. Panton. Part II. (*See O.S. 39.*) — 1874
  57. Cursor Mundi, in four Texts, ed. R. Morris. Part I. (*Reprinted 1961.*) 40s. „
  58, 63, 73. The Blickling Homilies, ed. R. Morris. Parts I, II, and III. (*Reprinted as one volume*
1967.) 70s. „
E.S. **20.** Lovelich's History of the Holy Grail, ed. F. J. Furnivall. Part I. (*Out of print.*) „
  21, 29. Barbour's Bruce, ed. W. W. Skeat. Parts II and III. (*Reprinted as Volume II 1968.*) 90s.
  22. Henry Brinklow's Complaynt of Roderyck Mors and The Lamentacyon of a Christen Agaynst
the Cytye of London, made by Roderigo Mors, ed. J. M. Cowper. (*Out of print.*) „
  23. Early English Pronunciation, by A. J. Ellis. Part IV. (*Out of print.*) „
O.S. **59.** Cursor Mundi, in four Texts, ed. R. Morris. Part II. (*Reprinted 1966.*) 50s. — 1875
  60. Meditacyuns on the Soper of our Lorde, by Robert of Brunne, ed. J. M. Cowper. (*Out of print.*) „
  61. The Romance and Prophecies of Thomas of Erceldoune, ed. J. A. H. Murray. (*Out of print.*) „
E.S. **24.** Lovelich's History of the Holy Grail, ed. F. J. Furnivall. Part II. (*Out of print.*) „
  25, 26. Guy of Warwick, 15th-century Version, ed. J. Zupitza. Pts. I and II. (*Reprinted as one volume*
1966.) 75s. „
O.S. **62.** Cursor Mundi, in four Texts, ed. R. Morris. Part III. (*Reprinted 1966.*) 40s. — 1876
  63. The Blickling Homilies, ed. R. Morris. Part II. (*See O.S. 58.*) „
  64. Francis Thynne's Embleames and Epigrams, ed. F. J. Furnivall. (*Out of print.*) „
  65. Be Domes Dæge (Bede's *De Die Judicii*), &c., ed. J. R. Lumby. (*Reprinted 1964.*) 30s. „
E.S. **26.** Guy of Warwick, 15th-century Version, ed. J. Zupitza. Part II. (*See E.S. 25*) „
  27. The English Works of John Fisher, ed. J. E. B. Mayor. Part I. (*Out of print.*) „
O.S. **66.** Cursor Mundi, in four Texts, ed. R. Morris. Part IV. (*Reprinted 1966.*) 40s. — 1877
  67. Notes on Piers Plowman, by W. W. Skeat. Part I. (*Out of print.*) „
E.S. **28.** Lovelich's Holy Grail, ed. F. J. Furnivall. Part III. (*Out of print.*) „
  29. Barbour's Bruce, ed. W. W. Skeat. Part III. (*See E.S. 21.*) „
O.S. **68.** Cursor Mundi, in 4 Texts, ed. R. Morris. Part V. (*Reprinted 1966.*) 40s. — 1878
  69. Adam Davie's 5 Dreams about Edward II, &c., ed. F. J. Furnivall. 30s. „
  70. Generydes, a Romance, ed. W. Aldis Wright. Part II. (*Out of print.*) „
E.S. **30.** Lovelich's Holy Grail, ed. F. J. Furnivall. Part IV. (*Out of print.*) „
  31. The Alliterative Romance of Alexander and Dindimus, ed. W. W. Skeat. (*Out of print.*) „
  32. Starkey's England in Henry VIII's Time. Part I. Starkey's Life and Letters, ed. S. J. Herrtage.
(*Out of print.*) „
O.S. **71.** The Lay Folks Mass-Book, four texts, ed. T. F. Simmons. (*Reprinted 1968.*) 90s. — 1879
  72. Palladius on Husbondrie, englisht, ed. S. J. Herrtage. Part II. 42s. „
E.S. **33.** Gesta Romanorum, ed. S. J. Herrtage. (*Reprinted 1962.*) 100s. „
  34. The Charlemagne Romances: 1. Sir Ferumbras, from Ashm. MS. 33, ed. S. J. Herrtage. (*Re-*
printed 1966.) 54s. „
O.S. **73.** The Blickling Homilies, ed. R. Morris. Part III. (*See O.S. 58.*) — 1880
  74. English Works of Wyclif, hitherto unprinted, ed. F. D. Matthew. (*Out of print.*) „
E.S. **35.** Charlemagne Romances: 2. The Sege of Melayne, Sir Otuell, &c., ed. S. J. Herrtage. (*Out of*
print.) „
  36, 37. Charlemagne Romances: 3 and 4. Lyf of Charles the Grete, ed. S. J. Herrtage. Parts I and II.
(*Reprinted as one volume 1967.*) 54s. „
O.S. **75.** Catholicon Anglicum, an English-Latin Wordbook, from Lord Monson's MS., A.D. 1483, ed.,
with Introduction and Notes, by S. J. Herrtage and Preface by H. B. Wheatley. (*Out of print.*) — 1881
  76, 82. Ælfric's Lives of Saints, in MS. Cott. Jul. E vii, ed. W. W. Skeat. Parts I and II. (*Reprinted as*
Volume I 1966.) 60s. „

E.S. 37. Charlemagne Romances : 4. Lyf of Charles the Grete, ed. S. J. Herrtage. Part II. (*See* E.S. 36.) 1881
38. Charlemagne Romances : 5. The Sowdone of Babylone, ed. E. Hausknecht. (*Out of print*.) „
O.S. 77. Beowulf, the unique MS. autotyped and transliterated, ed. J. Zupitza. (*Re-issued as* No. 245. *See under* 1958.) 1882
78. The Fifty Earliest English Wills, in the Court of Probate, 1387–1439, ed. F. J. Furnivall. (*Reprinted* 1964.) 50s.
E.S. 39. Charlemagne Romances : 6. Rauf Coilyear, Roland, Otuel, &c., ed. S. J. Herrtage. (*Out of print*.) „
40. Charlemagne Romances : 7. Huon of Burdeux, by Lord Berners, ed. S. L. Lee. Part I. (*Out of print*.)
O.S. 79. King Alfred's Orosius, from Lord Tollemache's 9th-century MS., ed. H. Sweet. Part I. (*Reprinted* 1959.) 55s. 1883
79 b. *Extra Volume*. Facsimile of the Epinal Glossary, ed. H. Sweet. (*Out of print*.) „
E.S. 41. Charlemagne Romances : 8. Huon of Burdeux, by Lord Berners, ed. S. L. Lee. Part II. (*Out of print*.)
42, 49, 59. Guy of Warwick : 2 texts (Auchinleck MS. and Caius MS.), ed. J. Zupitza. Parts I, II, and III. (*Reprinted as one volume* 1966). 110s.
O.S. 80. The Life of St. Katherine, B.M. Royal MS. 17 A. xxvii, &c., and its Latin Original, ed. E. Einenkel. (*Out of print*.) 1884
81. Piers Plowman : Glossary, &c., ed. W. W. Skeat. Part IV, completing the work. (*Out of print*.) „
E.S. 43. Charlemagne Romances : 9. Huon of Burdeux, by Lord Berners, ed. S. L. Lee. Part III. (*Out of print*.)
44. Charlemagne Romances : 10. The Foure Sonnes of Aymon, ed. Octavia Richardson. Part I. (*Out of print*.)
O.S. 82. Ælfric's Lives of Saints, MS. Cott. Jul. E vII. ed. W. W. Skeat. Part II. (*See* O.S. 76.) 1885
83. The Oldest English Texts, Charters, &c., ed. H. Sweet. (*Reprinted* 1966.) 110s. „
E.S. 45. Charlemagne Romances : 11. The Foure Sonnes of Aymon, ed. O. Richardson. Part II. (*Out of print*.)
46. Sir Beves of Hamtoun, ed. E. Kölbing. Part I. (*Out of print*.) „
O.S. 84. Additional Analogs to 'The Wright's Chaste Wife', O.S. 12, by W. A. Clouston. (*Out of print*.) 1886
85. The Three Kings of Cologne, ed. C. Horstmann. (*Out of print*.) „
86. Prose Lives of Women Saints, ed. C. Horstmann. (*Out of print*.) „
E.S. 47. The Wars of Alexander, ed. W. W. Skeat. (*Out of print*.) „
48. Sir Beves of Hamtoun, ed. E. Kölbing. Part II. (*Out of print*.) „
O.S. 87. The Early South-English Legendary, Laud MS. 108, ed. C. Hortsmann. (*Out of print*.) 1887
88. Hy. Bradshaw's Life of St. Werburghe (Pynson, 1521), ed. C. Horstmann. (*Out of print*.) „
E.S. 49. Guy of Warwick, 2 texts (Auchinleck and Caius MSS.), ed. J. Zupitza. Part II. (*See* E.S. 42.) „
50. Charlemagne Romances : 12. Huon of Burdeux, by Lord Berners, ed. S. L. Lee. Part IV. (*Out of print*.)
51. Torrent of Portyngale, ed. E. Adam. (*Out of print*.) „
O.S. 89. Vices and Virtues, ed. F. Holthausen. Part I. (*Reprinted* 1967.) 40s. 1888
90. Anglo-Saxon and Latin Rule of St. Benet, interlinear Glosses, ed. H. Logeman. (*Out of print*.) „
91. Two Fifteenth-Century Cookery-Books, ed. T. Austin. (*Reprinted* 1964.) 42s. „
E.S. 52. Bullein's Dialogue against the Feuer Pestilence, 1578, ed. M. and A. H. Bullen. (*Out of print*.) „
53. Vicary's Anatomie of the Body of Man, 1548, ed. 1577, ed. F. J. and Percy Furnivall. Part I. (*Out of print*.)
54. The Curial made by maystere Alain Charretier, translated by William Caxton, 1484, ed. F. J. Furnivall and P. Meyer. (*Reprinted* 1965.) 13s.
O.S. 92. Eadwine's Canterbury Psalter, from the Trin. Cambr. MS., ed. F. Harsley, Part II. (*Out of print*.) 1889
93. Defensor's Liber Scintillarum, ed. E. Rhodes. (*Out of print*.) „
E.S. 55. Barbour's Bruce, ed. W. W. Skeat. Part IV. (*See* E.S. 11.) „
56. Early English Pronunciation, by A. J. Ellis. Part V, the present English Dialects. (*Out of print*.) „
O.S. 94, 114. Ælfric's Lives of Saints, MS. Cott. Jul. E vII, ed. W. W. Skeat. Parts III and IV. (*Reprinted as Volume II* 1966.) 60s. 1890
95. The Old-English Version of Bede's Ecclesiastical History, re-ed. T. Miller. Part I, 1. (*Reprinted* 1959.) 54s.
E.S. 57. Caxton's Eneydos, ed. W. T. Culley and F. J. Furnivall. (*Reprinted* 1962.) 50s. „
58. Caxton's Blanchardyn and Eglantine, c. 1489, ed. L. Kellner. (*Reprinted* 1962.) 63s. „
O.S. 96. The Old-English Version of Bede's Ecclesiastical History, re-ed. T. Miller. Part I, 2. (*Reprinted* 1959.) 54s. 1891
97. The Earliest English Prose Psalter, ed. K. D. Buelbring. Part I. (*Out of print*.) „
E.S. 59. Guy of Warwick, 2 texts (Auchinleck and Caius MSS.), ed. J. Zupitza. Part III. (*See* E.S. 42.) „
60. Lydgate's Temple of Glas, re-ed. J. Schick. (*Out of print*.) „
O.S. 98. Minor Poems of the Vernon MS., ed. C. Horstmann. Part I. (*Out of print*.) 1892
99. Cursor Mundi. Preface, Notes, and Glossary, Part VI, ed. R. Morris. (*Reprinted* 1962.) 35s. „
E.S. 61. Hoccleve's Minor Poems, I, from the Phillipps and Durham MSS., ed. F. J. Furnivall. (*Out of print*.)
62. The Chester Plays, re-ed. H. Deimling. Part I. (*Reprinted* 1967.) 38s. „
O.S. 100. Capgrave's Life of St. Katharine, ed. C. Horstmann, with Forewords by F. J. Furnivall. (*Out of print*.) 1893
O.S. 101. Cursor Mundi. Essay on the MSS., their Dialects, &c., by H. Hupe. Part VII. (*Reprinted* 1962.) 35s.
E.S. 63. Thomas à Kempis's De Imitatione Christi, ed. J. K. Ingram. (*Out of print*.) „
64. Caxton's Godeffroy of Boloyne, or The Siege and Conqueste of Jerusalem, 1481, ed. Mary N. Colvin. (*Out of print*.)
O.S. 102. Lanfranc's Science of Cirurgie, ed. R. von Fleischhacker. Part I. (*Out of print*.) 1894

4

O.S. 103. The Legend of the Cross, &c., ed. A. S. Napier. (*Out of print.*)   1894
E.S. 65. Sir Beves of Hamtoun, ed. E. Kölbing. Part III. (*Out of print.*)   „
     66. Lydgate's and Burgh's Secrees of Philisoffres ('Governance of Kings and Princes'), ed. R. Steele. (*Out of print.*)   „
O.S. 104. The Exeter Book (Anglo-Saxon Poems), re-ed. I. Gollancz. Part I. (*Reprinted 1958.*) 55s.   1895
    105. The Prymer or Lay Folks' Prayer Book, Camb. Univ. MS., ed. H. Littlehales. Part I. (*Out of print.*)   „
E.S. 67. The Three Kings' Sons, a Romance, ed. F. J. Furnivall. Part I, the Text. (*Out of print.*)   „
     68. Melusine, the prose Romance, ed. A. K. Donald. Part I, the Text. (*Out of print.*)   „
O.S. 106. R. Misyn's Fire of Love and Mending of Life (Hampole), ed. R. Harvey. (*Out of print.*)   1896
    107. The English Conquest of Ireland, A.D. 1166–1185, 2 Texts, ed. F. J. Furnivall. Part I. (*Out of print.*) „
E.S. 69. Lydgate's Assembly of the Gods, ed. O. L. Triggs. (*Reprinted 1957.*) 42s.   „
     70. The Digby Plays, ed. F. J. Furnivall. (*Reprinted 1967.*) 30s.   „
O.S. 108. Child-Marriages and -Divorces, Trothplights, &c. Chester Depositions, 1561–6, ed. F. J. Furnivall. (*Out of print.*)   1897
    109. The Prymer or Lay Folks' Prayer Book, ed. H. Littlehales. Part II. (*Out of print.*)   „
E.S. 71. The Towneley Plays, ed. G. England and A. W. Pollard. (*Reprinted 1966.*) 45s.   „
     72. Hoccleve's Regement of Princes, and 14 Poems, ed. F. J. Furnivall. (*Out of print.*)   „
     73. Hoccleve's Minor Poems, II, from the Ashburnham MS., ed. I. Gollancz. (*Out of print.*)   „
O.S. 110. The Old-English Version of Bede's Ecclesiastical History, ed. T. Miller. Part II, 1. (*Reprinted 1963.*) 55s.   1898
    111. The Old-English Version of Bede's Ecclesiastical History, ed. T. Miller. Part II, 2. (*Reprinted 1963.*) 55s.
E.S. 74. Secreta Secretorum, 3 prose Englishings, one by Jas. Yonge, 1428, ed. R. Steele. Part I. 55s.   „
     75. Speculum Guidonis de Warwyk, ed. G. L. Morrill. (*Out of print.*)   „
O.S. 112. Merlin. Part IV. Outlines of the Legend of Merlin, by W. E. Mead. (*Out of print.*)   1899
    113. Queen Elizabeth's Englishings of Boethius, Plutarch, &c., ed. C. Pemberton. (*Out of print.*)   „
E.S. 76. George Ashby's Poems, &c., ed. Mary Bateson. (*Reprinted 1965.*) 30s.   „
     77. Lydgate's DeGuilleville's Pilgrimage of the Life of Man, ed. F. J. Furnivall. Part I. (*Out of print.*)   „
     78. The Life and Death of Mary Magdalene, by T. Robinson, c. 1620, ed. H. O. Sommer. 30s.   „
O.S. 114. Ælfric's Lives of Saints, ed. W. W. Skeat. Part IV and last. (*See* O.S. 94.)   1900
    115. Jacob's Well, ed. A. Brandeis. Part I. (*Out of print.*)   „
    116. An Old-English Martyrology, re-ed. G. Herzfeld. (*Out of print.*)   „
E.S. 79. Caxton's Dialogues, English and French, ed. H. Bradley. (*Out of print.*)   „
     80. Lydgate's Two Nightingale Poems, ed. O. Glauning. (*Out of print.*)   „
  80A. Selections from Barbour's Bruce (Books I–X), ed. W. W. Skeat. (*Out of print.*)   „
     81. The English Works of John Gower, ed. G. C. Macaulay. Part I. (*Reprinted 1957.*) 60s.   „
O.S. 117. Minor Poems of the Vernon MS., ed. F. J. Furnivall. Part II. (*Out of print.*)   1901
    118. The Lay Folks' Catechism, ed. T. F. Simmons and H. E. Nolloth. (*Out of print.*)   „
    119. Robert of Brunne's Handlyng Synne, and its French original, re-ed. F. J. Furnivall. Part I. (*Out of print.*)   „
E.S. 82. The English Works of John Gower, ed. G. C. Macaulay. Part II. (*Reprinted 1957.*) 60s.   „
     83. Lydgate's DeGuilleville's Pilgrimage of the Life of Man, ed. F. J. Furnivall. Part II. (*Out of print.*)   „
     84. Lydgate's Reson and Sensuallyte, ed. E. Sieper. Vol. I. (*Reprinted 1965.*) 50s.   „
O.S. 120. The Rule of St. Benet in Northern Prose and Verse, and Caxton's Summary, ed. E. A. Kock. (*Out of print.*)   1902
    121. The Laud MS. Troy-Book, ed. J. E. Wülfing. Part I. (*Out of print.*)   „
E.S. 85. Alexander Scott's Poems, 1568, ed. A. K. Donald. (*Out of print.*)   „
     86. William of Shoreham's Poems, re-ed. M. Konrath. Part I. (*Out of print.*)   „
     87. Two Coventry Corpus Christi Plays, re-ed. H. Craig. (*See under* 1952.)   „
O.S. 122. The Laud MS. Troy-Book, ed. J. E. Wülfing. Part II. (*Out of print.*)   1903
    123. Robert of Brunne's Handlyng Synne, and its French original, re-ed. F. J. Furnivall. Part II. (*Out of print.*)   „
E.S. 88. Le Morte Arthur, re-ed. J. D. Bruce. (*Reprinted 1959.*) 45s.   „
     89. Lydgate's Reson and Sensuallyte, ed. E. Sieper. Vol. II. (*Reprinted 1965.*) 35s.   „
     90. English Fragments from Latin Medieval Service-Books, ed. H. Littlehales. (*Out of print.*)   „
O.S. 124. Twenty-six Political and other Poems from Digby MS. 102, &c., ed. J. Kail. Part I. 50s.   1904
    125. Medieval Records of a London City Church, ed. H. Littlehales. Part I. (*Out of print.*)   „
    126. An Alphabet of Tales, in Northern English, from the Latin, ed. M. M. Banks. Part I. (*Out of print.*) „
E.S. 91. The Macro Plays, ed. F. J. Furnivall and A. W. Pollard. (*Out of print; see* 262.)   „
     92. Lydgate's DeGuilleville's Pilgrimage of the Life of Man, ed. Katherine B. Locock. Part III. (*Out of print.*)   „
     93. Lovelich's Romance of Merlin, from the unique MS., ed. E. A. Kock. Part I. (*Out of print.*)   „
O.S. 127. An Alphabet of Tales, in Northern English, from the Latin, ed. M. M. Banks. Part II. (*Out of print.*)   1905
    128. Medieval Records of a London City Church, ed. H. Littlehales. Part II. (*Out of print.*)   „
    129. The English Register of Godstow Nunnery, ed. A. Clark. Part I. 63s.   „
E.S. 94. Respublica, a Play on a Social England, ed. L. A. Magnus. (*Out of print. See under* 1946.)   „
     95. Lovelich's History of the Holy Grail. Part V. The Legend of the Holy Grail, ed. Dorothy Kempe. (*Out of print.*)   „
     96. Mirk's Festial, ed. T. Erbe. Part I. (*Out of print.*)   „
O.S. 130. The English Register of Godstow Nunnery, ed. A. Clark. Part II. 55s.   1906
    131. The Brut, or The Chronicle of England, ed. F. Brie. Part I. (*Reprinted 1960.*) 55s.   „
    132. John Metham's Works, ed. H. Craig. 50s.   „
E.S. 97. Lydgate's Troy Book, ed. H. Bergen. Part I, Books I and II. (*Out of print.*)   „

5

E.S. 98. Skelton's Magnyfycence, ed. R. L. Ramsay. (*Reprinted* 1958.) 55s.   1906
99. The Romance of Emaré, re-ed. Edith Rickert. (*Reprinted* 1958.) 30s.
O.S. 133. The English Register of Oseney Abbey, by Oxford, ed. A. Clark. Part I. 50s.   1907
134. The Coventry Leet Book, ed. M. Dormer Harris. Part I. (*Out of print.*)   „
E.S. 100. The Harrowing of Hell, and The Gospel of Nicodemus, re-ed. W. H. Hulme. (*Reprinted* 1961.)
50s.   „
101. Songs, Carols, &c., from Richard Hill's Balliol MS., ed. R. Dyboski. (*Out of print.*)   „
O.S. 135. The Coventry Leet Book, ed. M. Dormer Harris. Part II. (*Out of print.*)   1908
135 b. Extra Issue. Prof. Manly's Piers Plowman and its Sequence, urging the fivefold authorship
of the *Vision*. (*Out of print.*)   „
136. The Brut, or The Chronicle of England, ed. F. Brie. Part II. (*Out of print.*)   „
E.S. 102. Promptorium Parvulorum, the 1st English-Latin Dictionary, ed. A. L. Mayhew. (*Out of print.*) „
103. Lydgate's Troy Book, ed. H. Bergen. Part II, Book III. (*Out of print.*)   „
O.S. 137. Twelfth-Century Homilies in MS. Bodley 343, ed. A. O. Belfour. Part I, the Text. (*Reprinted*
1962.) 28s.   1909
138. The Coventry Leet Book, ed. M. Dormer Harris. Part III. (*Out of print.*)   „
E.S. 104. The Non-Cycle Mystery Plays, re-ed. O. Waterhouse. (*See end-note*, p. 8.)   „
105. The Tale of Beryn, with the Pardoner and Tapster, ed. F. J. Furnivall and W. G. Stone. (*Out
of print.*)   „
O.S. 139. John Arderne's Treatises of Fistula in Ano, &c., ed. D'Arcy Power. (*Reprinted* 1969.) 45s.   1910
139 b, c, d, e, f, Extra Issue. The Piers Plowman Controversy: b. Dr. Jusserand's 1st Reply to Prof.
Manly; c. Prof. Manly's Answer to Dr. Jusserand; d. Dr. Jusserand's 2nd Reply to Prof.
Manly; e. Mr. R. W. Chambers's Article; f. Dr. Henry Bradley's Rejoinder to Mr. R. W.
Chambers. (*Out of print.*)   „
140. Capgrave's Lives of St. Augustine and St. Gilbert of Sempringham, ed. J. Munro. (*Out of print.*) „
E.S. 106. Lydgate's Troy Book, ed. H. Bergen. Part III. (*Out of print.*)   „
107. Lydgate's Minor Poems, ed. H. N. MacCracken. Part I. Religious Poems. (*Reprinted* 1961.)
70s.   „
O.S. 141. Erthe upon Erthe, all the known texts, ed. Hilda Murray. (*Reprinted* 1964.) 30s.   1911
142. The English Register of Godstow Nunnery, ed. A. Clark. Part III. 42s.   „
143. The Prose Life of Alexander, Thornton MS., ed. J. S. Westlake. (*Out of print.*)   „
E.S. 108. Lydgate's Siege of Thebes, re-ed. A. Erdmann. Part I, the Text. (*Reprinted* 1960.) 50s. „
109. Partonope, re-ed. A. T. Bödtker. The Texts. (*Out of print.*)   „
O.S. 144. The English Register of Oseney Abbey, by Oxford, ed. A. Clark. Part II. 20s.   1912
145. The Northern Passion, ed. F. A. Foster. Part I, the four parallel texts. (*Out of print.*) „
E.S. 110. Caxton's Mirrour of the World, with all the woodcuts, ed. O. H. Prior. (*Reprinted* 1966.) 50s. „
111. Caxton's History of Jason, the Text, Part I, ed. J. Munro. (*Out of print.*)   „
O.S. 146. The Coventry Leet Book, ed. M. Dormer Harris. Introduction, Indexes, &c. Part IV. (*Out of print.*) 1913
147. The Northern Passion, ed . F. A. Foster, Introduction, French Text, Variants and Fragments,
Glossary. Part II. (*Out of print.*)   „
[An enlarged reprint of O.S. 26, Religious Pieces in Prose and Verse, from the Thornton MS.,
ed. G. G. Perry. (*Out of print.*)   „
E.S. 112. Lovelich's Romance of Merlin, ed. E. A. Kock. Part II. (*Reprinted* 1961.) 45s.   „
113. Poems by Sir John Salusbury, Robert Chester, and others, from Christ Church MS. 184, &c., ed.
Carleton Brown. (*Out of print.*)   „
O.S. 148. A Fifteenth-Century Courtesy Book and Two Franciscan Rules, ed. R. W. Chambers and W. W.
Seton. (*Reprinted* 1963.) 30s.   1914
149. Lincoln Diocese Documents, 1450–1544, ed. Andrew Clark. (*Out of print.*)   „
150. The Old-English Rule of Bp. Chrodegang, and the Capitula of Bp. Theodulf, ed. A. S. Napier.
(*Out of print.*)   „
E.S. 114. The Gild of St. Mary, Lichfield, ed. F. J. Furnivall. 27s.   „
115. The Chester Plays, re-ed. J. Matthews. Part II. (*Reprinted* 1967.) 38s.   „
O.S. 151. The Lanterne of Light, ed. Lilian M. Swinburn. (*Out of print.*)   1915
152. Early English Homilies, from Cott. Vesp. D. xiv, ed. Rubie Warner. Part I, Text. (*Out of
print.*)   „
E.S. 116. The Pauline Epistles, ed. M. J. Powell. (*Out of print.*)   „
117. Bp. Fisher's English Works, ed. R. Bayne. Part II. (*Out of print.*)   „
O.S. 153. Mandeville's Travels, ed. P. Hamelius. Part I, Text. (*Reprinted* 1960.) 40s.   1916
154. Mandeville's Travels, ed. P. Hamelius. Part II, Notes and Introduction. (*Reprinted* 1961.) 40s. „
E.S. 118. The Earliest Arithmetics in English, ed. R. Steele. (*Out of print.*)   „
119. The Owl and the Nightingale, 2 Texts parallel, ed. G. F. H. Sykes and J. H. G. Grattan. (*Out
of print.*)   „
O.S. 155. The Wheatley MS., ed. Mabel Day. 54s.   1917
E.S. 120. Ludus Coventriae, ed. K. S. Block. (*Reprinted* 1961.) 60s.   „
O.S. 156. Reginald Pecock's Donet, from Bodl. MS. 916, ed. Elsie V. Hitchcock. 63s.   1918
E.S. 121. Lydgate's Fall of Princes, ed. H. Bergen. Part I. (*Reprinted* 1967.) 63s.   „
122. Lydgate's Fall of Princes, ed. H. Bergen. Part II. (*Reprinted* 1967.) 63s.   „
O.S. 157. Harmony of the Life of Christ, from MS. Pepys 2498, ed. Margery Goates. (*Out of print.*) 1919
158. Meditations on the Life and Passion of Christ, from MS. Add., 11307, ed. Charlotte D'Evelyn.
(*Out of print.*)   „
E.S. 123. Lydgate's Fall of Princes, ed. H. Bergen. Part III. (*Reprinted* 1967.) 63s.   „
124. Lydgate's Fall of Princes, ed. H. Bergen. Part IV. (*Reprinted* 1967.) 90s.   „
O.S. 159. Vices and Virtues, ed. F. Holthausen. Part II. (*Reprinted* 1967.) 28s.   1920
[A re-edition of O.S. 18, Hali Meidenhad, ed. O. Cockayne, with a variant MS., Bodl. 34,
hitherto unprinted, ed. F. J. Furnivall. (*Out of print.*)   „
E.S. 125. Lydgate's Siege of Thebes, ed. A. Erdmann and E. Ekwall. Part II. (*Out of print.*)   „

6

E.S. 126. Lydgate's Troy Book, ed. H. Bergen. Part IV. (*Out of print.*) 1920
O.S. 160. The Old English Heptateuch, MS. Cott. Claud. B. IV, ed. S. J. Crawford. (*Reprinted 1969.*) 75s. 1921
161. Three O.E. Prose Texts, MS. Cott. Vit. A. xv, ed. S. Rypins. (*Out of print.*) „
162. Facsimile of MS. Cotton Nero A. x (Pearl, Cleanness, Patience and Sir Gawain), Introduction by I. Gollancz. (*Reprinted 1955.*) 200s. 1922
163. Book of the Foundation of St. Bartholomew's Church in London, ed. N. Moore. (*Out of print.*) 1923
164. Pecock's Folewer to the Donet, ed. Elsie V. Hitchcock. (*Out of print.*) „
165. Middleton's Chinon of England, with Leland's Assertio Arturii and Robinson's translation, ed. W. E. Mead. (*Out of print.*) „
166. Stanzaic Life of Christ, ed. Frances A. Foster. (*Out of print.*) 1924
167. Trevisa's Dialogus inter Militem et Clericum, Sermon by FitzRalph, and Bygynnyng of the World, ed. A. J. Perry. (*Out of print.*) „
168. Caxton's Ordre of Chyualry, ed. A. T. P. Byles. (*Out of print.*) 1925
169. The Southern Passion, ed. Beatrice Brown. (*Out of print.*) „
170. Walton's Boethius, ed. M. Science. (*Out of print.*) „
171. Pecock's Reule of Cristen Religioun, ed. W. C. Greet. (*Out of print.*) 1926
172. The Seege or Batayle of Troye, ed. M. E. Barnicle. (*Out of print.*) „
173. Hawes' Pastime of Pleasure, ed. W. E. Mead. (*Out of print.*) 1927
174. The Life of St. Anne, ed. R. E. Parker. (*Out of print.*) „
175. Barclay's Eclogues, ed. Beatrice White. (*Reprinted 1961.*) 55s. „
176. Caxton's Prologues and Epilogues, ed. W. J. B. Crotch. (*Reprinted 1956.*) 54s. „
177. Byrhtferth's Manual, ed. S. J. Crawford. (*Reprinted 1966.*) 63s. 1928
178. The Revelations of St. Birgitta, ed. W. P. Cumming. (*Out of print.*) „
179. The Castell of Pleasure, ed. B. Cornelius. (*Out of print.*) „
180. The Apologye of Syr Thomas More, ed. A. I. Taft. (*Out of print.*) 1929
181. The Dance of Death, ed. F. Warren. (*Out of print.*) „
182. Speculum Christiani, ed. G. Holmstedt. (*Out of print.*) „
183. The Northern Passion (Supplement), ed. W. Heuser and Frances Foster. (*Out of print.*) 1930
184. The Poems of John Audelay, ed. Ella K. Whiting. (*Out of print.*) „
185. Lovelich's Merlin, ed. E. A. Kock. Part III. (*Out of print.*) „
186. Harpsfield's Life of More, ed. Elsie V. Hitchcock and R. W. Chambers. (*Reprinted 1963.*) 105s. 1931
187. Whittinton and Stanbridge's Vulgaria, ed. B. White. (*Out of print.*) „
188. The Siege of Jerusalem, ed. E. Kölbing and Mabel Day. (*Out of print.*) „
189. Caxton's Fayttes of Armes and of Chyualrye, ed. A. T. Byles. (*Out of print.*) 1932
190. English Mediæval Lapidaries, ed. Joan Evans and Mary Serjeantson. (*Reprinted 1960.*) 50s. „
191. The Seven Sages, ed. K. Brunner. (*Out of print.*) „
191A. On the Continuity of English Prose, by R. W. Chambers. (*Reprinted 1966.*) 25s.
192. Lydgate's Minor Poems, ed. H. N. MacCracken. Part II, Secular Poems. (*Reprinted 1961.*) 75s. 1933
193. Seinte Marherete, re-ed. Frances Mack. (*Reprinted 1958.*) 50s. „
194. The Exeter Book, Part II, ed. W. S. Mackie. (*Reprinted 1938.*) 42s. „
195. The Quatrefoil of Love, ed. I. Gollancz and M. Weale. (*Out of print.*) 1934
196. A Short English Metrical Chronicle, ed. E. Zettl. (*Out of print.*) „
197. Roper's Life of More, ed. Elsie V. Hitchcock. (*Reprinted 1958.*) 35s. „
198. Firumbras and Otuel and Roland, ed. Mary O'Sullivan. (*Out of print.*) „
199. Mum and the Sothsegger, ed. Mabel Day and R. Steele. (*Out of print.*) „
200. Speculum Sacerdotale, ed. E. H. Weatherly. (*Out of print.*) 1935
201. Knyghthode and Bataile, ed. R. Dyboski and Z. M. Arend. (*Out of print.*) „
202. Palsgrave's Acolastus, ed. P. L. Carver. (*Out of print.*) „
203. Amis and Amiloun, ed. McEdward Leach. (*Reprinted 1960.*) 50s. „
204. Valentine and Orson, ed. Arthur Dickson. (*Out of print.*) 1936
205. Tales from the Decameron, ed. H. G. Wright. (*Out of print.*) „
206. Bokenham's Lives of Holy Women (Lives of the Saints), ed. Mary S. Serjeantson. (*Out of print.*) „
207. Liber de Diversis Medicinis, ed. Margaret S. Ogden. (*Out of print.*) „
208. The Parker Chronicle and Laws (facsimile), ed. R. Flower and A. H. Smith. (*Out of print.*) 1937
209. Middle English Sermons from MS. Roy. 18 B. xxiii, ed. W. O. Ross. (*Reprinted 1960.*) 75s. 1938
210. Sir Gawain and the Green Knight, ed. I. Gollancz. With Introductory essays by Mabel Day and M. S. Serjeantson. (*Reprinted 1966.*) 25s. „
211. Dictes and Sayings of the Philosophers, ed. C. F. Bühler. (*Reprinted 1961.*) 75s. 1939
212. The Book of Margery Kempe, Part I, ed. S. B. Meech and Hope Emily Allen. (*Reprinted 1961.*) 70s. „
213. Ælfric's De Temporibus Anni, ed. H. Henel. (*Out of print.*) 1940
214. Morley's Translation of Boccaccio's De Claris Mulieribus, ed. H. G. Wright. (*Out of print.*) „
215. English Poems of Charles of Orleans, Part I, ed. R. Steele. (*Out of print.*) 1941
216. The Latin Text of the Ancrene Riwle, ed. Charlotte D'Evelyn. (*Reprinted 1957.*) 45s. „
217. The Book of Vices and Virtues, ed. W. Nelson Francis. (*Reprinted 1968.*) 75s. 1942
218. The Cloud of Unknowing and the Book of Privy Counselling, ed. Phyllis Hodgson. (*Reprinted 1958.*) 40s. 1943
219. The French Text of the Ancrene Riwle, B.M. Cotton MS. Vitellius. F. VII, ed. J. A. Herbert. (*Reprinted 1967.*) 55s. „
220. English Poems of Charles of Orleans, Part II, ed. R. Steele and Mabel Day. (*Out of print.*) 1944
221. Sir Degrevant, ed. L. F. Casson. (*Out of print.*) „
222. Ro. Ba.'s Life of Syr Thomas More, ed. Elsie V. Hitchcock and Mgr. P. E. Hallett. (*Reprinted 1957.*) 63s. 1945
223. Tretyse of Loue, ed. J. H. Fisher. (*Out of print.*) „
224. Athelston, ed. A. McI. Trounce. (*Reprinted 1957.*) 42s. 1946
225. The English Text of the Ancrene Riwle, B.M. Cotton MS. Nero A. XIV, ed. Mabel Day. (*Reprinted 1957.*) 50s. „

7

226. Respublica, re-ed. W. W. Greg. (*Out of print.*) 1946
227. Kyng Alisaunder, ed. G. V. Smithers. Vol. I, Text. (*Reprinted* 1961.) 75s. 1947
228. The Metrical Life of St. Robert of Knaresborough, ed. J. Bazire. (*Reprinted* 1968.) 42s. „
229. The English Text of the Ancrene Riwle, Gonville and Caius College MS. 234/120, ed. R. M. Wilson. With Introduction by N. R. Ker. (*Reprinted* 1957.) 35s. 1948
230. The Life of St. George by Alexander Barclay, ed. W. Nelson. (*Reprinted* 1960.) 40s. „
231. Deonise Hid Diuinite, and other treatises related to *The Cloud of Unknowing*, ed. Phyllis Hodgson. (*Reprinted* 1958.) 50s. 1949
232. The English Text of the Ancrene Riwle, B.M. Royal MS. 8 C. 1, ed. A. C. Baugh. (*Reprinted* 1958.) 30s. „
233. The Bibliotheca Historica of Diodorus Siculus translated by John Skelton, ed. F. M. Salter and H. L. R. Edwards. Vol. I, Text. (*Reprinted* 1968.) 80s. 1950
234. Caxton: Paris and Vienne, ed. MacEdward Leach. (*Out of print.*) 1951
235. The South English Legendary, Corpus Christi College Cambridge MS. 145 and B.M. M.S. Harley 2277, &c., ed. Charlotte D'Evelyn and Anna J. Mill. Text, Vol. I. (*Reprinted* 1967.) 63s. „
236. The South English Legendary. Text, Vol. II. (*Reprinted* 1967.) 63s. 1952
[E.S. 87. Two Coventry Corpus Christi Plays, re-ed. H. Craig. Second Edition. (*Reprinted* 1967.) 30s.]
237. Kyng Alisaunder, ed. G. V. Smithers. Vol. II, Introduction, Commentary, and Glossary. 50s. 1953
238. The Phonetic Writings of Robert Robinson, ed. E. J. Dobson. (*Reprinted* 1968.) 30s. „
239. The Bibliotheca Historica of Diodorus Siculus translated by John Skelton, ed. F. M. Salter and H. L. R. Edwards. Vol. II. Introduction, Notes, and Glossary. 30s. 1954
240. The French Text of the Ancrene Riwle, Trinity College, Cambridge, MS. R. 14, 7, ed. W. H. Trethewey. 55s. „
241. Þe Wohunge of ure Lauerd, and other pieces, ed. W. Meredith Thompson. 45s. 1955
242. The Salisbury Psalter, ed. Celia Sisam and Kenneth Sisam. (*Reprinted* 1969.) 90s. 1955–56
243. George Cavendish: The Life and Death of Cardinal Wolsey, ed. Richard S. Sylvester. (*Reprinted* 1961.) 45s. 1957
244. The South English Legendary. Vol. III, Introduction and Glossary, ed. C. D'Evelyn. 30s. „
245. Beowulf (facsimile). With Transliteration by J. Zupitza, new collotype plates, and Introduction by N. Davis. (*Reprinted* 1967.) 100s. 1958
246. The Parlement of the Thre Ages, ed. M. Y. Offord. (*Reprinted* 1967.) 40s. 1959
247. Facsimile of MS. Bodley 34 (Katherine Group). With Introduction by N. R. Ker. 63s. „
248. Þe Liflade ant te Passiun of Seinte Iuliene, ed. S. R. T. O. d'Ardenne. 40s. 1960
249. Ancrene Wisse, Corpus Christi College, Cambridge, MS. 402, ed. J. R. R. Tolkien. With an Introduction by N. R. Ker. 50s. „
250. La3amon's Brut, ed. G. L. Brook and R. F. Leslie. Vol. I, Text (first part). 100s. 1961
251. Facsimile of the Cotton and Jesus Manuscripts of the Owl and the Nightingale. With Introduction by N. R. Ker. 50s. 1962
252. The English Text of the Ancrene Riwle, B.M. Cotton MS. Titus D. xviii, ed. Frances M. Mack, and Lanhydrock Fragment, ed. A. Zettersten. 50s. „
253. The Bodley Version of Mandeville's Travels, ed. M. C. Seymour. 50s. 1963
254. Ywain and Gawain, ed. Albert B. Friedman and Norman T. Harrington. 50s. „
255. Facsimile of B.M. MS. Harley 2253 (The Harley Lyrics). With Introduction by N. R. Ker. 100s. 1964
256. Sir Eglamour of Artois, ed. Frances E. Richardson. 50s. 1965
257. Sir Thomas Chaloner: The Praise of Folie, ed. Clarence H. Miller. 50s. „
258. The Orcherd of Syon, ed. Phyllis Hodgson and Gabriel M. Liegey. Vol. I, Text. 100s. 1966
259. Homilies of Ælfric: A Supplementary Collection, ed. J. C. Pope. Vol. I. 100s. 1967
260. Homilies of Ælfric: A Supplementary Collection, ed. J. C. Pope. Vol. II. 100s. 1968
261. Lybeaus Desconus, ed. M. Mills. 50s. 1969
262. The Macro Plays, re-ed. Mark Eccles. 50s. „

Forthcoming volumes

263. Caxton's History of Reynard the Fox, ed. N. F. Blake. (*At press.*) 50s. 1970
264. Scrope's Epistle of Othea, ed. C. F. Bühler. (*At press.*) 50s. „
265. The Cyrurgie of Guy de Chauliac, ed. Margaret S. Ogden. Vol. I, Text. (*At Press.*) 100s. 1971
266. Wulfstan's Canons of Edgar, ed. R. G. Fowler. (*At press.*) 50s. 1972
267. The English Text of the Ancrene Riwle, B. M. Cotton MS. Cleopatra C. vi, ed. E. J. Dobson. (*At press.*) 50s. „

Other texts are in preparation.

Supplementary Texts

The Society proposes to issue some Supplementary Texts from time to time as funds allow. These will be sent to members as part of the normal issue and will also be available to non-members at listed prices. The first of these, Supplementary Text 1, expected to appear in 1970, will be *Non-Cycle Plays and Fragments*, ed. Norman Davis (about 50s.). This is a completely revised and re-set edition of the texts in Extra Series 104 with some additional pieces. Supplementary Text 2, expected to appear in 1971, will be *Caxton's Knight of La Tour Landry*, ed. M. Y. Offord (at press, about 50s.).

April 1969

Publisher: LONDON · THE OXFORD UNIVERSITY PRESS, ELY HOUSE, 37 DOVER ST., W. 1